SELECTED WORKS BY **FRAN FORMAN**

THE REST BETWEEN TWO NOTES

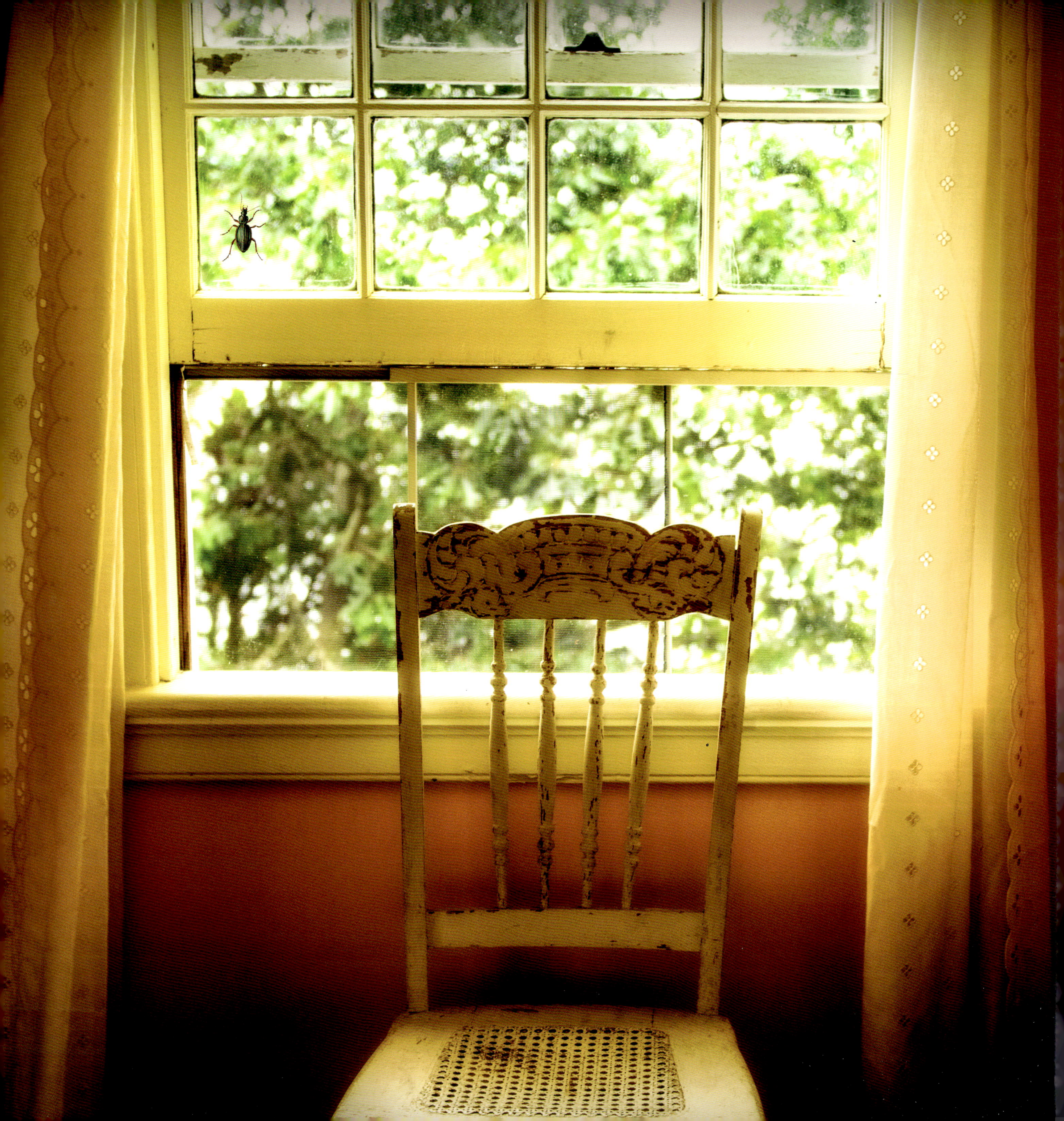

SELECTED WORKS BY **FRAN FORMAN**

THE REST BETWEEN TWO NOTES

UNICORN

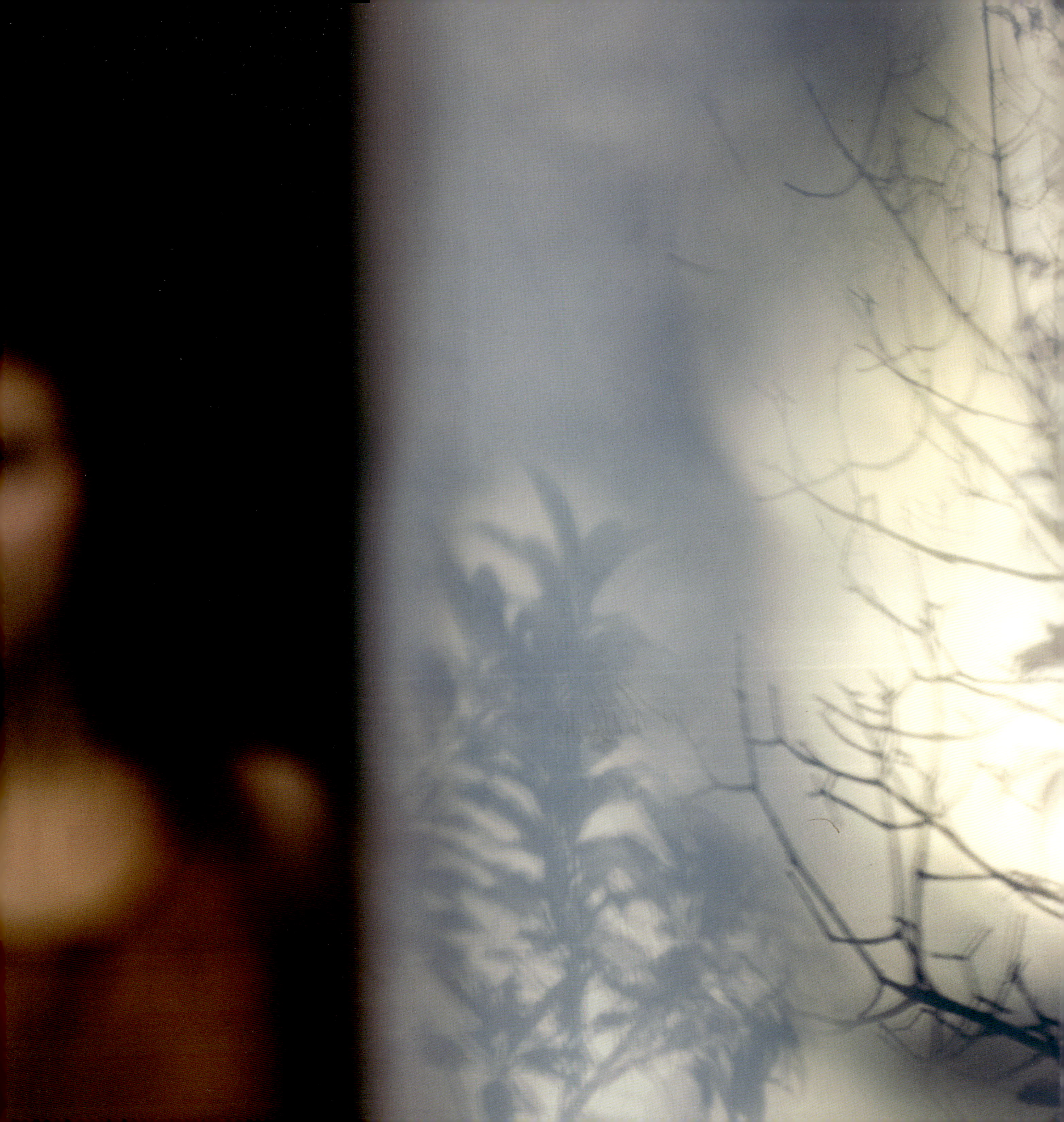

I AM **THE REST BETWEEN TWO NOTES**,

WHICH ARE SOMEHOW ALWAYS IN DISCORD

because Death's note wants to climb over—
but in the dark interval, reconciled,
they stay there trembling.
And the song goes on, beautiful.

—Rainer Maria Rilke

Published in 2019 by Unicorn, an imprint
of Unicorn Publishing Group LLP
5 Newburgh Street
London W1F 7RG
www.unicornpublishing.org

978-1-912690-38-1

Designed by Connie Hwang Design

Printed in China by Artron Art Printing
(HK) Ltd through Crash Paper

This book is dedicated to those

who take the time to participate

IN THE CONVERSATION

THAT IS **ART**.

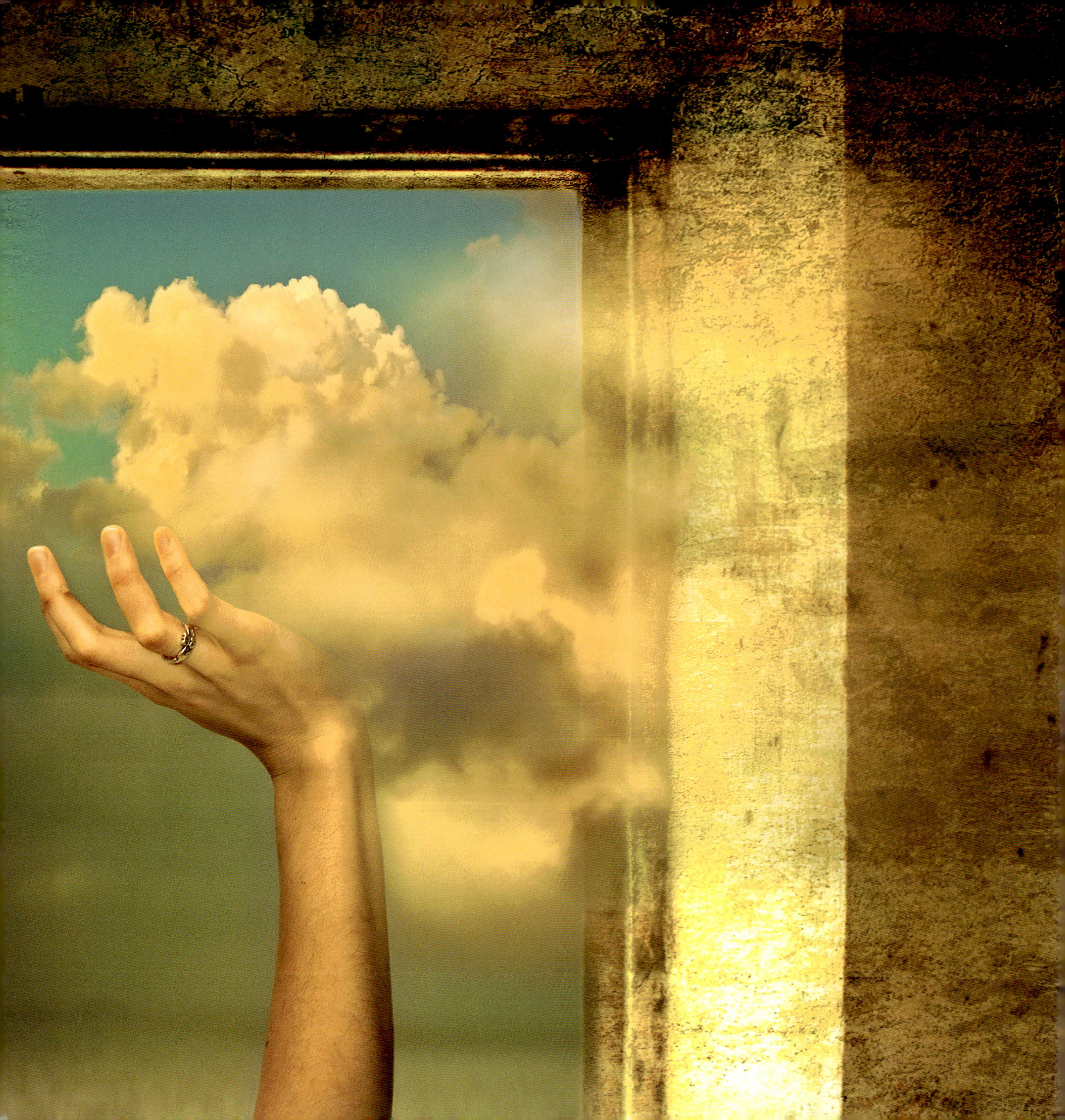

FOREWORD

Fran Forman christened our first satellite gallery of the Griffin Museum of Photography in 2008 with *Alchemy of Memory* and in 2017 she revisited another with *Return to the Clouds*. She has delighted our patrons in workshops and lectures, leaving them always calling for more. Our New England audience has loved Fran for well over a decade, though her name is now known throughout the United States and abroad. She has reached a point in life where the number of gallery representations, exhibitions held, and awards received are plentiful. She is collected widely with her most recent acquisition close to home by the Museum of Fine Arts, Boston.

At the time of Fran's entry into photomontage in the early '90s, the process was a relatively novel approach to making artwork and practiced by few. Although the tools she works with might be similar to other photo artists today, her library of photographs is unique to her, as all are made by her or handed down by her family over generations. I have always recognized Fran's hand in every one of her art pieces. The narratives she tells are her stories, her fears, and her delights. Her work engages because it blends a dash of certainty with a pinch of whimsy and straight-faced irony.

Through metaphor, references to art and social history, classical mythology, as well as her empathic heart, Fran articulates themes of freedom, migration, and the concept of hope. Her characters are transported from one dimension to another, whether it be in time, place, or circumstance. Some characters are culled from the animal kingdom, the pages of literature, and even the museum wall. The bird cage, for example, shows itself in many of Forman's images as if she is in conversation with her muse, René Magritte.

The bird is a reoccurring character in her narratives that could speak to freedom, escape, and the natural world. Even as a young woman, Fran Forman championed equal rights for all. The bird in flight or an empty room as a holding area provokes Fran's poetic imagination, just as it did for Maya Angelou in the poignant poem called *Caged Bird*. "A free bird leaps on the back of the wind." (*The Complete Collected Poems of Maya Angelou*, Random House Inc., 1994)

Fran's personal journey is described in the Afterword of this book. Every layer of her life has contributed in some way to the woman and artist that she has become. Her trajectories are circuitous, often leading to unexpected outcomes. Other pathways are more deliberate and considered. Her title of this book *The Rest Between Two Notes* is a certain bellwether of more to come from Fran Forman.

What has always impressed me over the course of following Fran's career is her ability to make light where there is none, coupled with the intensity of her color palette. In this new book her light sources, color usage, and shadow details are richer in every way. This makes perfect sense. As we age, we ripen. We pause at sunsets. We've learned patience. And Fran's subjects seem to linger for longer looks. The mystery, the hesitation, and uncertainty are ever present in the geometry and design of each page. And what silence there is in waiting.

As viewers of Fran Forman's artwork, we travel across continents and time. Her Golden Age portraits are wrested from history books and the author's imagination. The scenes are populated using friends and family, and random people Fran meets in her travels. She places her subjects inside rooms colored in regal tones on textured walls or lined with lavish drapes and wallpapers. If walls could talk, we could know their many layers of experience as witness.

There are wrinkles in reason scattered purposefully throughout this book. I found it satisfying to find Fran's trickery. Her playfulness adds so much to the viewers' interaction with the artwork. Mirrors deliver surprises. Subjects appear in contemporary clothing next to their historical counterpart in black and white in a frame on a blood red wall. We are aware of other puzzles, too, regarding what we know. For example, we find a woman in a ruff as if it were the 17th century in Holland, yet she holds a cell phone with her selfie on the screen. She holds our gaze as if daring us to say what is amiss. We interrupt another woman as she writes a letter; she stares directly as well. She wears a yellow coat with spotted white fur, just as in the Vermeer painting called *A Lady Writing* and just like a coat Vermeer is said to have owned. Fran created this image in homage to Vermeer. With a second take we see that instead of sitting below a static still life, the woman sits below a photograph of Frank Gehry's Stata Center at MIT in Cambridge, Massachusetts. The Stata building is comprised of a series of angular structures that appear to be falling on top of each other in contrast to the unrecognizable and inert object in Vermeer's painting.

Fran has spent a lifetime fine-tuning the journey. She has never been shy about trying new roads. And here she is again refining her voice. With *The Rest Between Two Notes* Fran uncovers a greater range of her artistic expression. In these in-between moments she too waits. She stretches more. She inhales, then breathes out in anticipation of the next note. It's not the end that follows the rest but another beginning. As Rilke tells us, after the silent interval, the song goes on.

Paula Tognarelli

Paula Tognarelli is the Executive Director and Curator of the internationally renowned Griffin Museum of Photography.

She has juried and curated exhibitions internationally, is a regular participant in national and local portfolio reviews, has been a panelist and featured speaker at photography events and conferences worldwide. She is a past member of the Xerox Technical Advisory Board. She is on the advisory committee for the New England School of Photography and the Arnold Newman Portrait Prize facilitated by Maine Media Workshops.

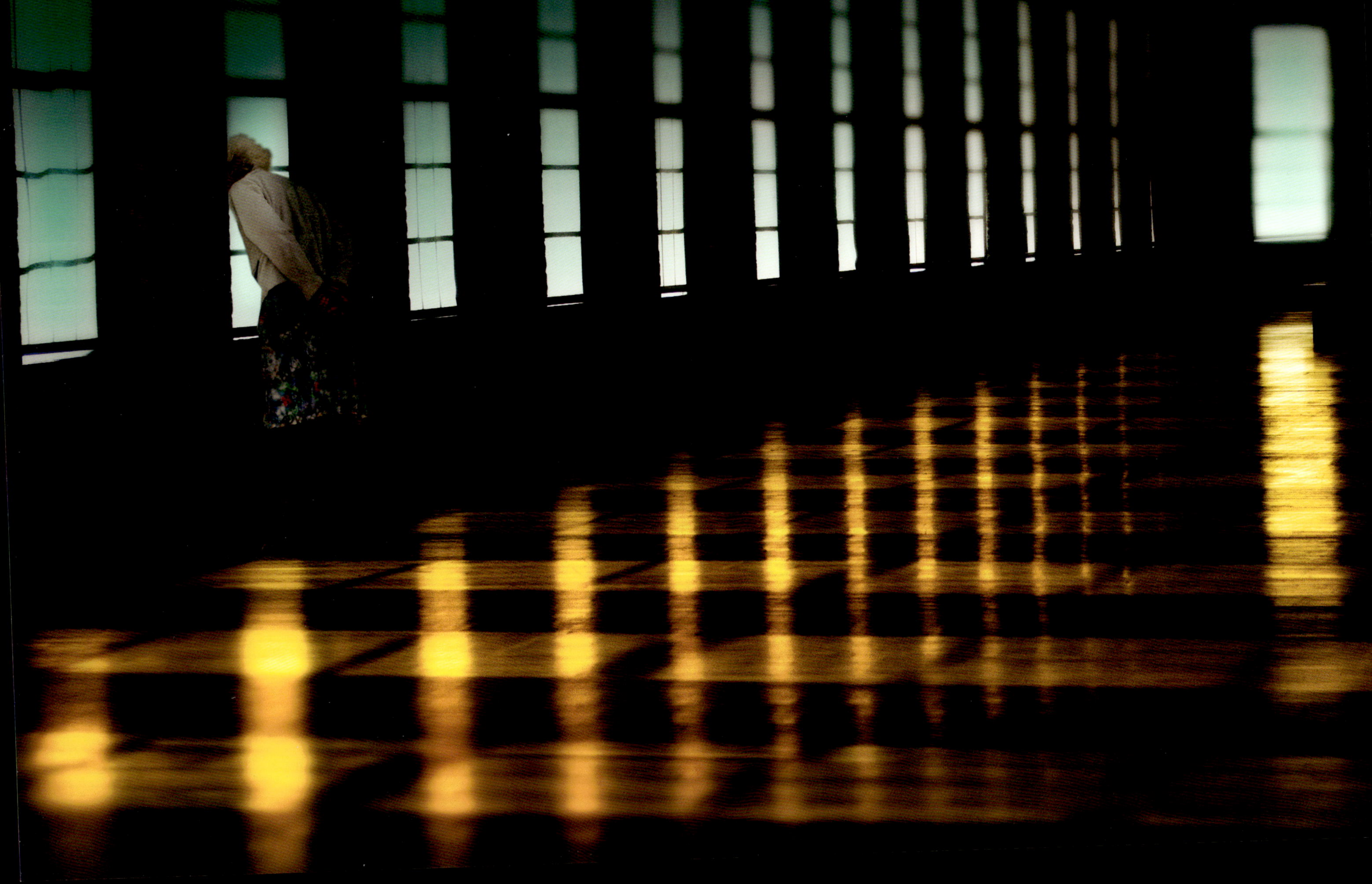

ECHOES AND REFLECTIONS

Art is a conversation between the artist and the viewer, as much as it is between the artist's hand and her mind, and every artist hopes to make an emotional connection with the viewer. As Todd Hido has written, "The real story in photography happens outside the frame … in the viewer's mind when they look at it."

I have always been fascinated by how different people respond to an image, bringing in their own memories, hopes, dreams, and world views. Each person brings a specific frame of reference to an image—fictional, academic, poetic, or just something more purely intuitive, all reflecting who they are as individuals.

Pictures are in two dimensions. Words add a third. For this book, I have asked several artists, writers, and others who have commented on my work in the past if they would share some thoughts, stories, or poems inspired by a particular image.

Their words appear adjacent to their selected image. I am delighted to share them with you here.

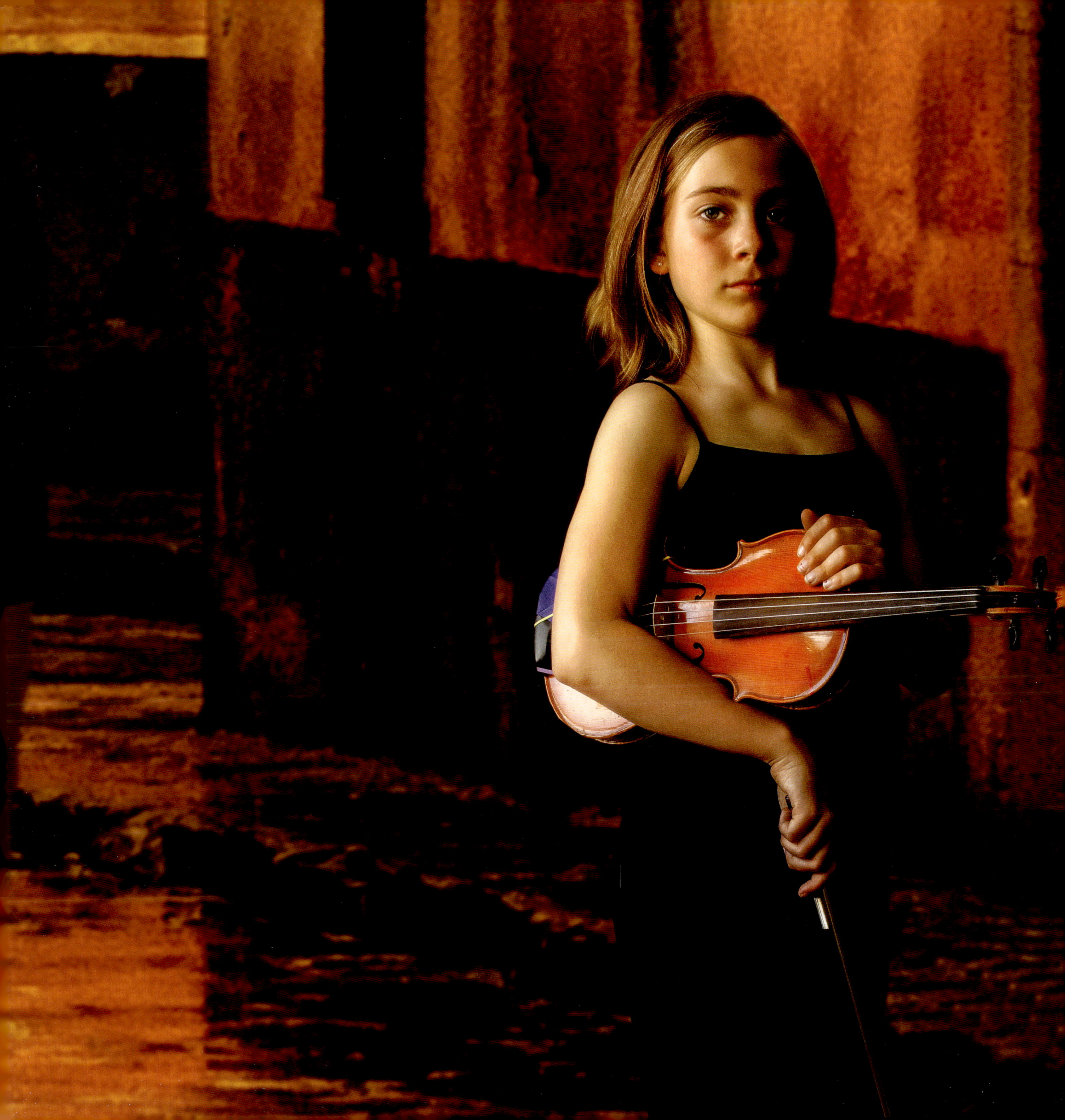

"HOW CAN I BE SUBSTANTIAL IF I DO NOT CAST A SHADOW?

I MUST HAVE A DARK SIDE ALSO IF I AM TO BE WHOLE." —Carl Jung

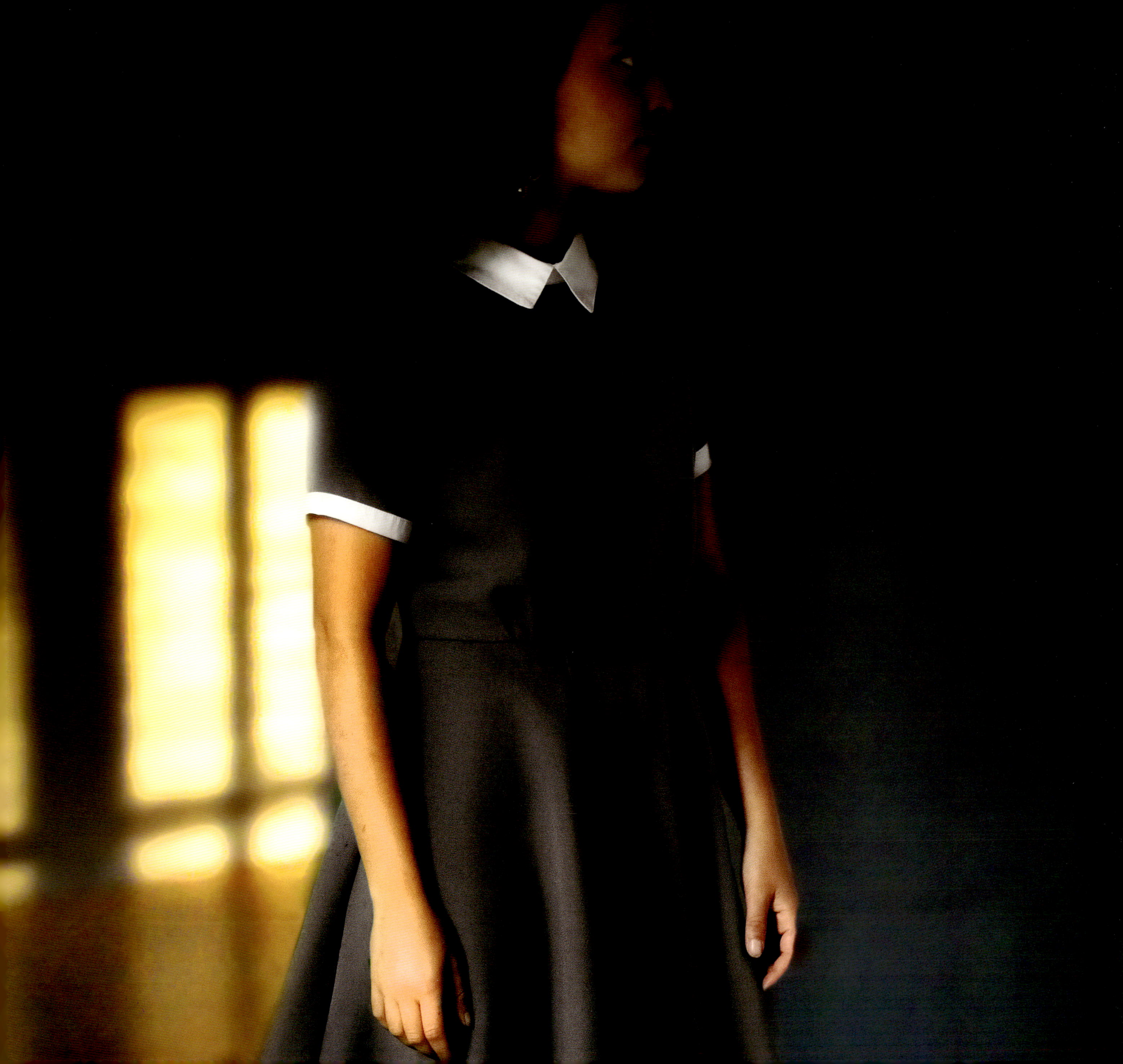

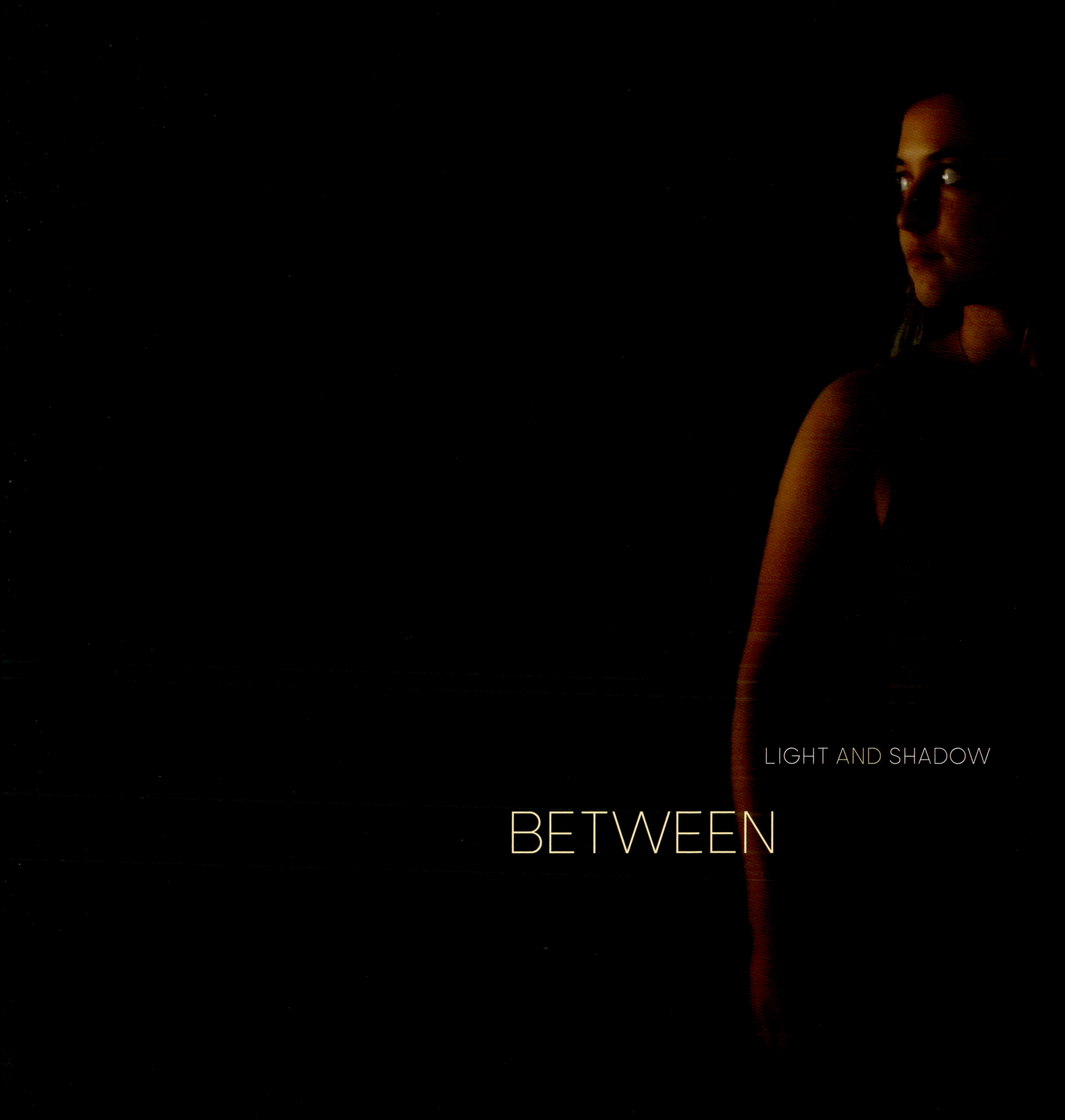

LIGHT AND SHADOW

BETWEEN

LIGHT DANCES ON THE COBBLESTONES ILLUMINATING A WELL-WORN PASSAGE.

A woman stands strong, like a siren, beckoning us by an open door. The brilliant sunlight glows like an aura around her and the vaulted ceilings and round columns are echoed in her posture. She seems to be waiting patiently for the pixie-like child, hiding in the wings, to emerge.

Sarah Hadley

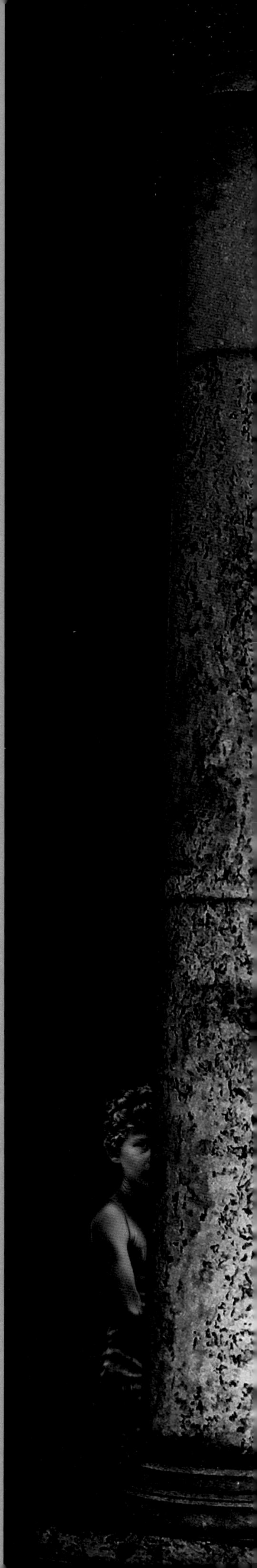

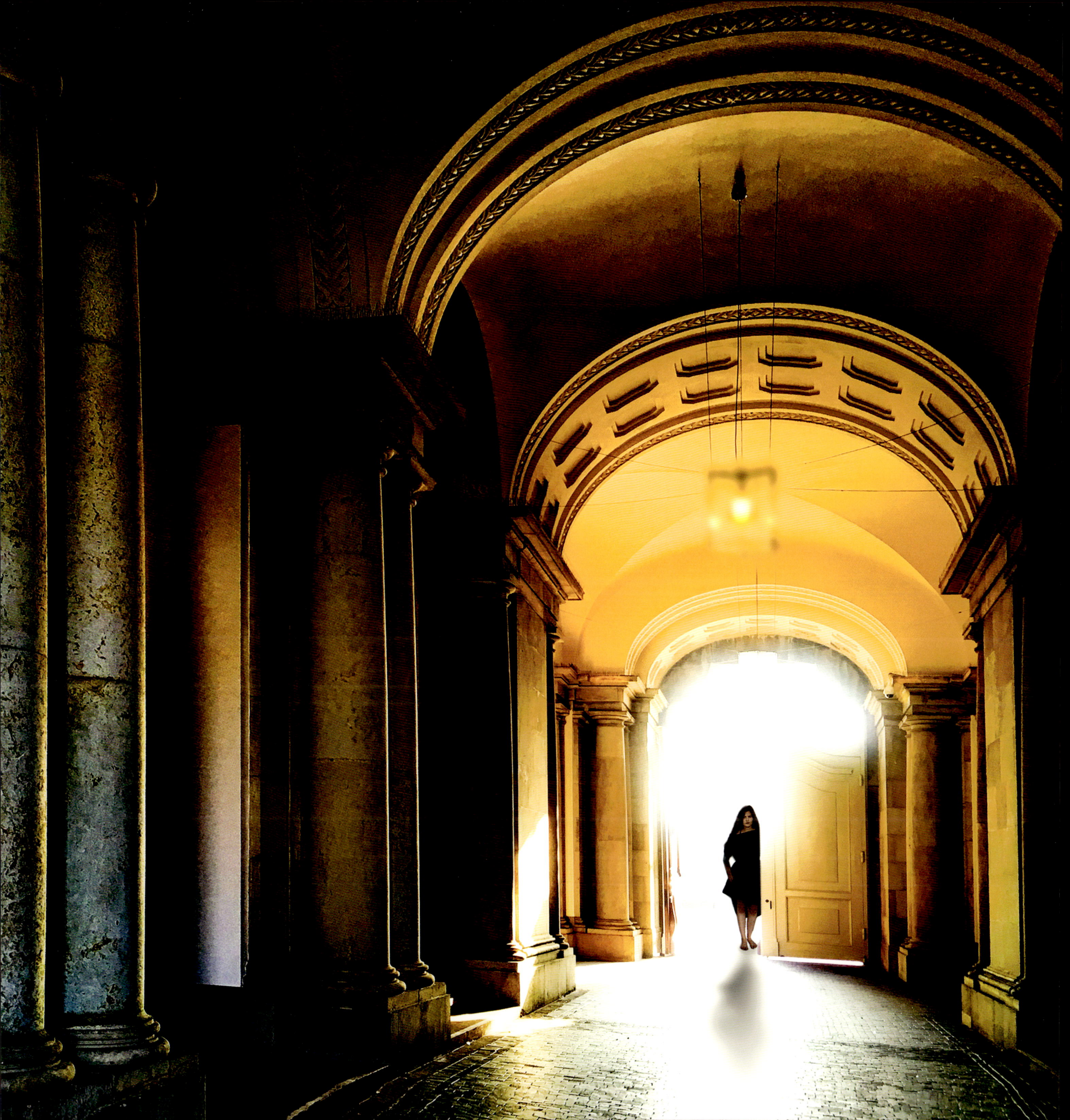

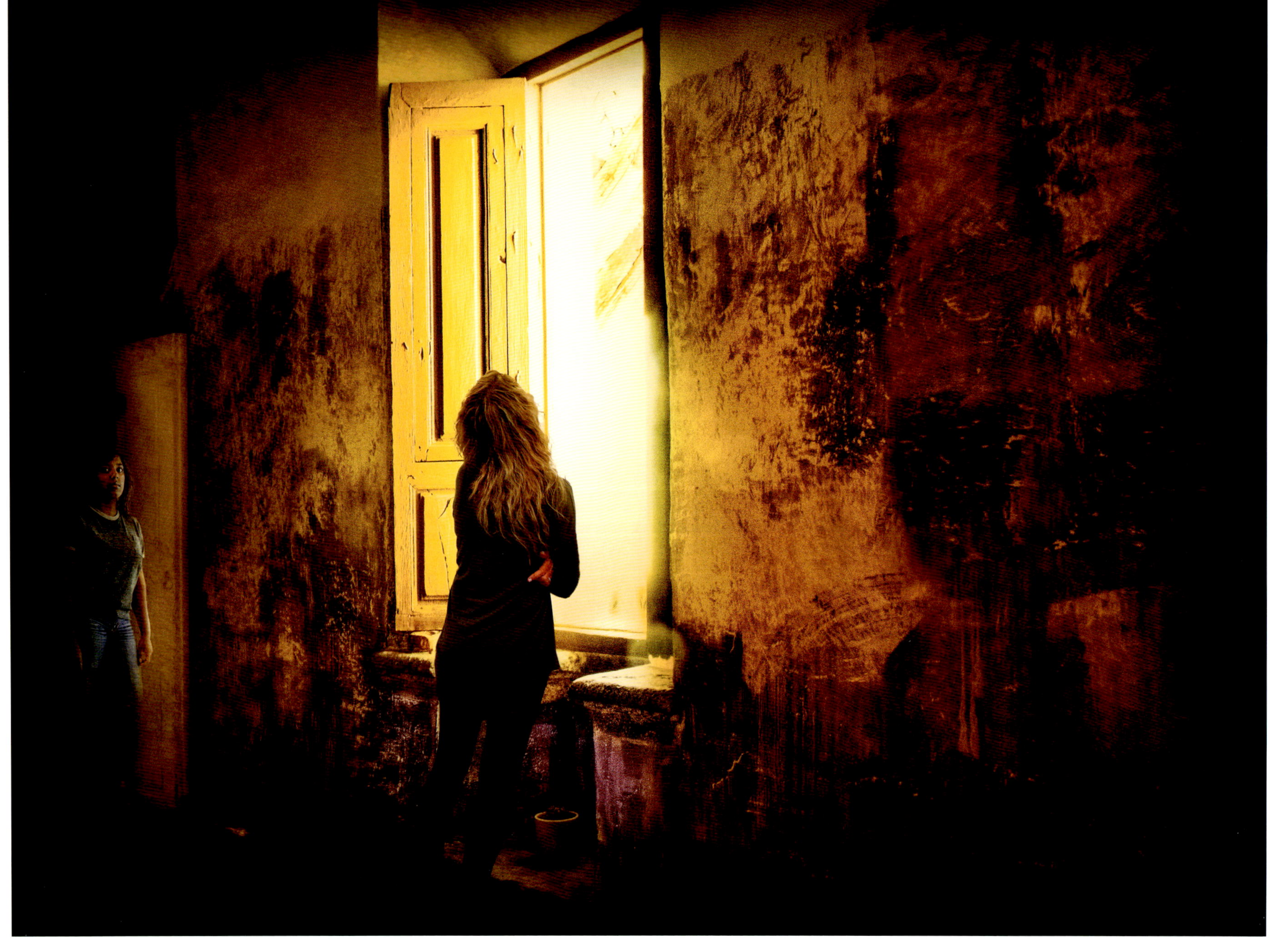

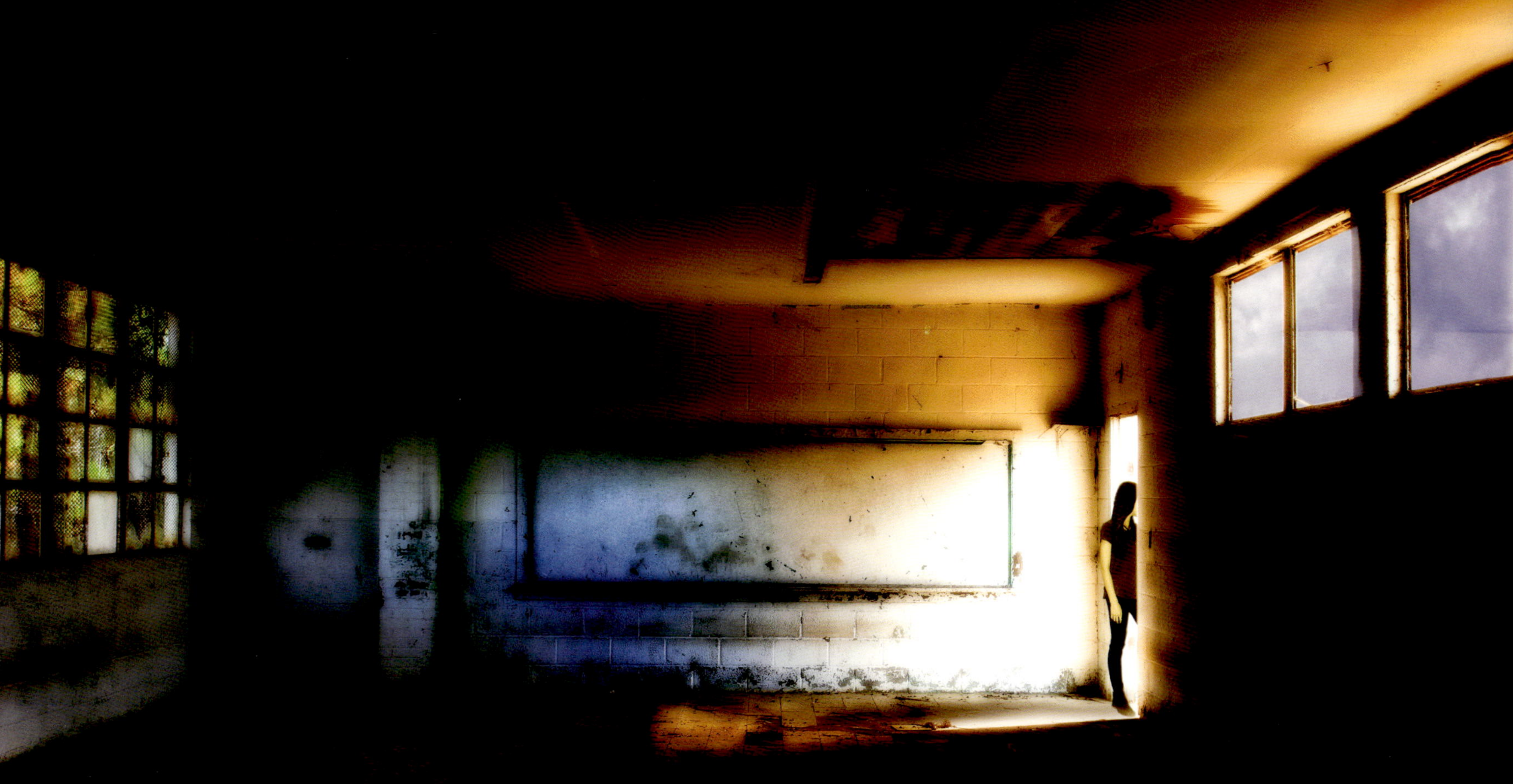

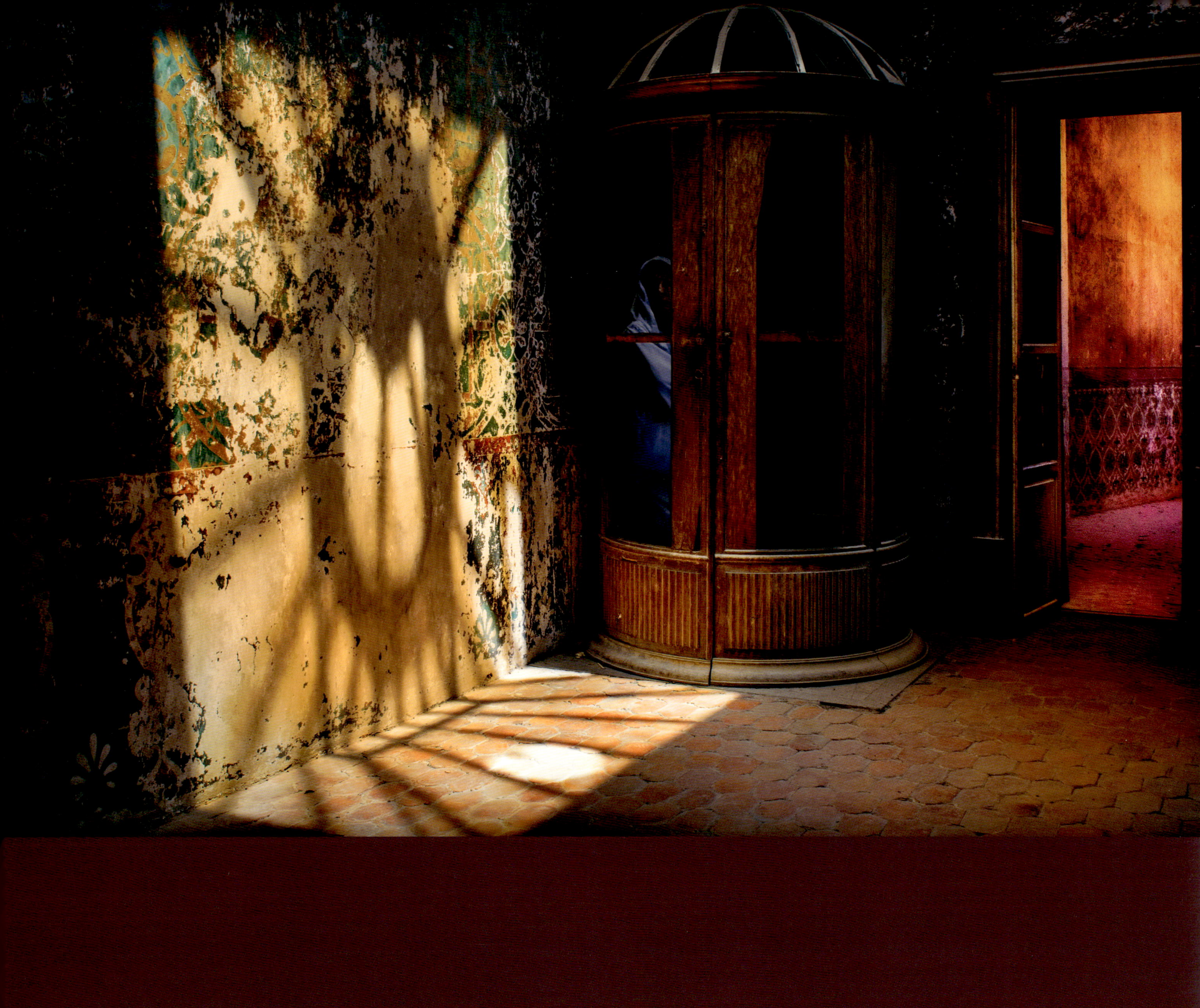

ASCENDANT

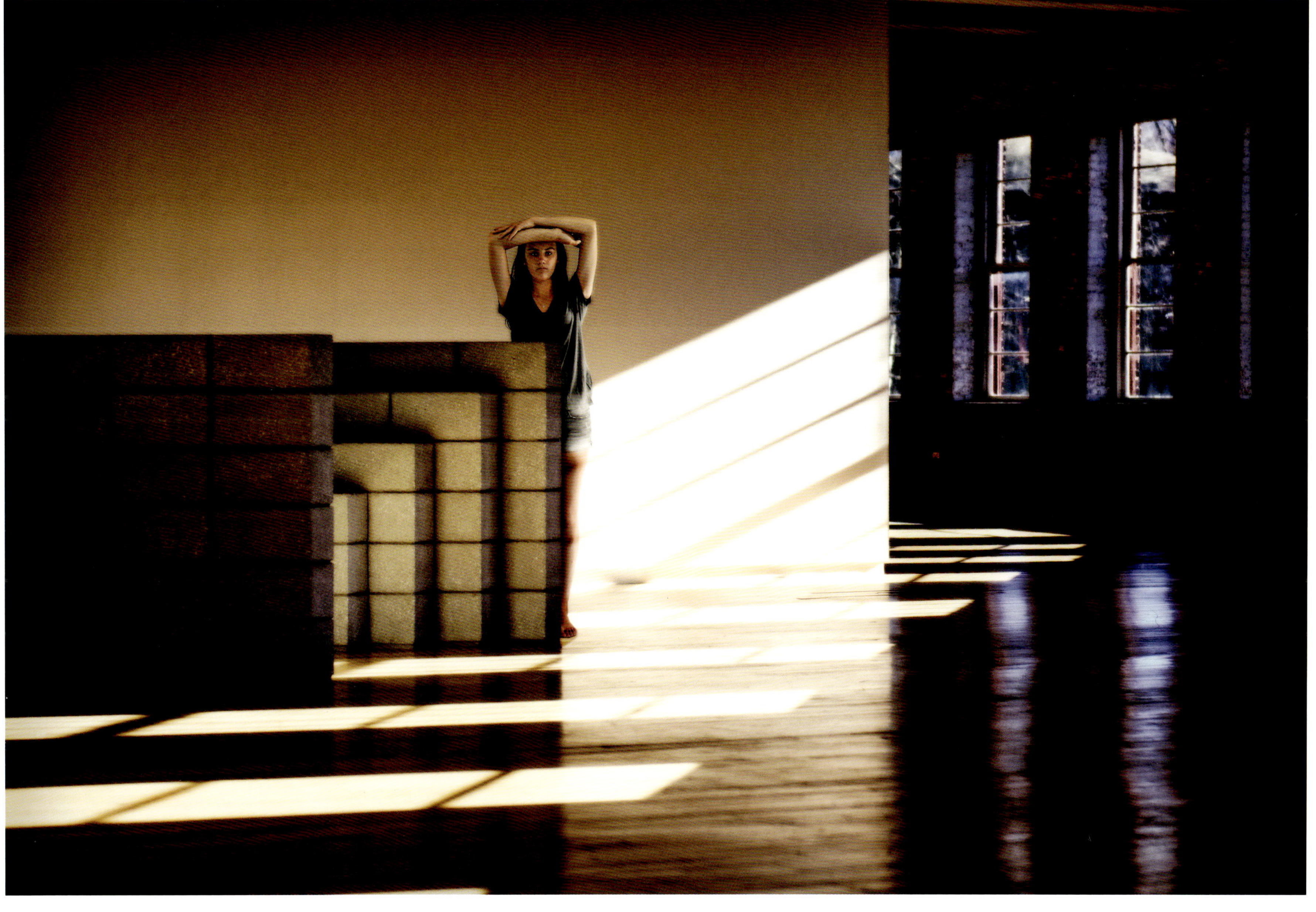

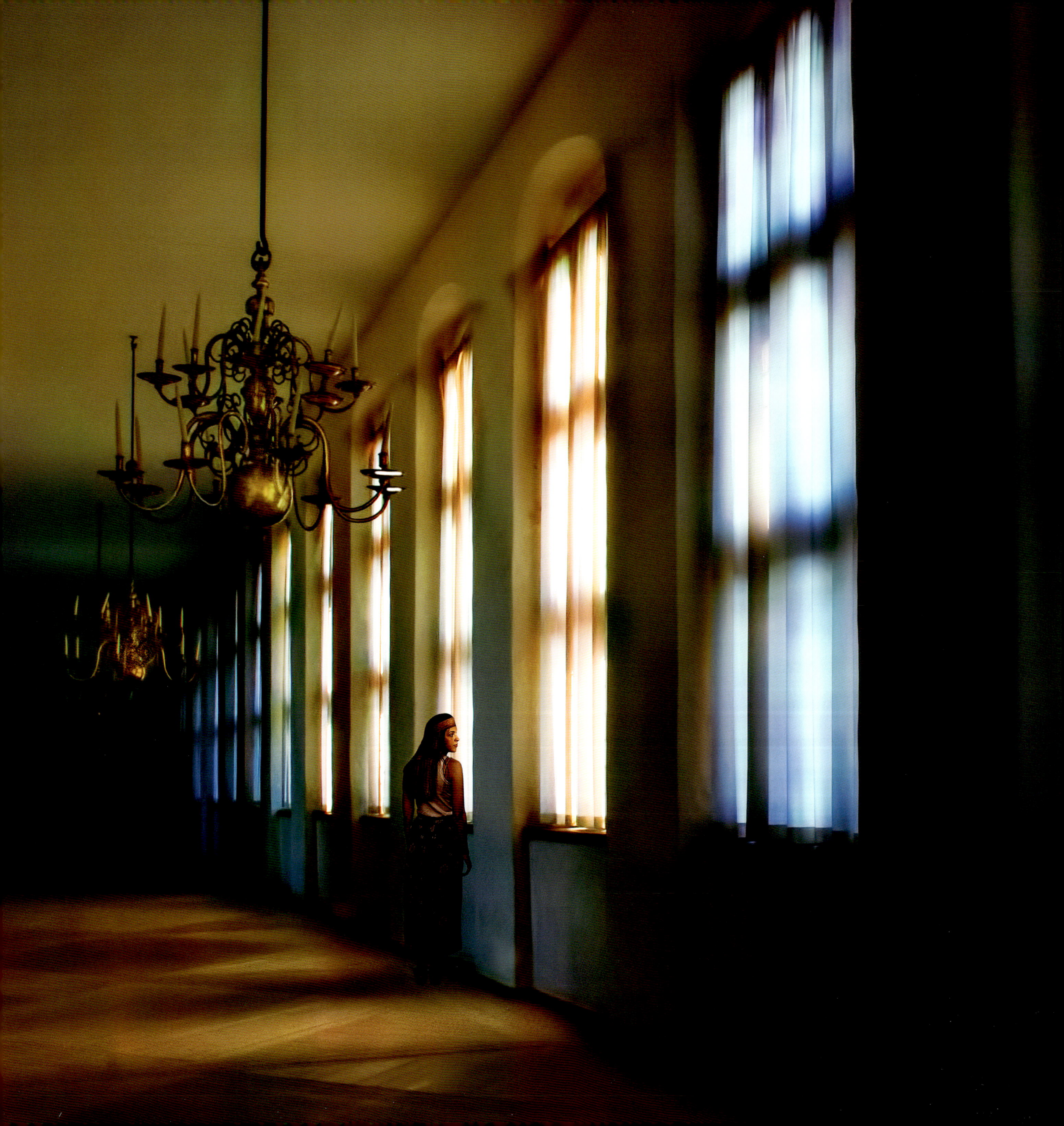

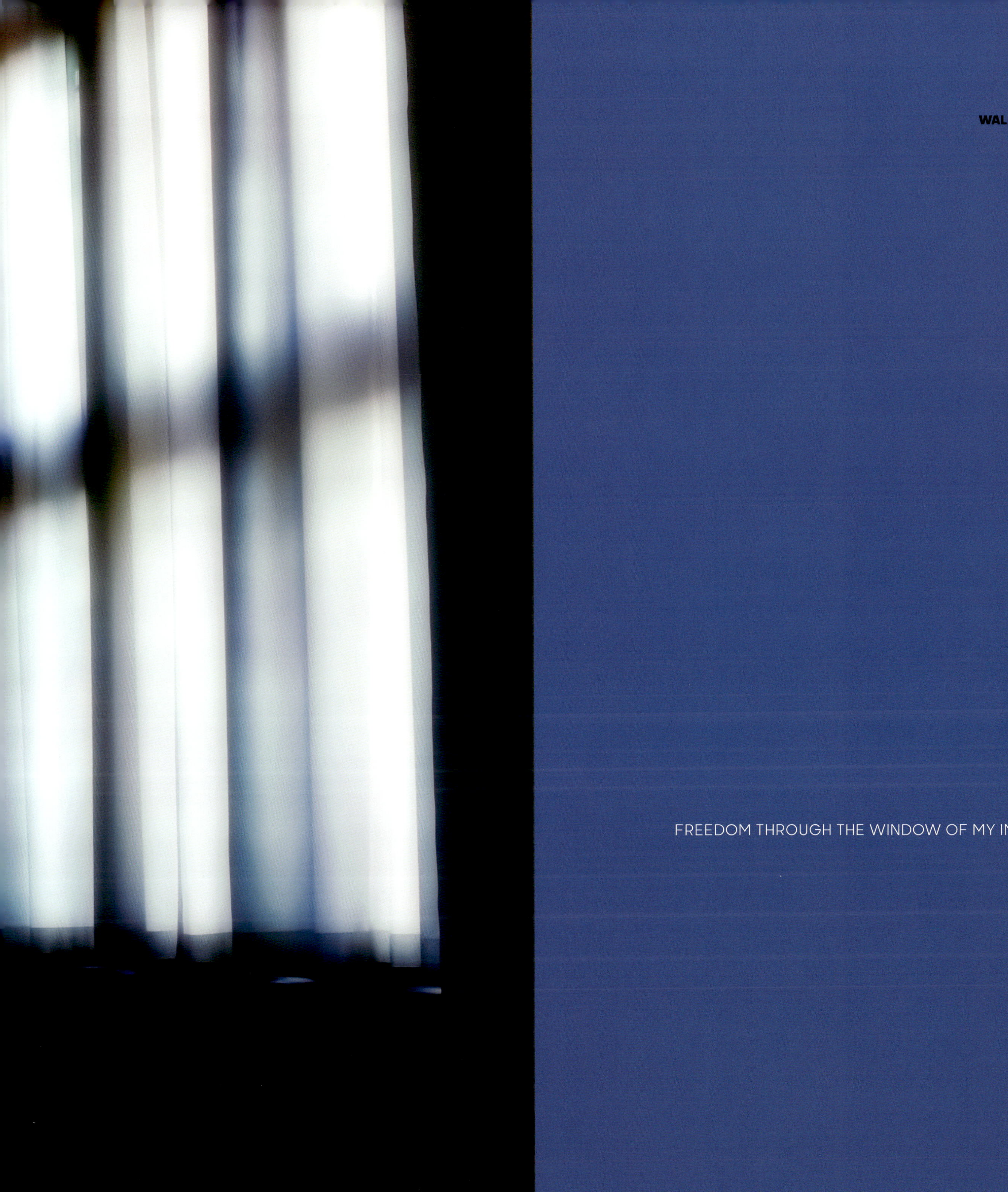

FREEDOM THROUGH THE WINDOW OF MY IMAGINATION.

Victor Rosario

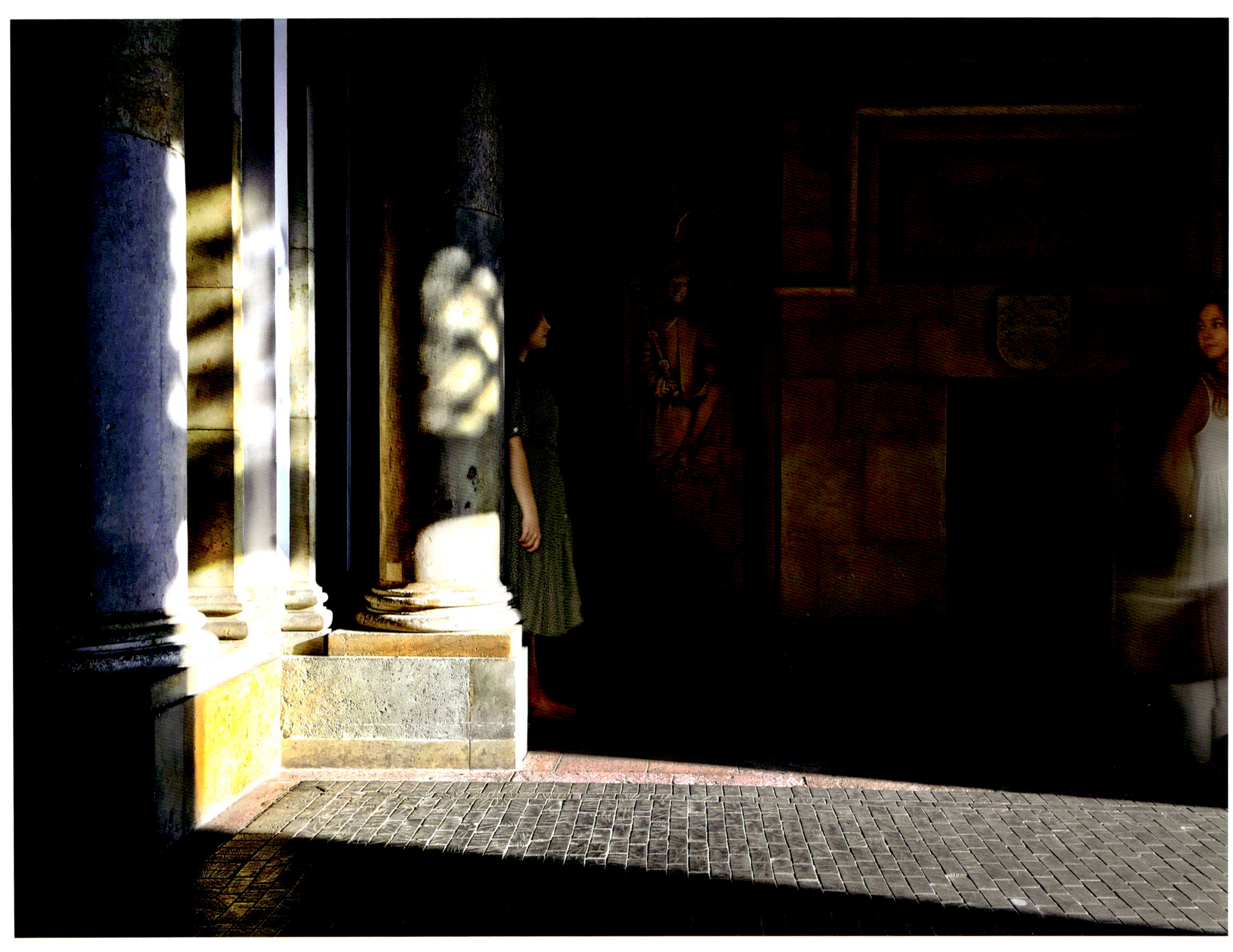

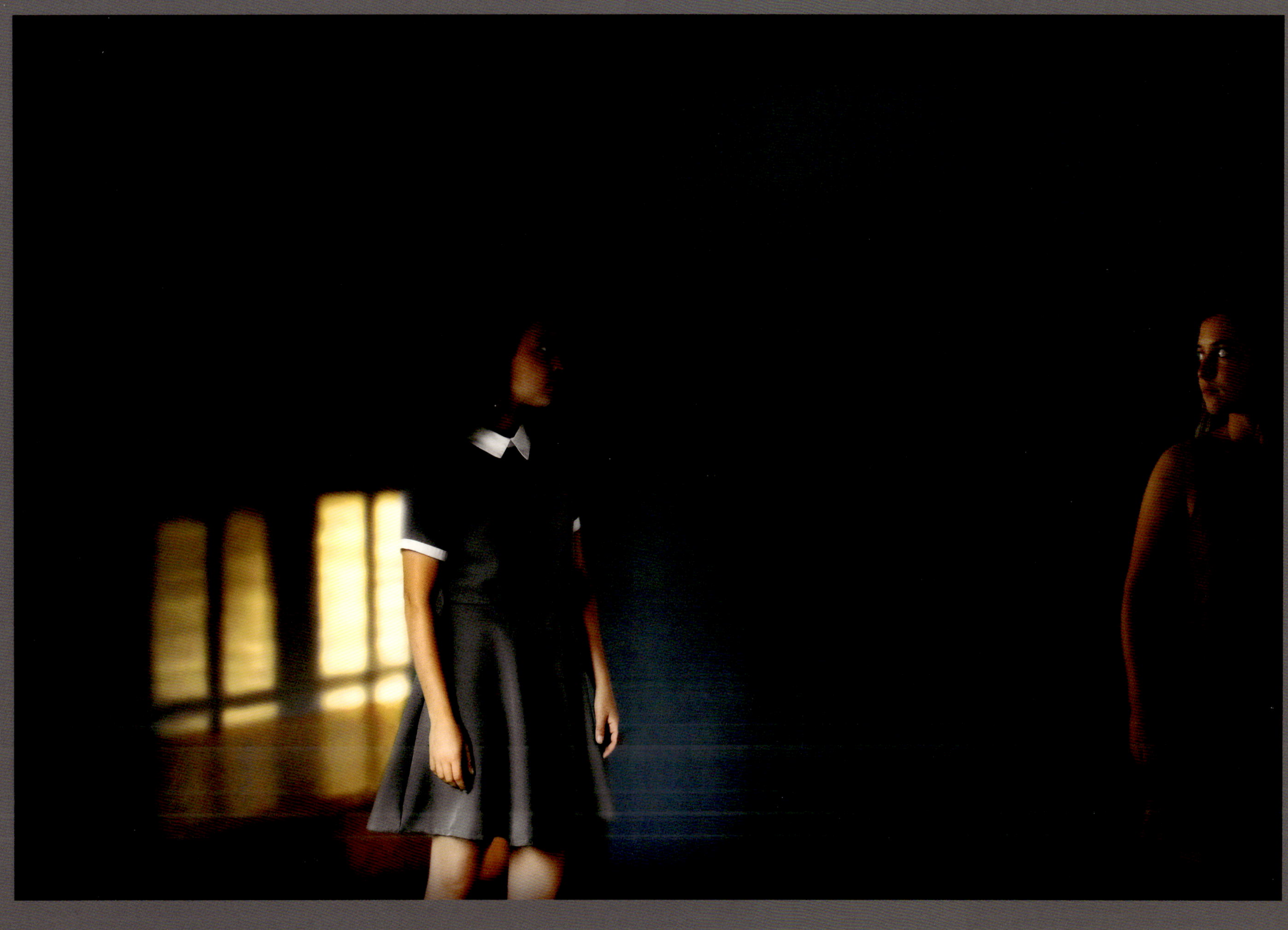

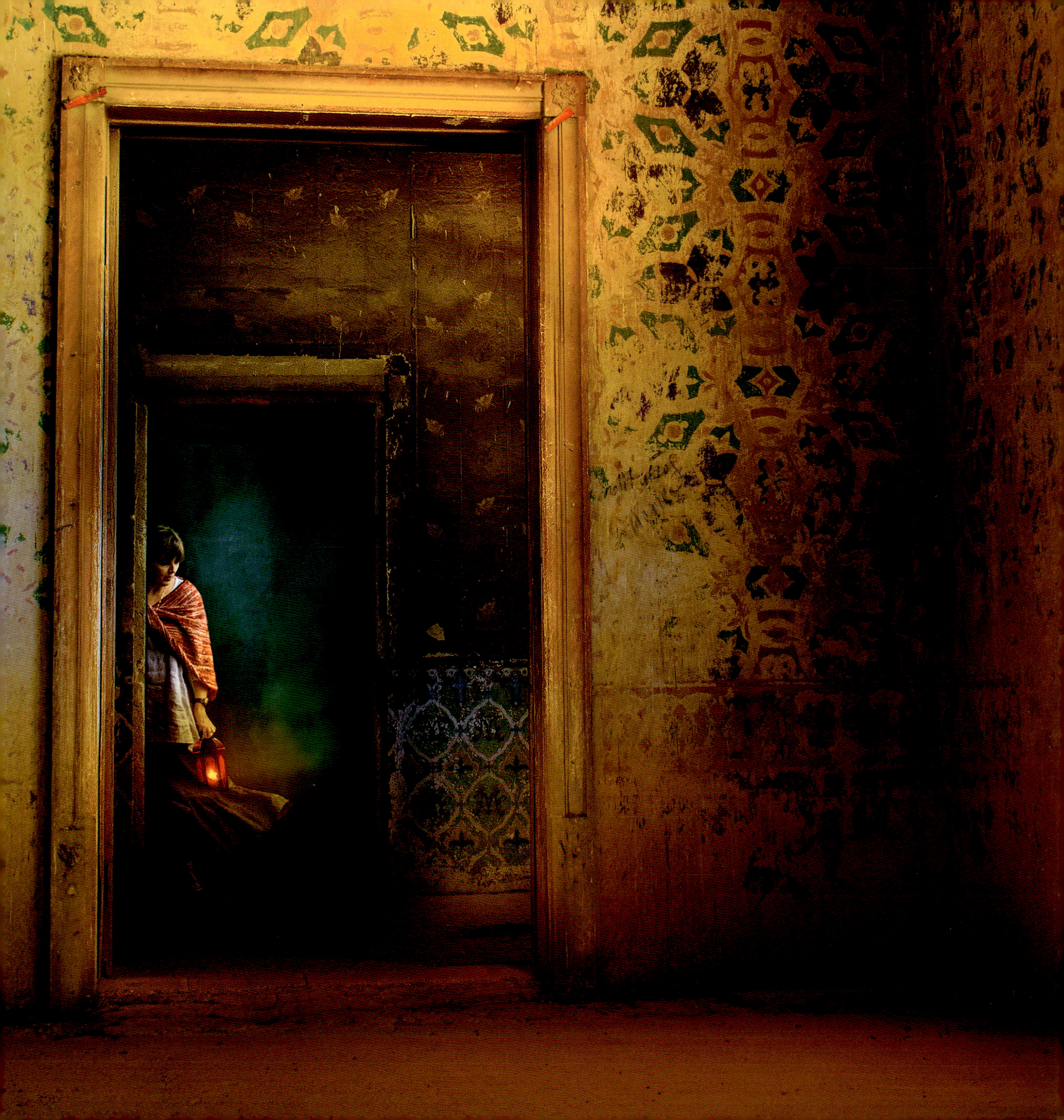

ROOM WITH THREE DOORS

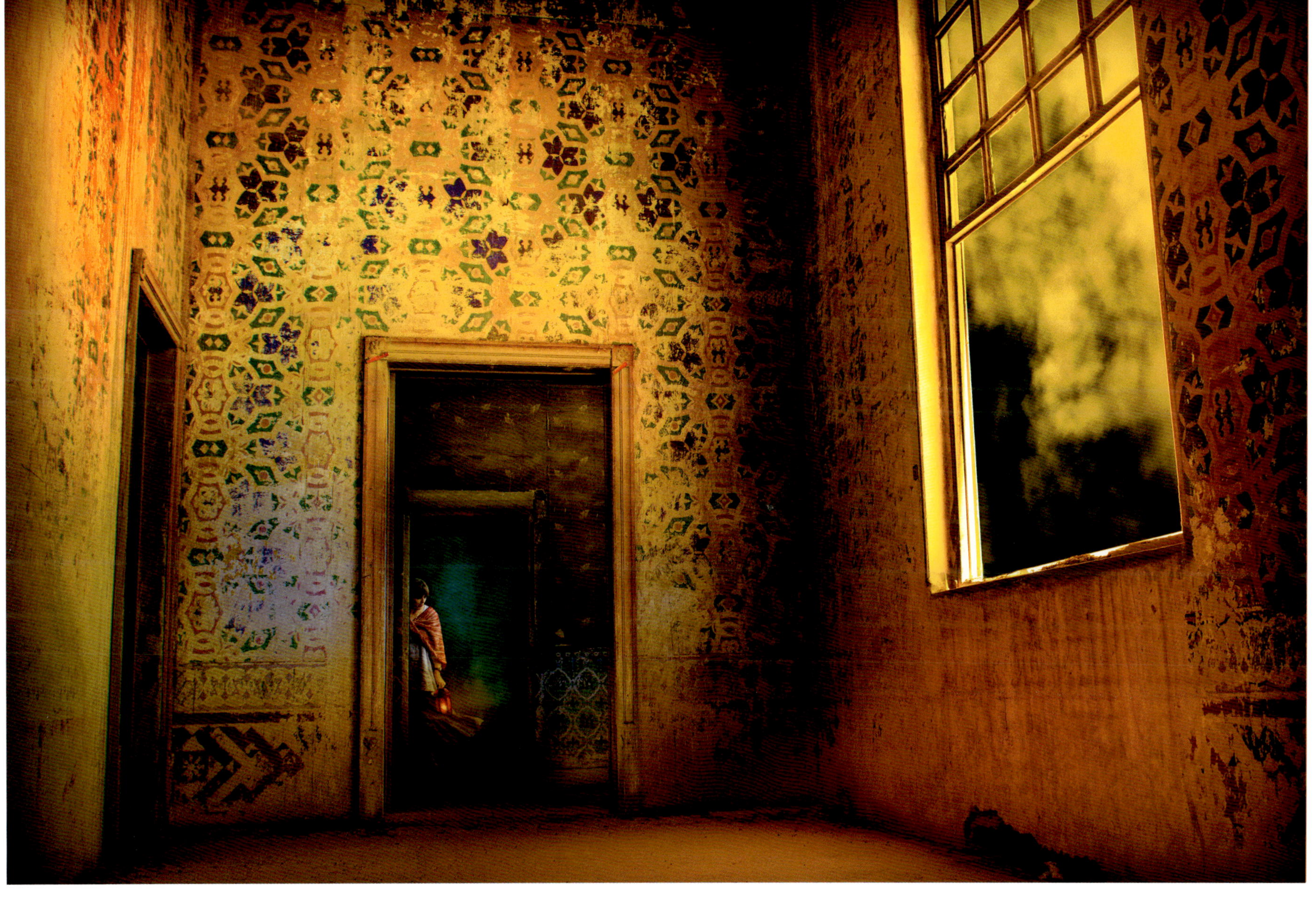

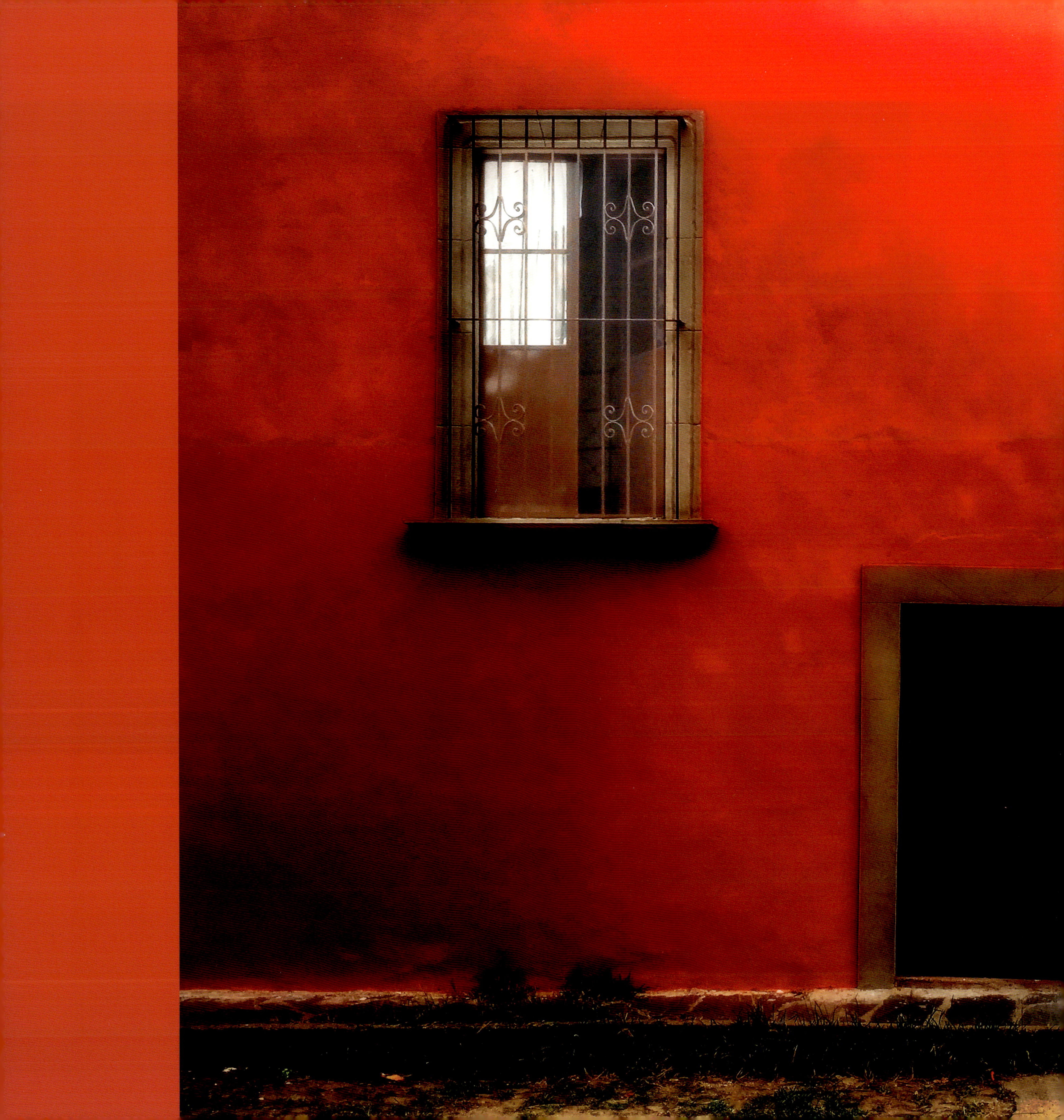

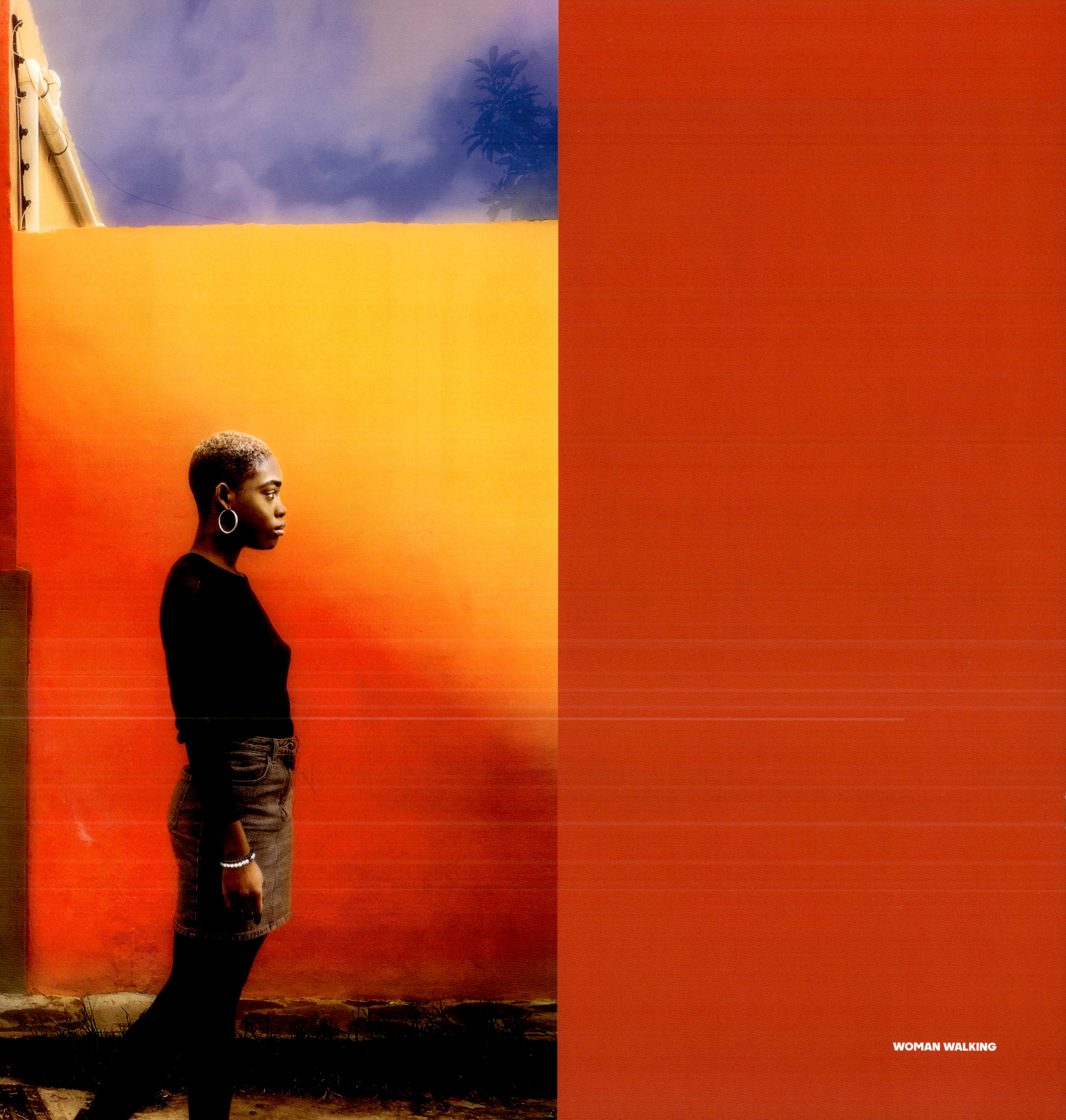

WOMAN WALKING

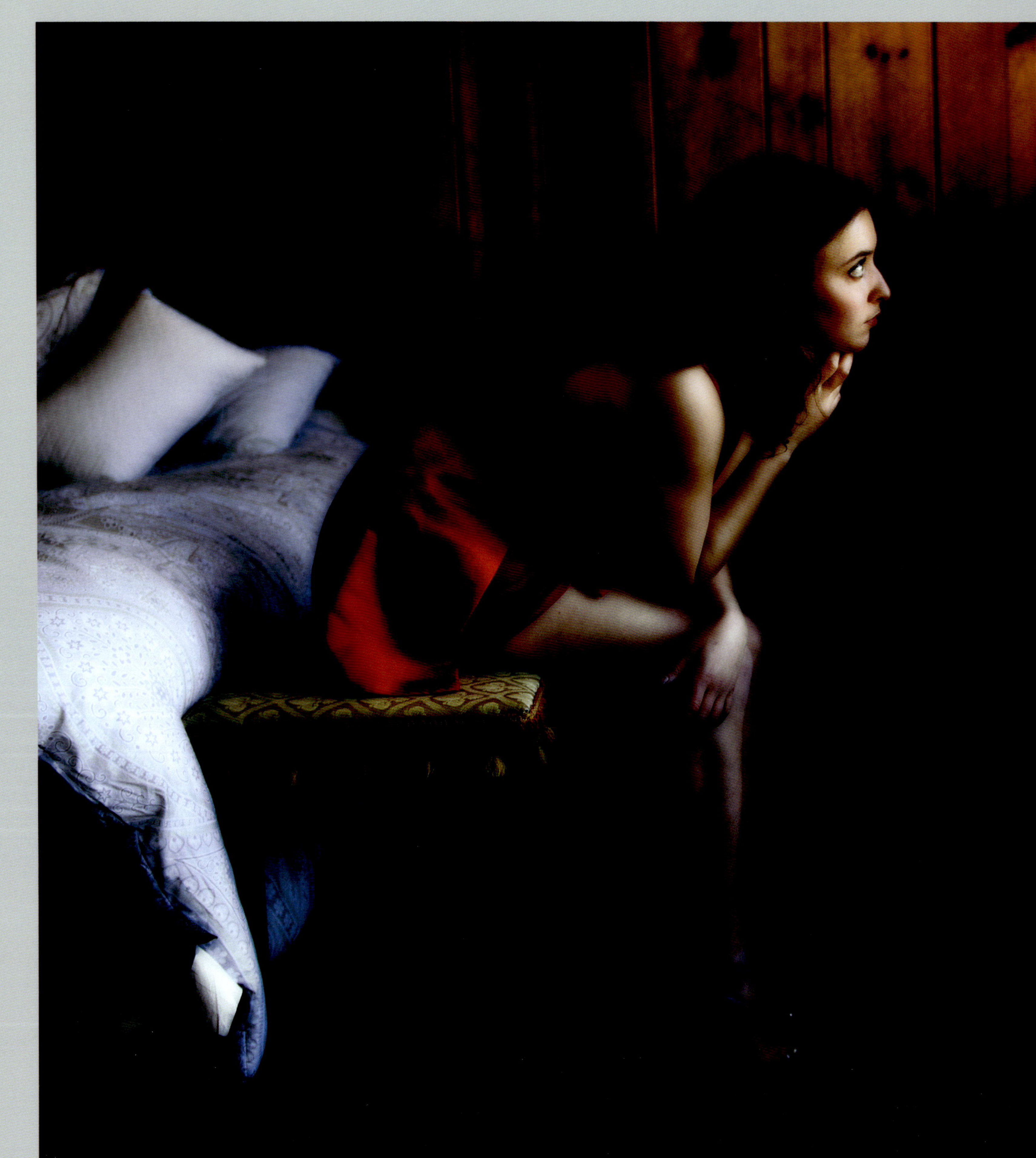

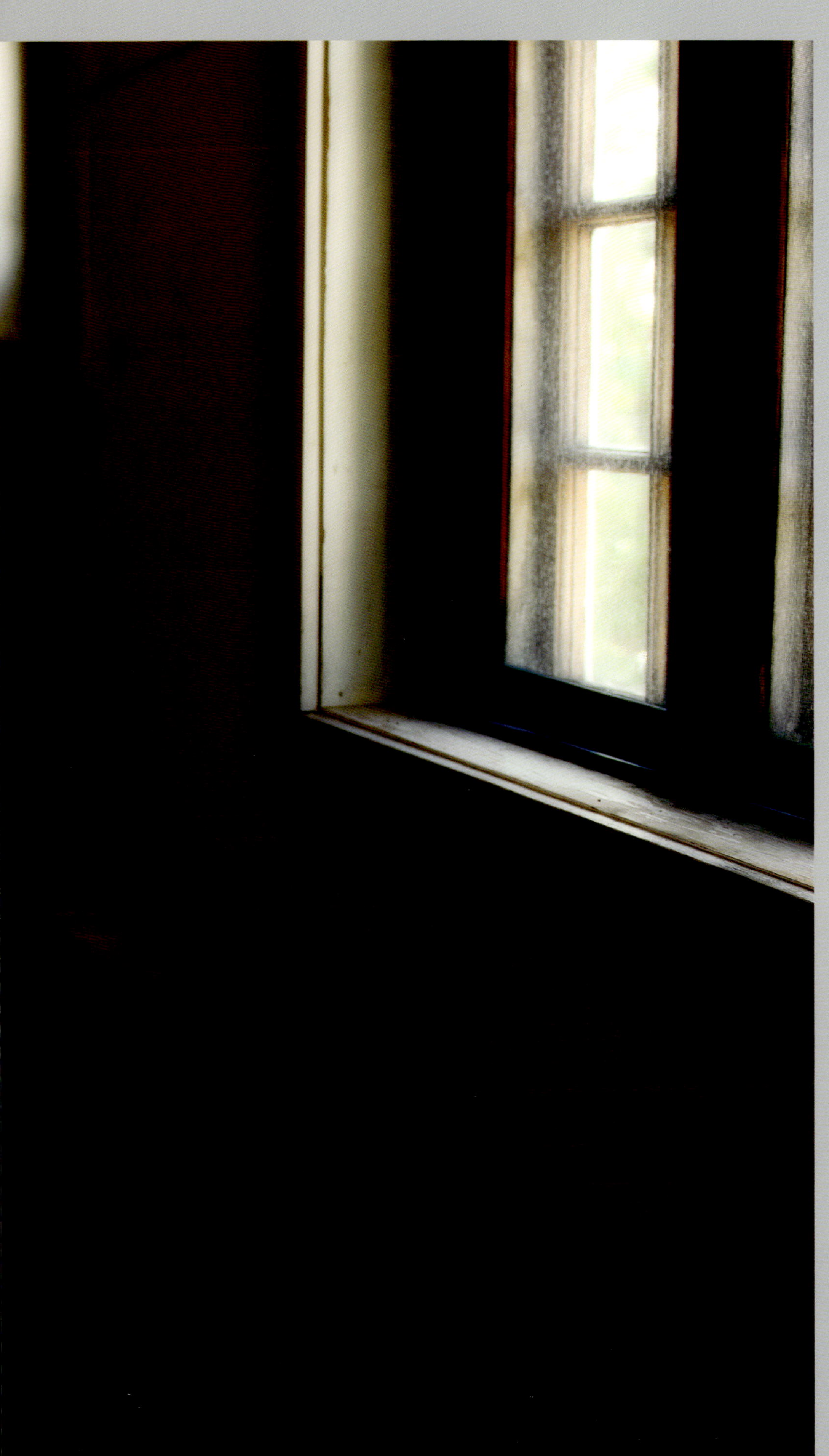

IN THE BEDROOM

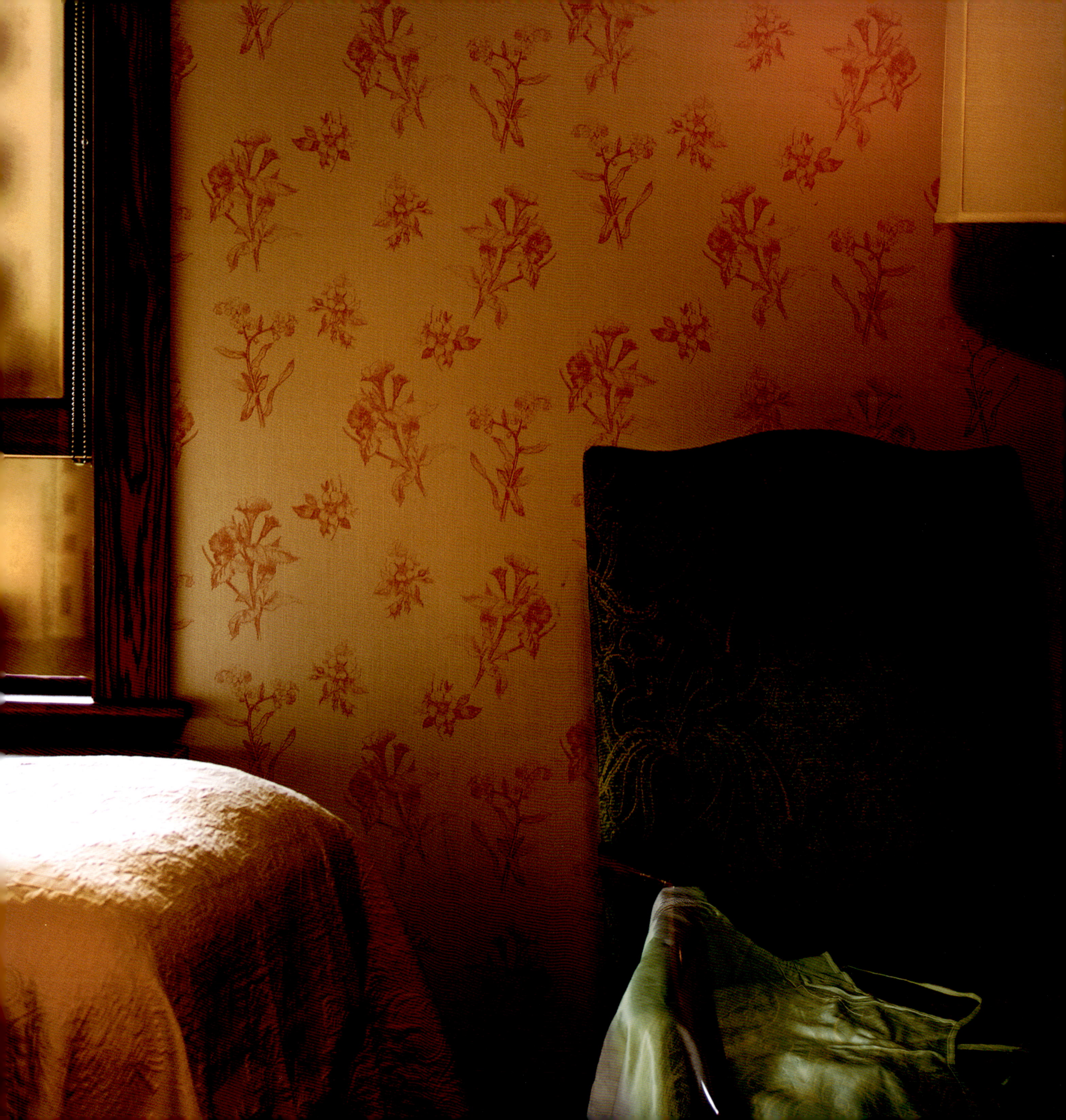

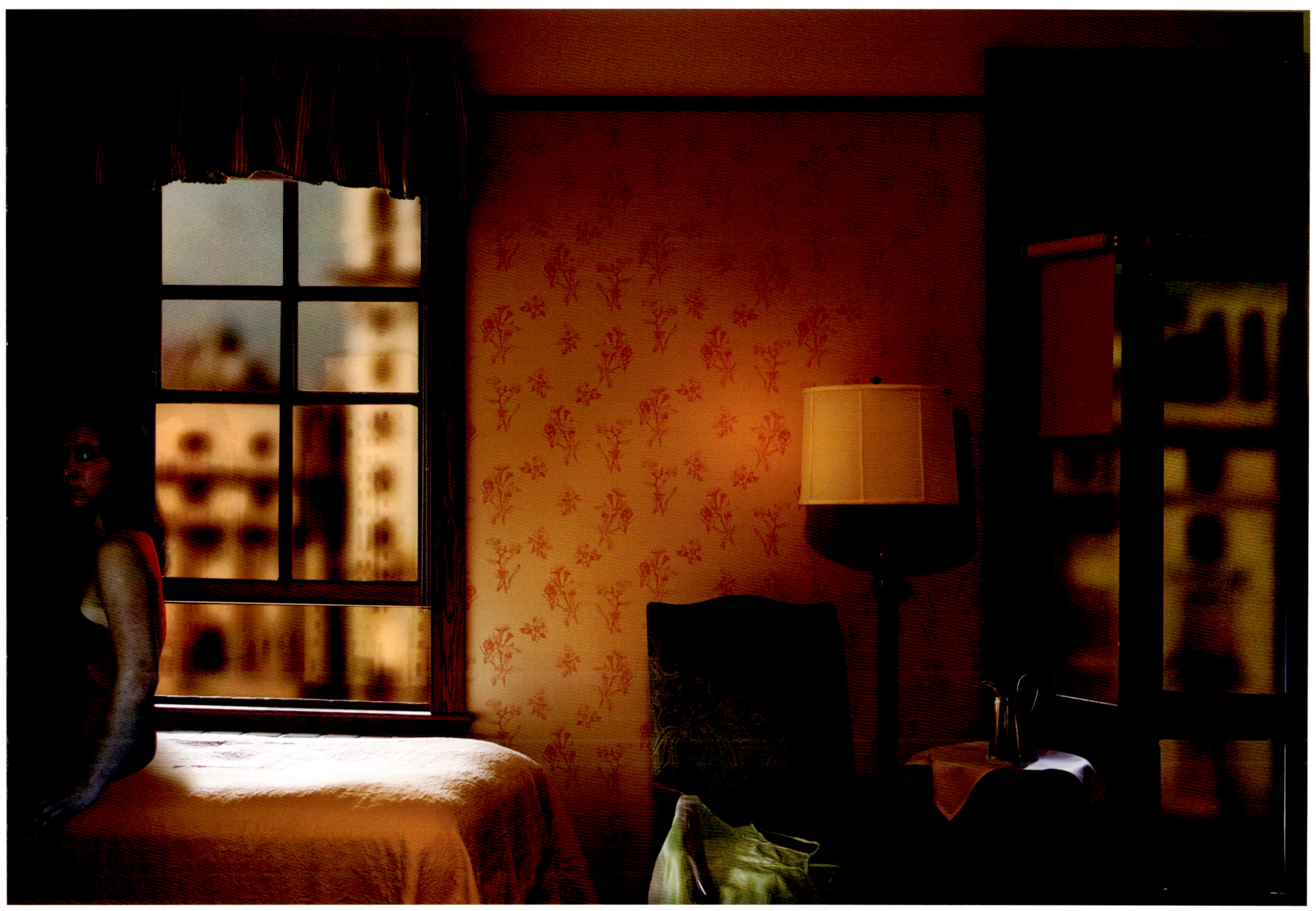

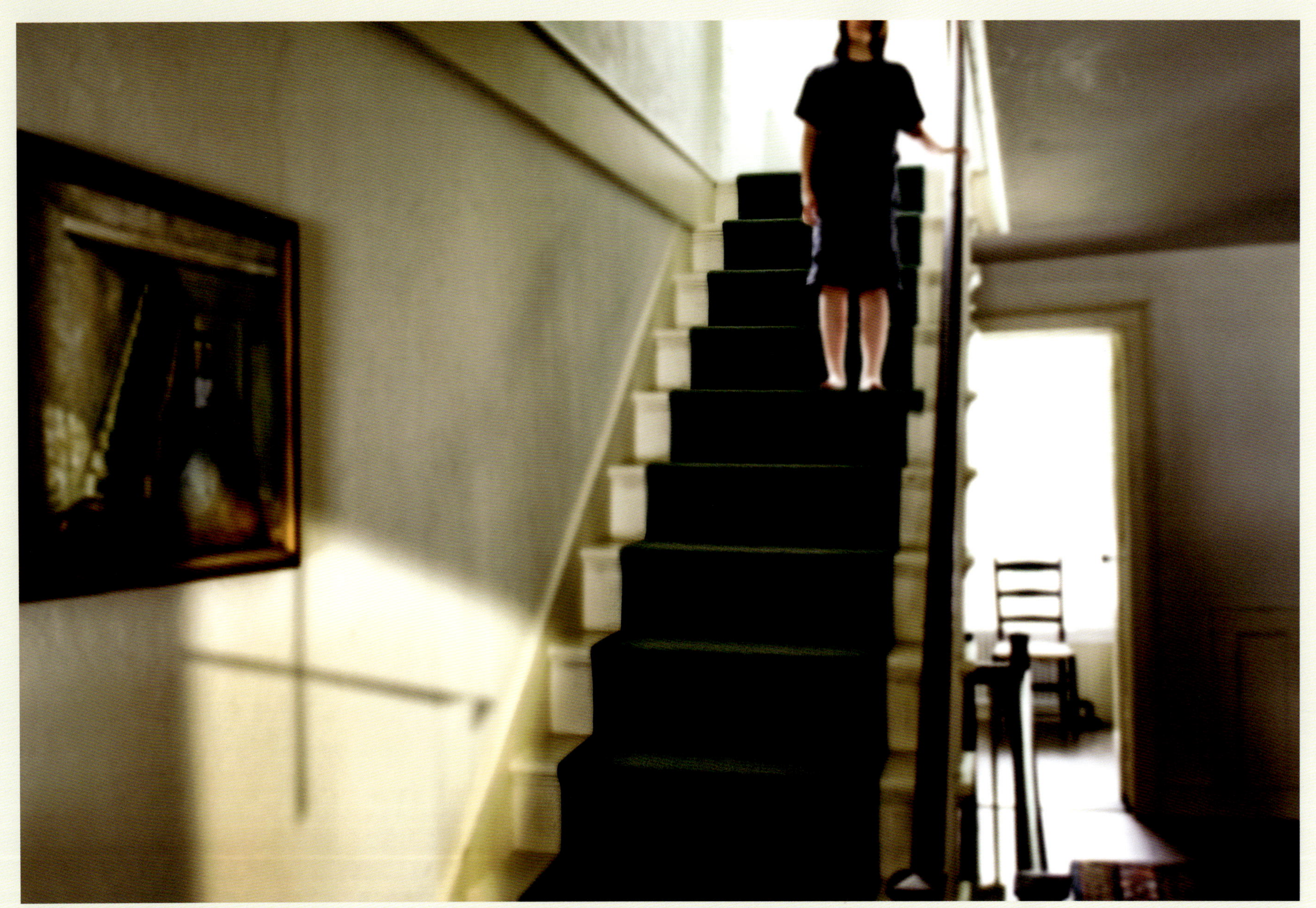

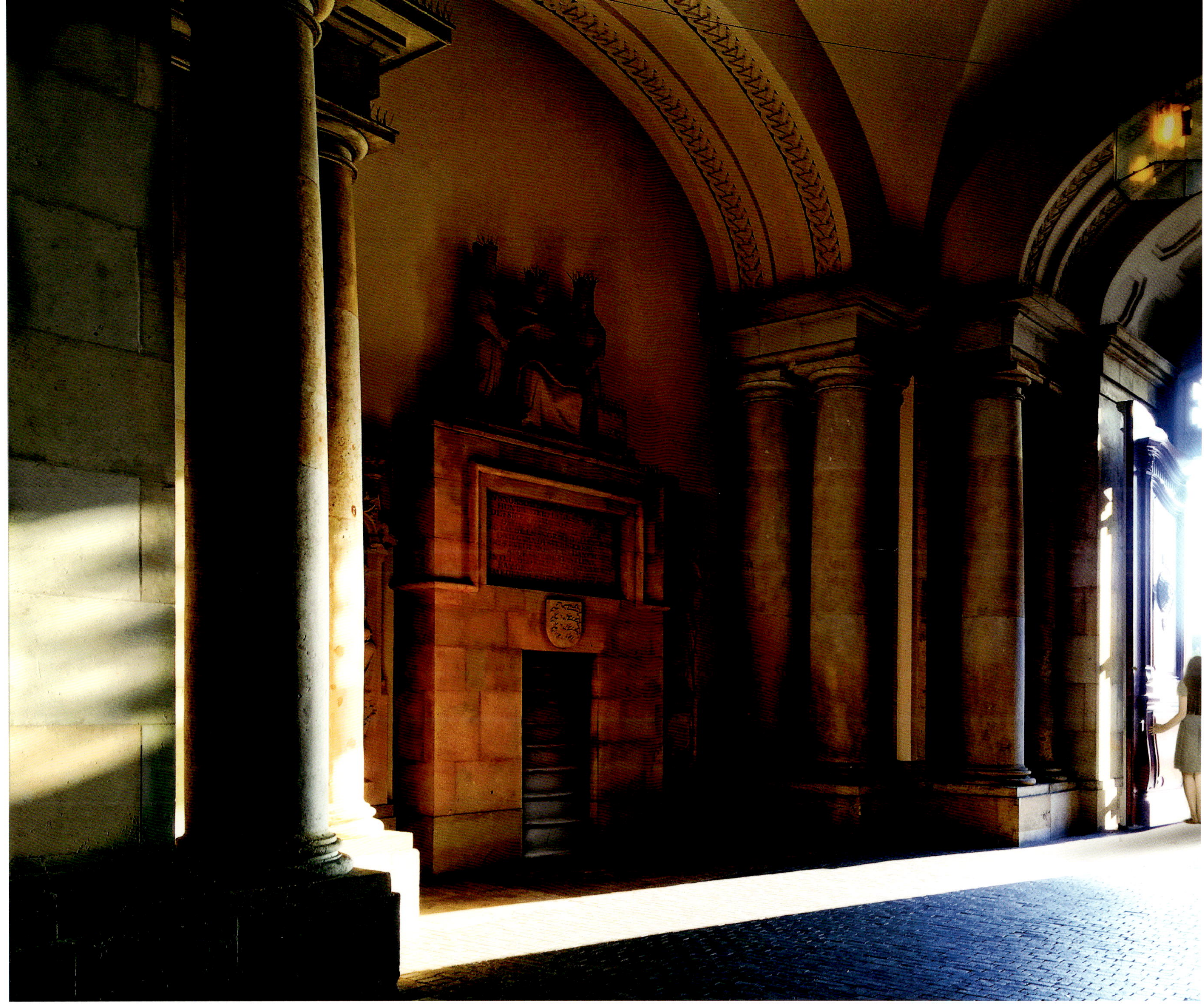

BETWEEN EACH BEAT OF THE HEART

THERE IS A STATE OF REST.

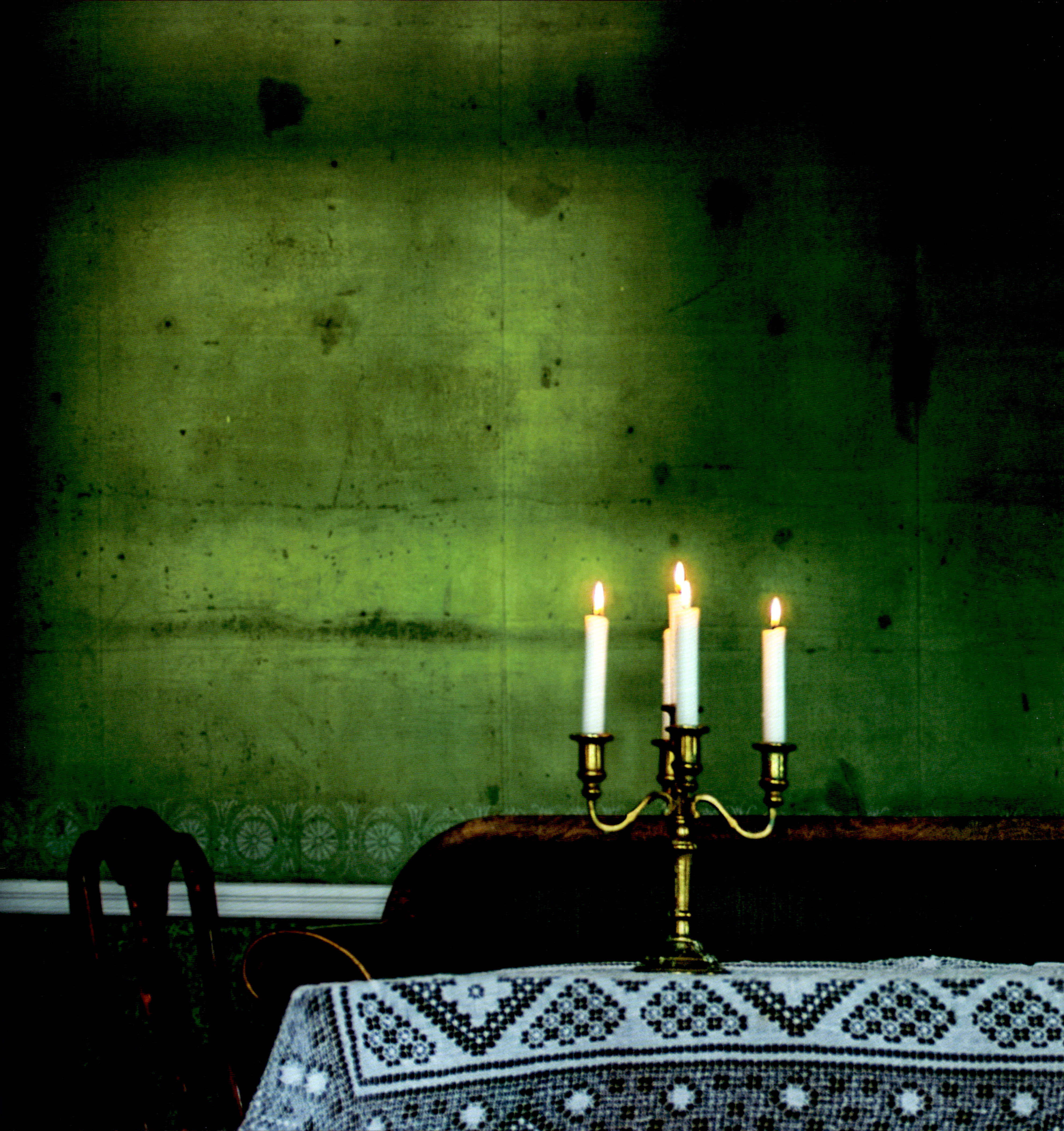

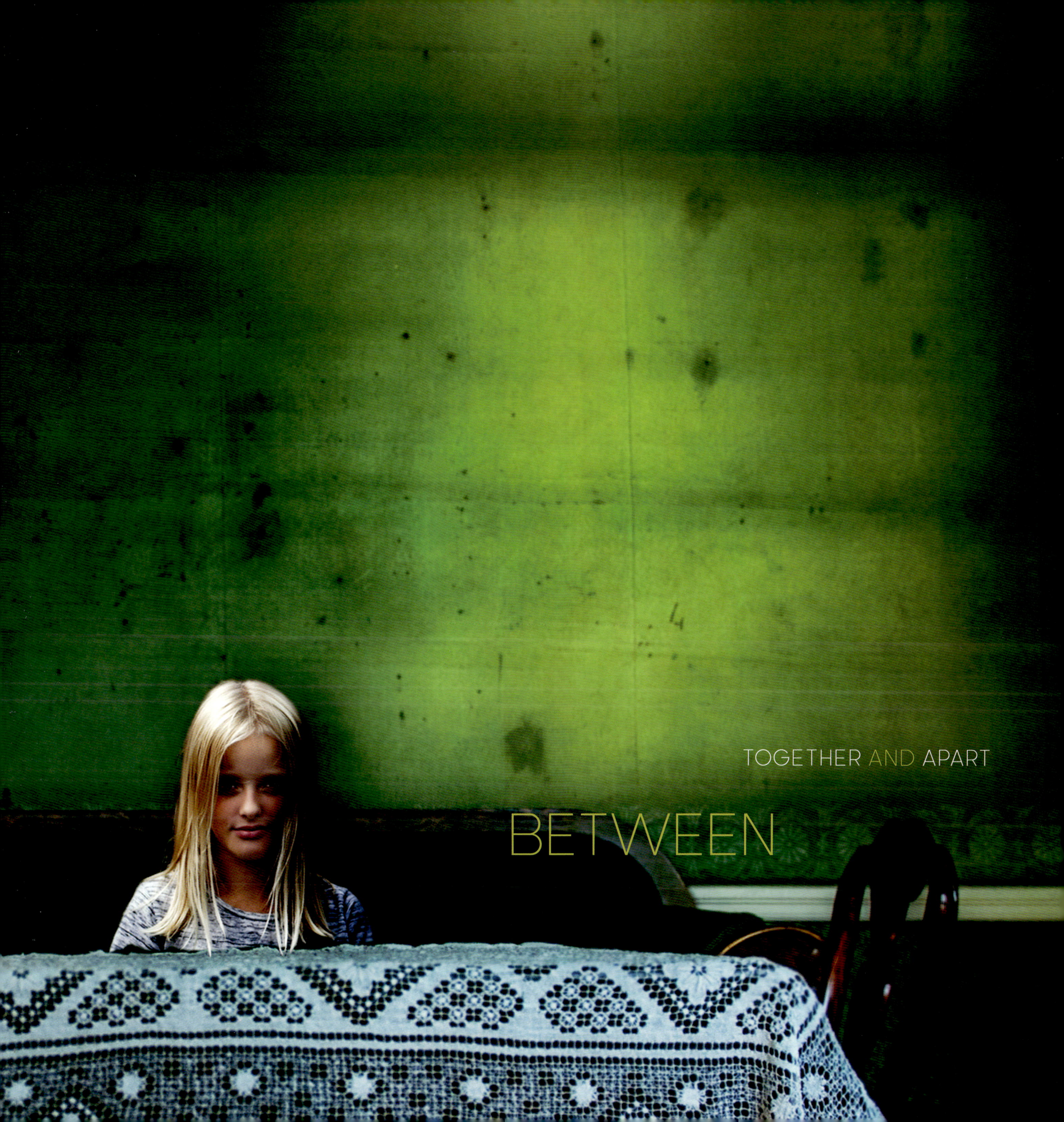
TOGETHER AND APART
BETWEEN

Lily lives in a room
that is shrinking
or her limbs
are growing

Ever since she ate the cookie
marked, "eat me"
her green dress began to glow
like a stalk
pushing through winter's dream

From her lookout
a new view

Nadine Boughton

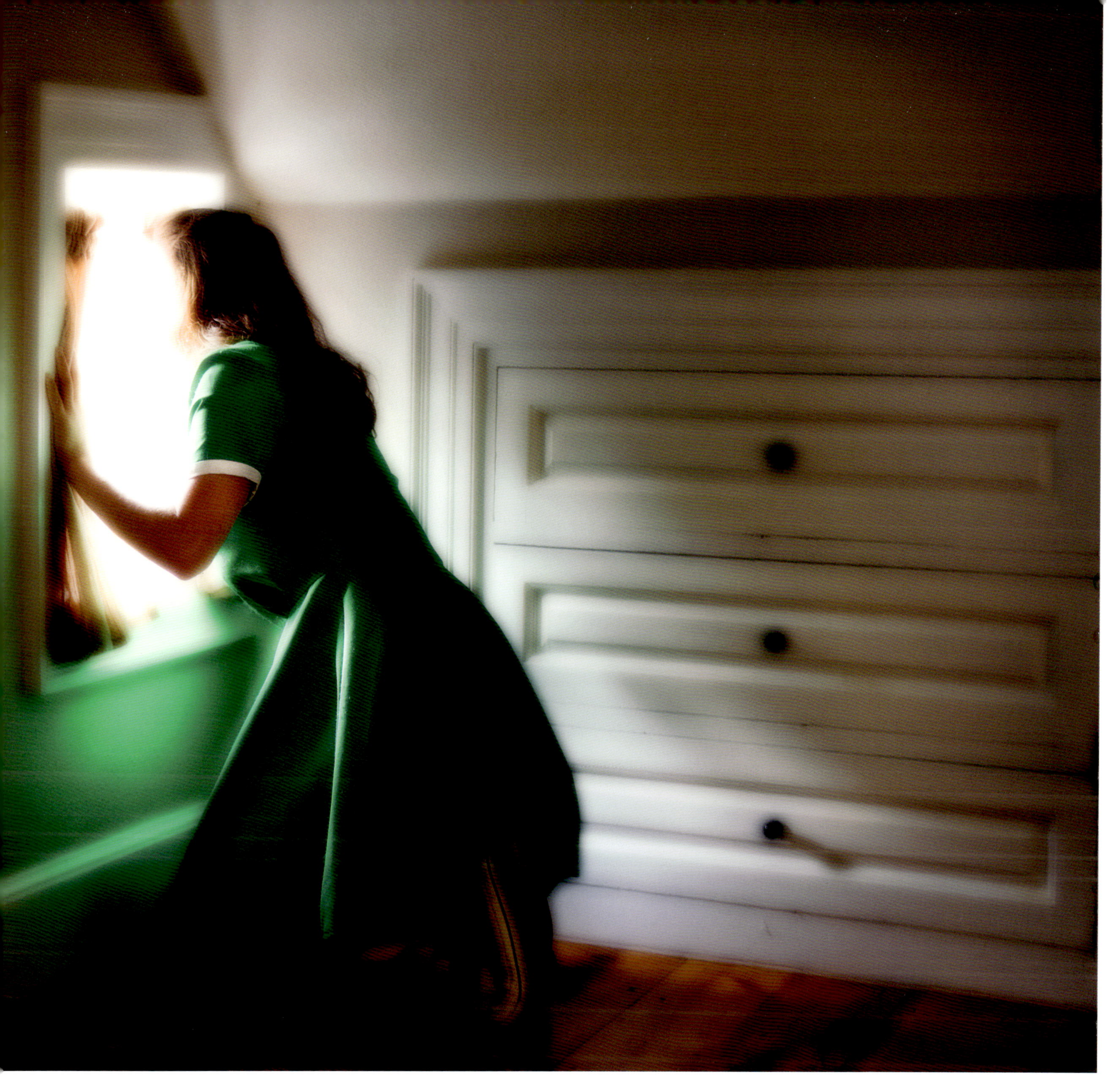

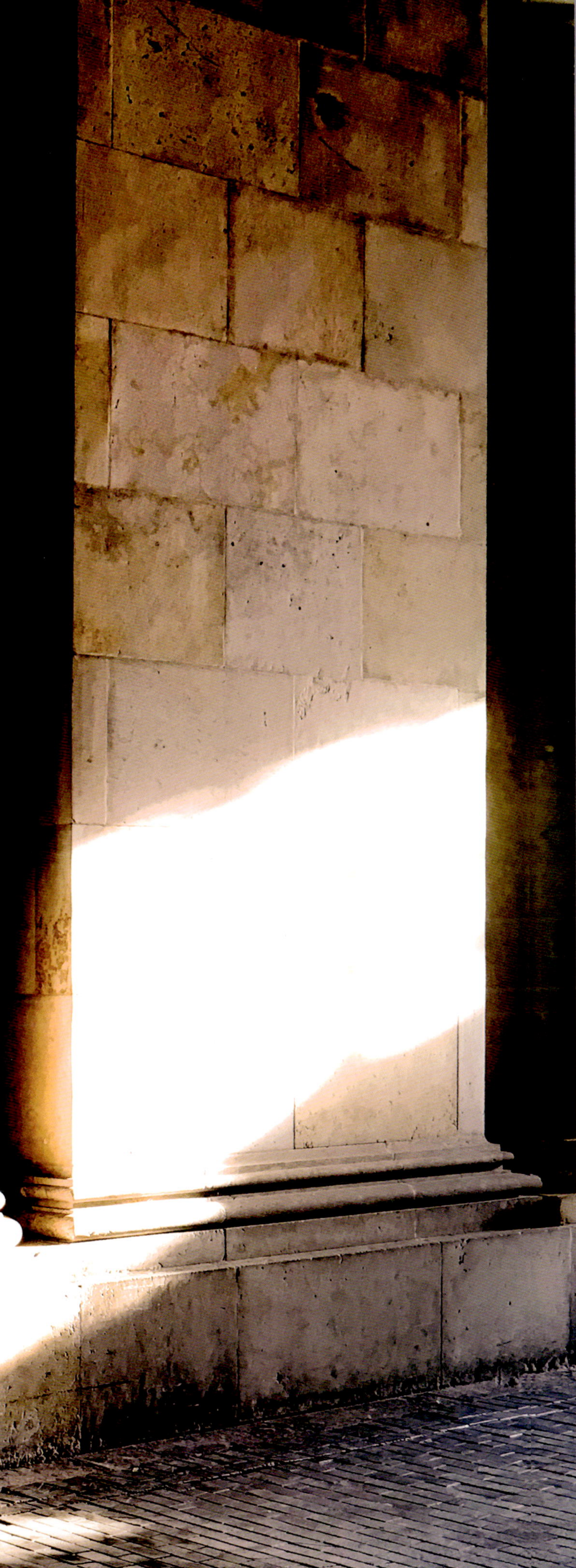

CYAN WAITING

It shouldn't be a surprise that a teacher of architecture is drawn to an image that reflects his interest. The play of light and shadow created by natural and artificial light, especially at the beginning of the stairs, the choice of materials and their different surfaces.

The cobblestone in the entranceway, the chiseled masonry walls, the somewhat different columns, the polished marble stairs, the original stucco, the white element that seems to be a later addition to emphasize a piece of art and finally the monumental wooden double door ... all provide such a rich environment in addition to the spatial experience of the architecture.

Is Cyan waiting for these doors to open to allow for more exploration of architectural treasures or is he/she waiting for a person potentially coming out of these doors?

Reinhold Mahler

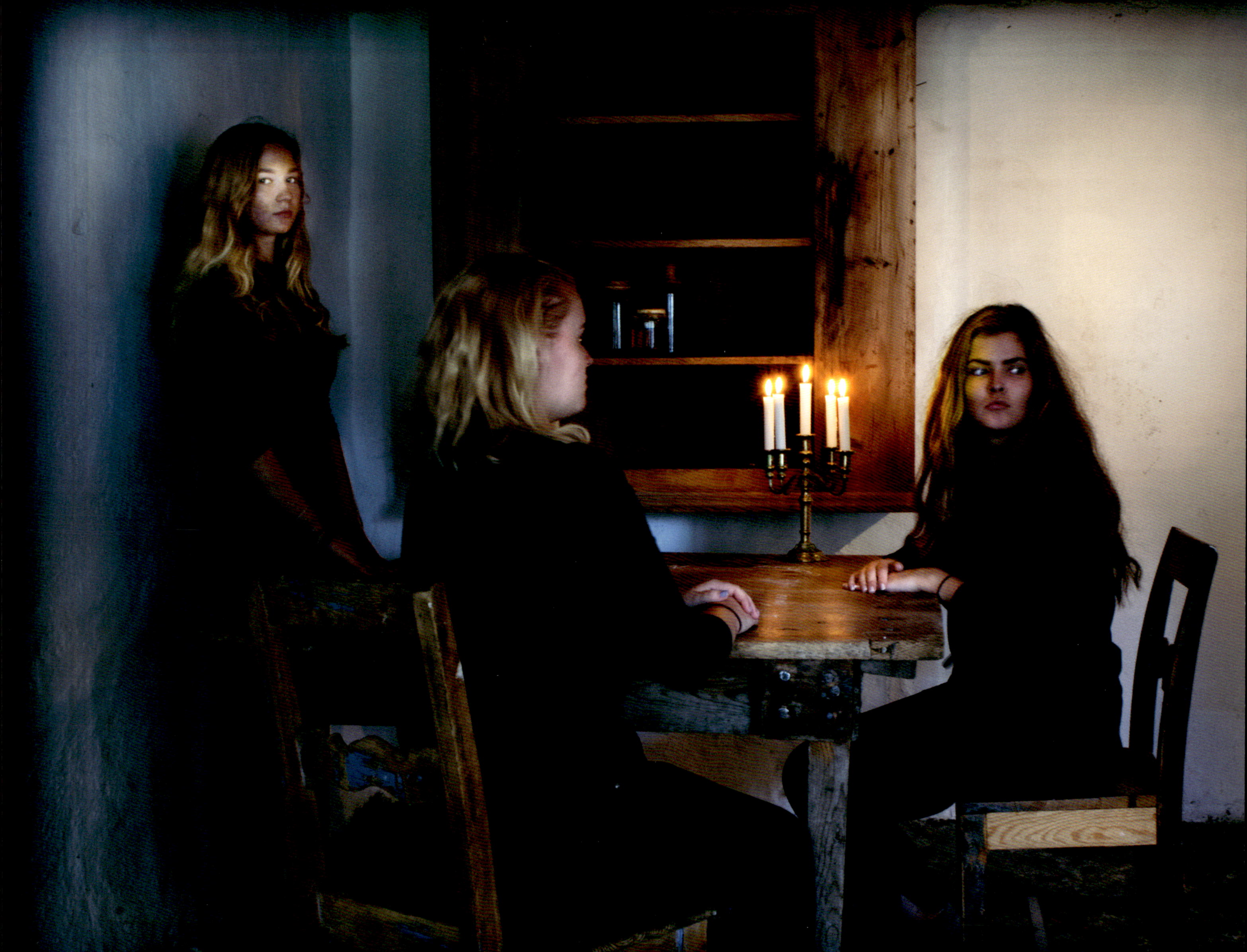

CANDLELIGHT

a family meeting—

three sisters light five tapers

listening for ghosts

Nancer Ballard

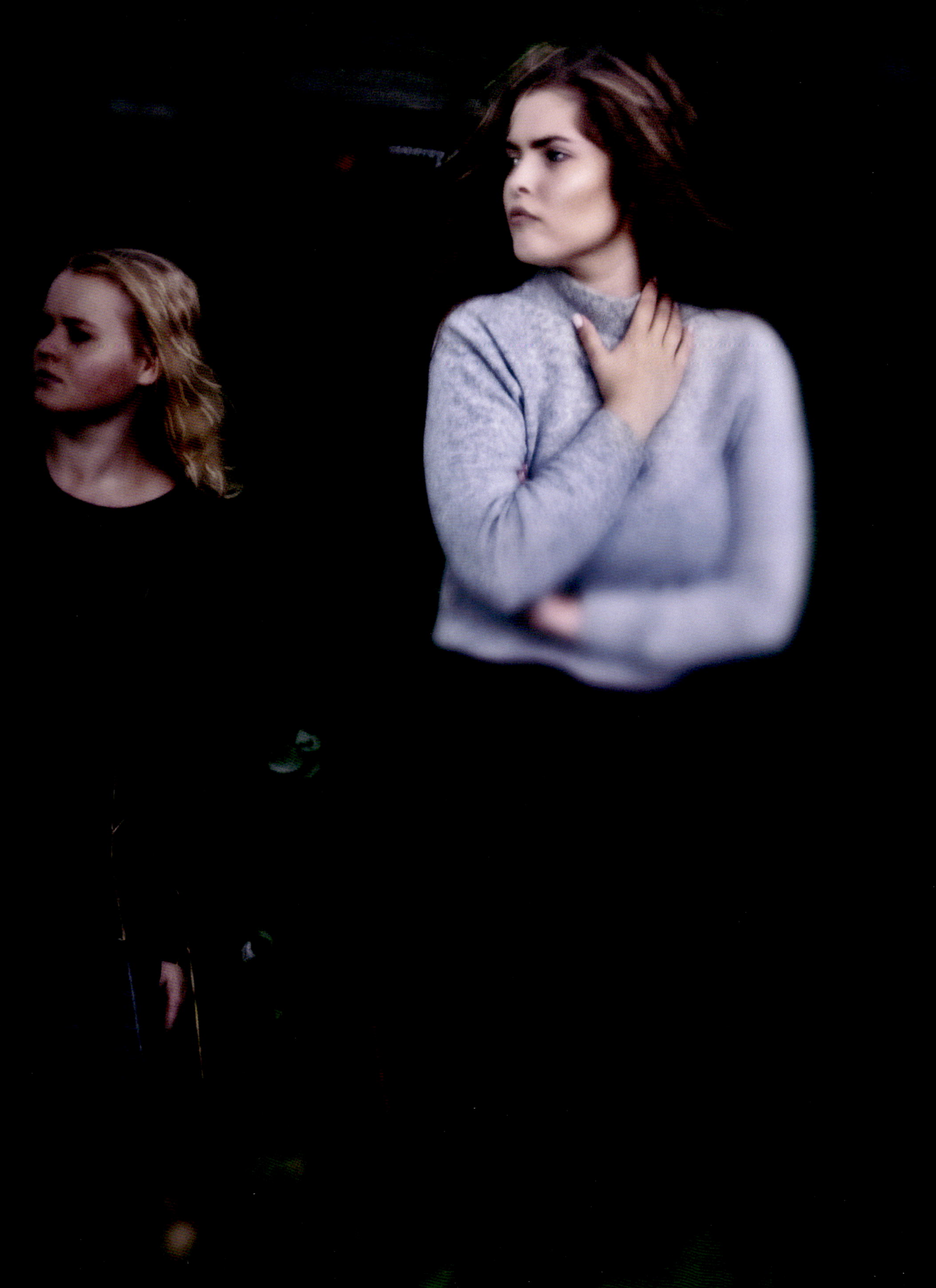

Upon first glance I notice what appears to be a sweet girl helping another sweet girl dress for a play.

Upon second glance my observation shifted. The clouds, which are the brightest part of the photo, have an ominous quality, almost sinister. The girl dressed in black may represent darkness as she appears to be tense; her mouth drawn and toes lifted to avoid the uncomfortable debris-ridden floor. The white dress, representing light as it shifts attention between darkness and light, a constant struggle. Life—so solid and limited—and clouds—so translucent and eternal—cross paths with these two girls. The helper's white dress with clouds projected from some unknown source bring to mind the theatrical nature of life.

Jamie Gordon

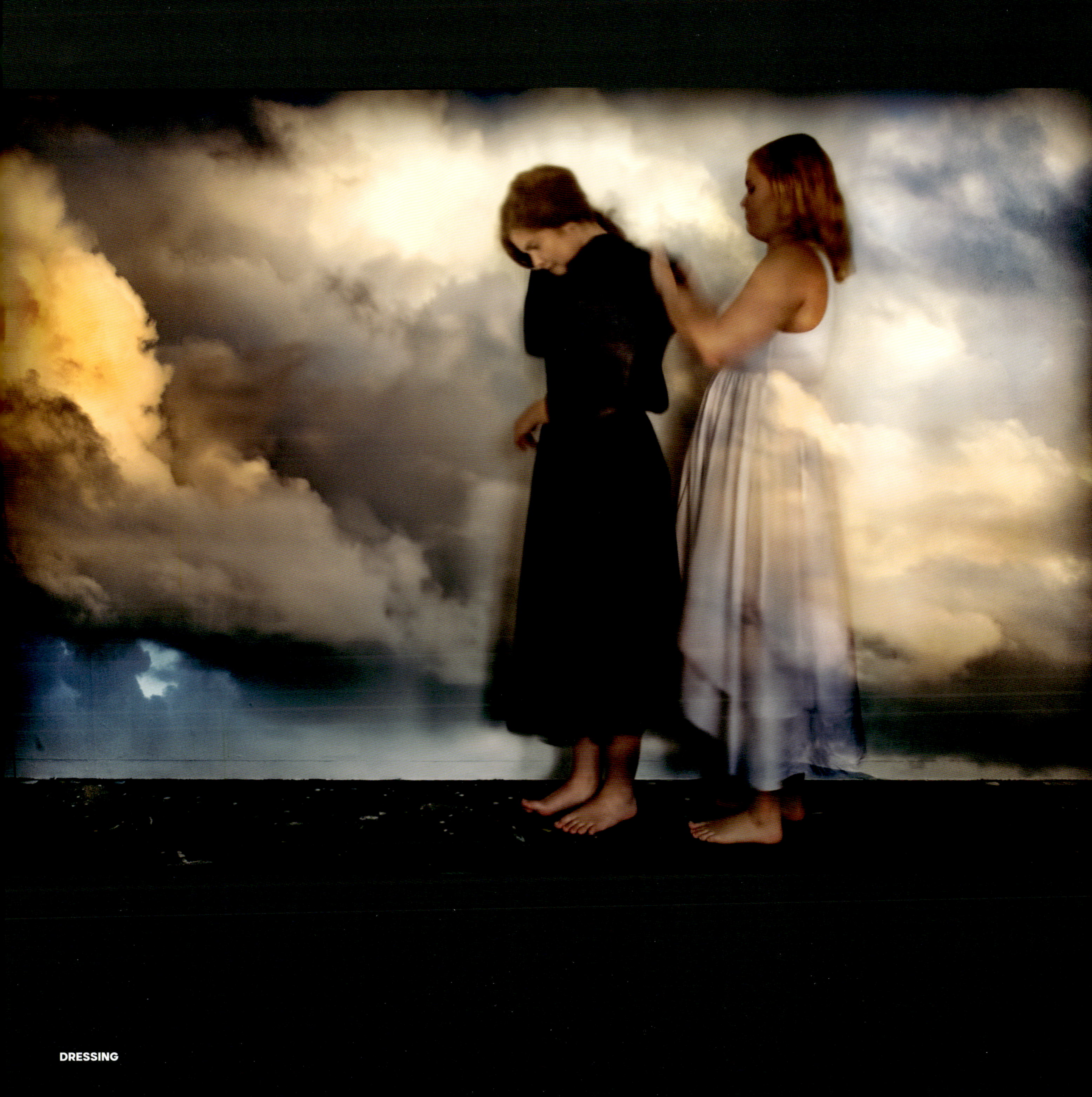

DRESSING

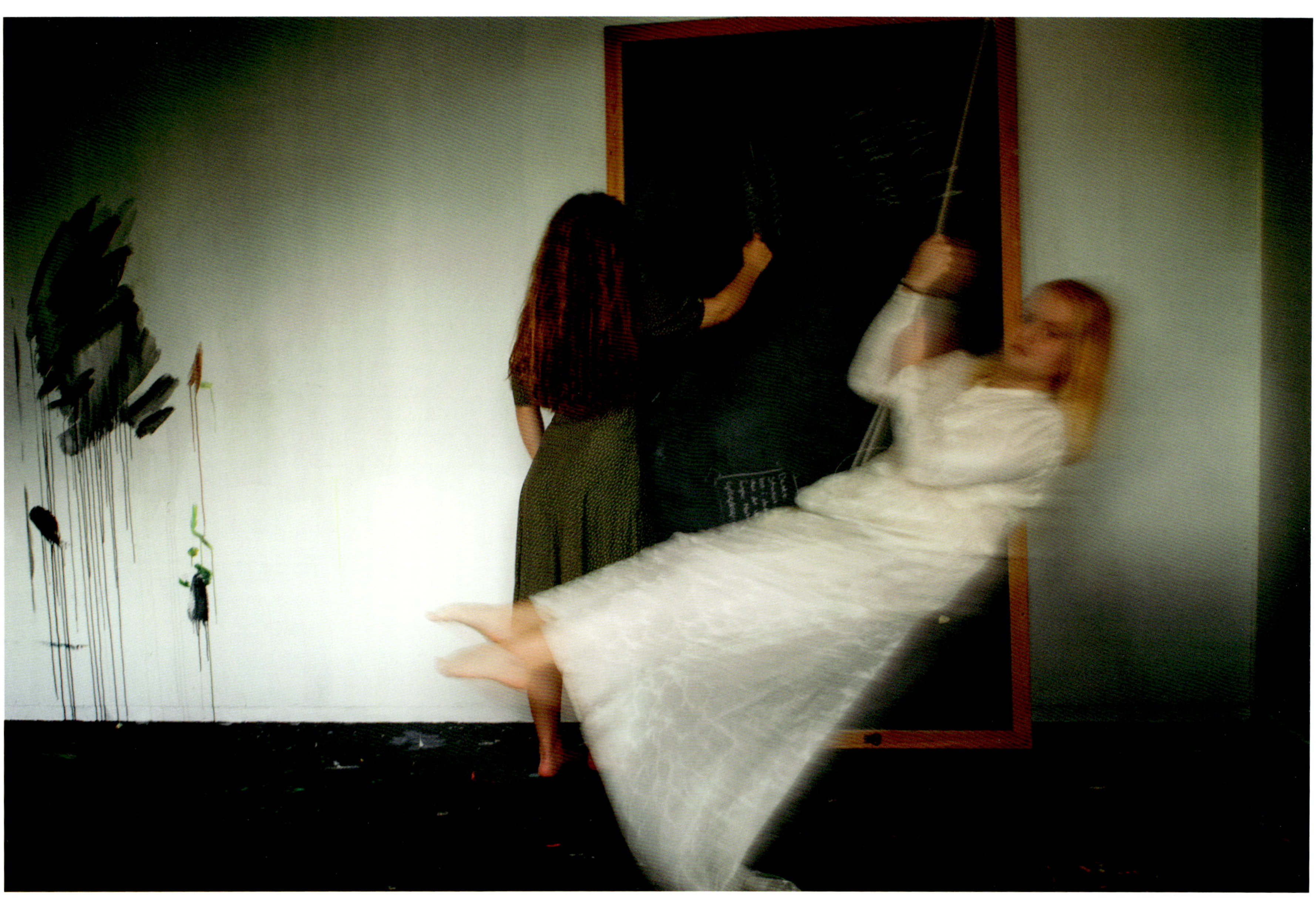

Is the world continuous or discrete? This question has preoccupied physicists since … since there were physicists.

A girl swings on a rope from shadow into light. We see her foot at the apogee of her swing, just as it ends its upward arc and retraces its way down gravity's well. But how does it get to that point?

Plato cites a vexing observation by Zeno to the effect that, at any point before the foot reaches its apogee, it must still travel to the midpoint of the remaining distance—and from that midpoint to yet another midpoint at half of the remaining distance, and so on in a frustrating lather of infinitesimals. We are momentarily compelled to stop and wonder how the foot can ever get anywhere at all.

"And yet it moves," we protest. It moves because … it is in the nature of the foot of a girl on a swing to move.

Swing reminds us of motions too obvious to ponder. Of positions and extents that don't need labelling. What we might label the "apogee" is simply the foot at rest, caught by the camera. A rest between two opposing motions—or between two phases of one harmonic motion.

A girl swings on a rope from shadow into light. She crosses a threshold. Our very act of observation causes her to be in one state or another. The wave function of her diaphonous gown collapses into a predefined level. For a hundred years, we have been constrained by quantum theories to believe that electrons have a similar discrete nature.

They only orbit at predefined levels. When they are forced to change levels, they don't comply smoothly. They shriek, emitting a photon of protest, and are suddenly somewhere else. The photons are colored with excitement and zip off through the universe until they hit us in the retina. And for a time—perhaps an immeasurably short time—the electron is at rest between colors.

We still can't seem to answer this question. Theoretical models we subscribe to still vacillate between particles and waves, between black holes of infinite density and loop dimensions of tiny but non-vanishing diameter. We explore with ever more refined instruments, but still absorb these new measurements with the same old sensorium. And on some questions, we are left swinging back and forth.

Is the world continuous or discrete?

David Ray

The caged giraffe, too,
dreams of song, the smell of grass,
ambling free again

Nancer Ballard

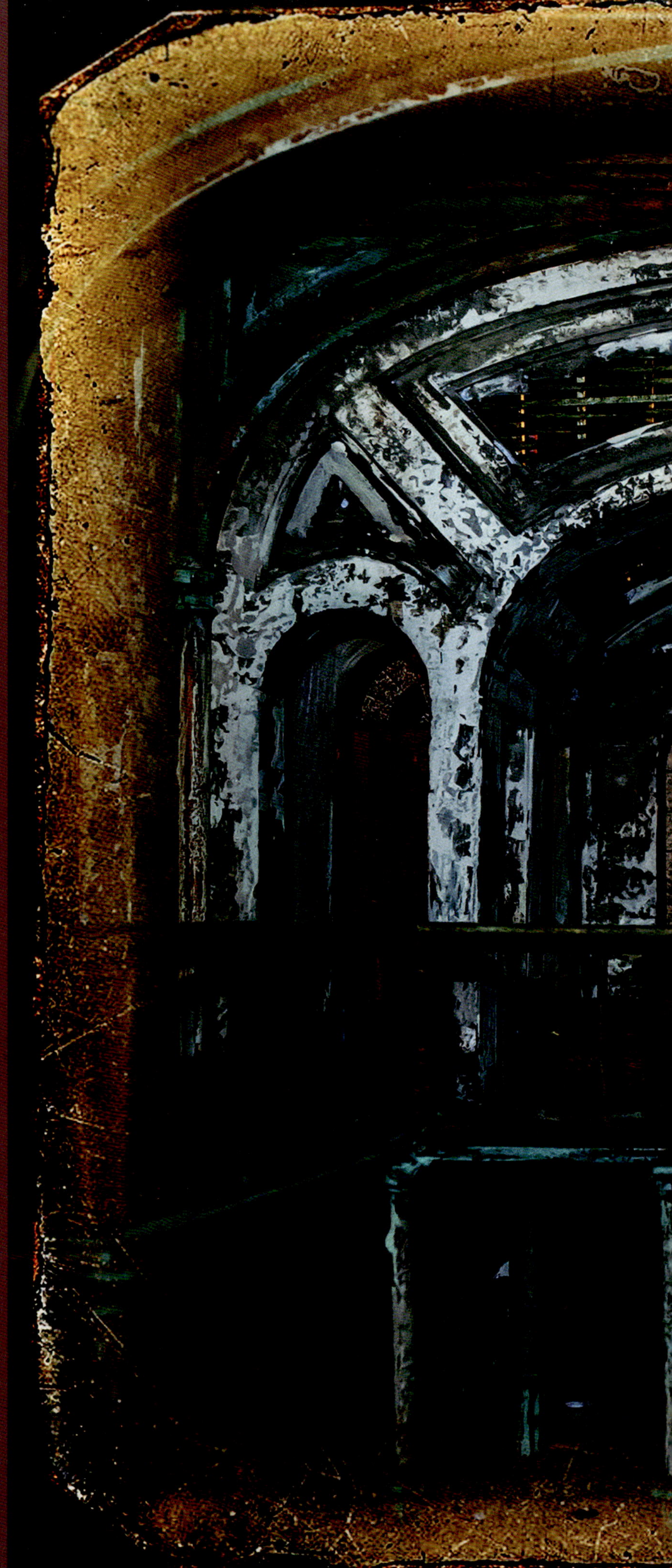

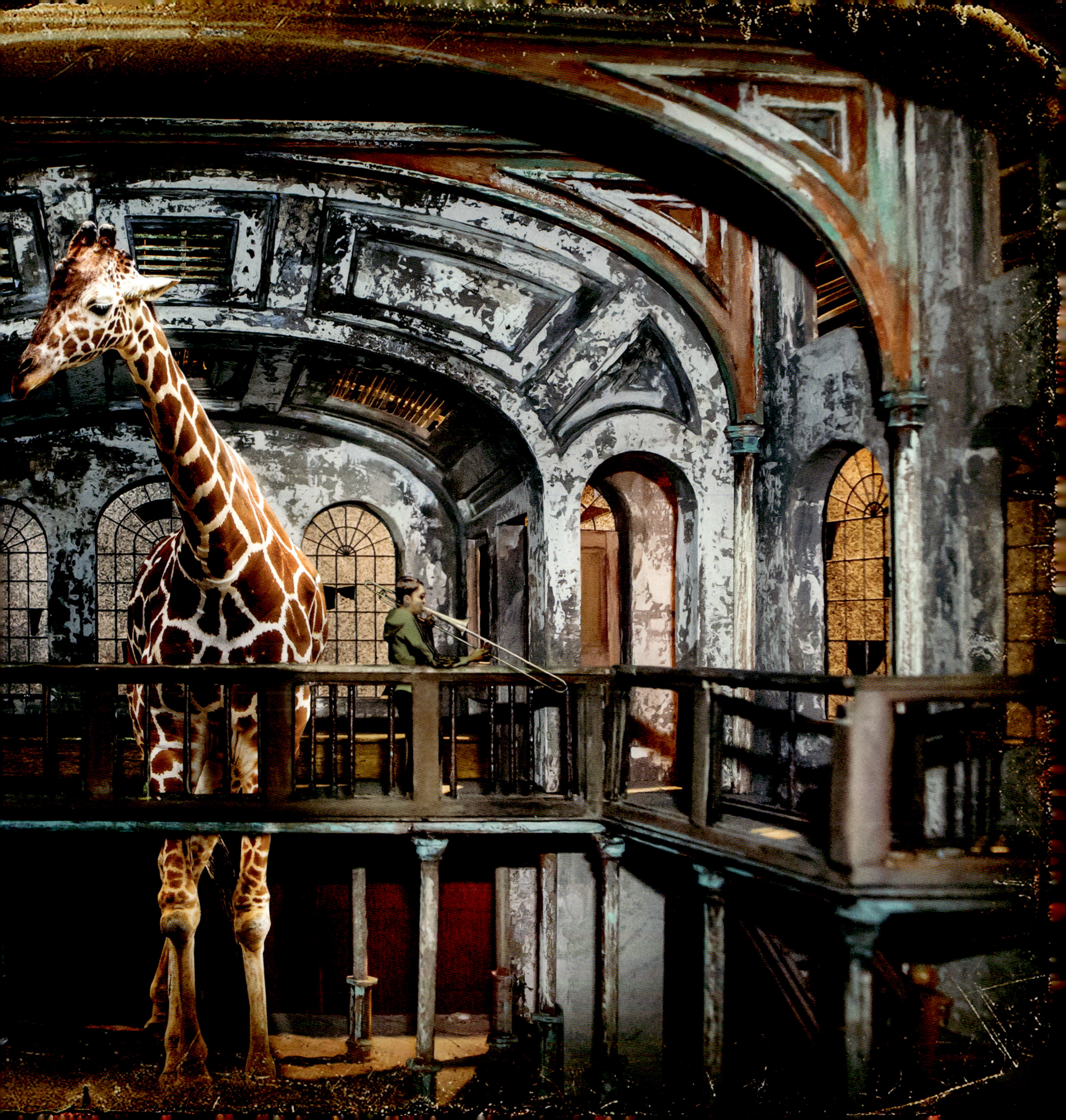

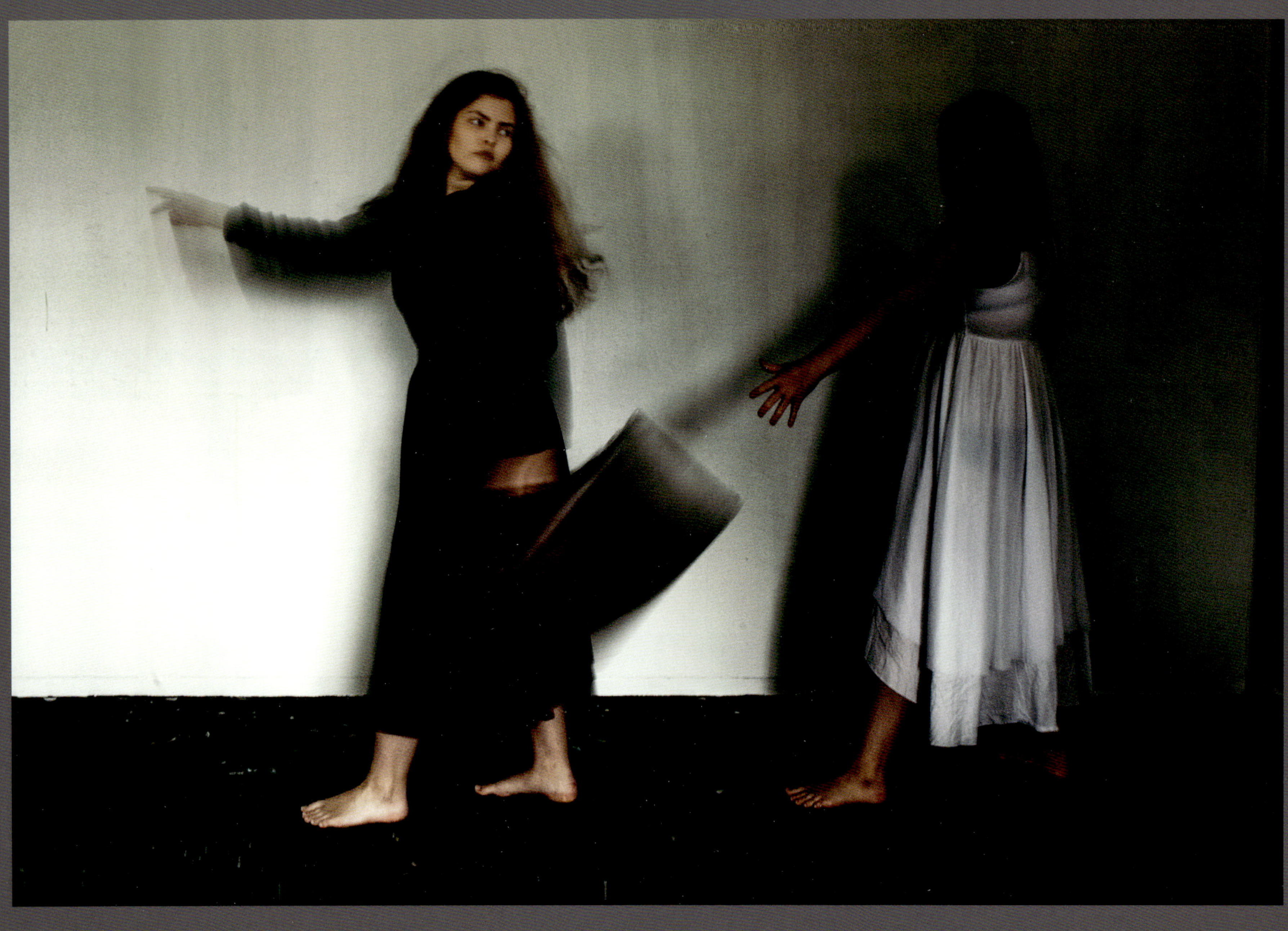

Something smacked my left ankle. I turned and saw that Marie had thrown my suitcase out after me. Surprised at my own quick response, I grabbed its bamboo handle, intercepting its progress towards the gutter. It seemed lighter than I had remembered.

I had left it behind partly on purpose, packed as it was with what seemed to mark so firmly my next station in life—a Bible, a pair of clogs, a brick of tan soap, a square-cut cream linen apron with vertical pockets, already showing faded stains of kitchen duty. But when, after setting it firmly on my hotel bed, I opened the brass clasps of the suitcase, I saw none of those. Instead, there was a throw of black feathers, cunningly woven together at the back, unbelievably soft and sensuous, at once rebellious and tender. I immediately spread it over the blue chenille of the hotel bedspread.

My coat, damp from the rain, I had already hung on the door hook. Now I took off my jacket with the grape cluster buttons, then the plain white silk shirt, my best. In my camisole, I rolled and squirmed on the feather throw, like the delicate pelt of some amazing bird. Then I called down to the bar to send up an absinthe, planning to pay with some of the money I'd reserved for my train ticket.

I was distracted by the sloshing sound of the suitcase. Made of woven rattan, now soaked from the downpour, it seemed to be at once melting and unravelling. When I got up to investigate, I saw there was something else in it, a pair of black feathered gloves with gold talons. Under them, as if the gloves had been balled up over its eyes to keep out the light, curled an eagle mask, a helmet of metallic wire threaded with more feathers, this time dappled and brown. I pulled the mask over my head. The beak seemed to be real keratin, not ivory or plastic. I ran to the bathroom mirror. Through two pinhole eye slits, I saw myself transformed—a creature suddenly savage and wise in the ways of savagery.

The suitcase was soaked and seemed to be falling apart the more I removed from it, as if its strange cargo had exhausted it. It would never be possible to fit these things back inside. The one thing left, which I had taken at first for part of the suitcase, was a black lanyard (or was it a little switch?) braided in what I would learn was the Japanese *kumihimo* pattern. I began to beat it on bedpost and bureau, aimless and imperious, a staccato tattoo: my sharp taps backed by the drone of wind and rain.

Eventually the wind was still. I heard only my own faint percussion. Then I stopped that, too. I slid off the mask, and put my silk shirt back on. Then, with an arabesque of intuition that seemed to come from beyond me, I reached up and undid the top collar button. Then, the one the below that, too.

I called down to say I would not need room service after all. I had changed my mind. I would come down and drink at the bar.

Monica Raymond

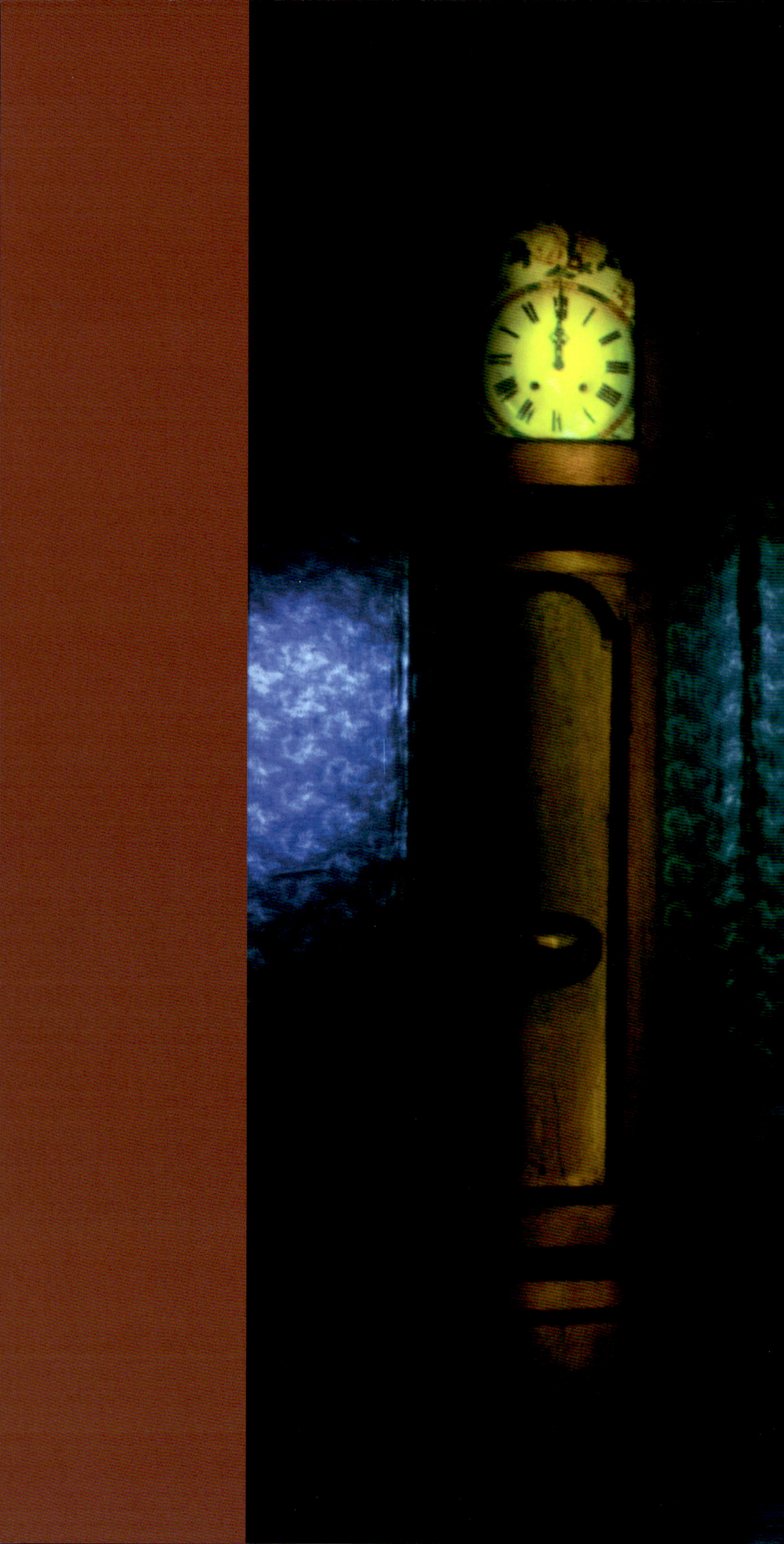

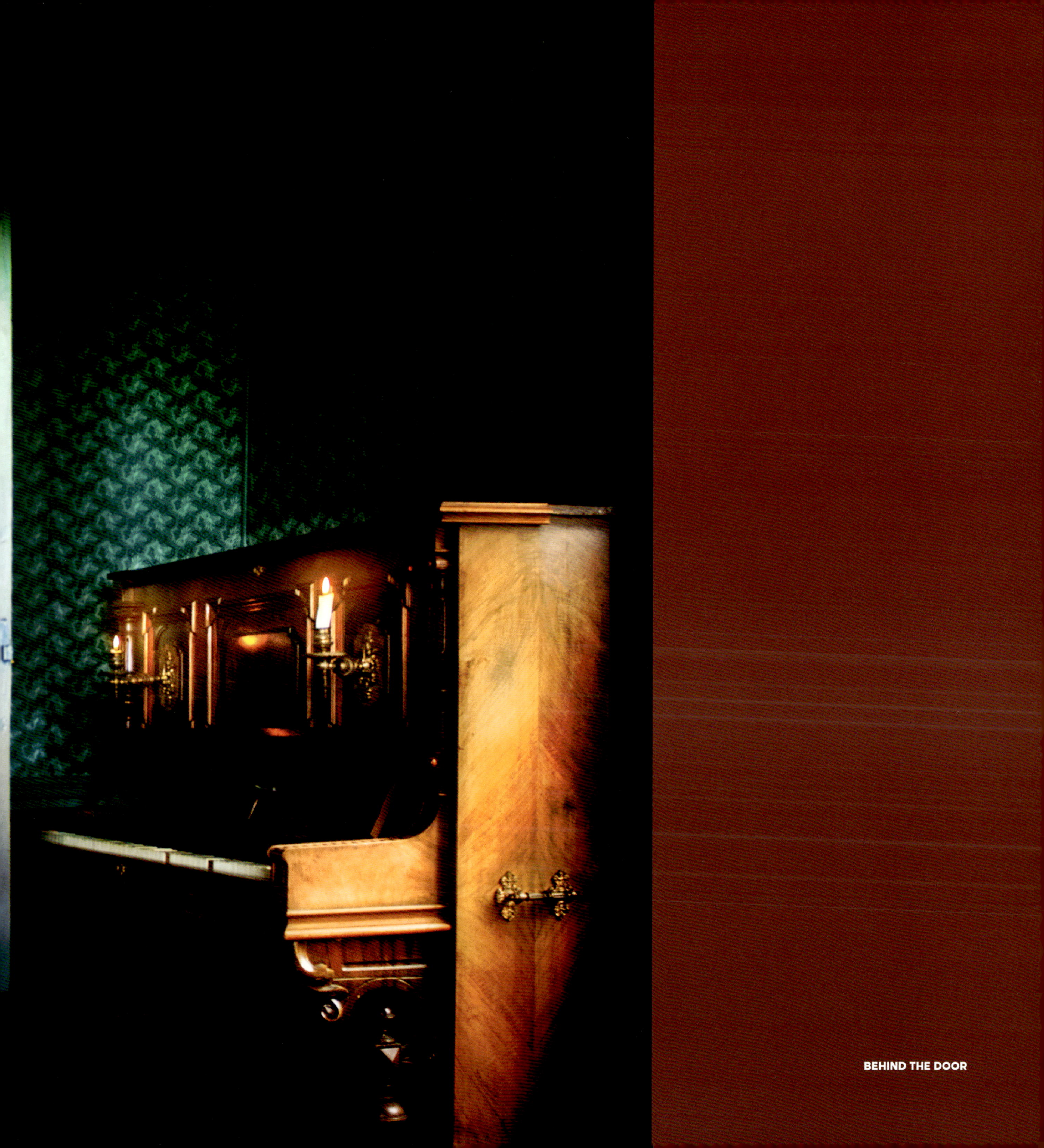

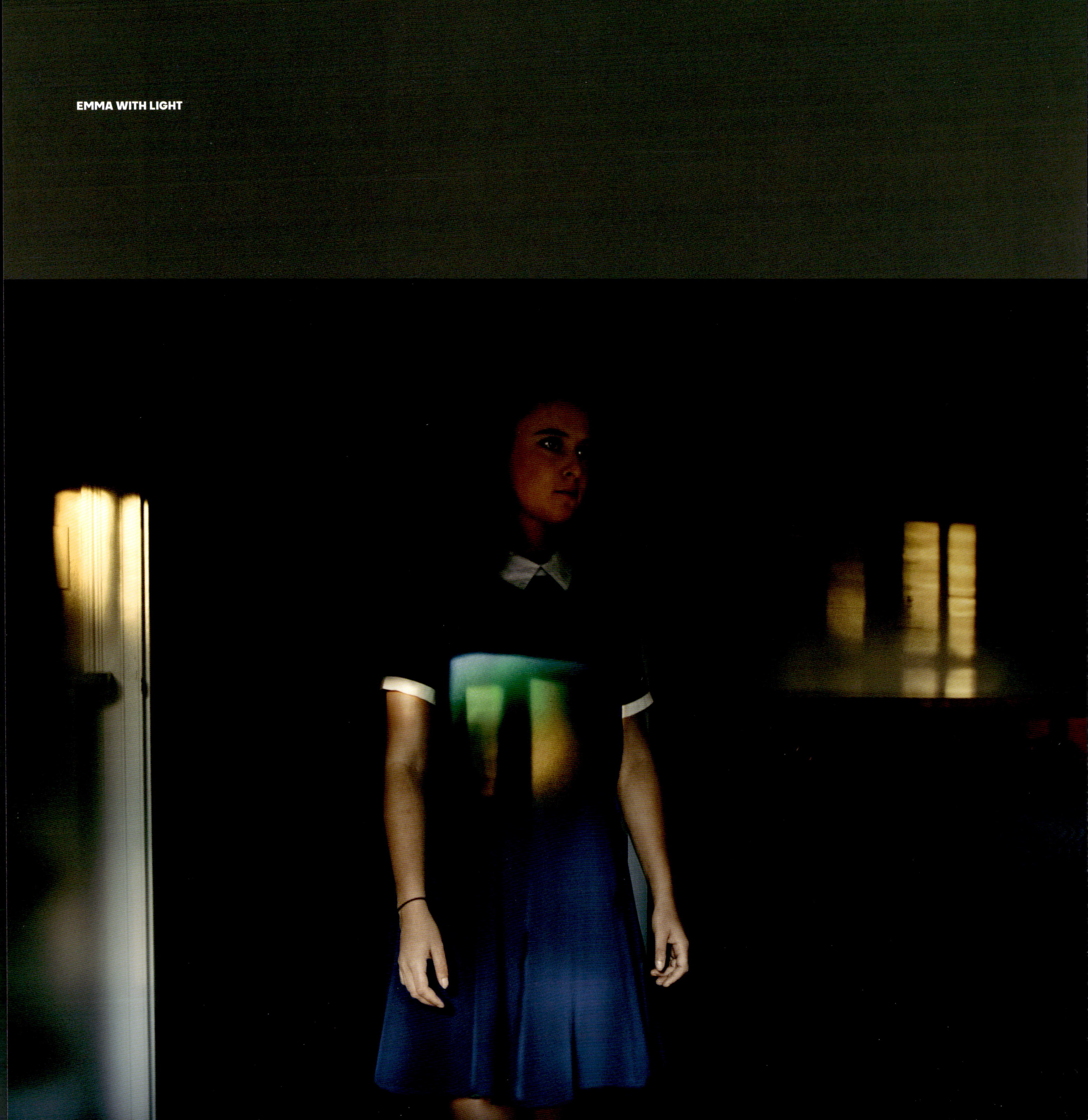

EMMA WITH LIGHT

For one hour a day, starting at eleven in the morning, a different world opened on to Emma's chest, smooth transparent slabs of topaz or aquamarine. She wasn't sure what it was. A palace or a prison? Boulders, glaciers, gelatin dessert? She couldn't tell the scale—infinite or infinitesimal? Mile high glass curtains, or carats cut under the jeweler's loupe, facets of dragonfly wing?

In physics, Mr Galanter had said light had two forms, particle and wave. But this was a third form, light as slab, which the stained glass remembered. There was no point in mentioning it, or arguing. She wondered if it was some kind of arcane radiation, if it would affect her tiny breasts, which were just starting to come in, swollen and sore. She sometimes experienced the light as a kind of soothing application, a menthol, a Tiger Balm of split cool prism, not as cold as ice, but like that.

She felt strangely proud and abashed, vessel or vehicle for what she did not know she was carrying.

One time she thought she sensed, just out of eyeshot, a rangy Nordic man with close cropped gray hair giving orders to someone to maneuver these prisms around in rope slings. She imagined he was a choreographer, and this was his stage. Another time she thought it must be the entry to an aerodrome or exquisite subway in a dangerous glassy universe like something from a Philip Pullman novel, and she tried to imagine what the laws of such a world might be.

She couldn't catch it clearly, only see the reflection of the reflection, see herself faint and fractured, diminished in the window through which the white shafts of light pulsed so strongly, knowing their own mind.

Monica Raymond

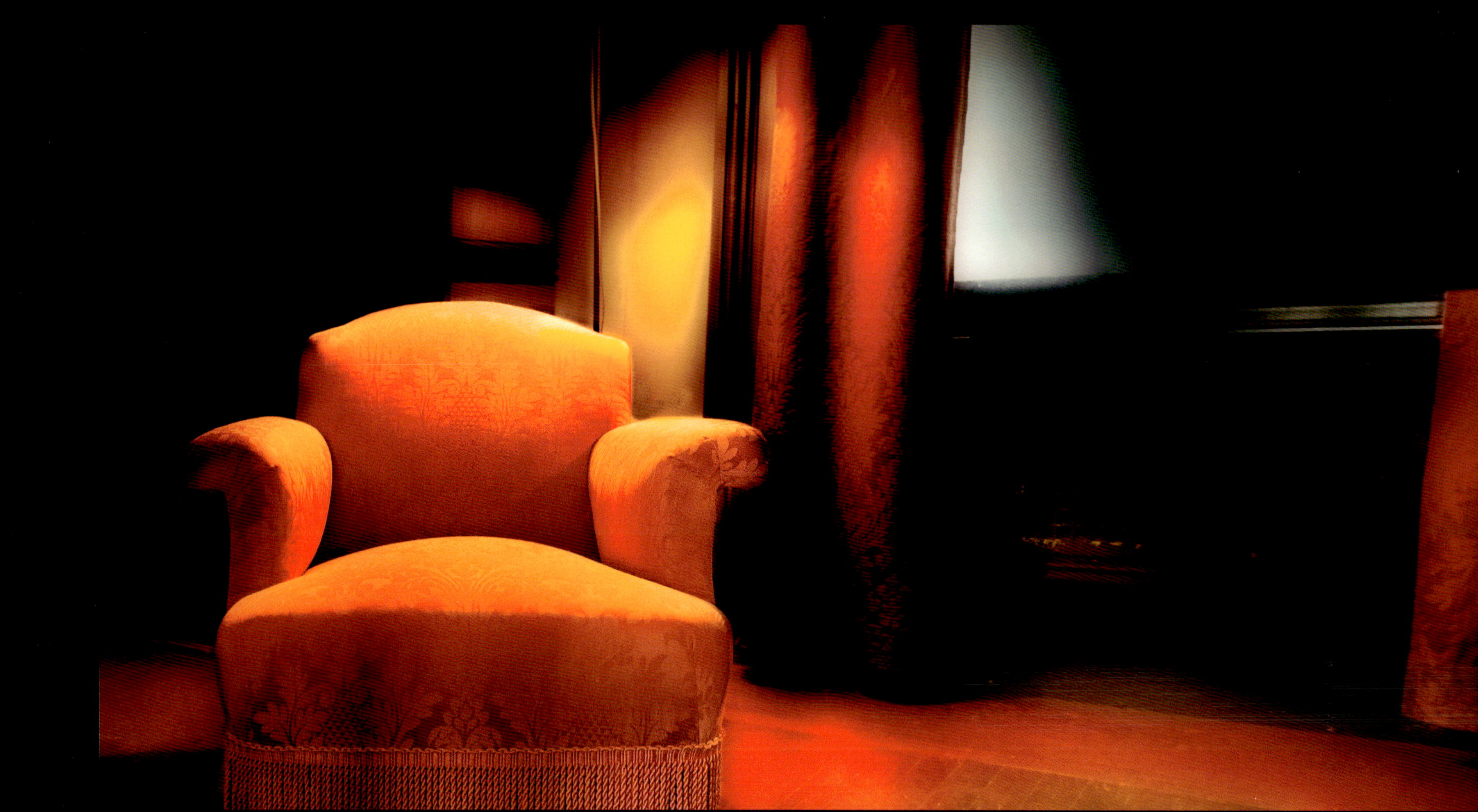

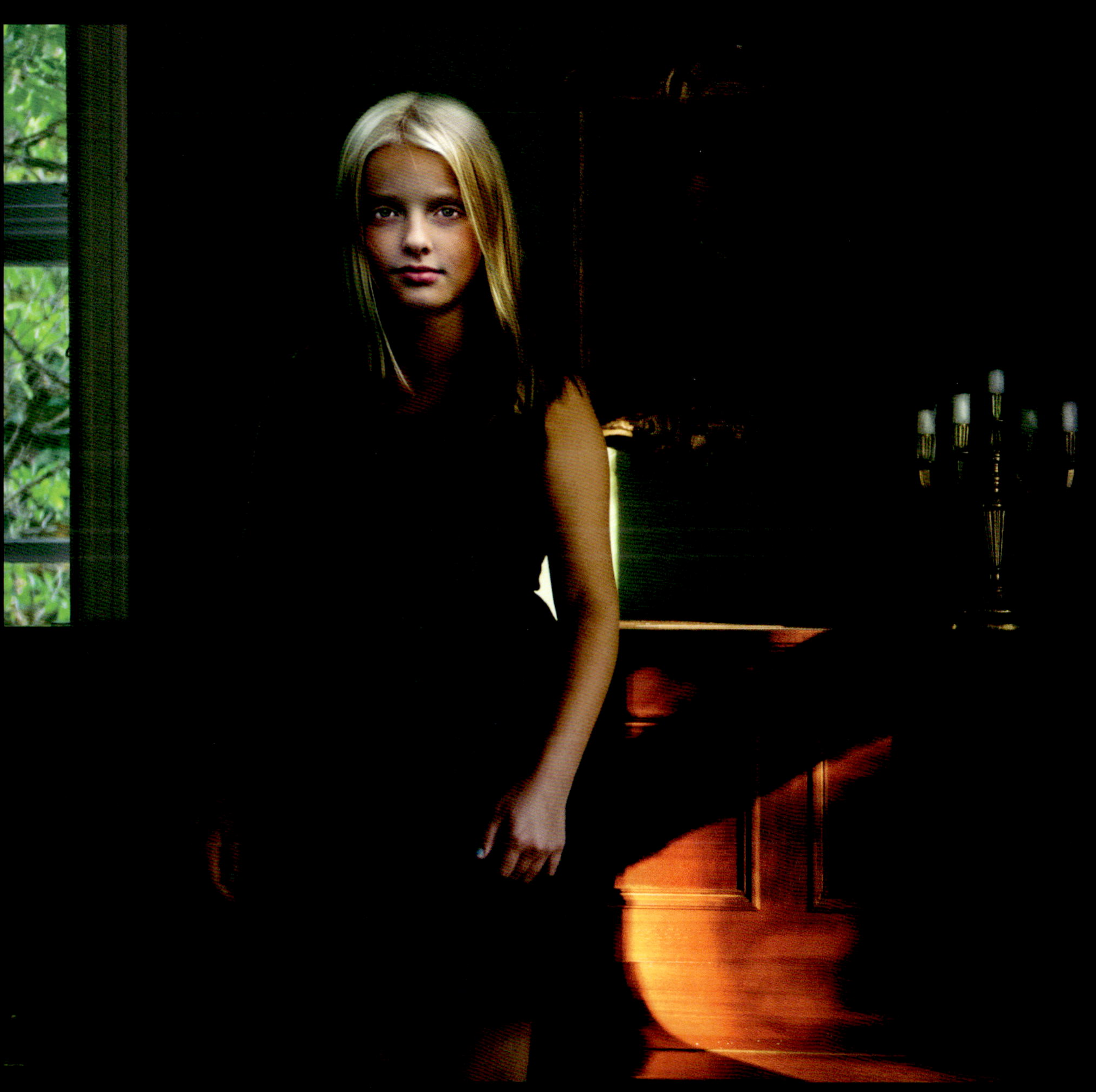

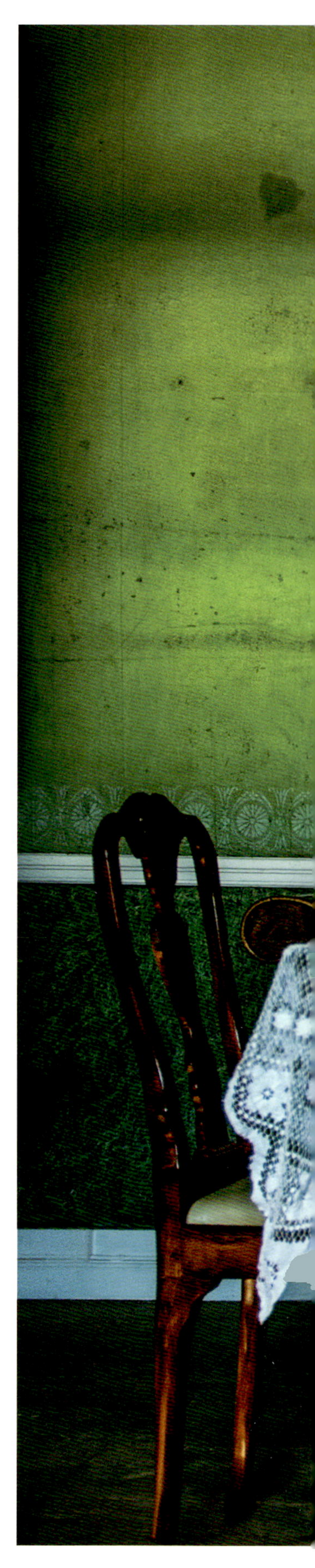

LEAH IN THE GREEN ROOM

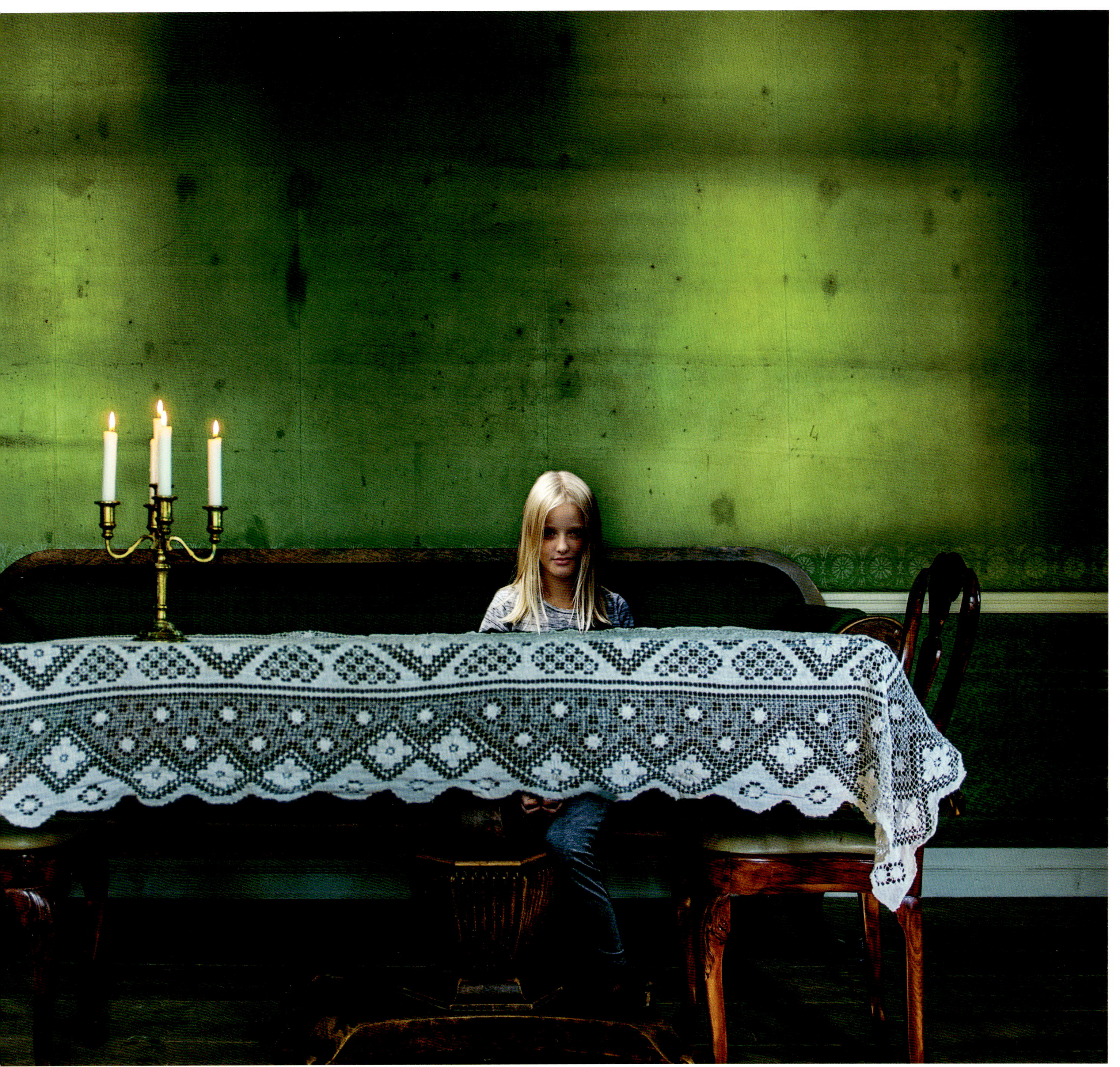

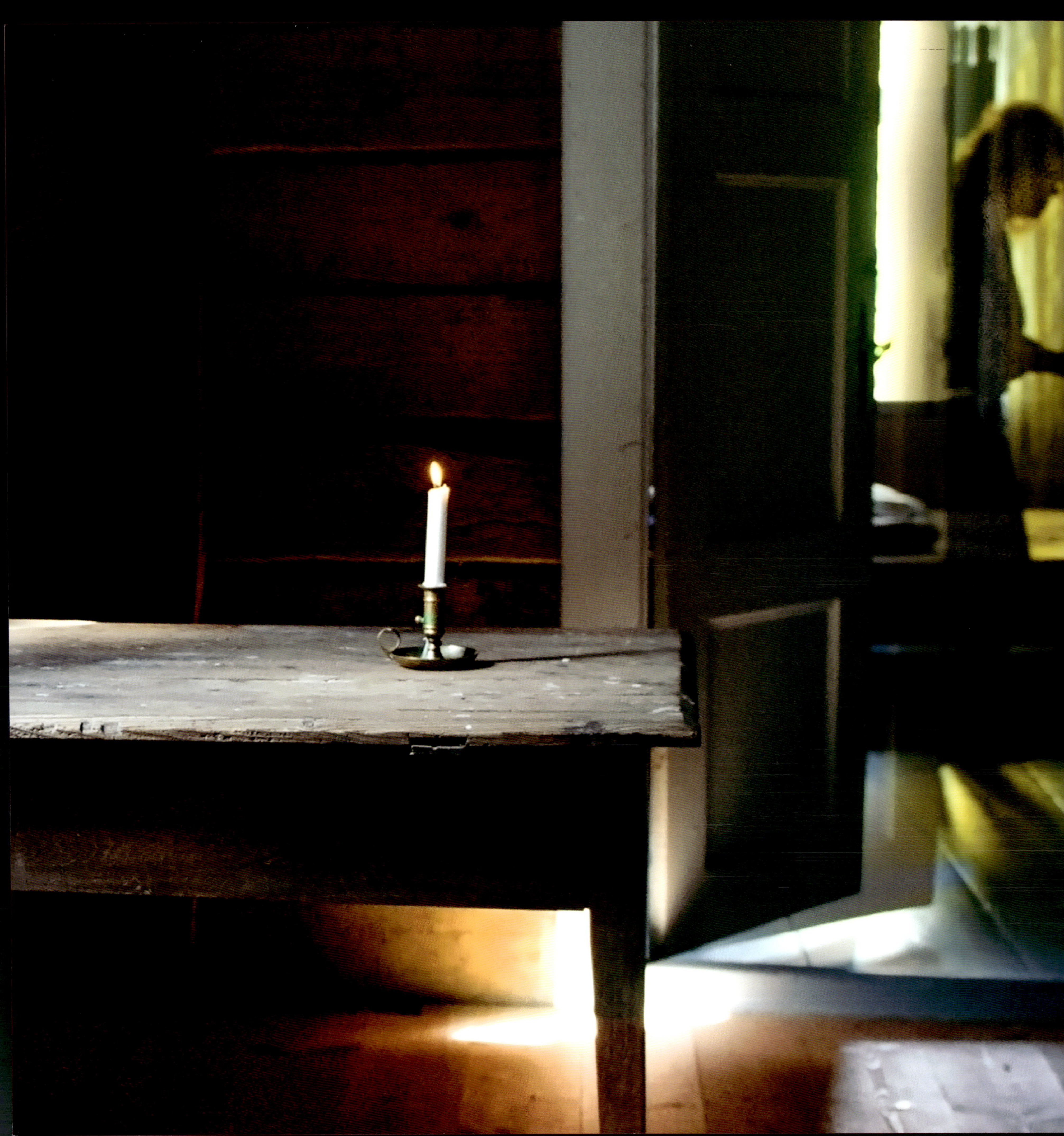

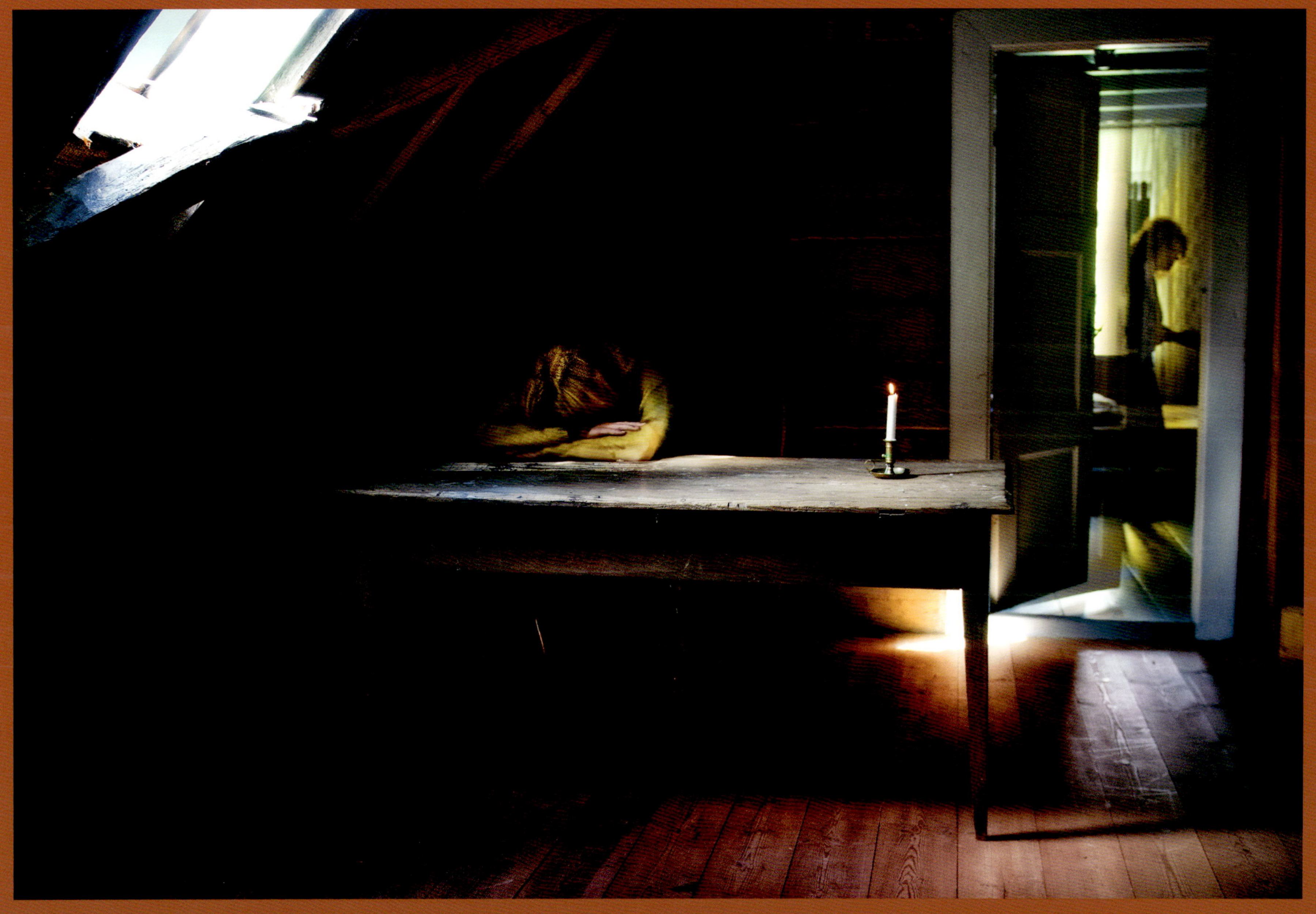

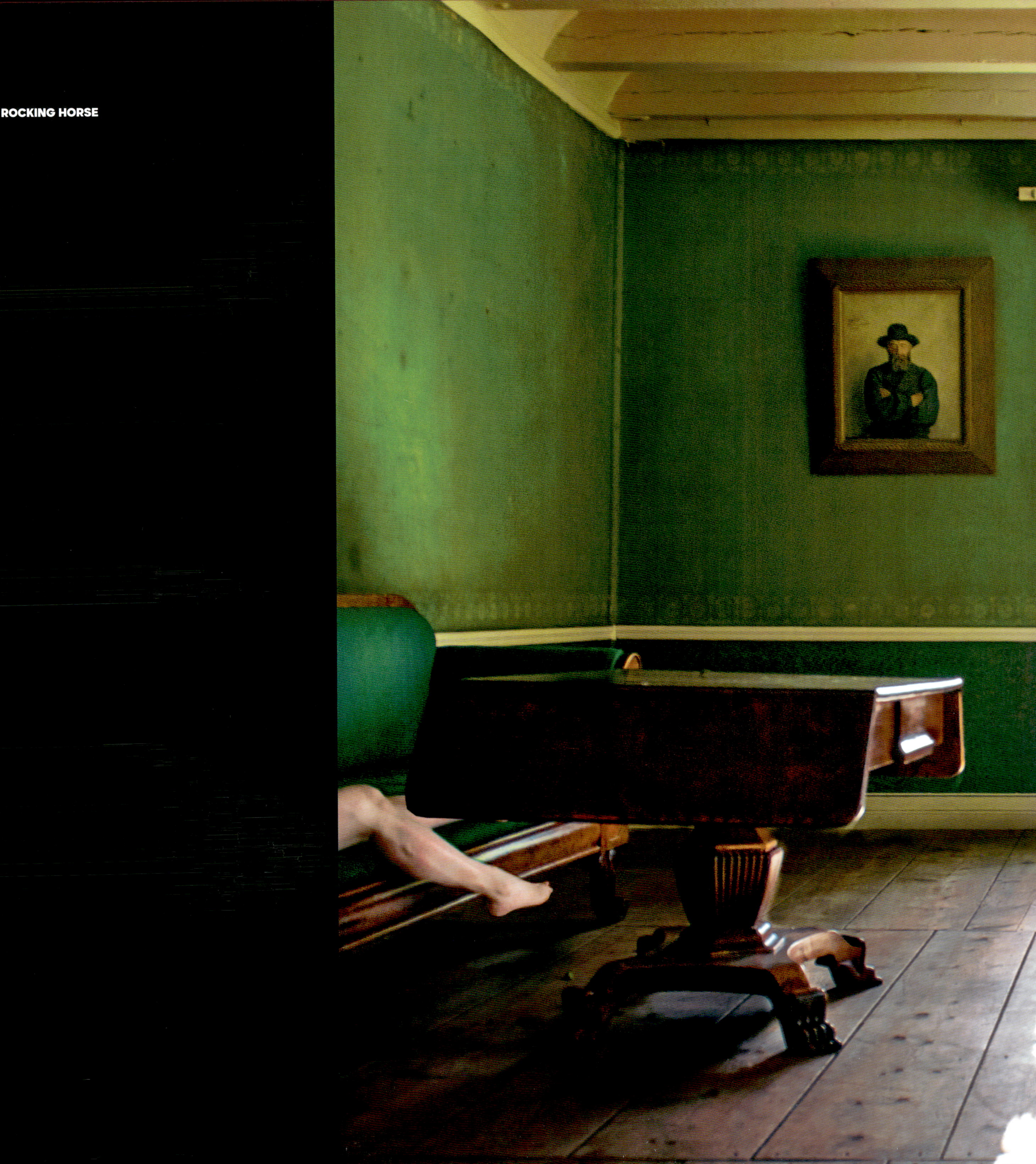
ROCKING HORSE

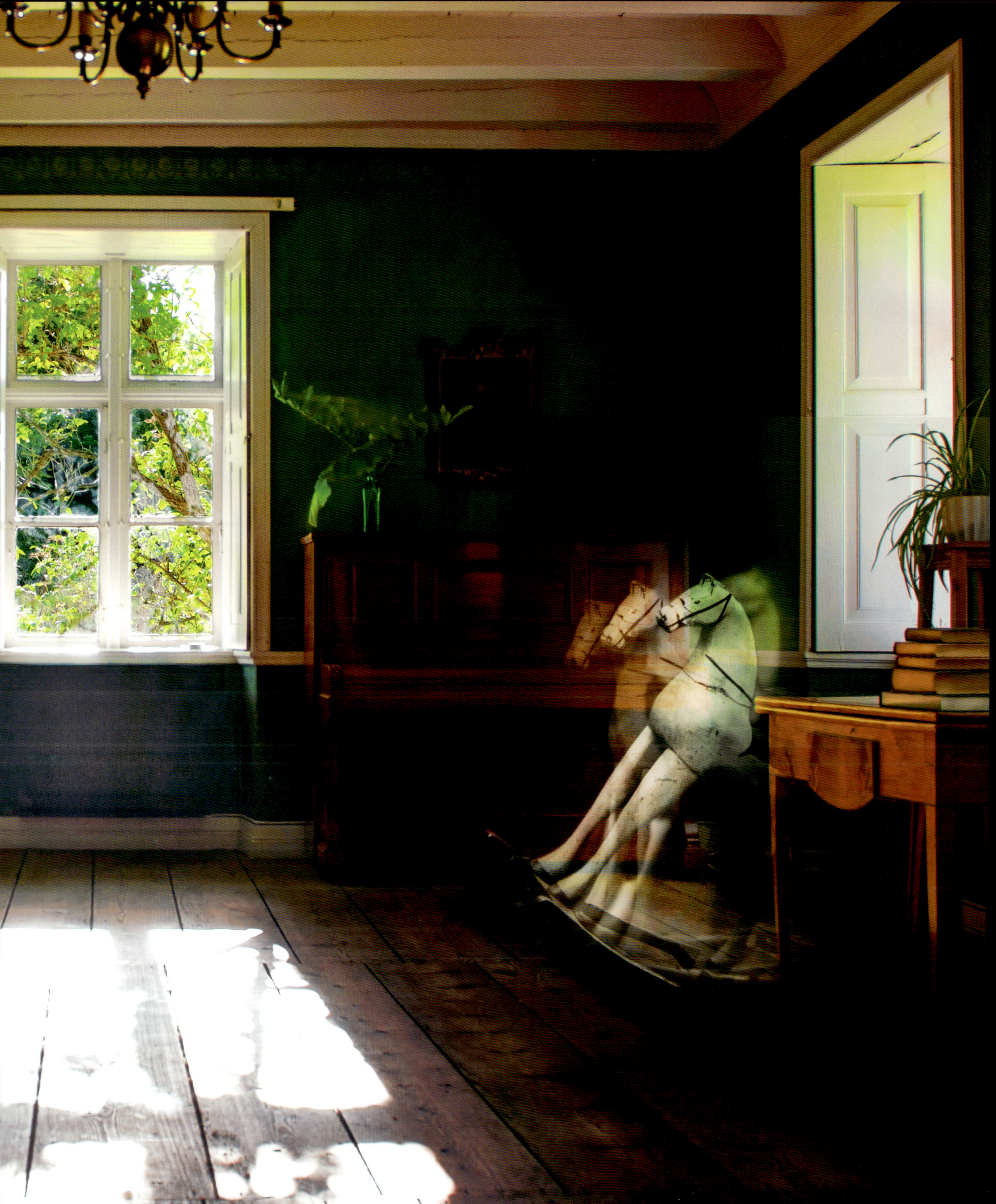

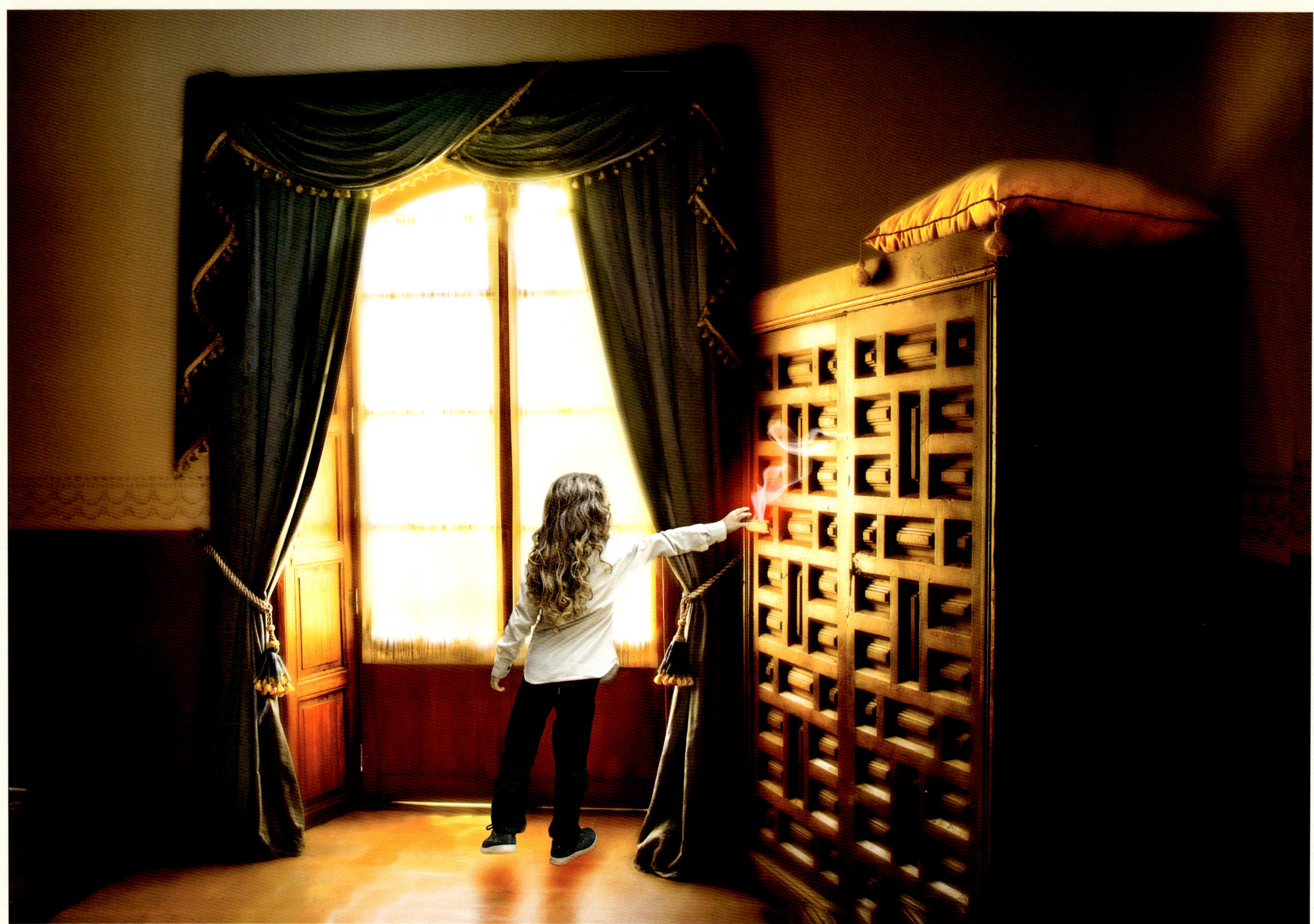

I am reminded of the O-mikuji, fortunes of both good and bad luck one chooses from many, many drawers in cabinets at Shinto shrines in Japan. In this wonderful image, the beautiful young child hopes for good luck in his future, as we all do. Although I see strong light coming through the window, illuminating him, the dark room reveals potential misfortune. Many of the images in this book remind me of jeweled Tarot cards, which can be read in many ways, depending on the mindset of the viewer.

Sandra Klein

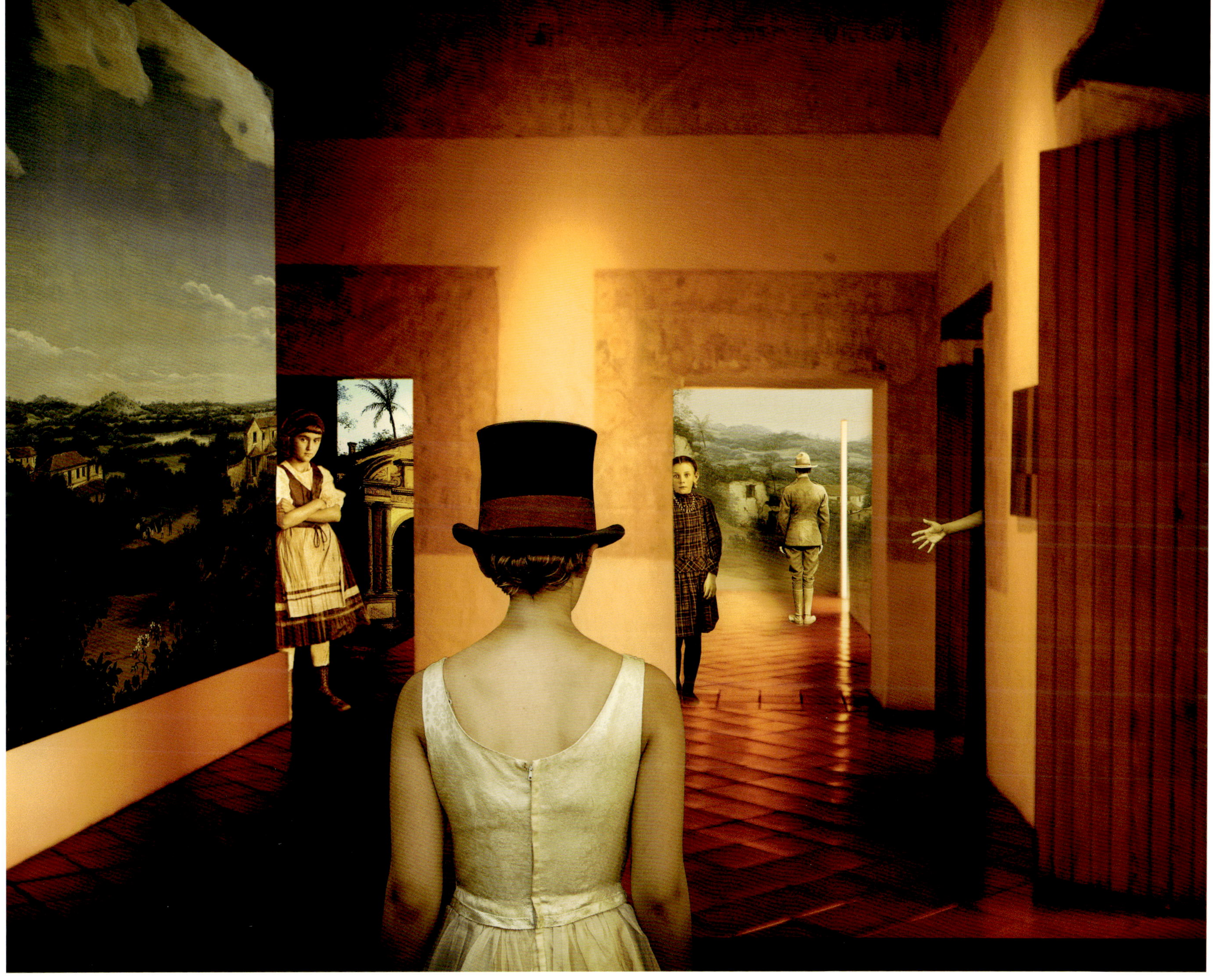

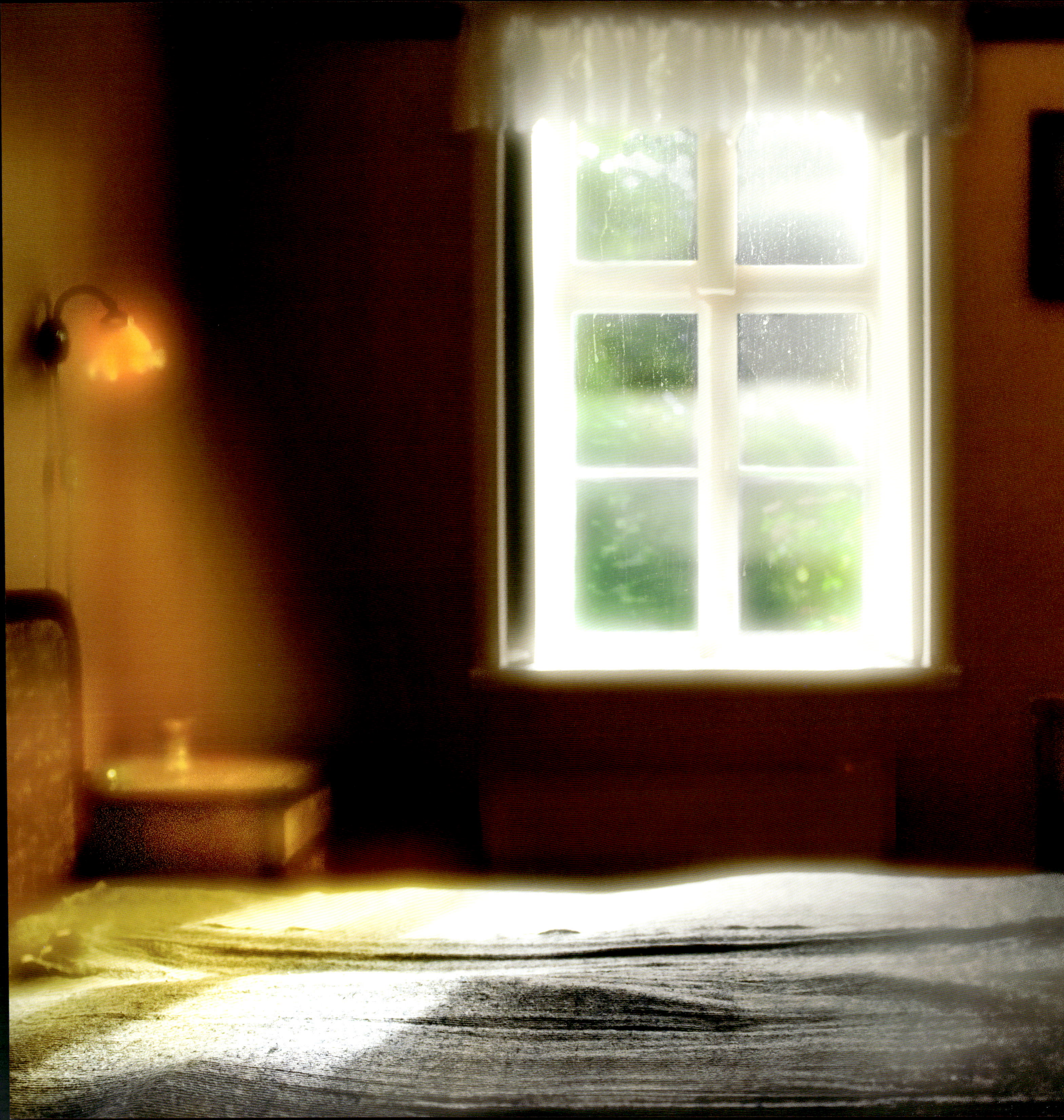

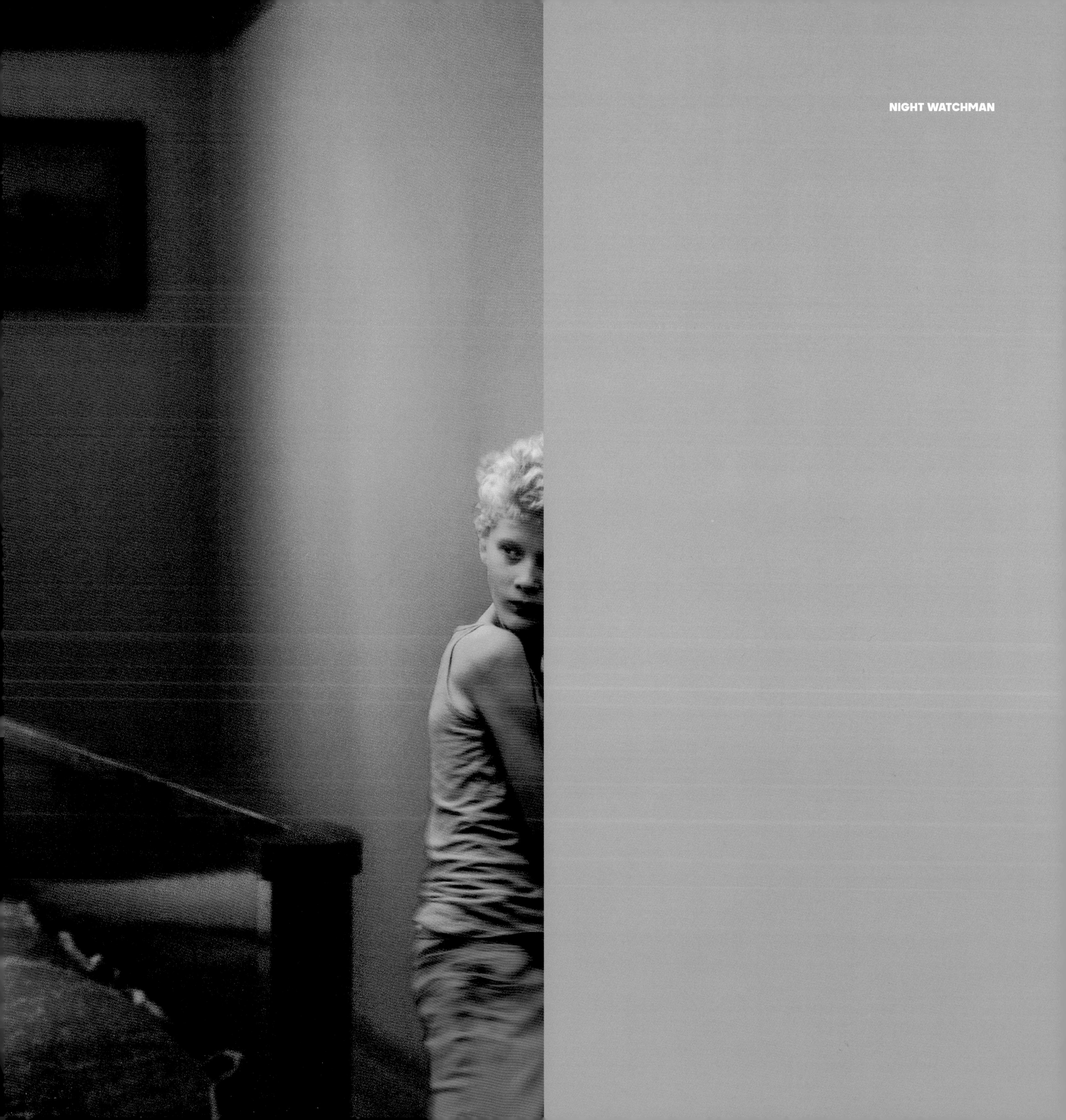

NIGHT WATCHMAN

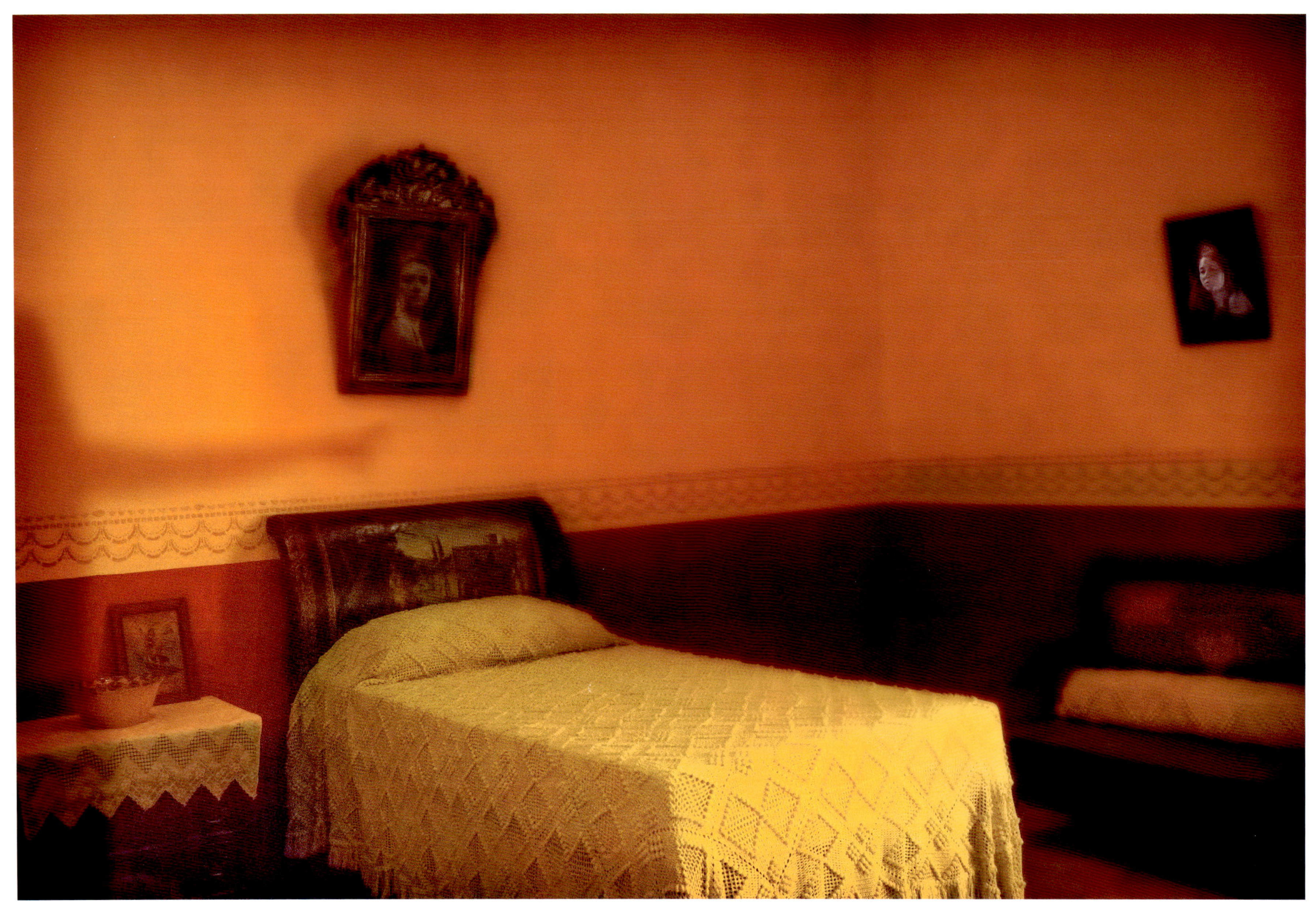

THE DANGERS OF FALSE CERTAINTY

"Promise me you will never change," was the last thing he asked of her before deploying.

The timing of his departure hit hard. They were set to be married the following month. From the moment they met, she knew they would be together forever. He said she was everything he had ever wanted. He loved how attentive she was to his needs, which made him feel like the most important man in the world.

They wrote regularly until one day his letters stopped coming. Many weeks passed with no correspondence. Her parents gently suggested he may have met someone else and moved on. She exploded, "I will not even consider that notion."

Shortly thereafter, she received an official letter from the military bearing the somber news her fiancé's ship had gone down. Hundreds of men died, and numerous others, her sweetheart included, went missing at sea. While they declared him MIA, her intuition insisted he had survived and it was simply a matter of time before they would be reunited.

A year passed and she waited patiently. She took pains to keep things exactly as they were, so when he reappeared they could go on as nothing had changed whatsoever. This worried her parents greatly. They tried to sway her to accept her beloved had most likely perished that fateful night. The more agitated they got about the situation the more firmly she stood her ground.

One morning her father called her into his study to show her a picture that caught his eye in the newspaper. It was a wedding announcement for a couple, and, without a doubt, the groom was the man she was once engaged to marry.

She immediately became excited and proclaimed, "I knew he would come back to me!"

Her father was dumbfounded. "How has he come back to you? He just married someone else."

"Their marriage is a mere technicality. He is my soulmate and a love as special as ours never changes."

Shaking his head, her father questioned, "If your love was so special wouldn't he have come back and married you?"

"Of course not. I'm sure the shipwreck threw him into a stupor and numbed his memory. I have complete faith when he sees me and remembers what we had he will divorce this woman and we will wed right away."

"And what if he won't leave his wife? What will you do?"

"I will stand by until he is widowed and we will marry thereafter."

"But what if you are to pass away first? Then you will have waited in vain and die alone."

"Father, it is clear you do not understand an oath of love. My heart is eternally bound to his and I will honor our commitment for evermore."

Her father sadly sighed, "None of this makes sense to me," and then implored, "How can you be so certain?"

She unabashedly looked him straight in the eye and asserted, **"Because he asked me to."**

Cat Gwynn

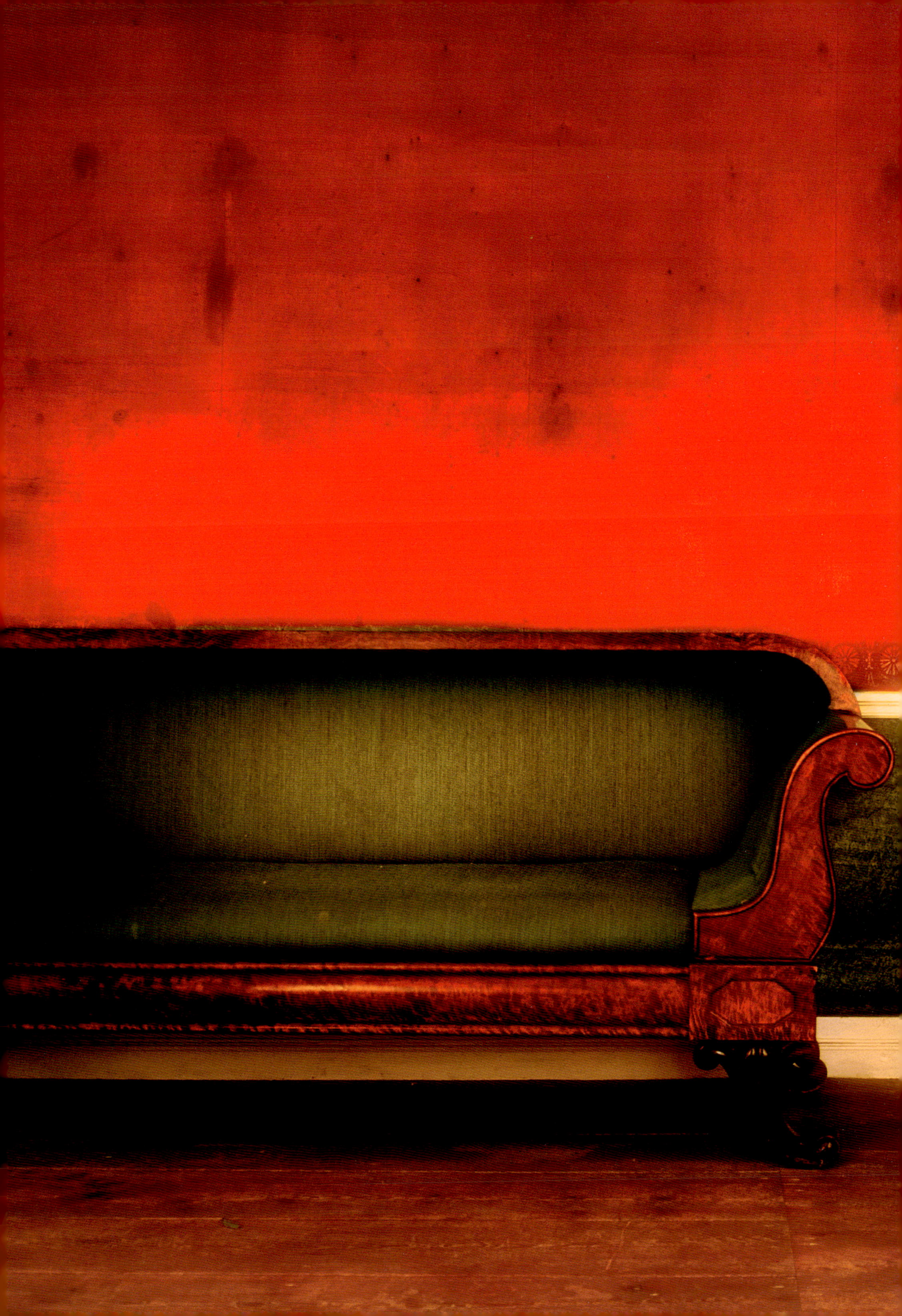

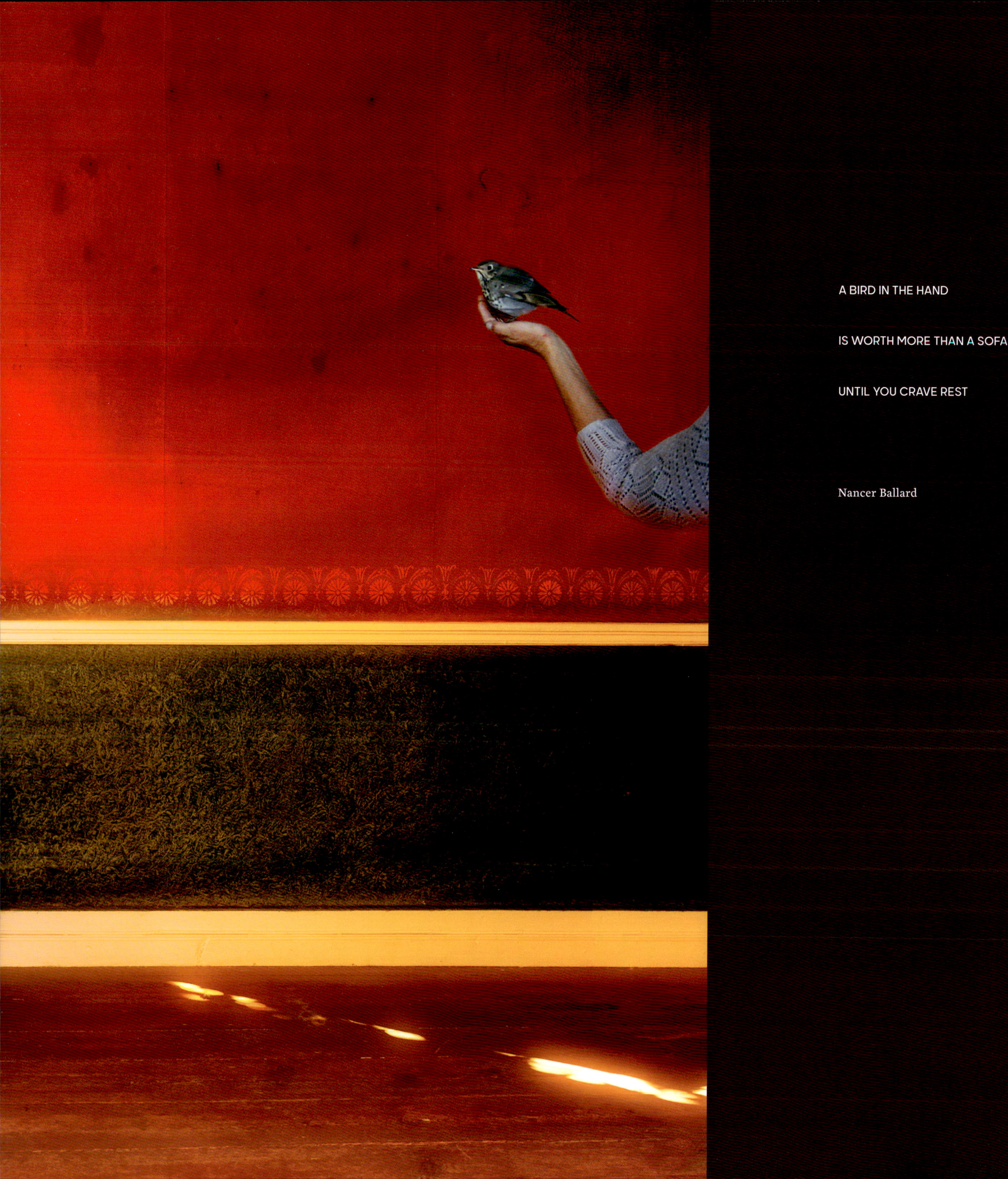

A BIRD IN THE HAND

IS WORTH MORE THAN A SOFA

UNTIL YOU CRAVE REST

Nancer Ballard

One can get truly lost in these images of magical realism, immersed in the evocative use of light and rich jewel tones, paving the way to a fantastical dream state.

Jane Fulton Alt

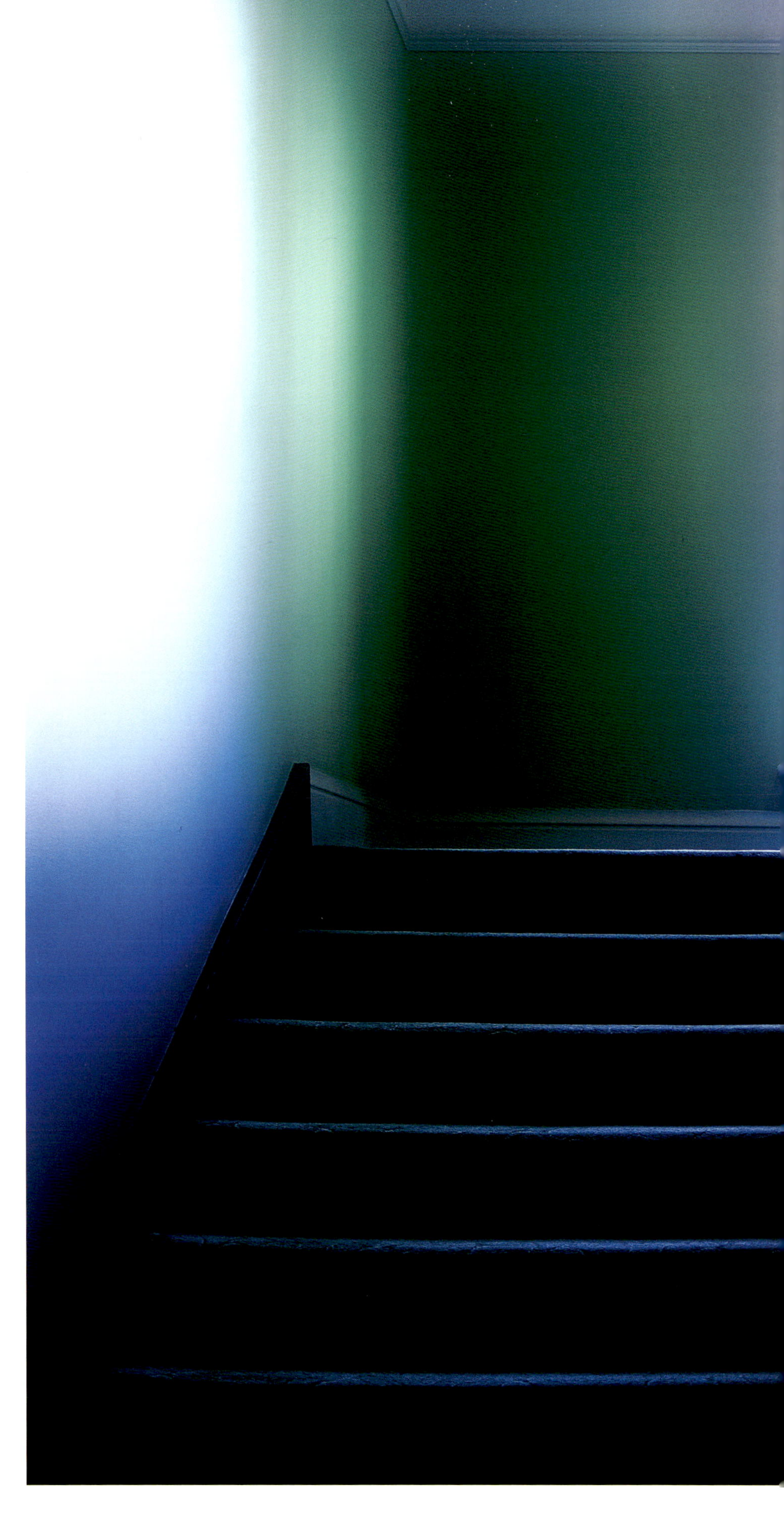

WOMAN DESCENDING

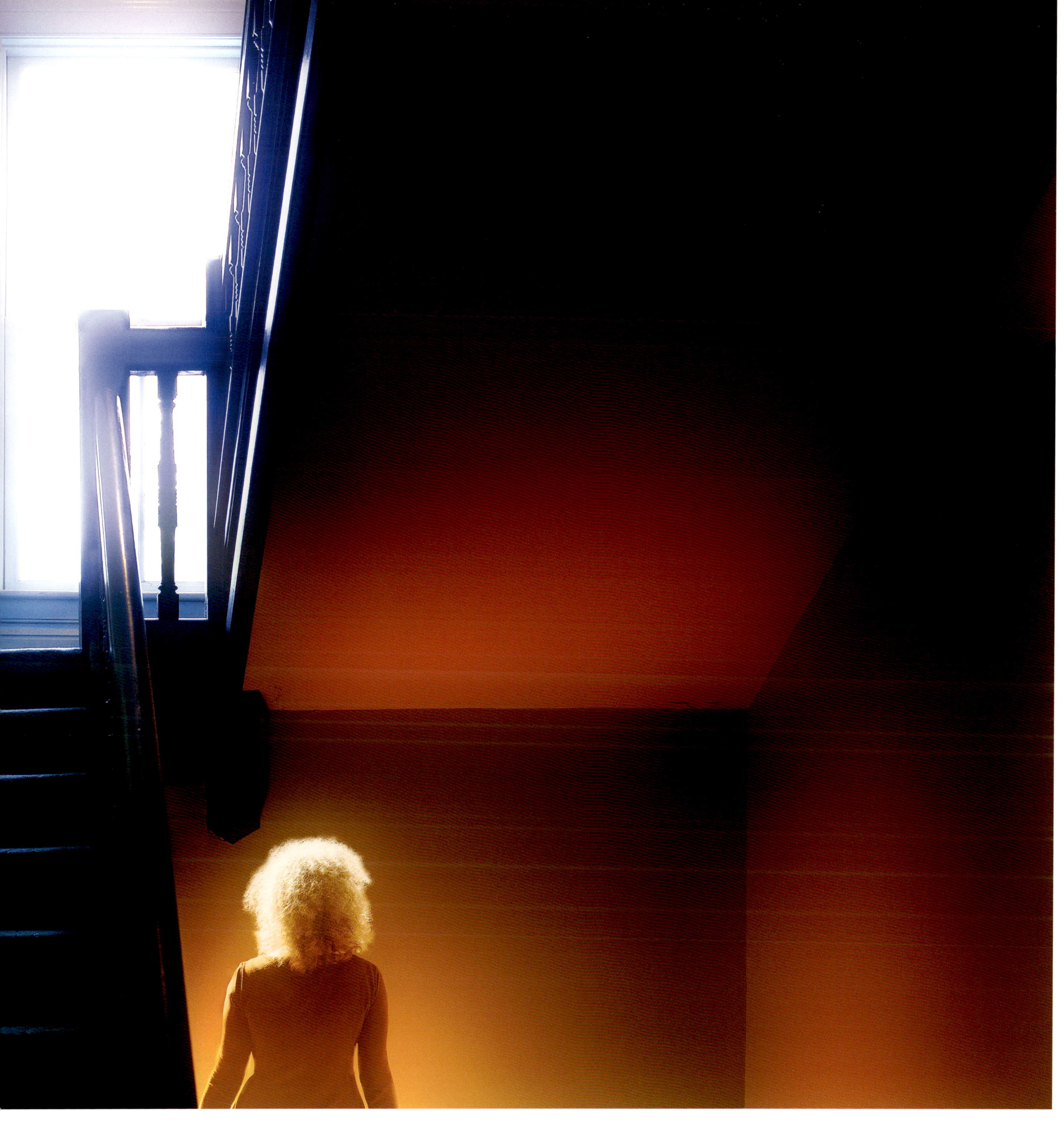

"IN DREAMS BEGIN RESPONSIBILITIES." —William Butler Yeats

FRAN'S WORLD, AN OVERVIEW

Do we dream in technicolor?
I ask myself as I wake but the dream runs away
lost in the morning light like quicksilver slipping between closed fingers.
Outlines of plot I remember, and characters,
and (when erotic) even the room with the bed.
Are they in color? I simply don't know.

For decades Fran's world has been peopled with polished polychrome mystery,
something better than run-of-the-millstream dreams.
Some mix of vision and drama, occasionally ecstasy, frequently dread,
But a benign, domestic dread, or dread in imaginary landscapes
and dimly-lit interiors.

How to put it? Dread without threat?
Maybe she is saying that all life is a dream, but that our standard waking image
of "reality" is lazy, cheap, unworthy,
that at any moment if we choose we can close our outer eyes and see a
seductive strangeness before us,
and plunge into that shimmering, haunted world
that was always right here an arm's length away,
that we can run away from home without rising from our easy chairs.

I once wrote a poem that ended, "If life is a dream we all die in our sleep."
Yet Fran's controlled creepiness is not about death:
it serves a glossier, more vibrant Otherworld.

As an older man, I feel I have been given a Special Pass to enter this
performance space
of mostly children,
mostly girls and women.

And yet as a fisherman I feel at home amid the boats,
those lapstraked dories marooned in summer fields.
And maybe a streak of girlish shyness and awe is not so alien to my
wandering mind.
And birds, and clouds: I am a shameless birdman, a ready cloudman.
And the charts and maps and gridworks I have always loved,
that imprint and measure and order the worlds of her people.

And with my own collection of sepia ancestors,
I feel at ease amid the slightly Golden Age ambiance
her creatures inhabit
with their funny hats
and stiff collars and boots and aprons.
She says, This is your world and this is your trip that was and is and will be,
available without closing your eyes,
this is your other home, unknown and familiar,
and I will heat up the hues and twist up the saturations,
and you will sail or fly or row from dream to dream
and phantom critters will approach, to lick your hand
and glowing better-than-Maxfield-Parrish clouds will follow you,
and you will disappear down long corridors of old mansions
unafraid of the dark, which is and was always your own, since your
childhood, which has never ended.

David Gullette

"THE PAST ISN'T DEAD.

IT ISN'T EVEN PAST." —William Faulkner

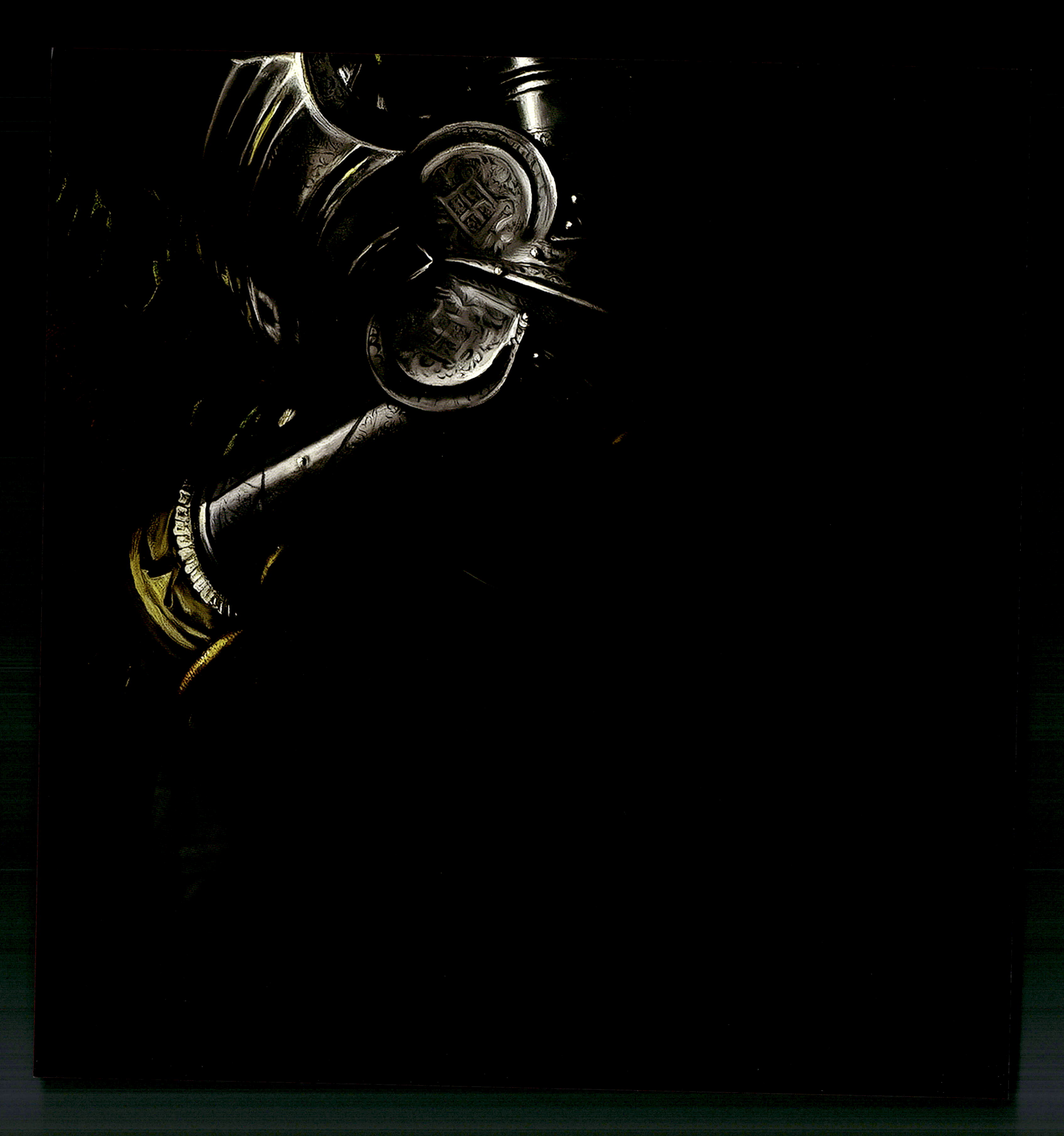

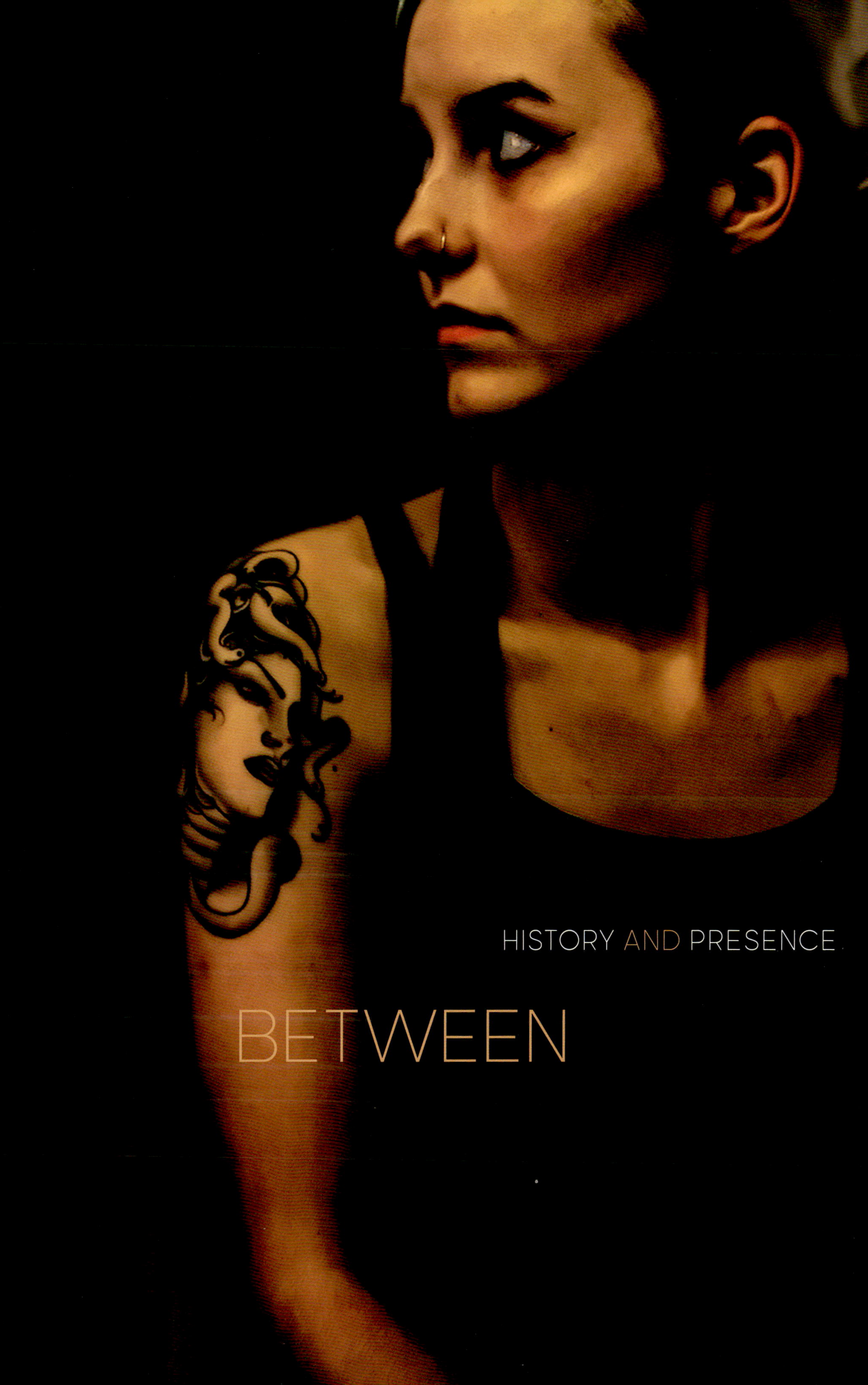

HISTORY AND PRESENCE

BETWEEN

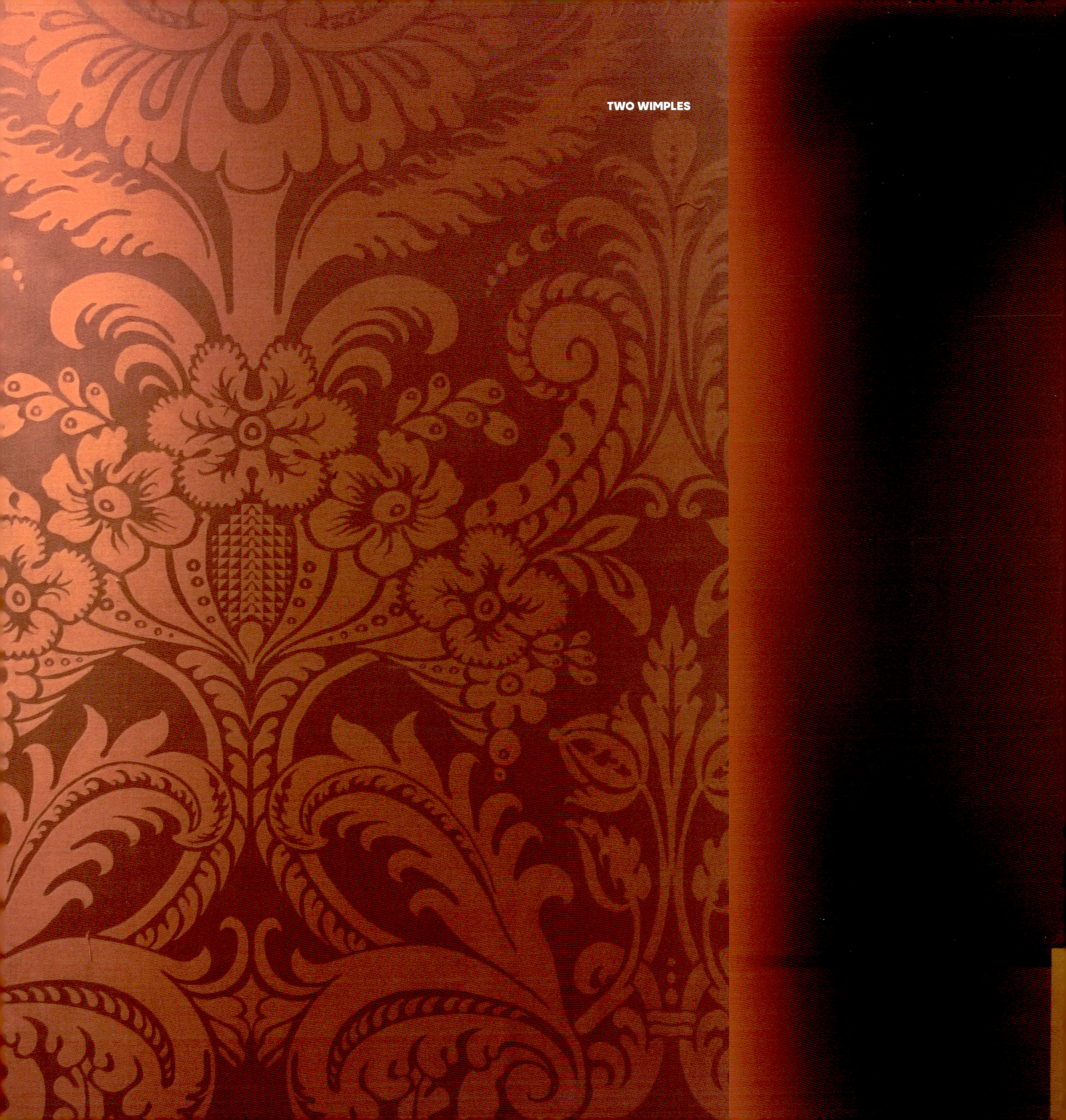
TWO WIMPLES

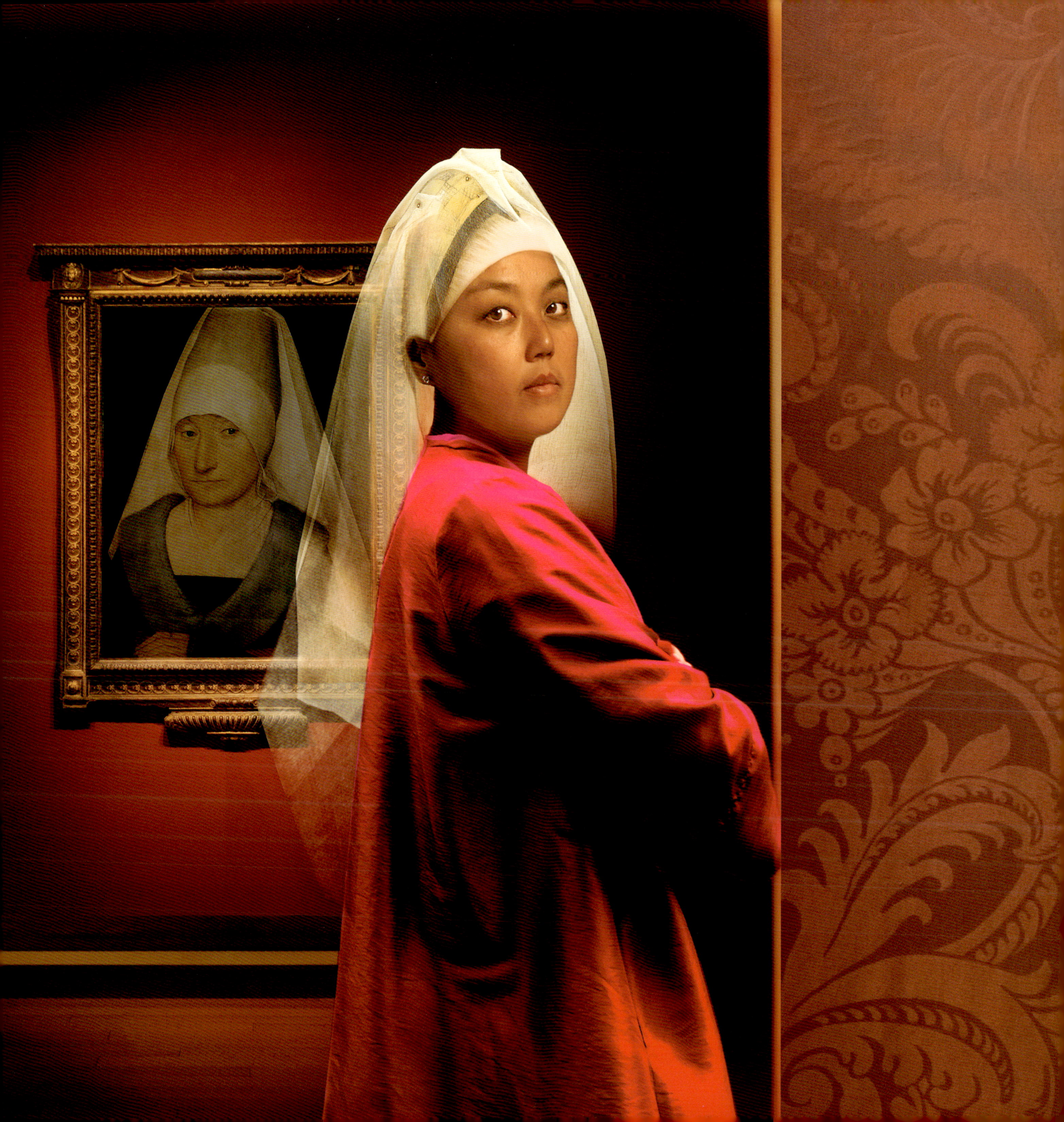

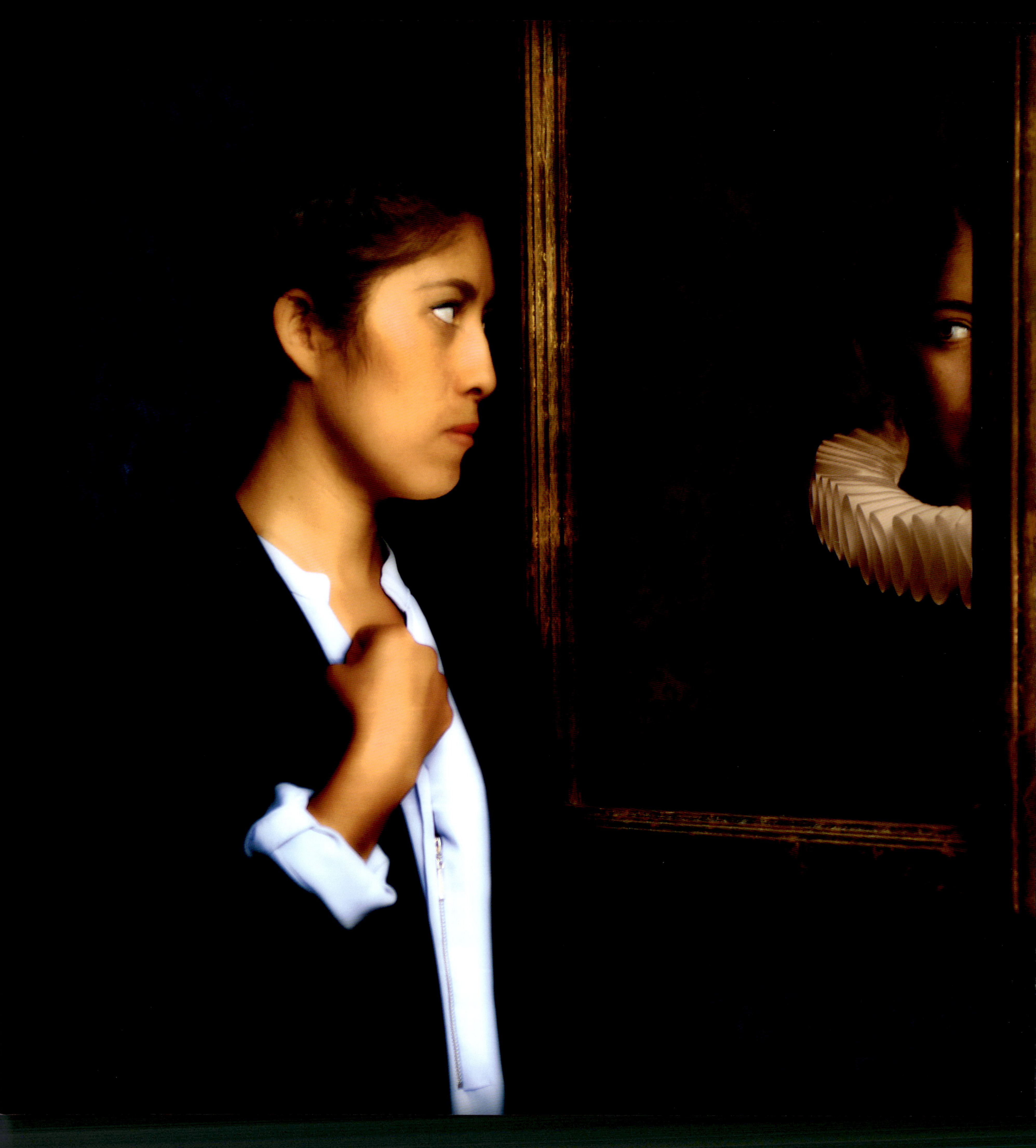

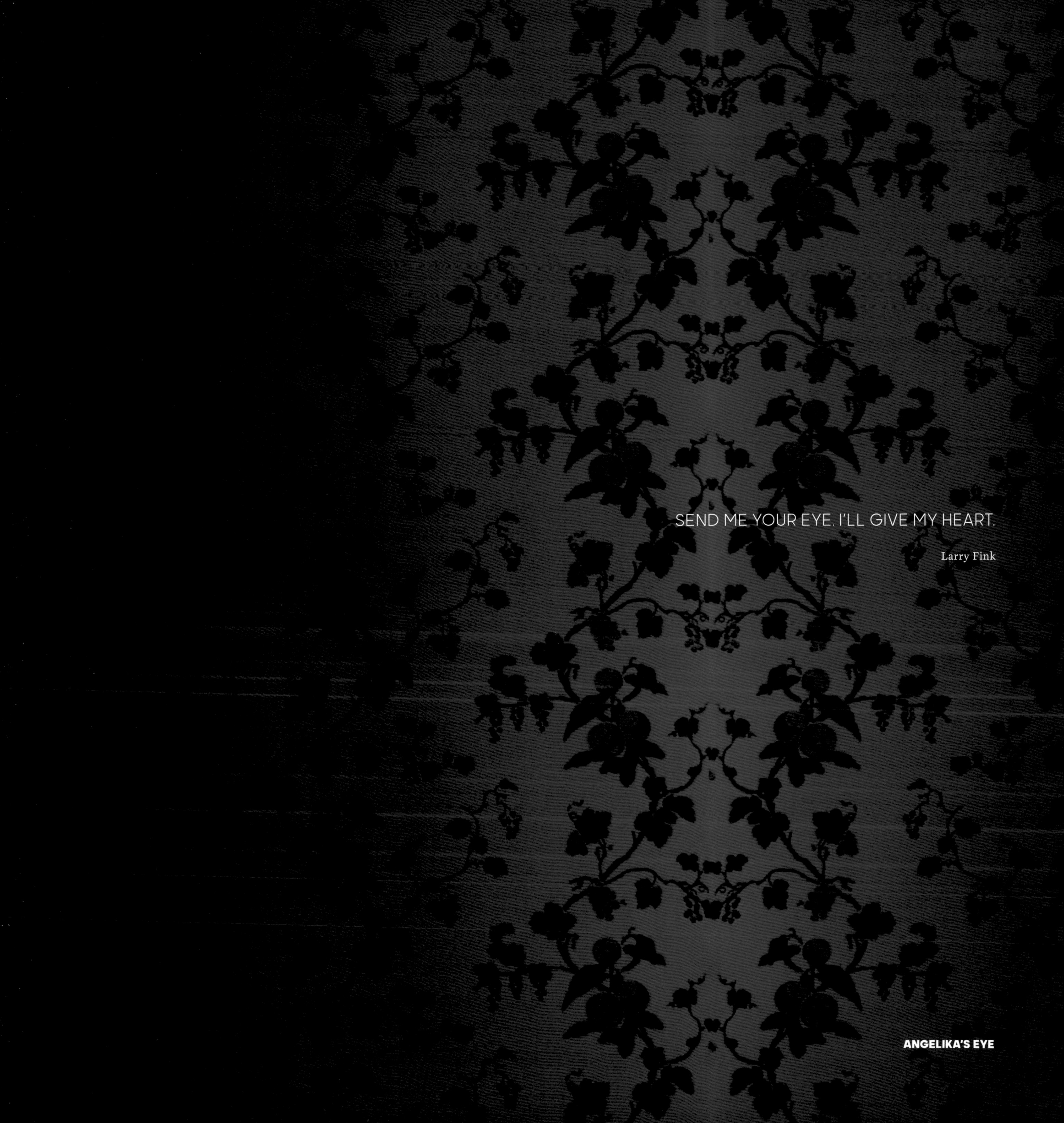

SEND ME YOUR EYE. I'LL GIVE MY HEART.

Larry Fink

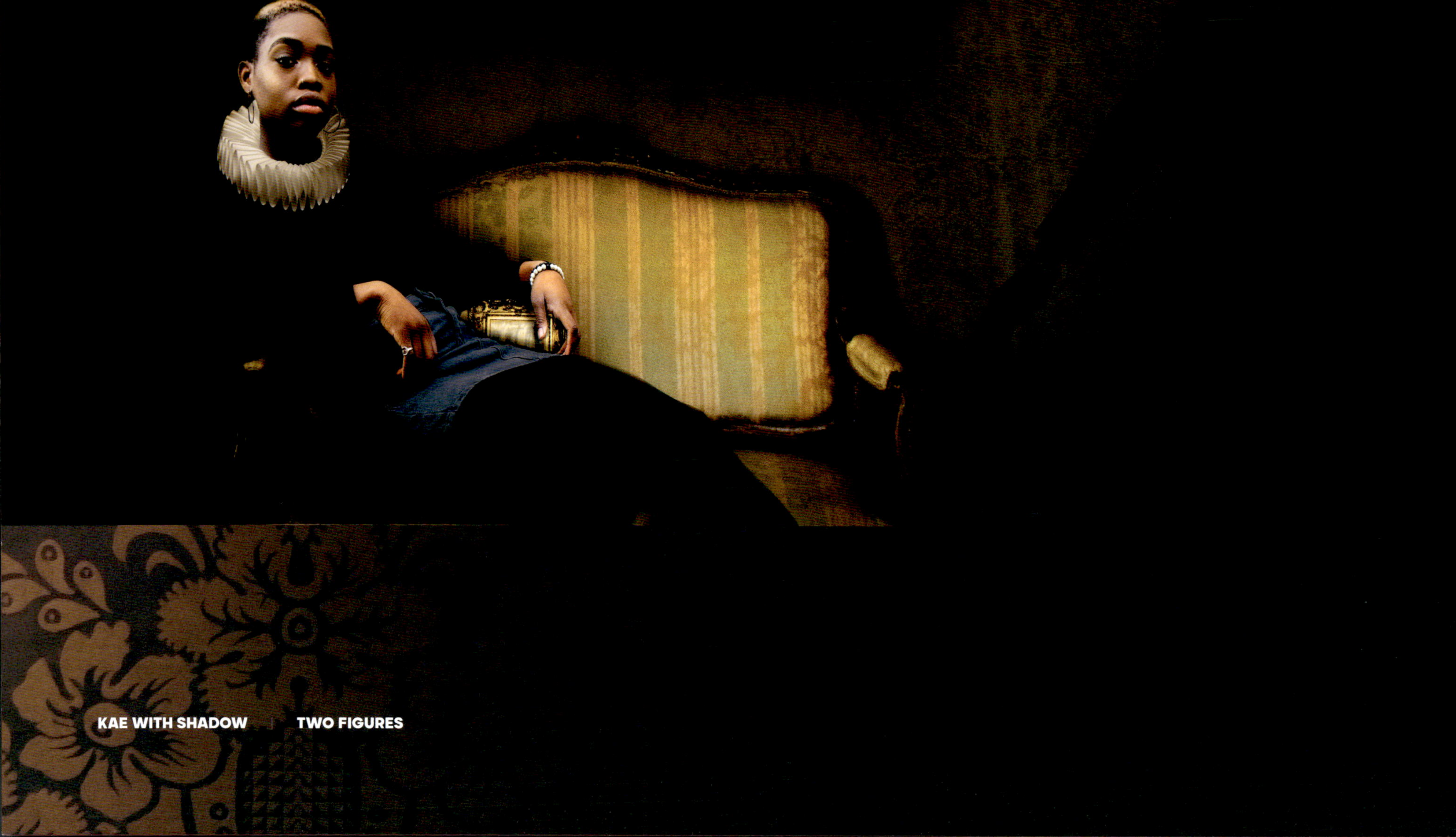

KAE WITH SHADOW | TWO FIGURES

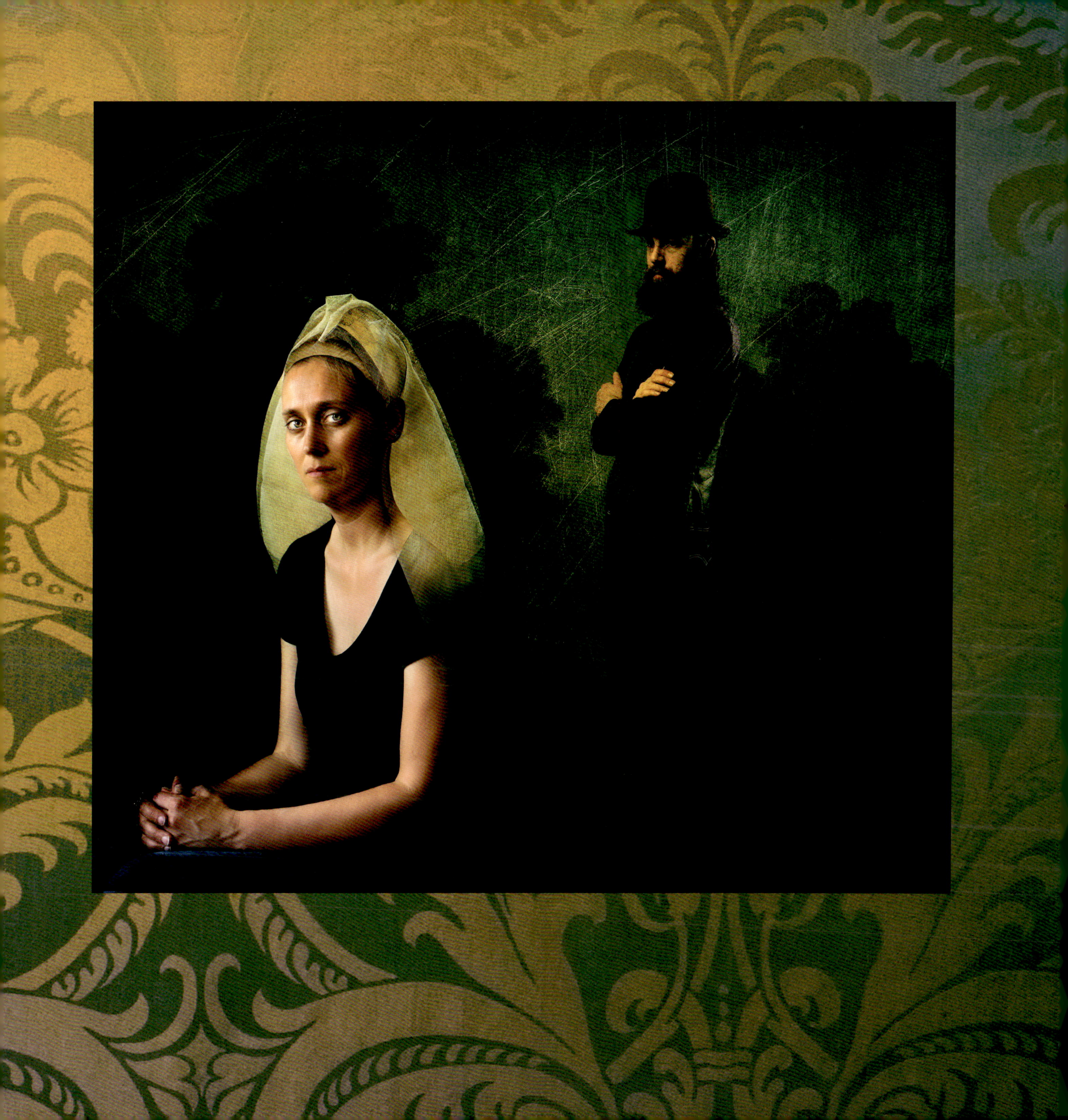

IN THE DARKEST PLACE IN MY MIND, I SEE THE LIGHT.

Victor Rosario

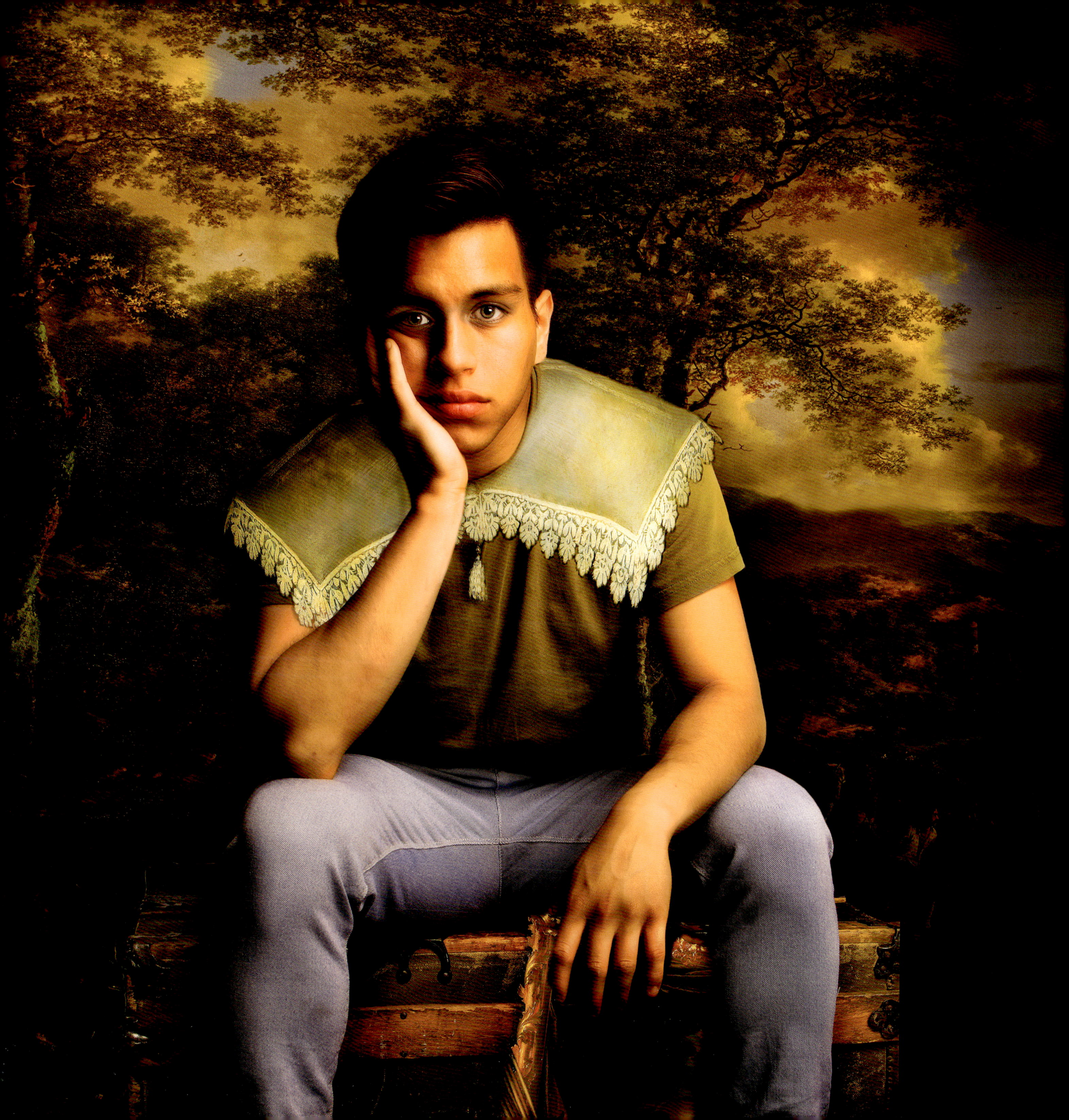

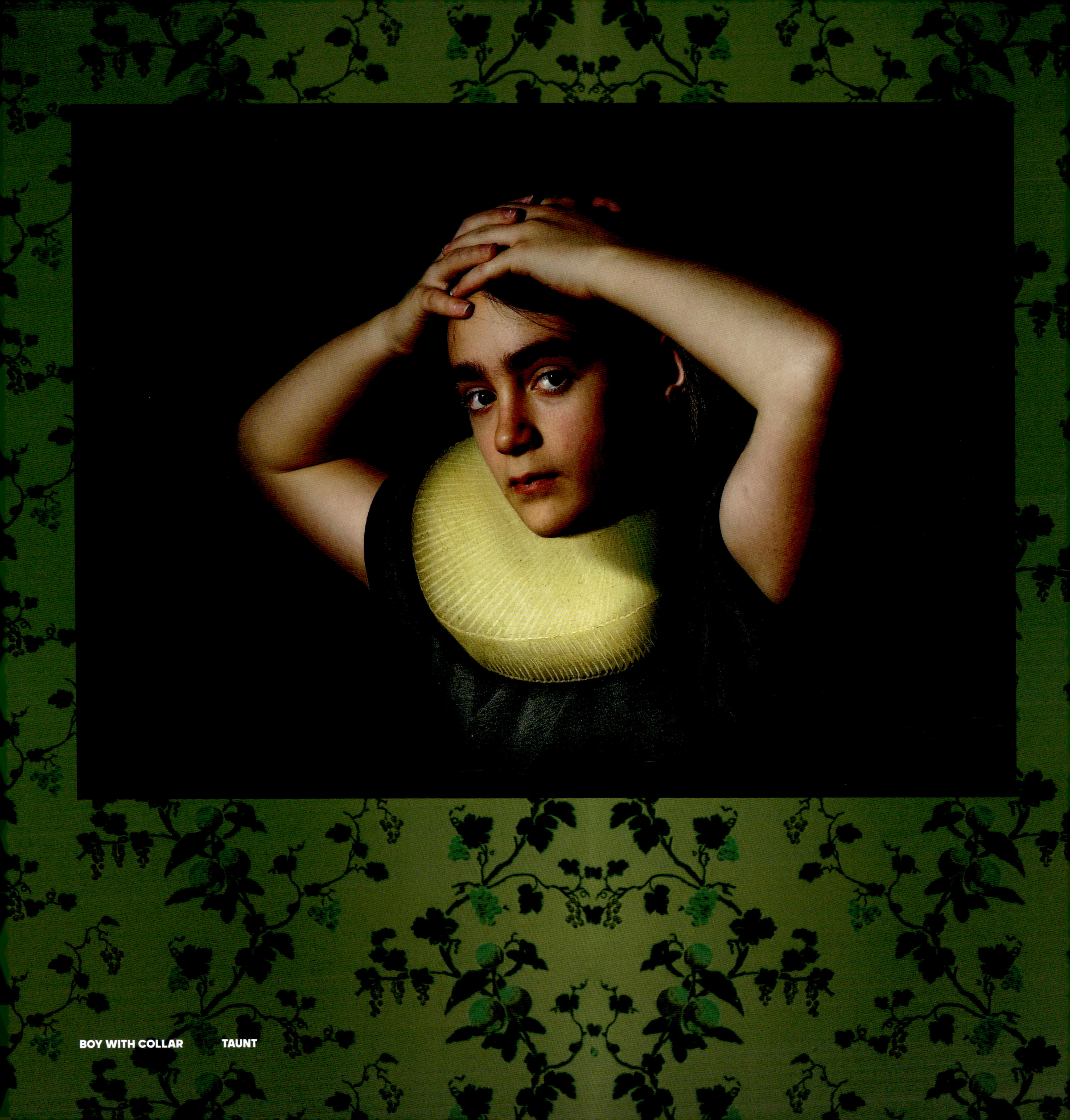

BOY WITH COLLAR | TAUNT

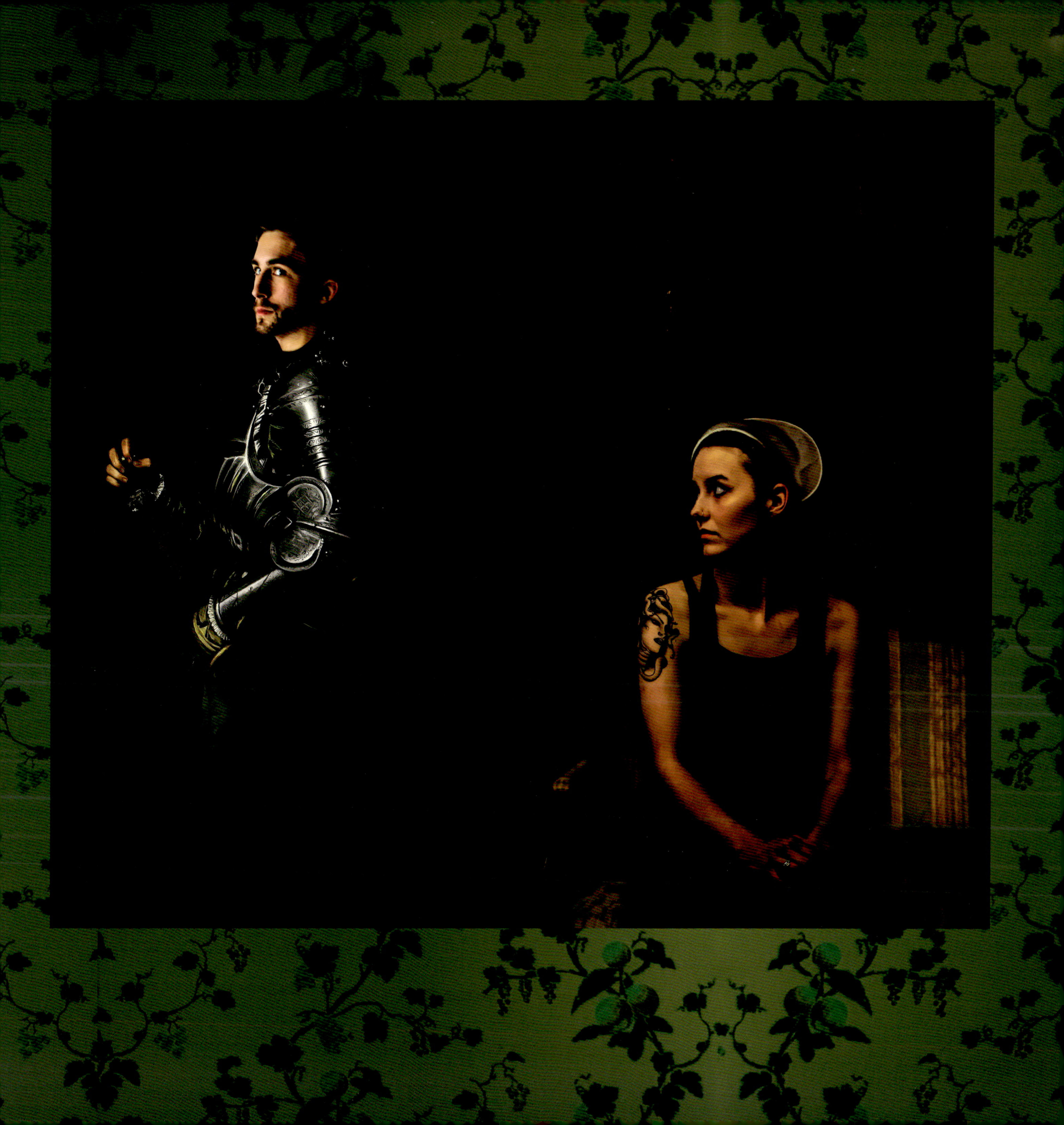

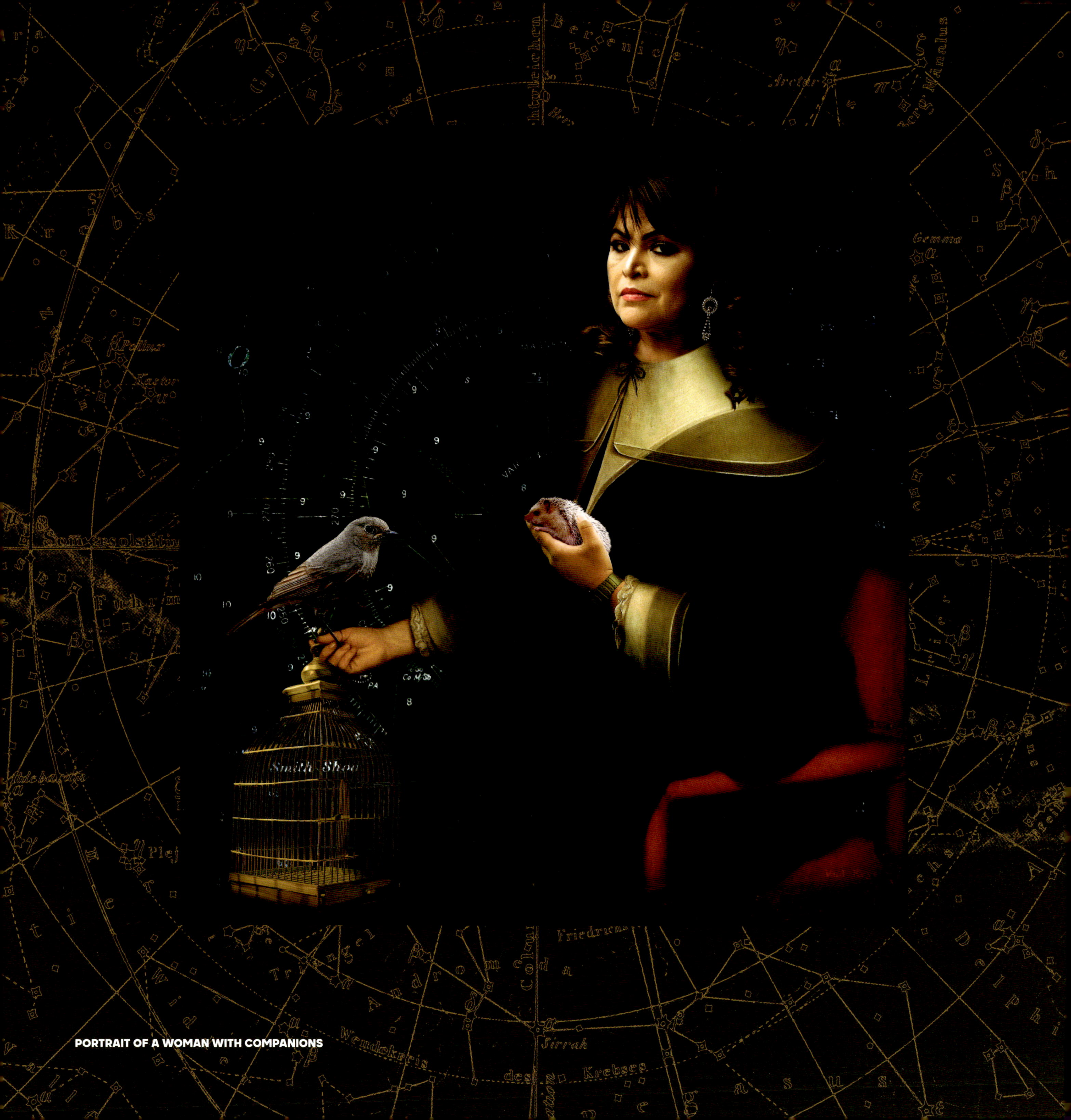

PORTRAIT OF A WOMAN WITH COMPANIONS

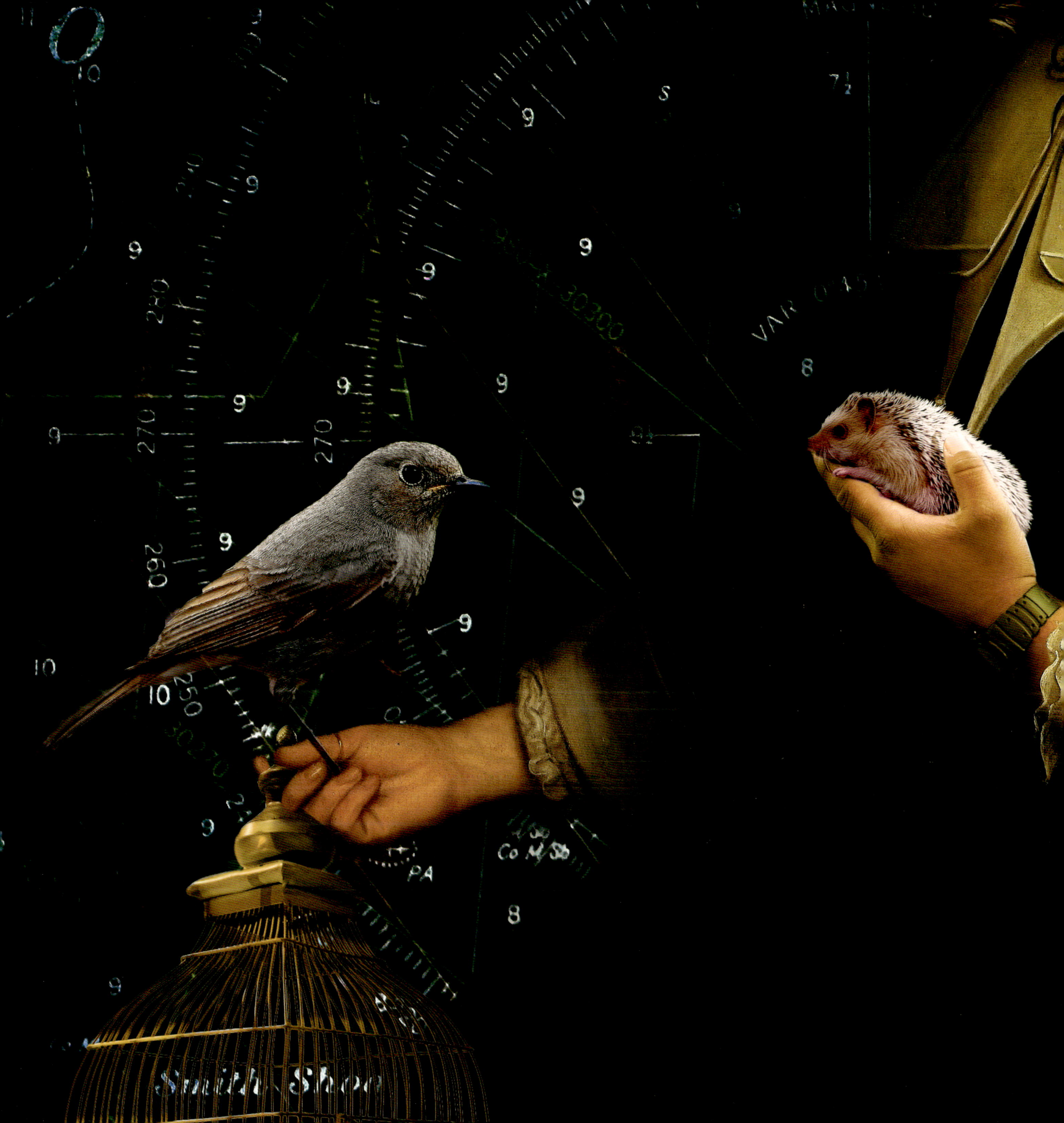

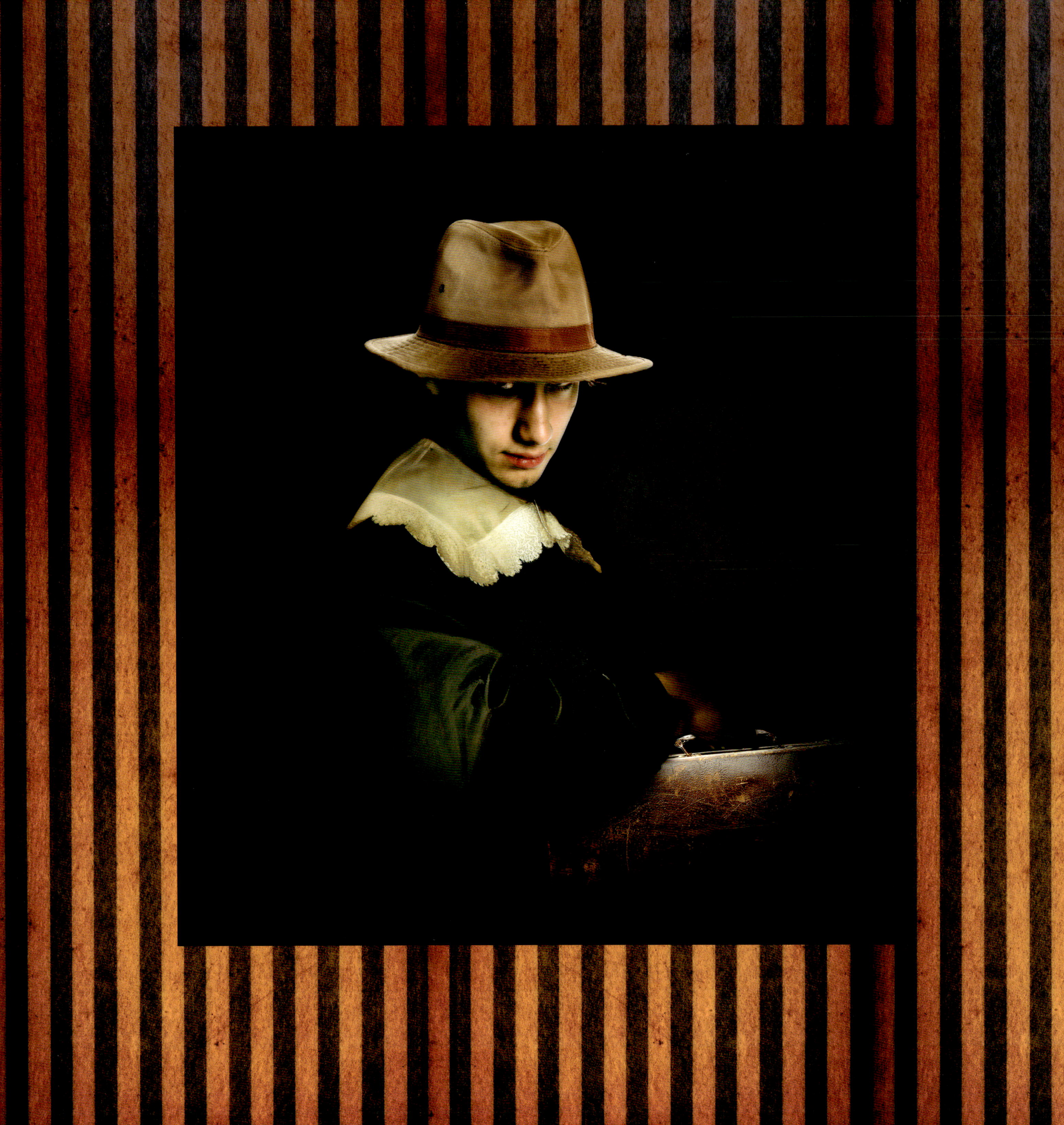

CLAPTRAP

Like the actor
forgetting his one line
and booed off the stage
we shall play the Fool
in floppy shoes and fright wig
peddling trash talk tragedies
and crocodile tears
to lords and groundlings
until our farewell tour
and final curtain

Anthony James

PORTRAIT OF A BOY WITH FEDORA

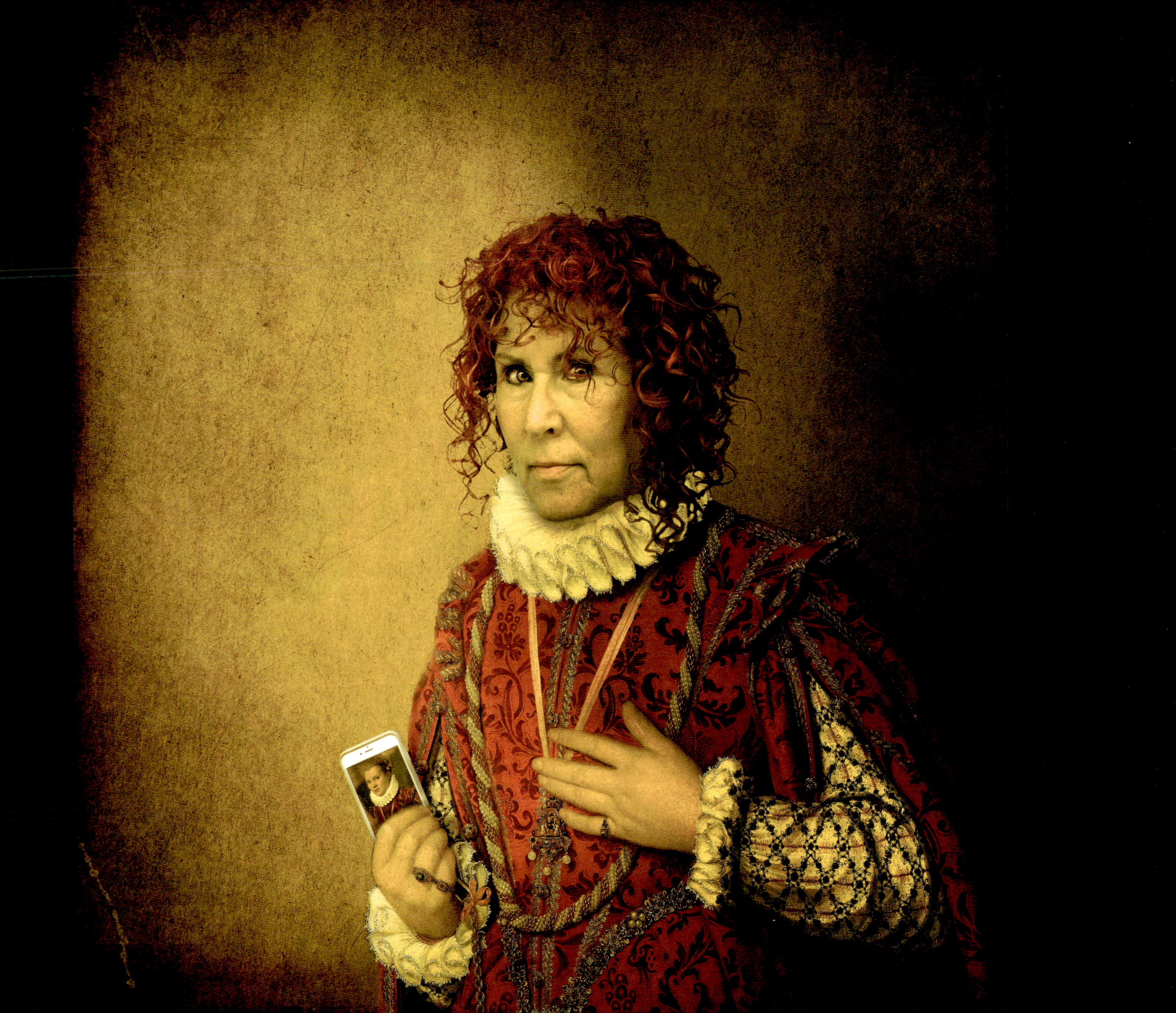

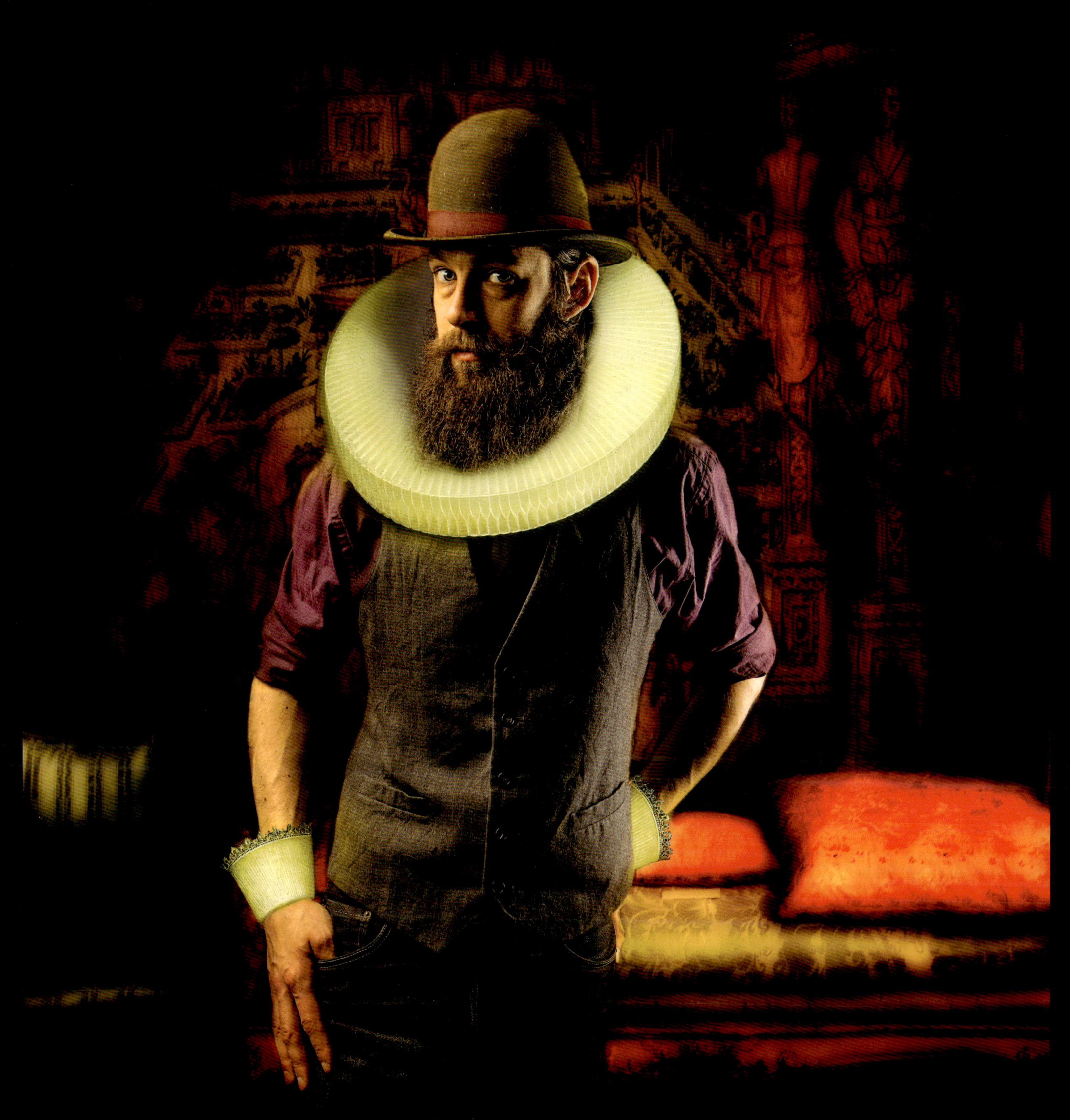

PORTRAIT OF A WOMAN WITH SELFIE | PORTRAIT OF MR JONES

Anaïs Nin describes best what I often think about my first exposure to a Fran Forman image:

"We see things as we are, Not as they are."

On first look I think I have taken the image in and am aware of all that is before me. It is only my second and longer gaze that shows me the anomaly in the picture or the small figure almost hidden next to the frame. I see what I choose to see until I surrender my willfulness and only then am I able to see all that the artist has chosen for me to see.

Barbara Hill

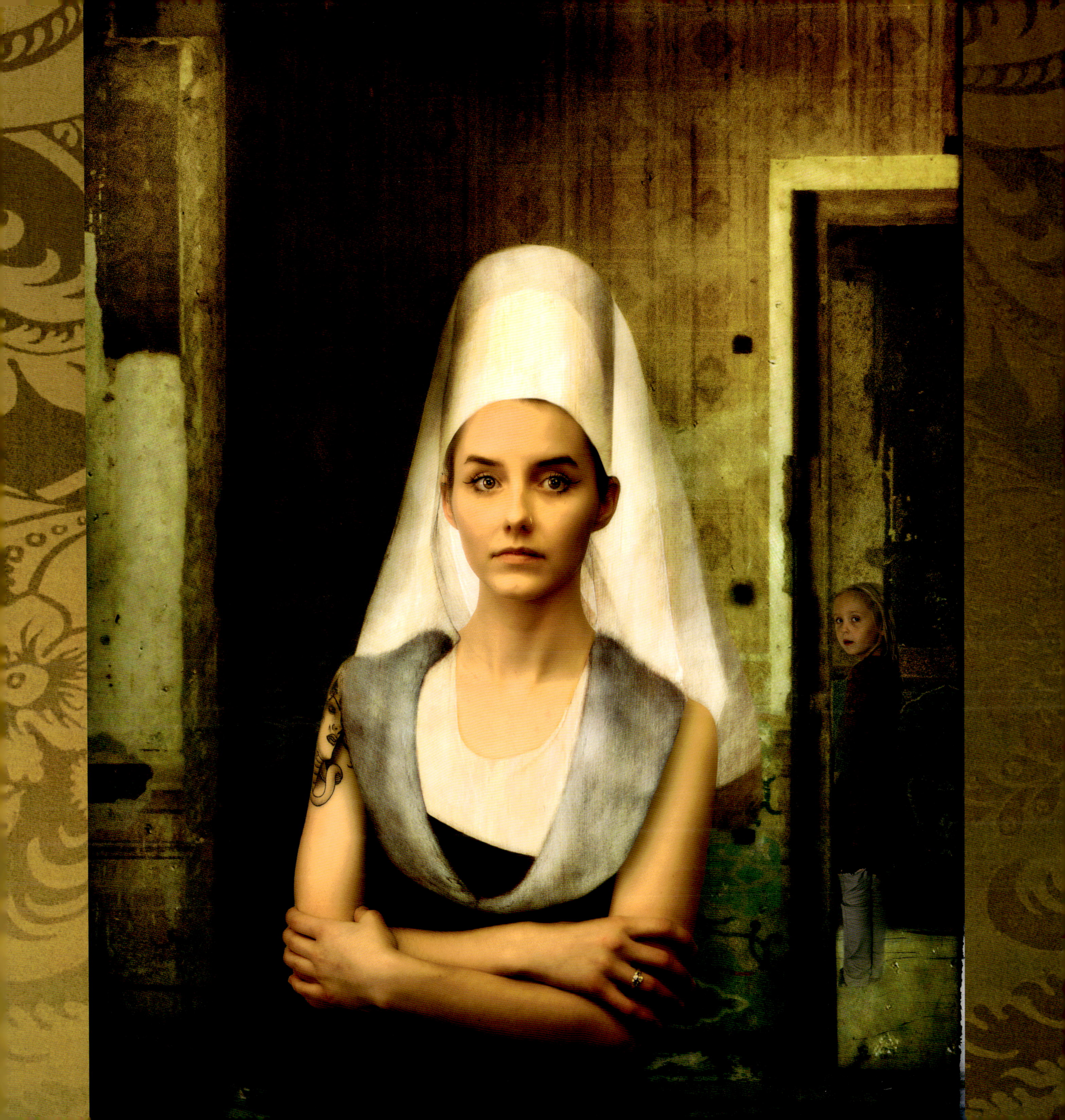

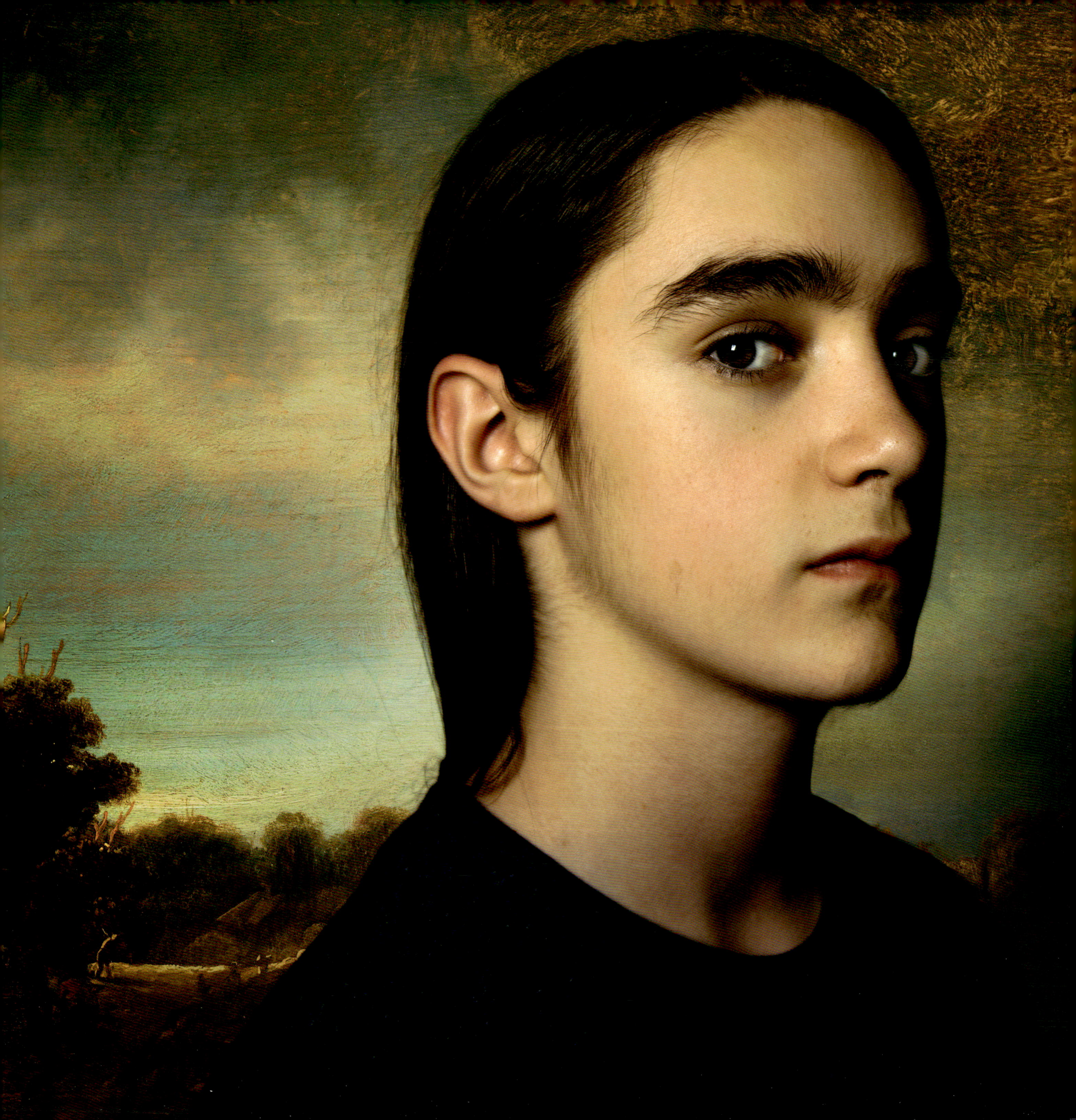

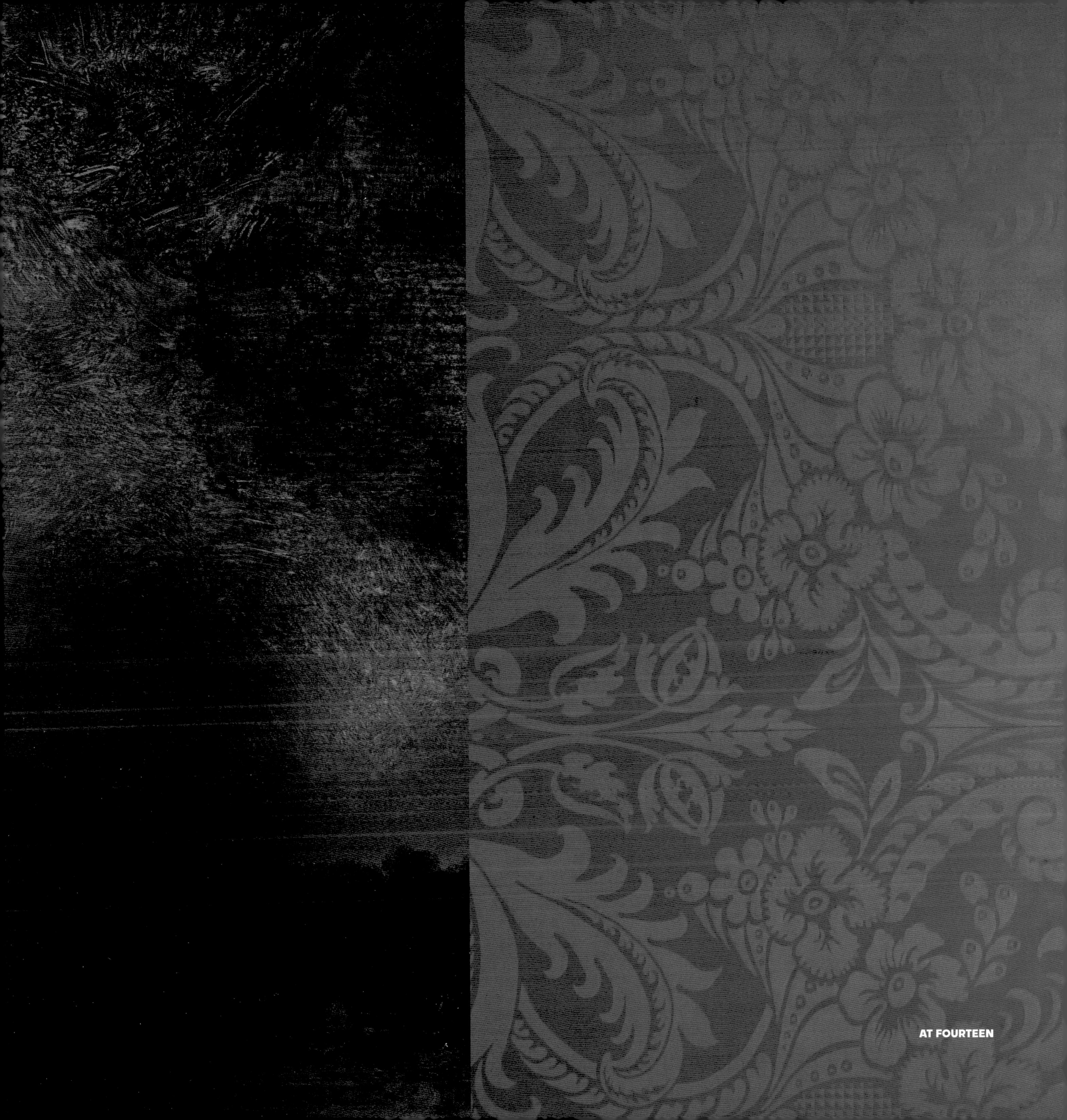
AT FOURTEEN

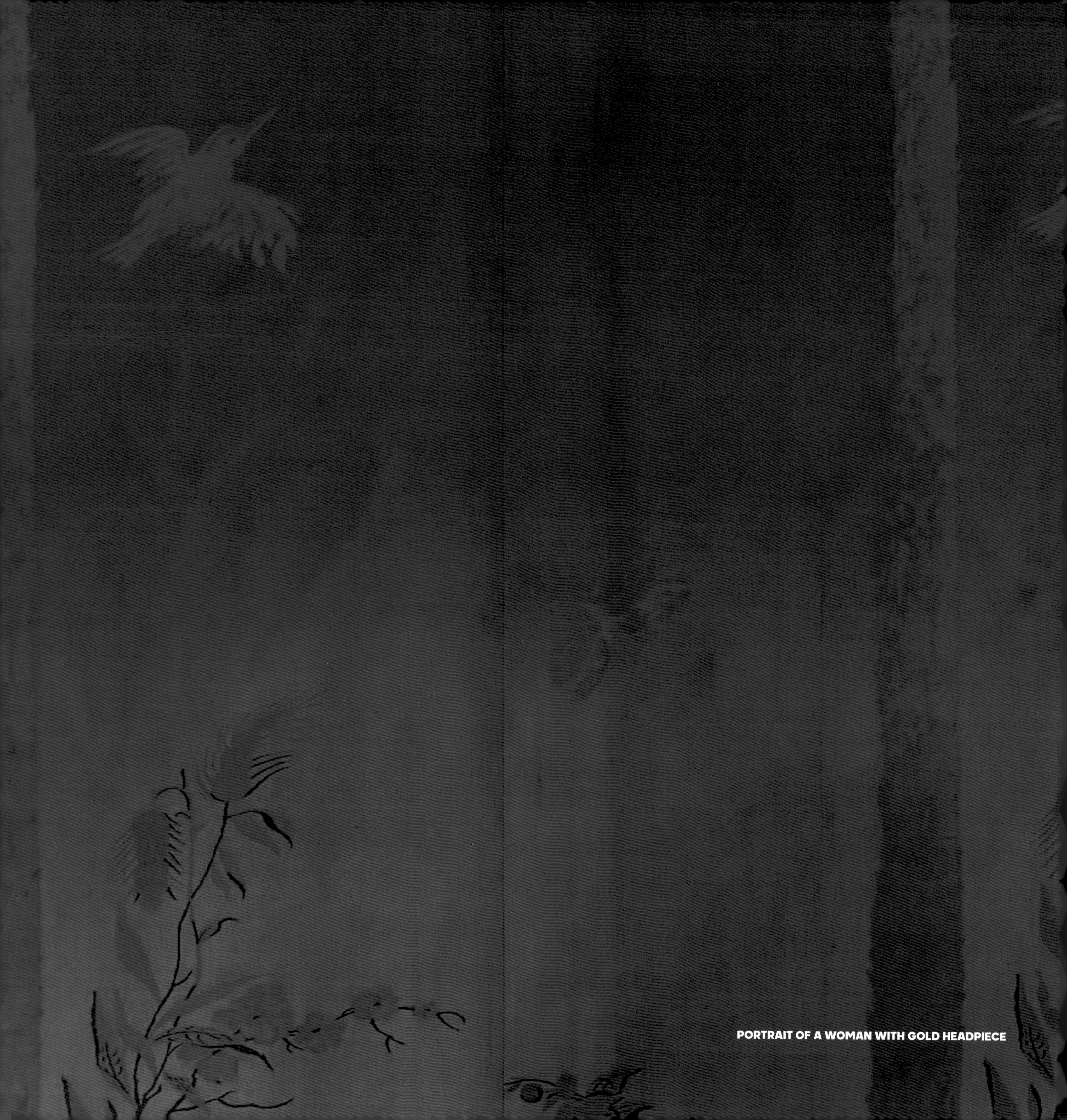

PORTRAIT OF A WOMAN WITH GOLD HEADPIECE

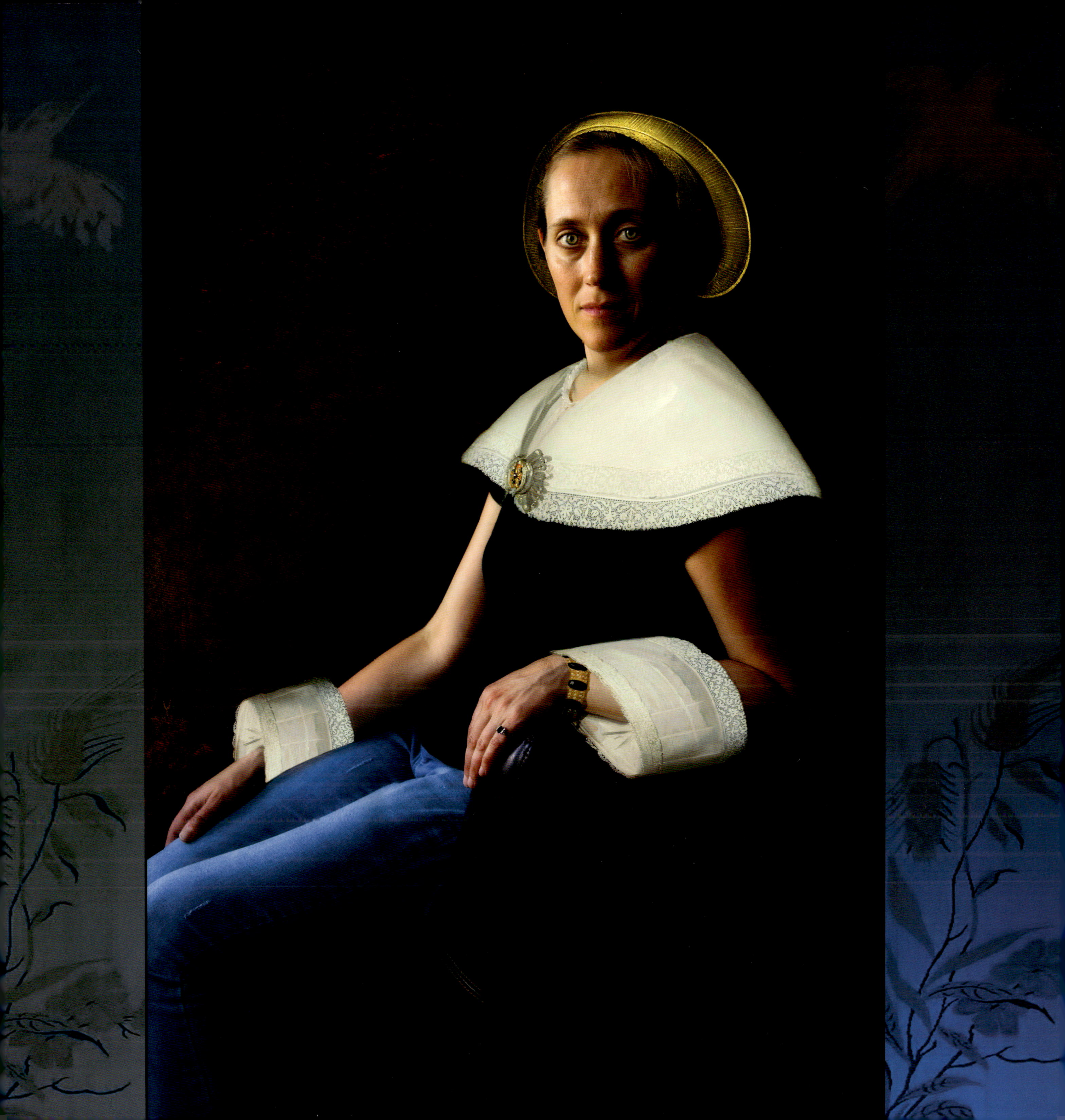

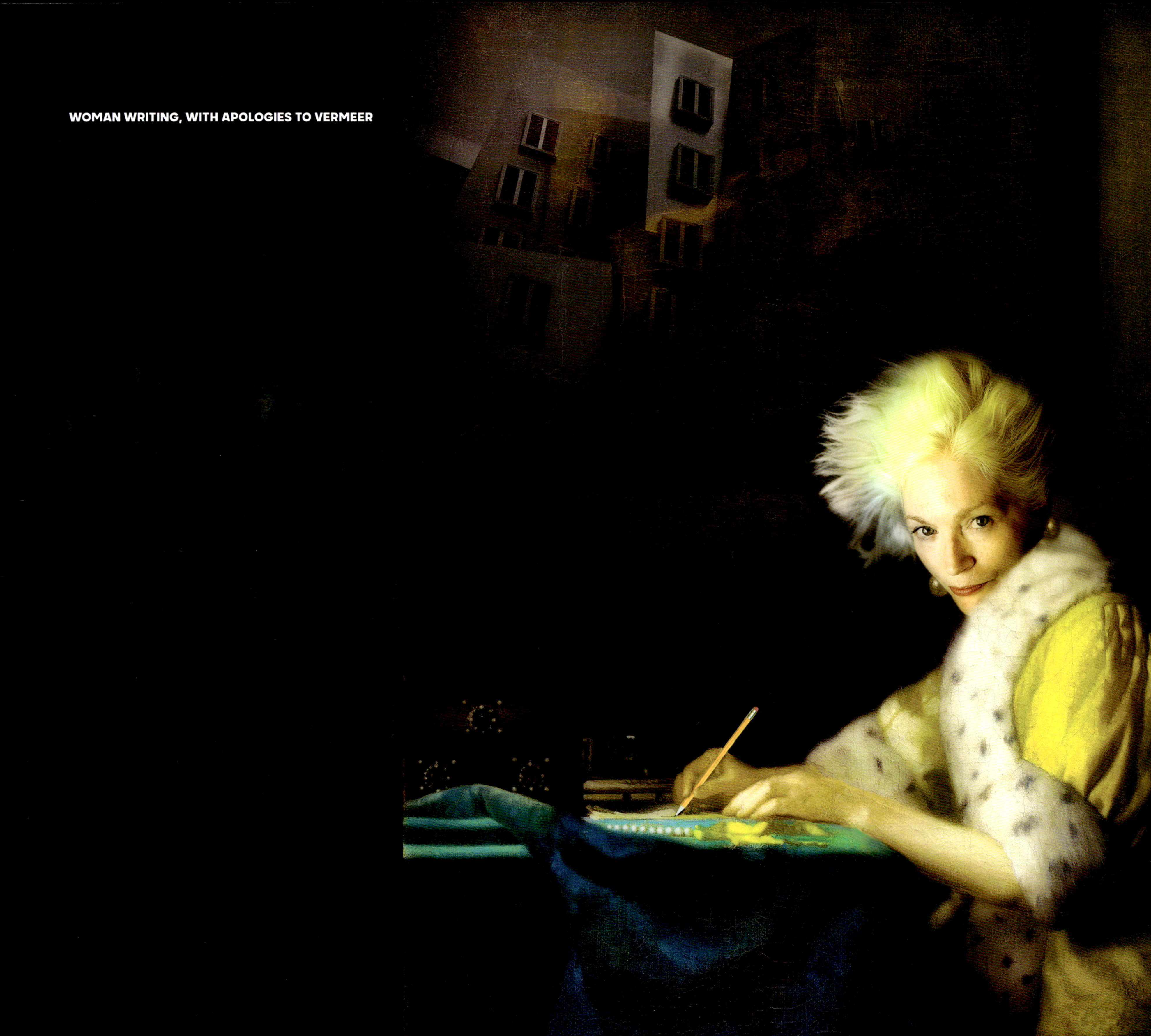

WOMAN WRITING, WITH APOLOGIES TO VERMEER

In a past life, I was *A Young Woman seated at a Virginal*,
and I was the bluff Dutchman, fingers dusted with black
chalk, red chalk, who painted her. "Sit
still, smile, not too much, yes, that's it, now

hold," and I was *A Lady Writing*,
at the Algonquin with Benchley, and Willy
kept me locked in my room, churning
out pages of *Claudine*. It's where I'm most

at home, happiest, backstage between
costume and undress, history and presence. "After I've cleaned
my brushes, we'll go for schnapps and sausage."
I slip off my white ermine. Moebius strip

tease. Like Escher drawing the hand he draws with,
I write myself. Into this life. In a past life.

Monica Raymond

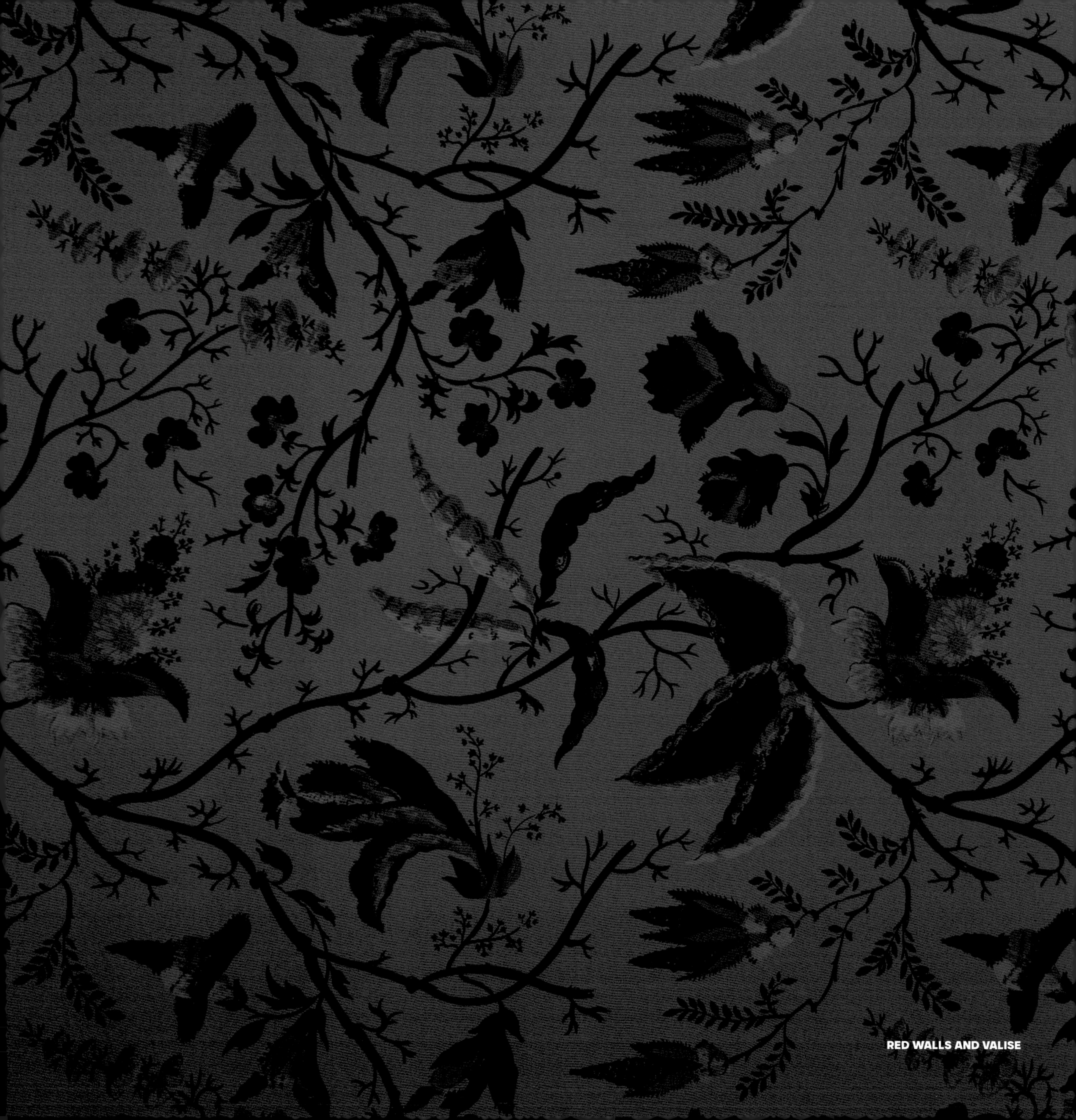
RED WALLS AND VALISE

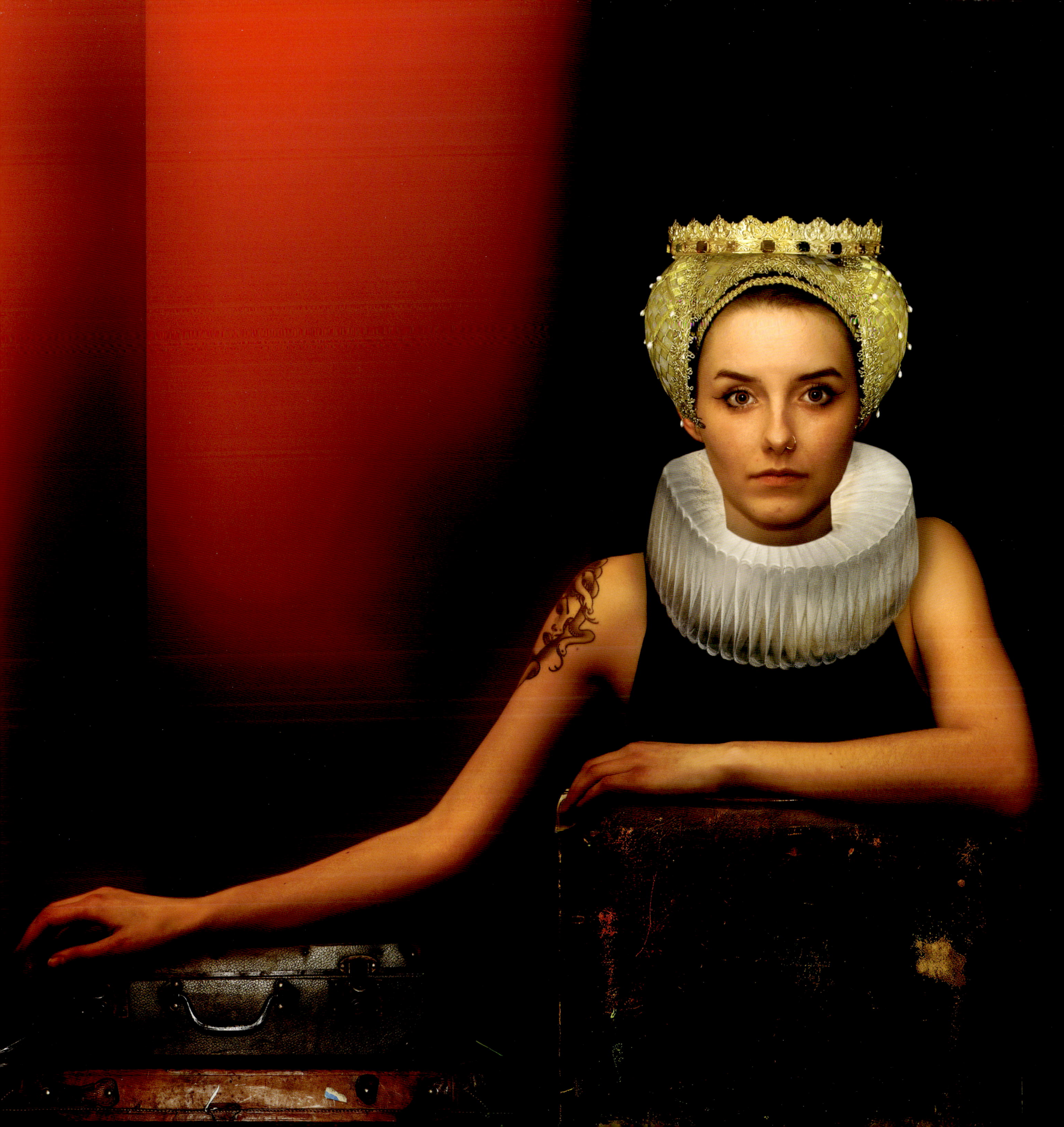

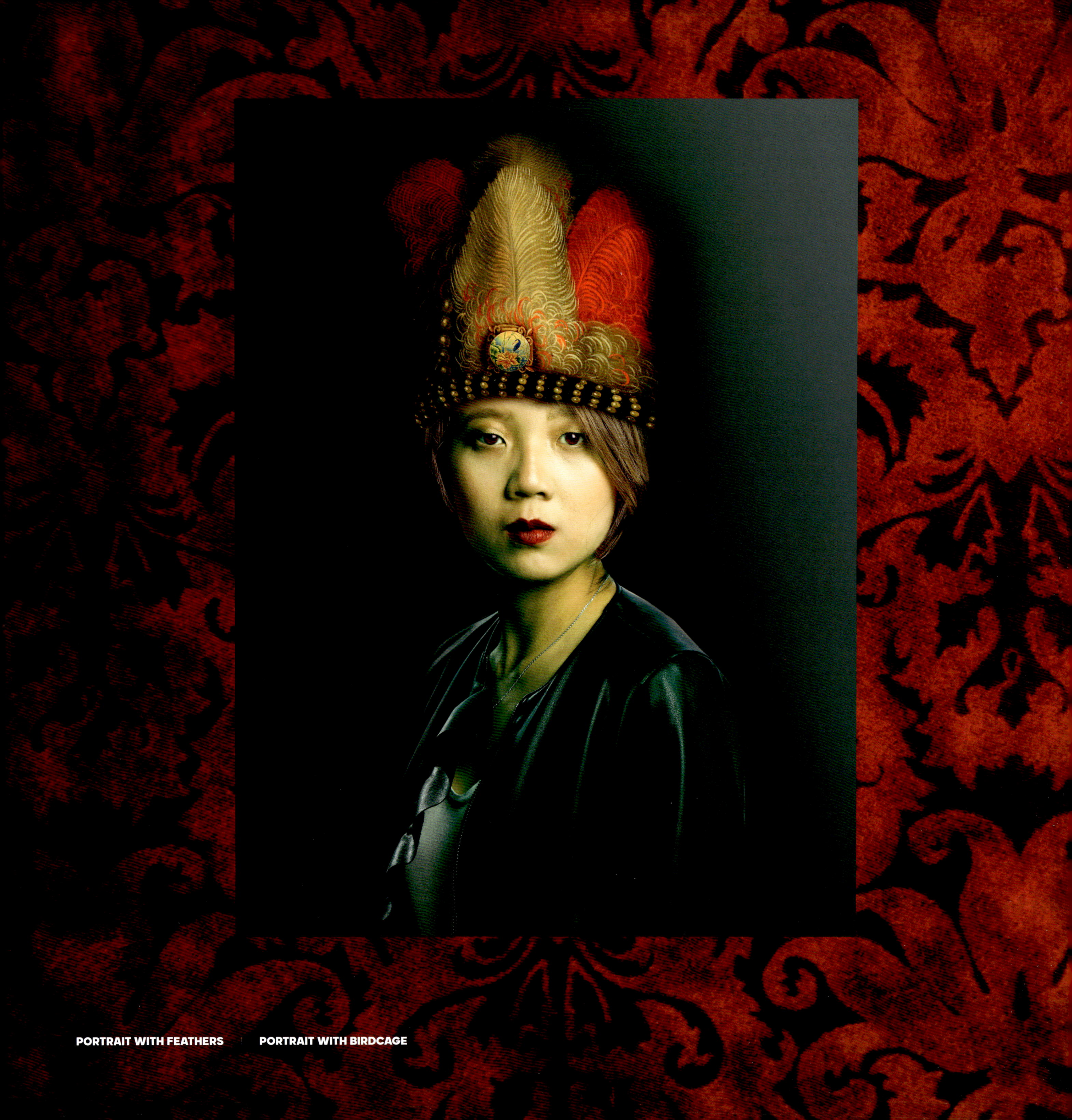

PORTRAIT WITH FEATHERS | PORTRAIT WITH BIRDCAGE

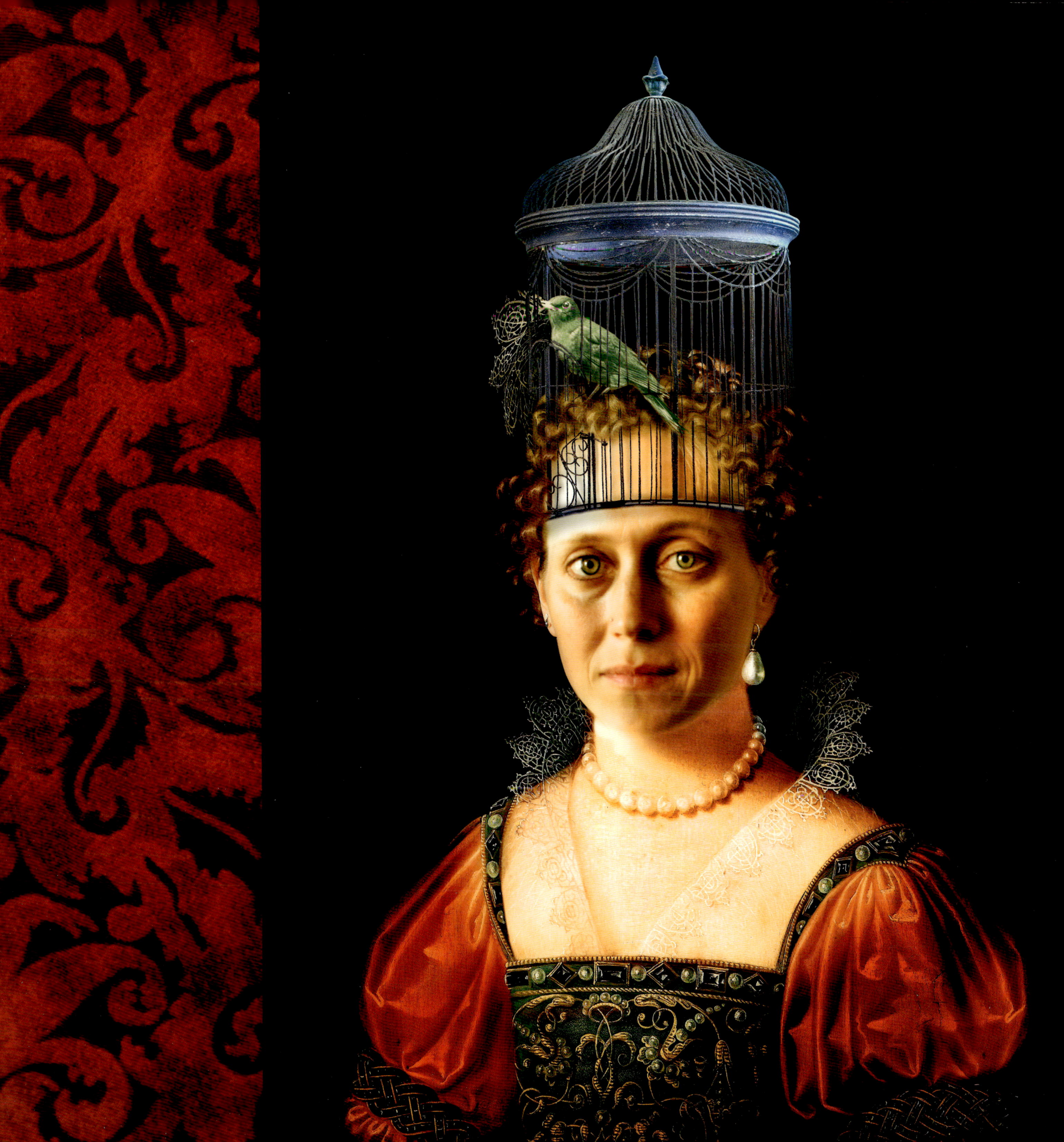

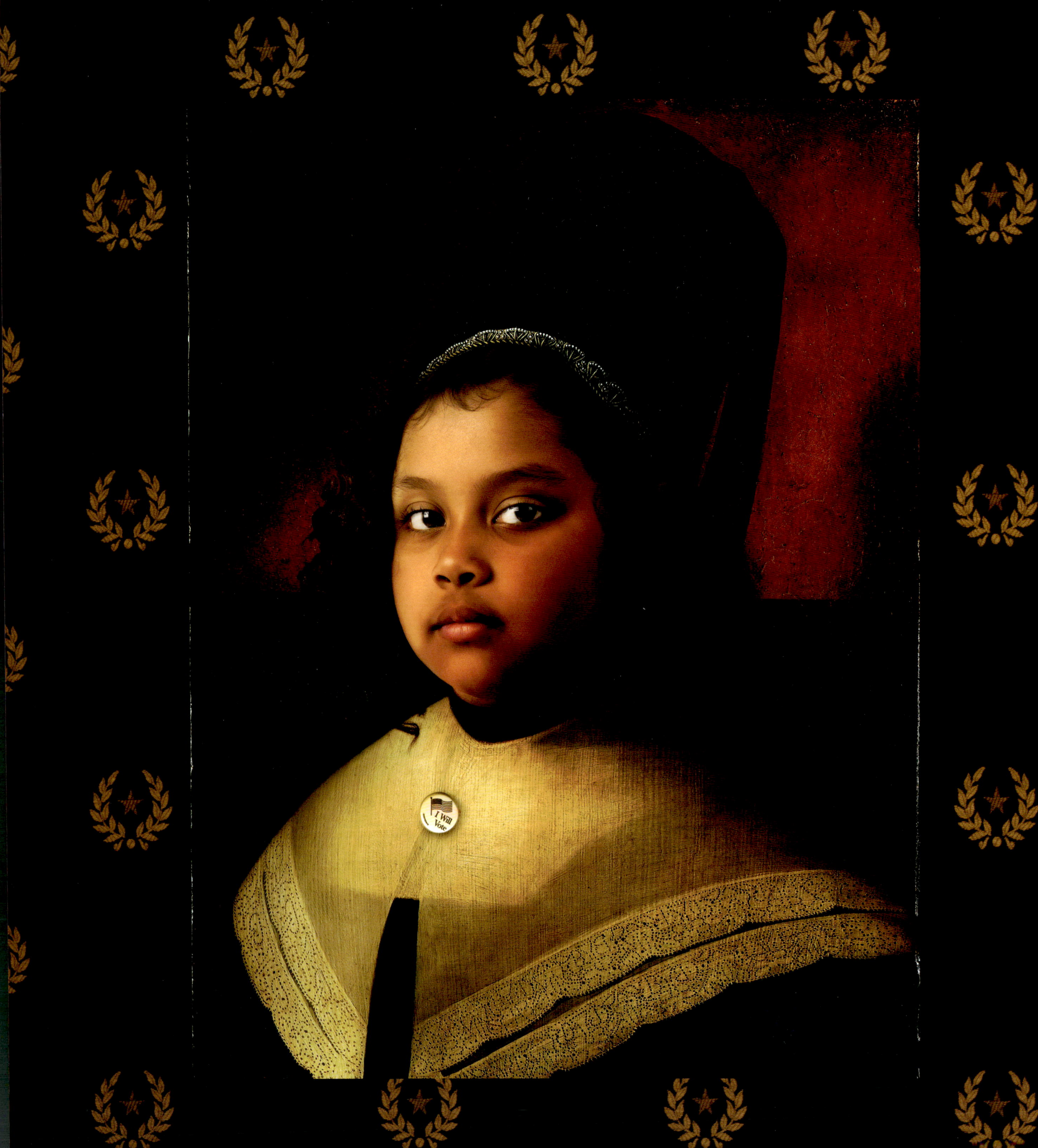
I Will Vote

Of course, it's saddening to see someone bound in chains or ropes or any harness that keeps them from the freedom they would enjoy. It's also saddening to witness people—children, old people, rich people, princes, beggars, refugees, or really anyone—bound by invisible but real social constraints, class expectations, stereotypes, or rigid gender roles. The complex restraints that keep people from being all that they could be naturally frustrate us. We wonder how they could have come to be so fettered, and how they might be unbound. Part of understanding how to undo such bondage is to envision it first. And often we can't envision the unleashing until we clearly see the leashing. We have to see what is binding someone, and then see in our mind's eye a vision of how they might look once liberated. Art often presents such images that intellectual projections cannot adequately accomplish.

Fran Forman's images do this imagining for me, and I love them for it. They take a portrait of a pinched and rigid character confined by historic social chains and constraints layered on by time and familiarity, and propose an opposite. With Fran's juxtapositioning of a person who may be representative of a category of people who—in another place and time—might be bound to another role, as indicated by clothing or accoutrements, and then placing that person into an alternative spot, opens up possibilities in our minds for what might be.

The brown-skinned girl in this photo might not have worn a collar like the one in Fran's photo, since typically such collars were reserved for a woman of the nobility in 15th-century Brugge. But seeing her wearing it with Fran's layering of images liberates the girl, and liberates the clothing, and suggests possibilities for what people bound by the conventions of that time might never have experienced. And once unbound, all kinds of ways people who might dress and be like this child burst forth to mind.

Judy Dushku

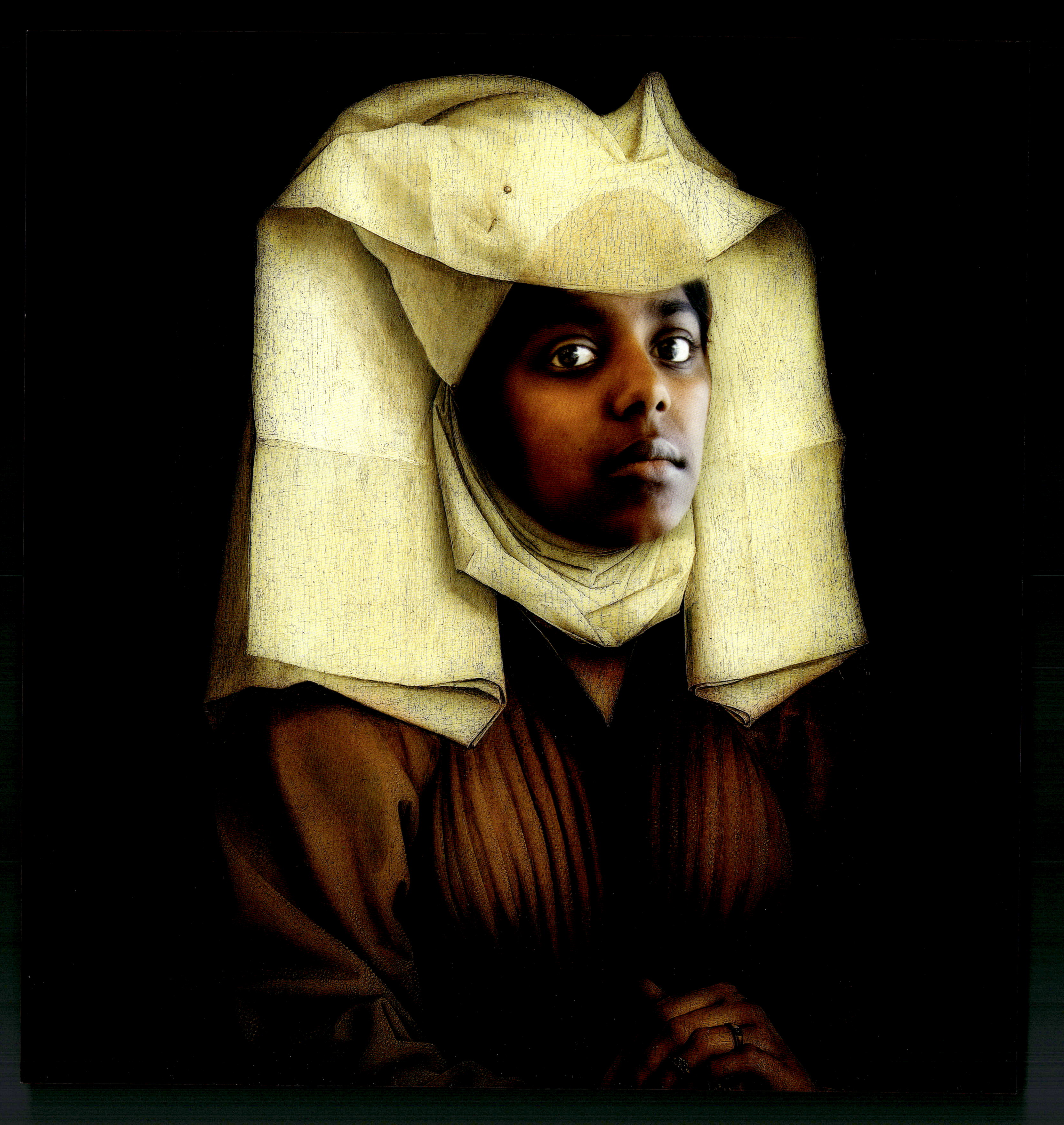

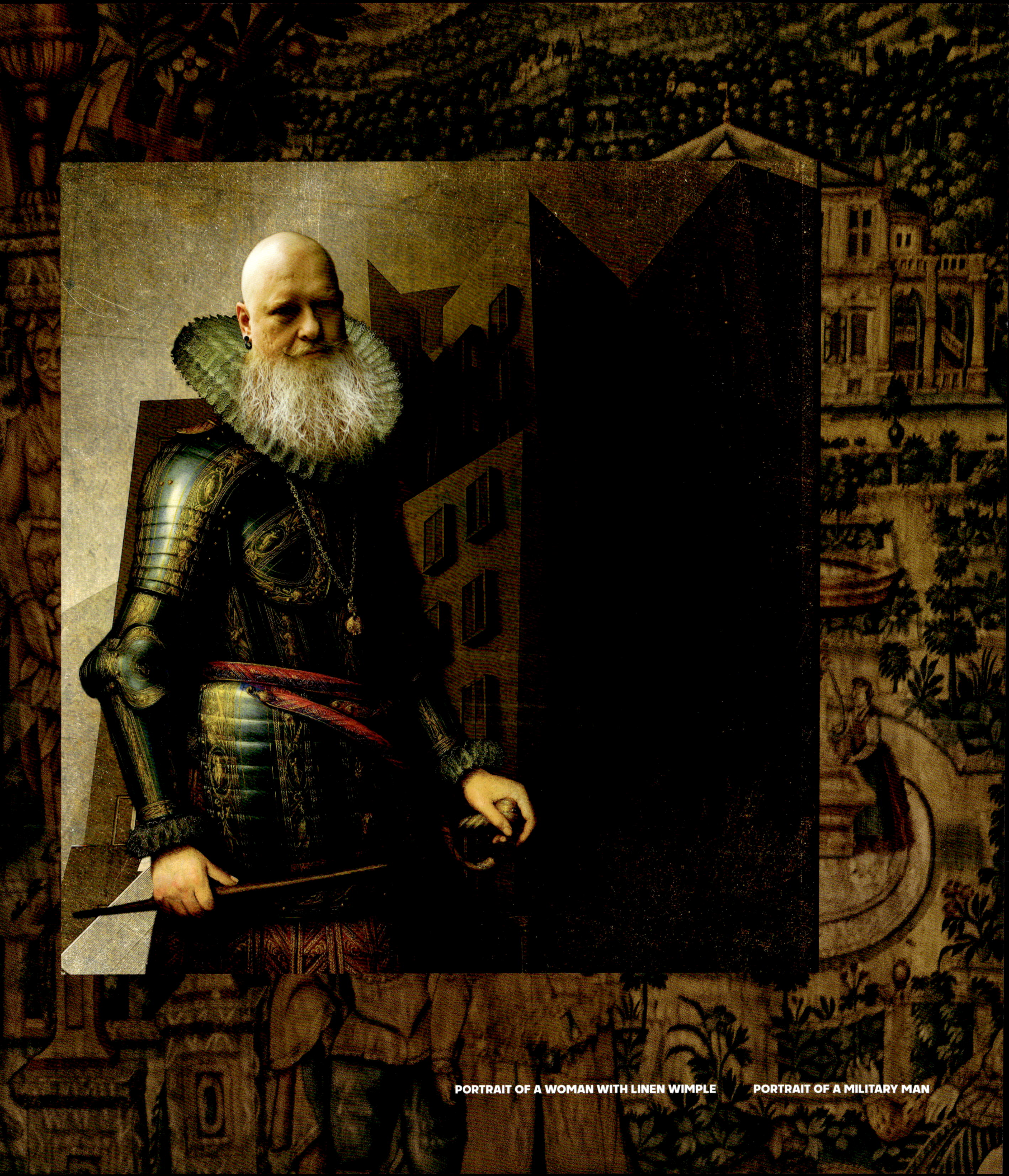

PORTRAIT OF A WOMAN WITH LINEN WIMPLE

PORTRAIT OF A MILITARY MAN

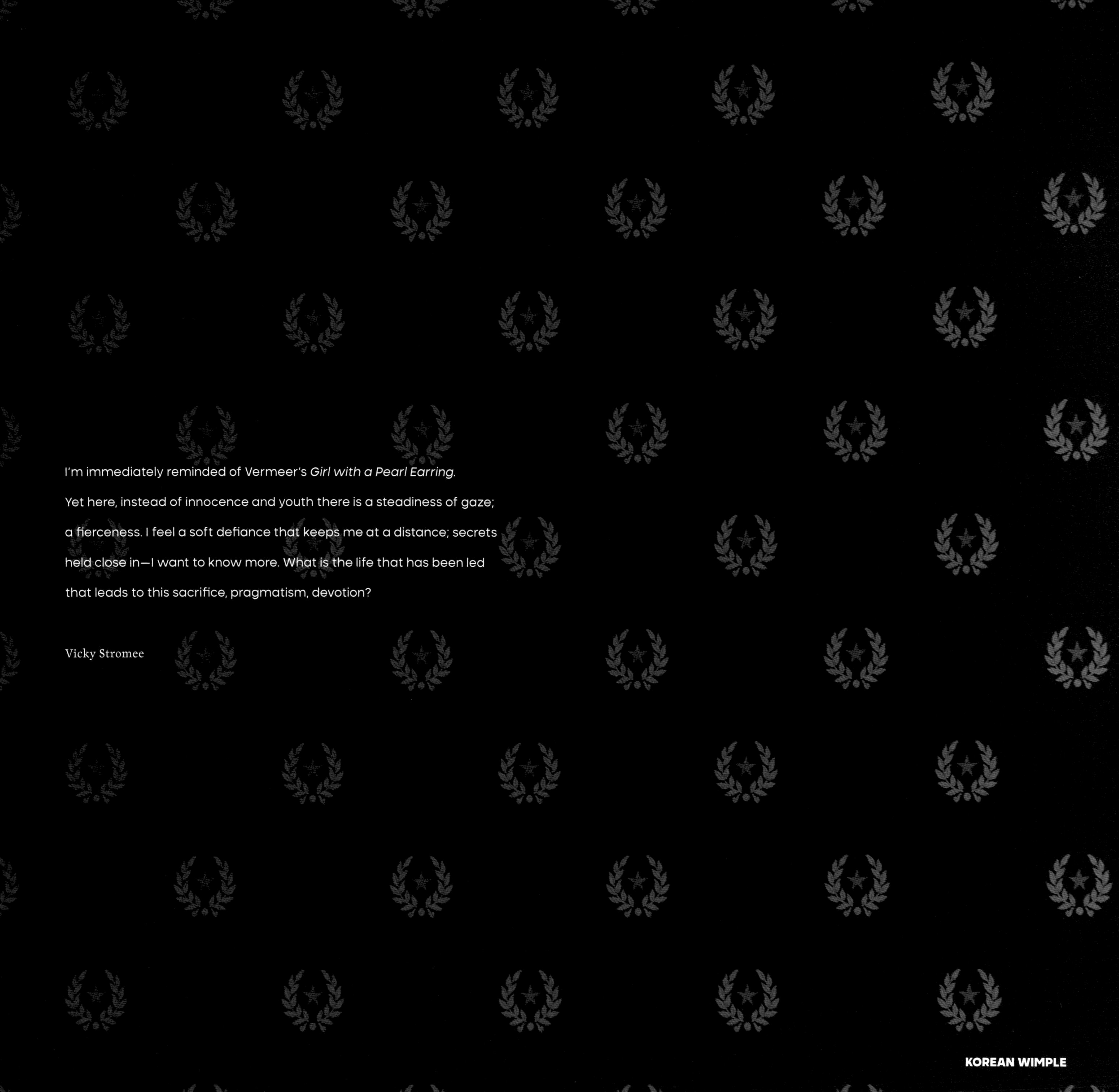

I'm immediately reminded of Vermeer's *Girl with a Pearl Earring.* Yet here, instead of innocence and youth there is a steadiness of gaze; a fierceness. I feel a soft defiance that keeps me at a distance; secrets held close in—I want to know more. What is the life that has been led that leads to this sacrifice, pragmatism, devotion?

Vicky Stromee

KOREAN WIMPLE

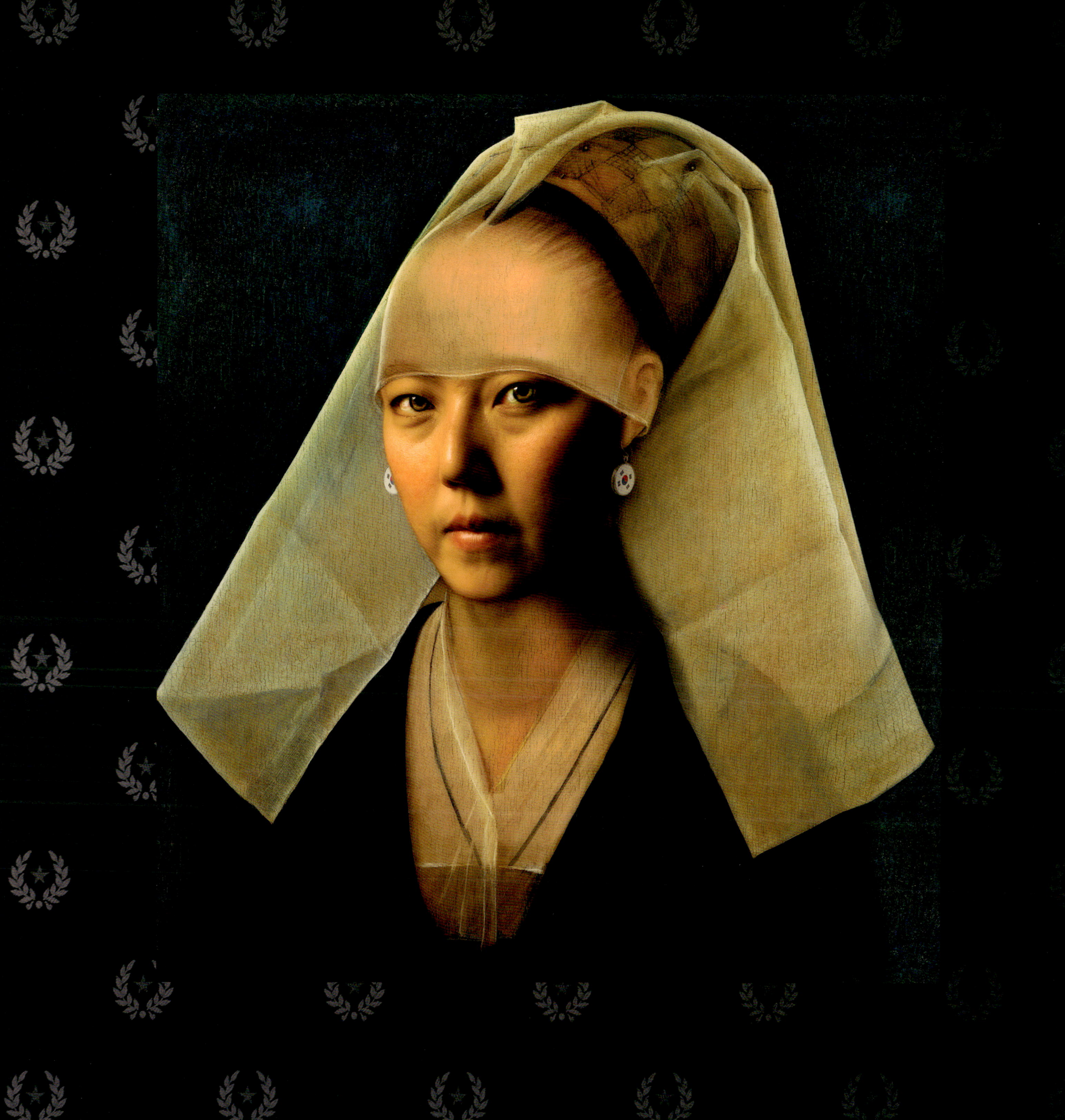

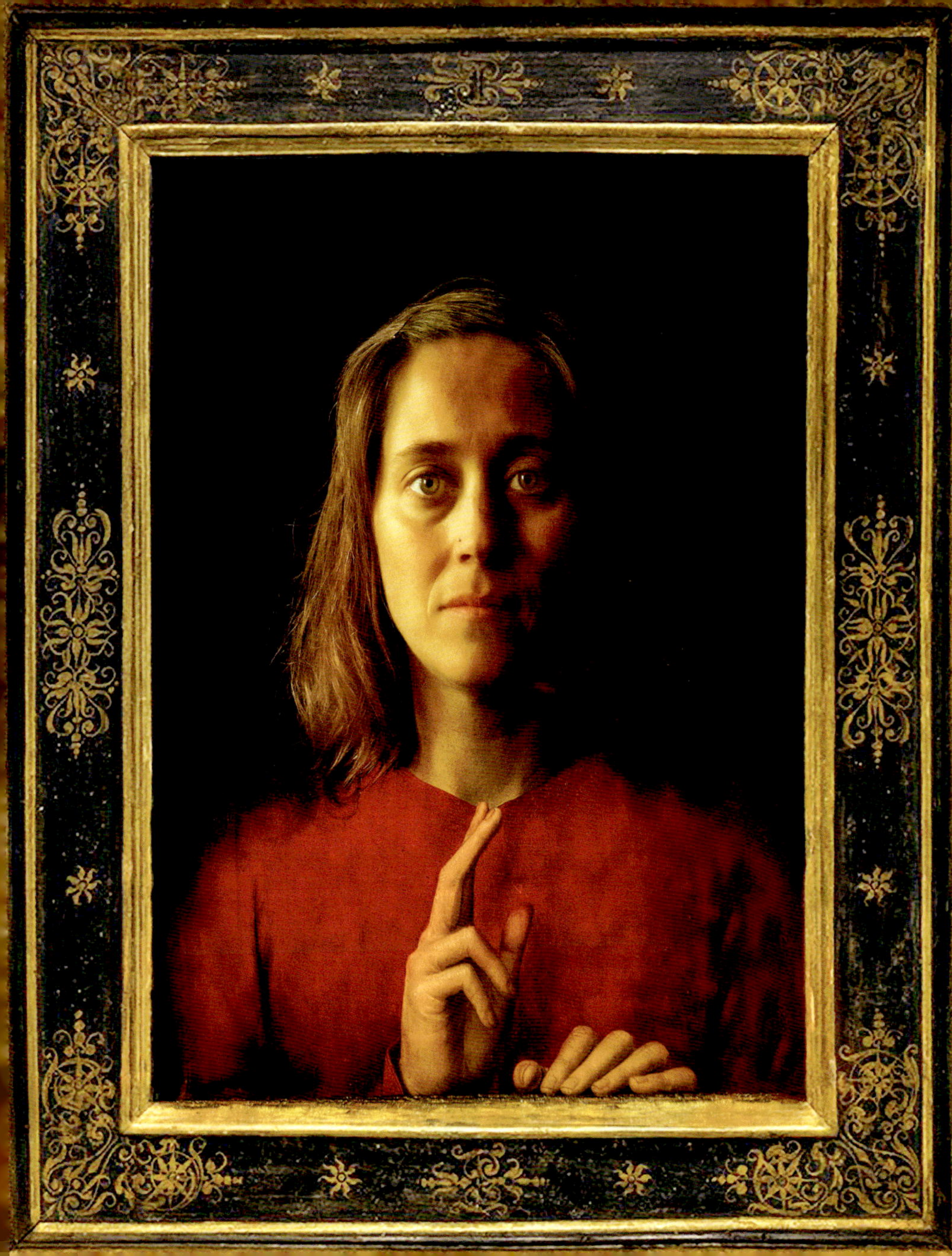

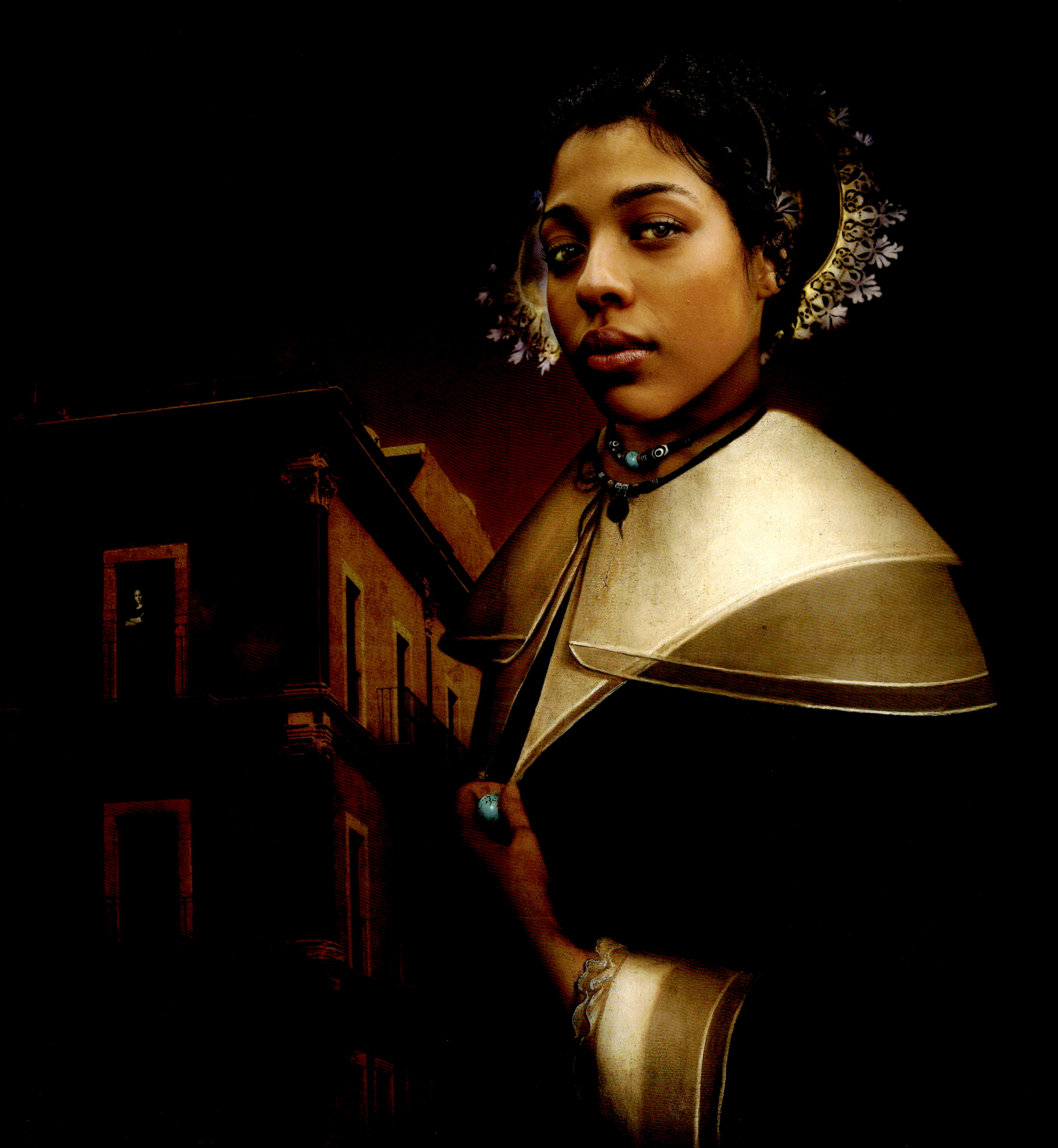

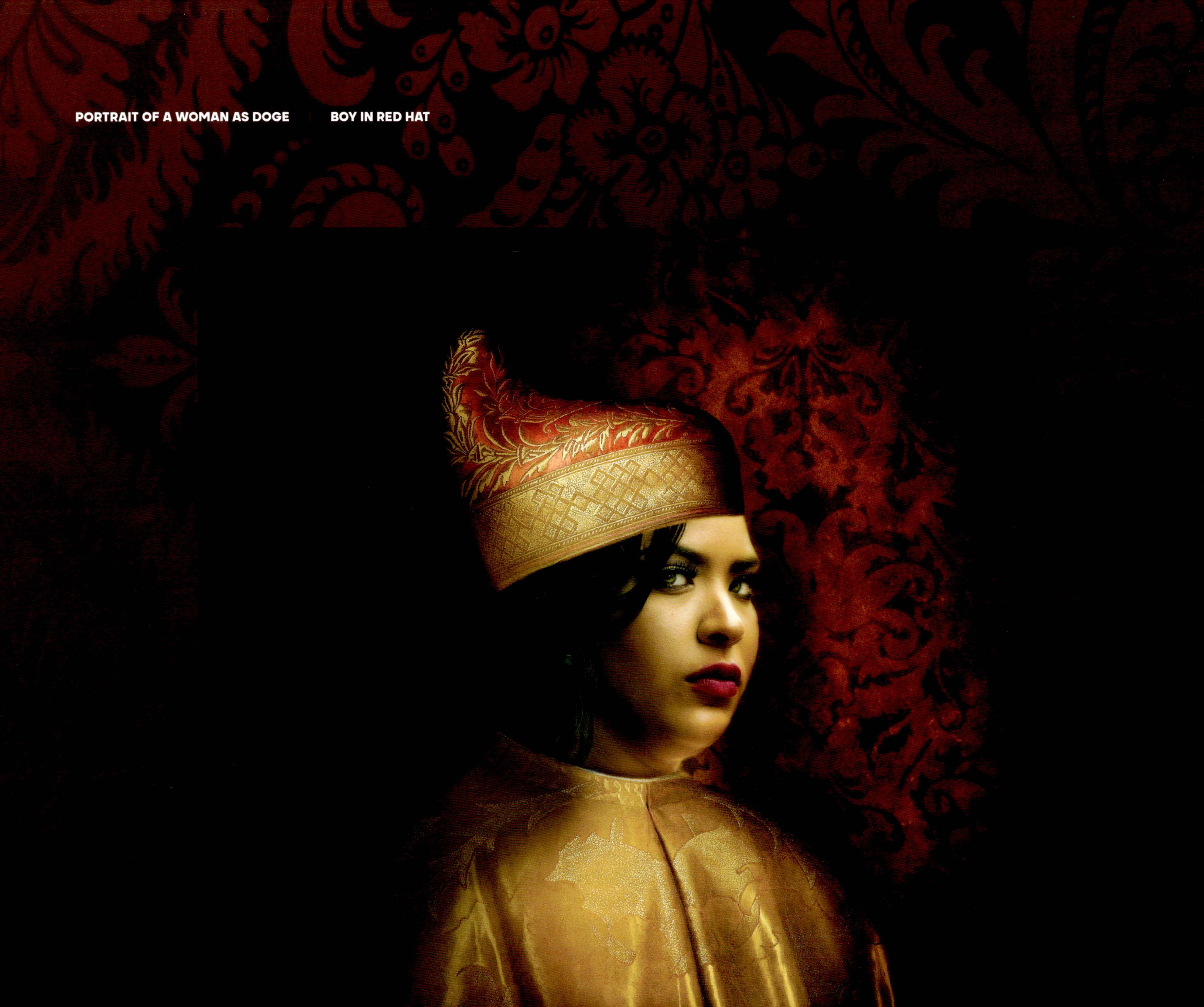

PORTRAIT OF A WOMAN AS DOGE | BOY IN RED HAT

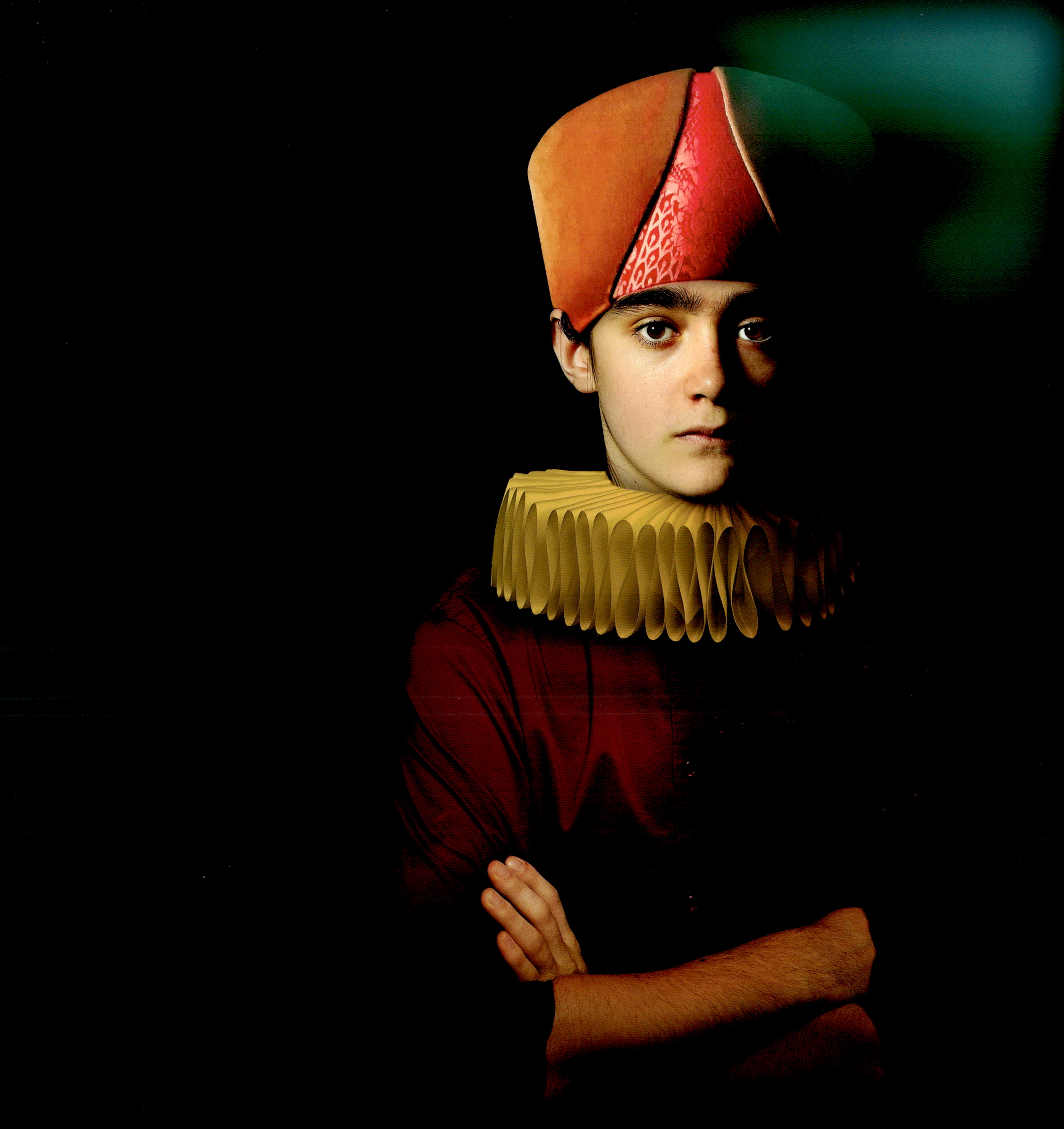

Sophisticated surprises engage me whenever I view Fran's images that play with an absurd blending of scale, composition, and most importantly time. Much of her work bridges my experience of art history, poetry, and private dreams. In *Portrait of a Young Woman after Anonymous* I want to ask this young woman what she cares about and what secrets she is harboring. This is my key to an effective portrait—do I want to know more about the person in the picture and, better yet, do I want to meet that person? To the young woman in this image, "The confidence exuded with your posture and firm jaw gives me hope for the future. Thank you."

Katrin Eismann

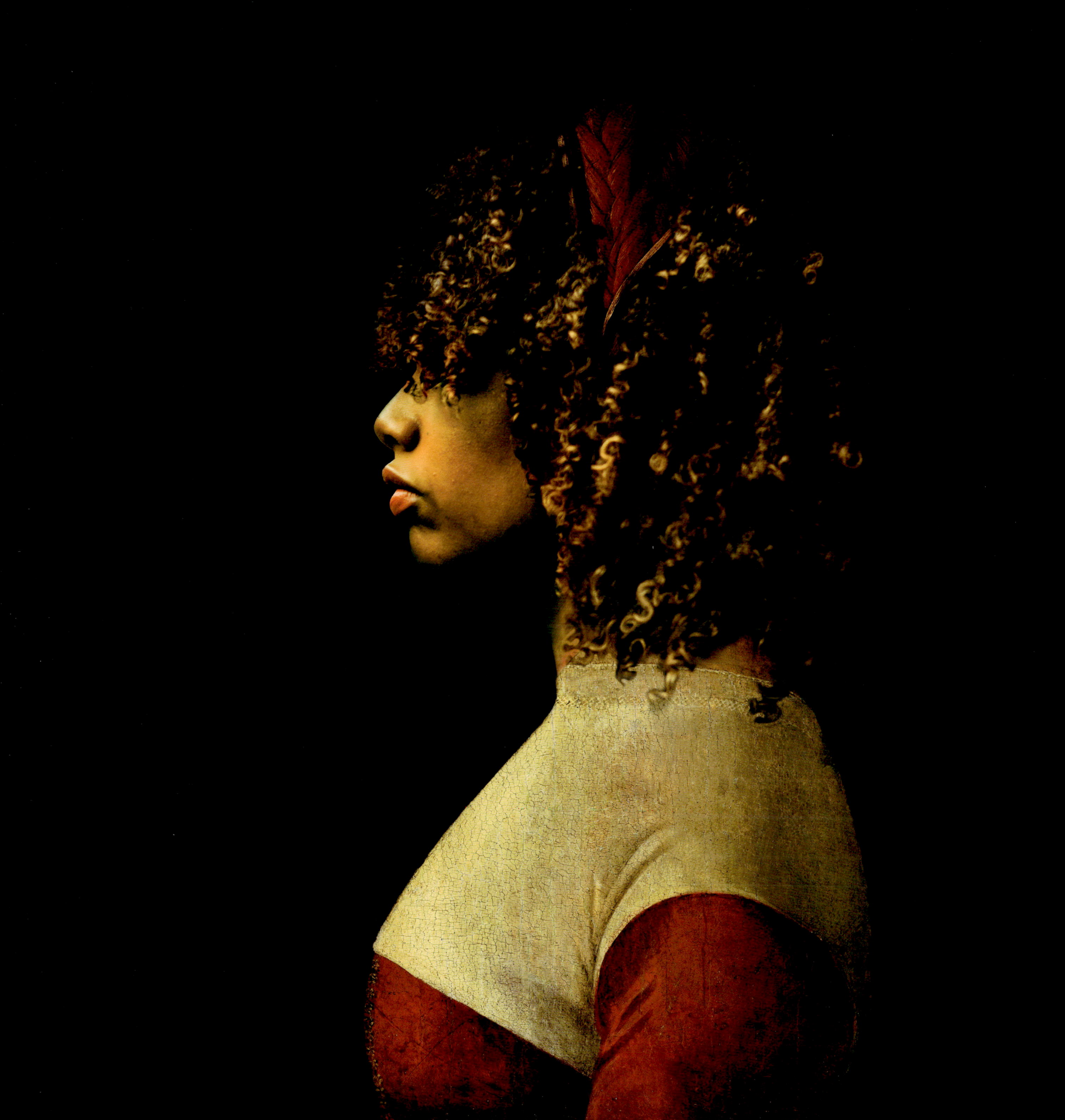

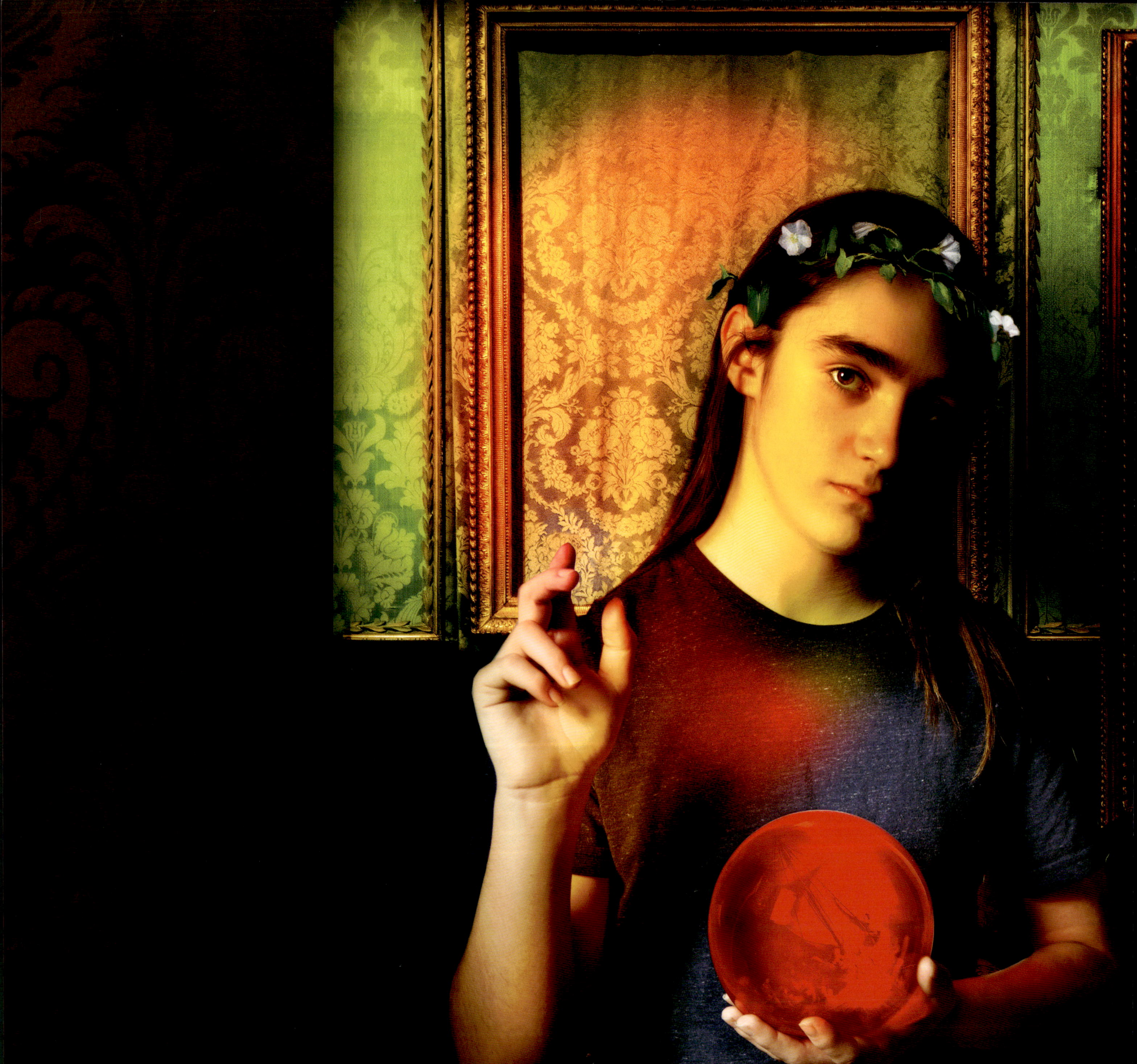

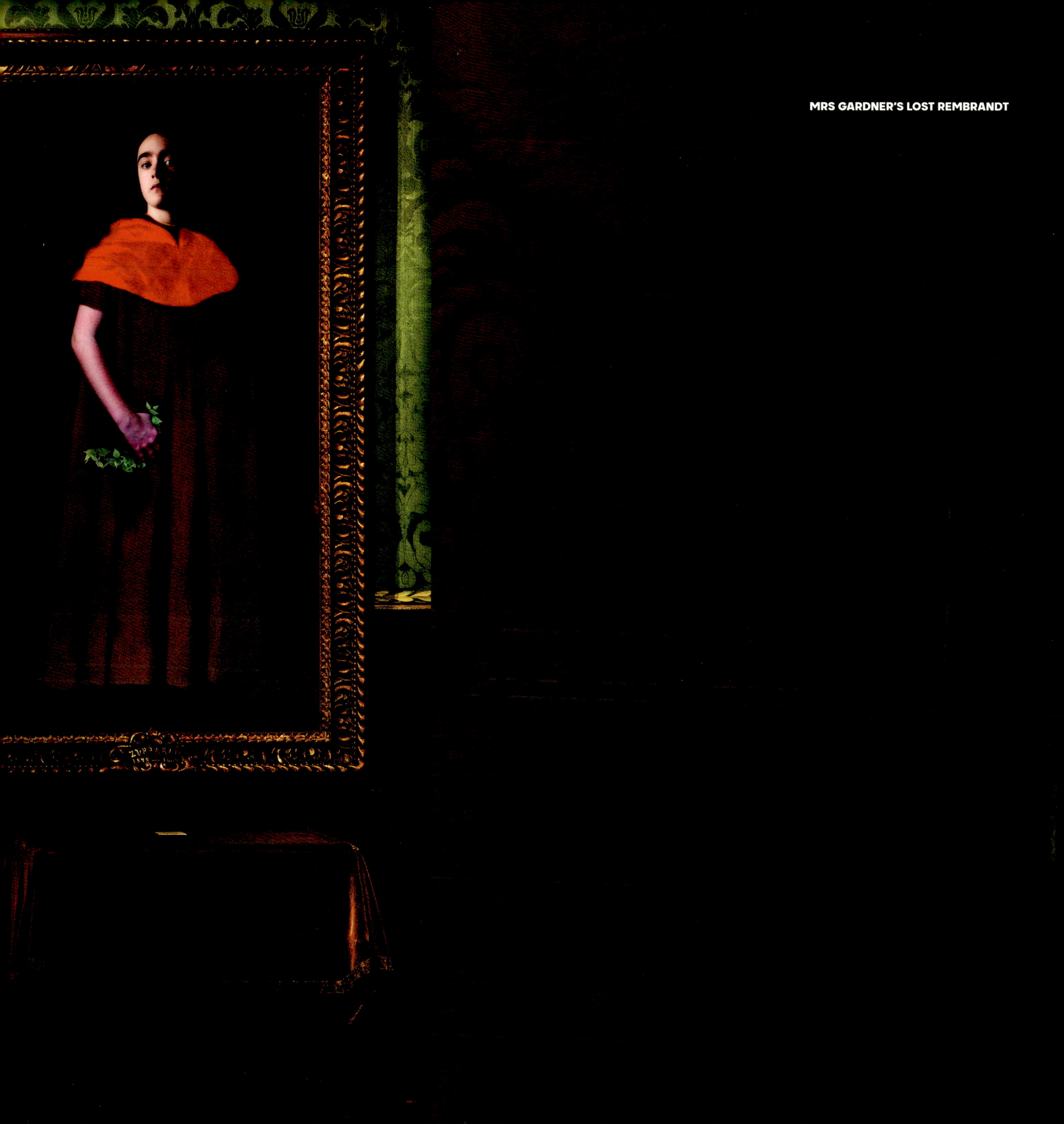

SOMEWHERE BETWEEN ARRIVAL AND DEPARTURE,

THERE IS A MOMENT OF BLISS.

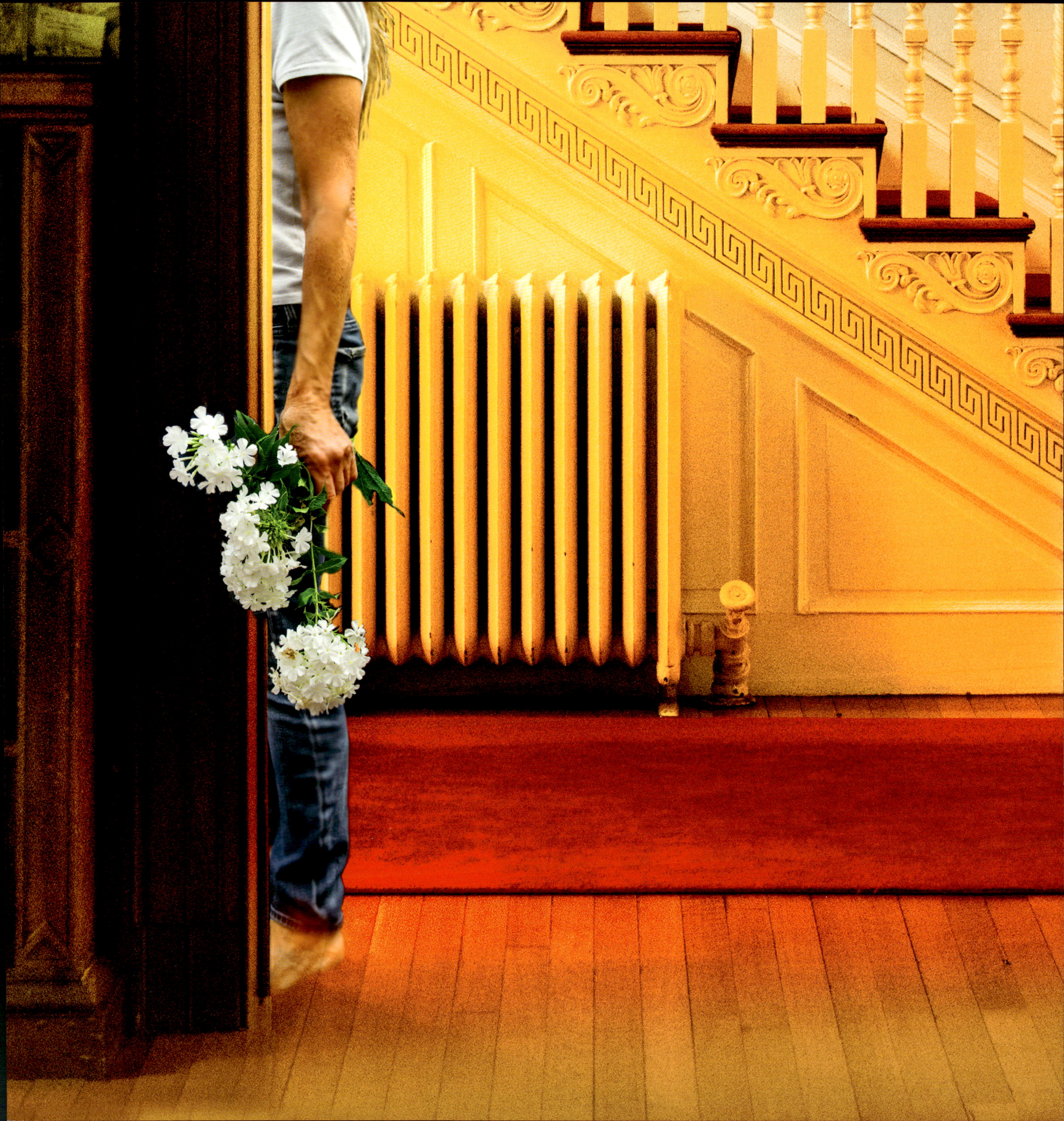

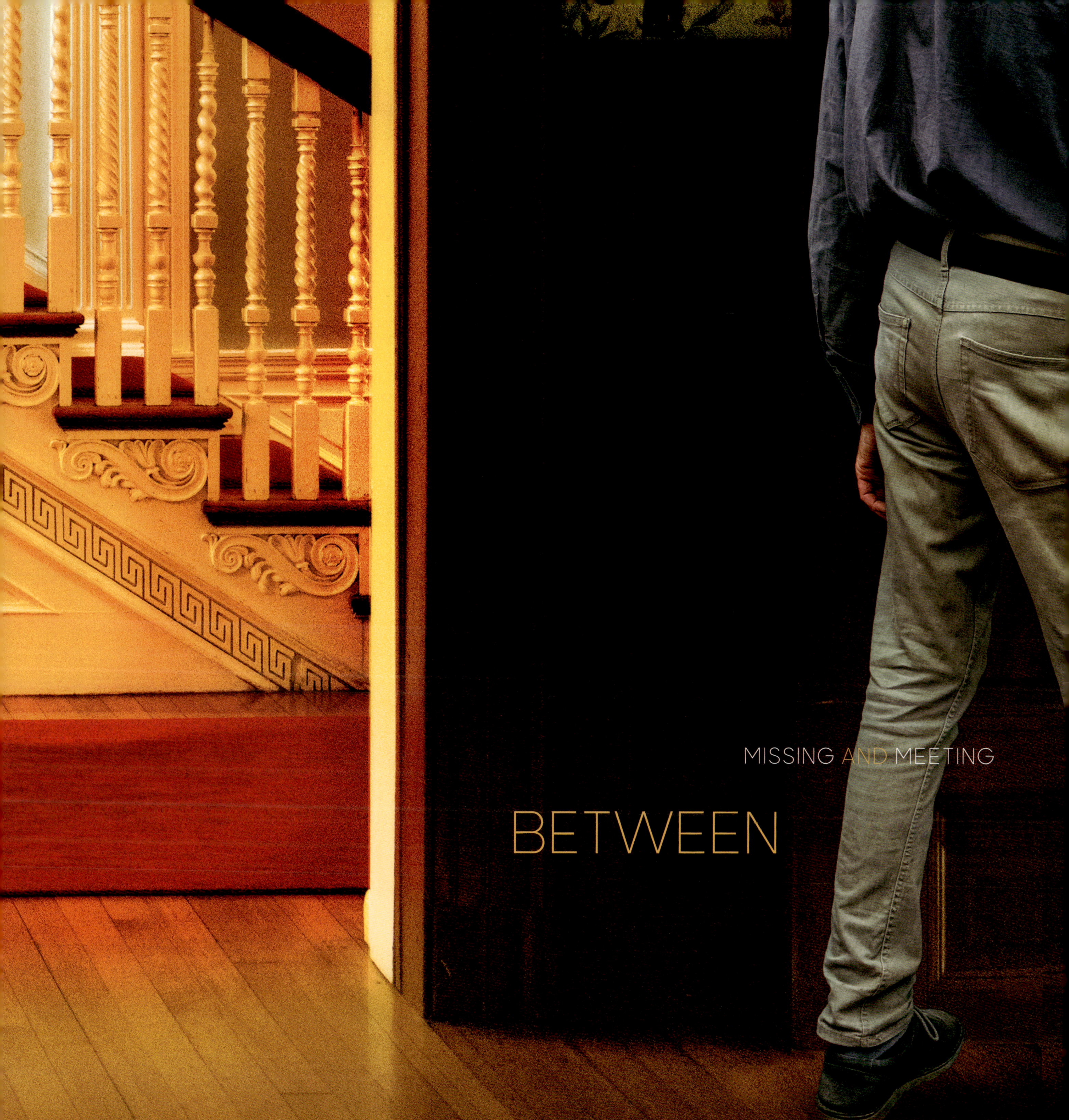
MISSING AND MEETING
BETWEEN

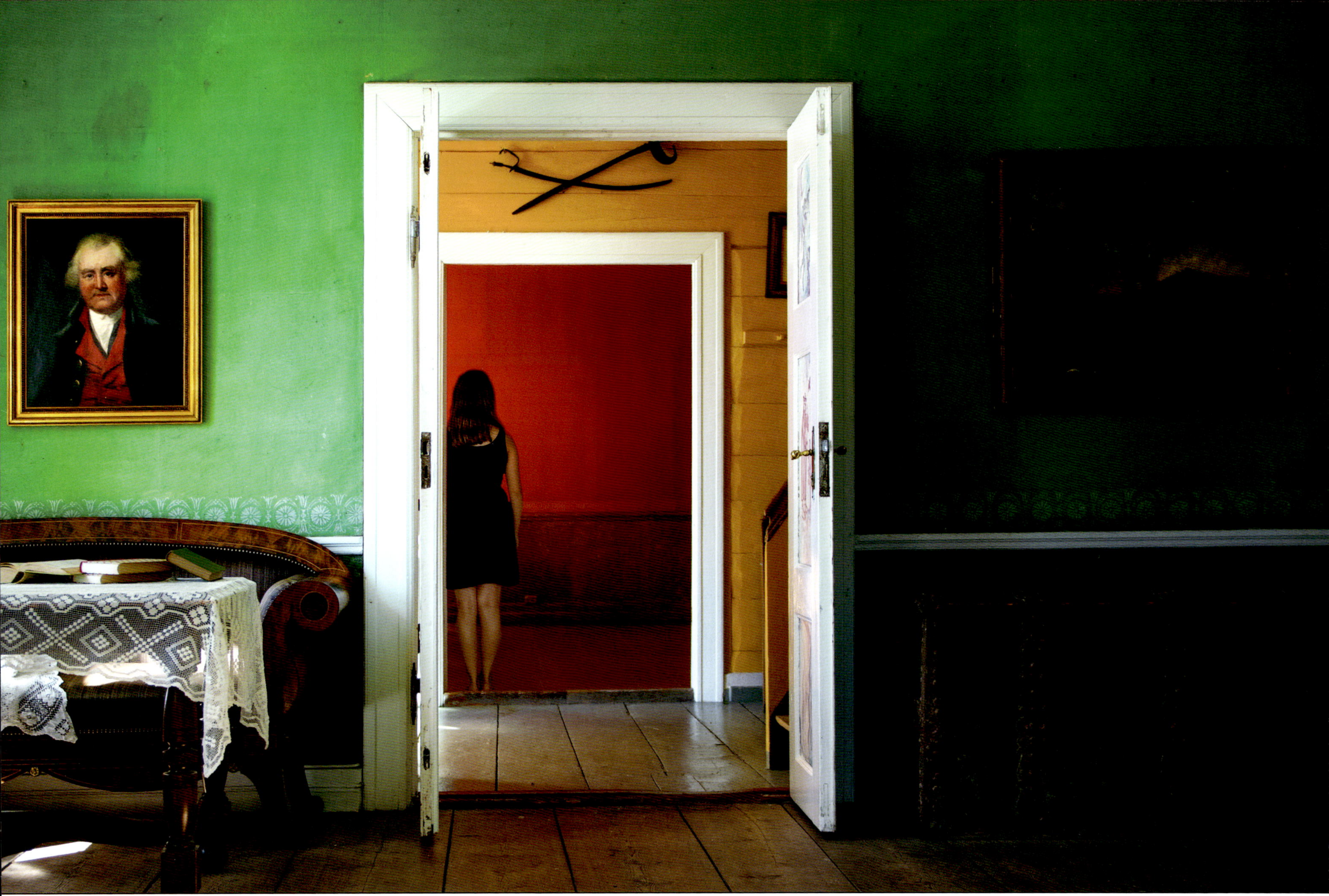

PORTALS

I knew the title of this image before I saw it in writing—it couldn't be about anything else.

The ancients knew the importance of portals, and they continue to represent powerful symbols. The Greek god Hermes, among his many roles, was also a god of boundaries and thresholds, and he guided souls into (and out of) the underworld. Hermes was sometimes referred to as "Guardian of the Gate." The psychologist Carl Jung considered Hermes to be the god the of the unconscious and the guide to inner journeys, and that portals symbolized this journey. Many ancient and modern rites of passage play on this unconscious meaning and involve traversing portals, symbolizing the ascent into another realm of being, either spiritual or social. Holy places are often entered through a small vestibule, which opens up into the grandeur of the place of worship, indicating a transition to the spiritual plane. Think of the transition symbolized by a groom carrying his bride across the threshold as they enter married life (probably an antiquated custom now). Portals figure prominently in initiation rituals. The initiate undergoes a transformation as he enters a new space and becomes a member of the group. Portals may also represent opportunity and new beginnings, as in the expression, "One door closes, another opens."

In this image, Fran Forman presents us with a young woman, as seen from behind, as she appears to be paused atop the second of two thresholds, about to enter the next room. The colors of the three visible rooms progress from green to yellow to red, perhaps as a warning of danger ahead in her final transition. The portrait in the first room is that of a stern paternal figure, and there are books piled on a lace-covered table. This may represent her childhood, comforting yet under the constraints of parental authority. The next room is yellow, a color that radiates optimism and hope, as the youth leaves the parental home and strikes out on her own. However, above the portal to the red room loom two threatening sabers, and the color signals passion and danger. She is about to enter a new, more mature phase of her life. She is drawn to the red room, yet hesitates on the threshold, sensing the risks that accompany adulthood. Like generations of women before her, she will enter that room and will take on the challenges ahead.

David Weinberg

The Vermeer-like ambiguity makes me return to this picture, imposing a different interpretation each time. And the color.

Andrea Petersen

AT THE THRESHOLD

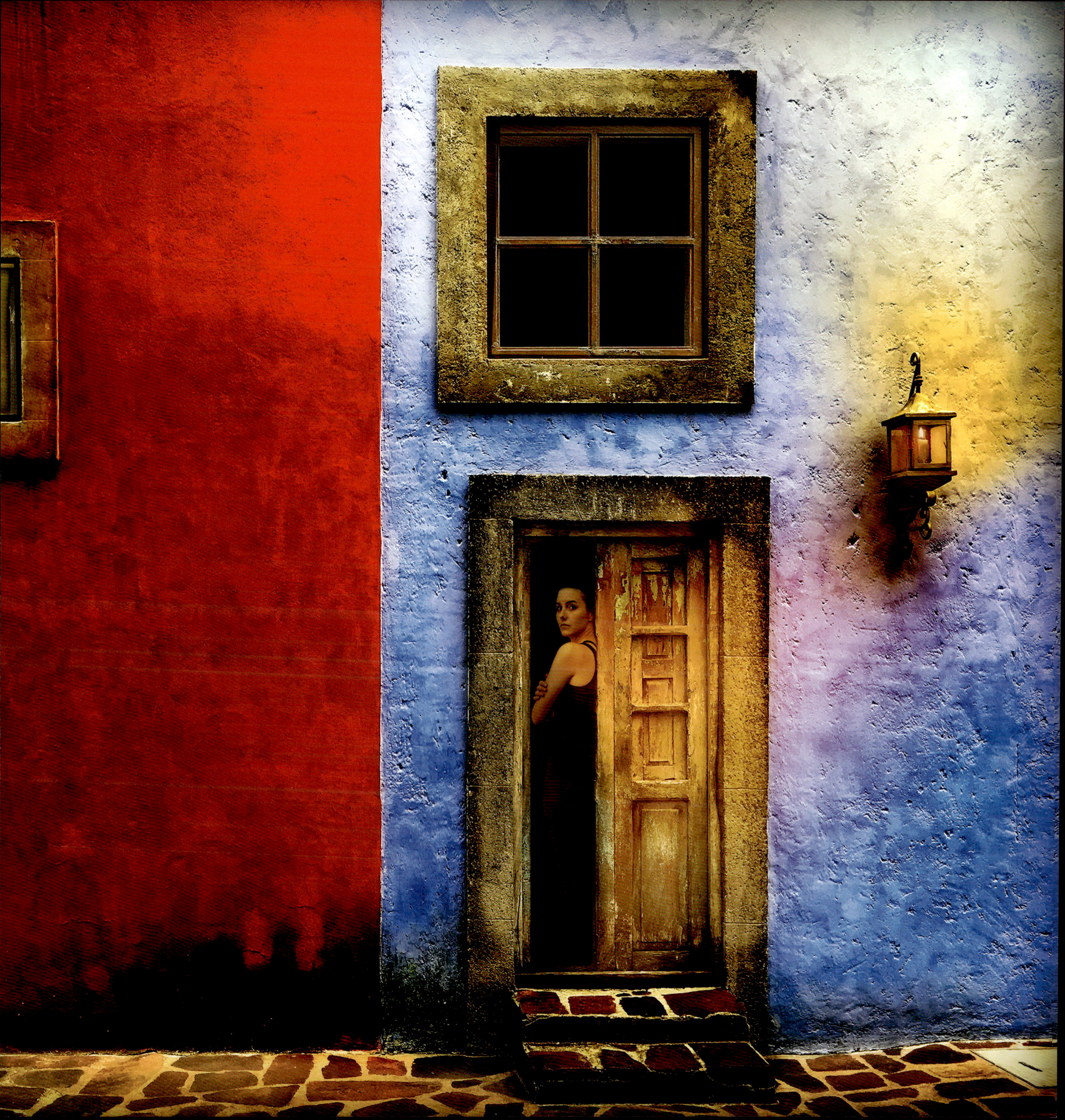

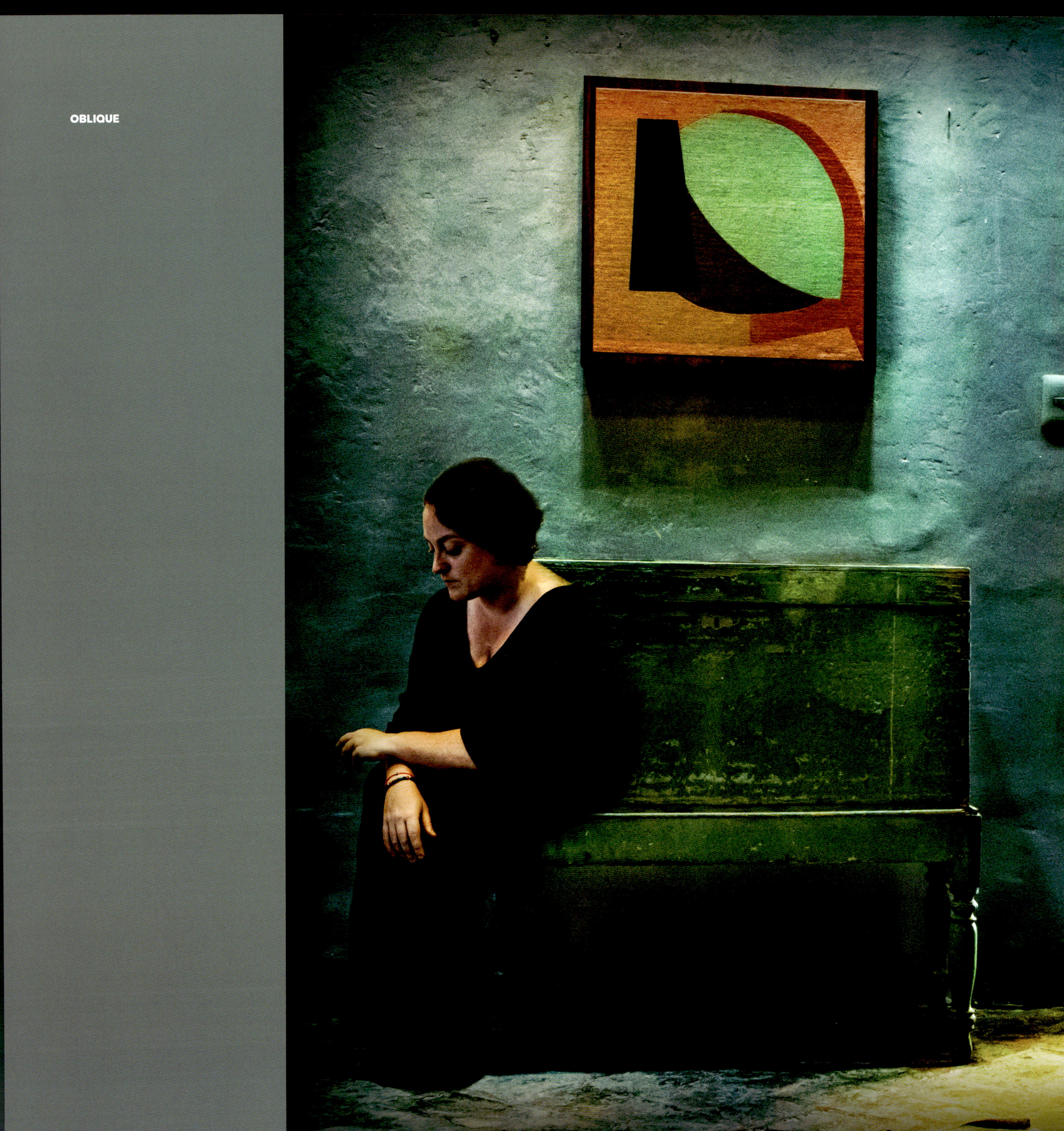

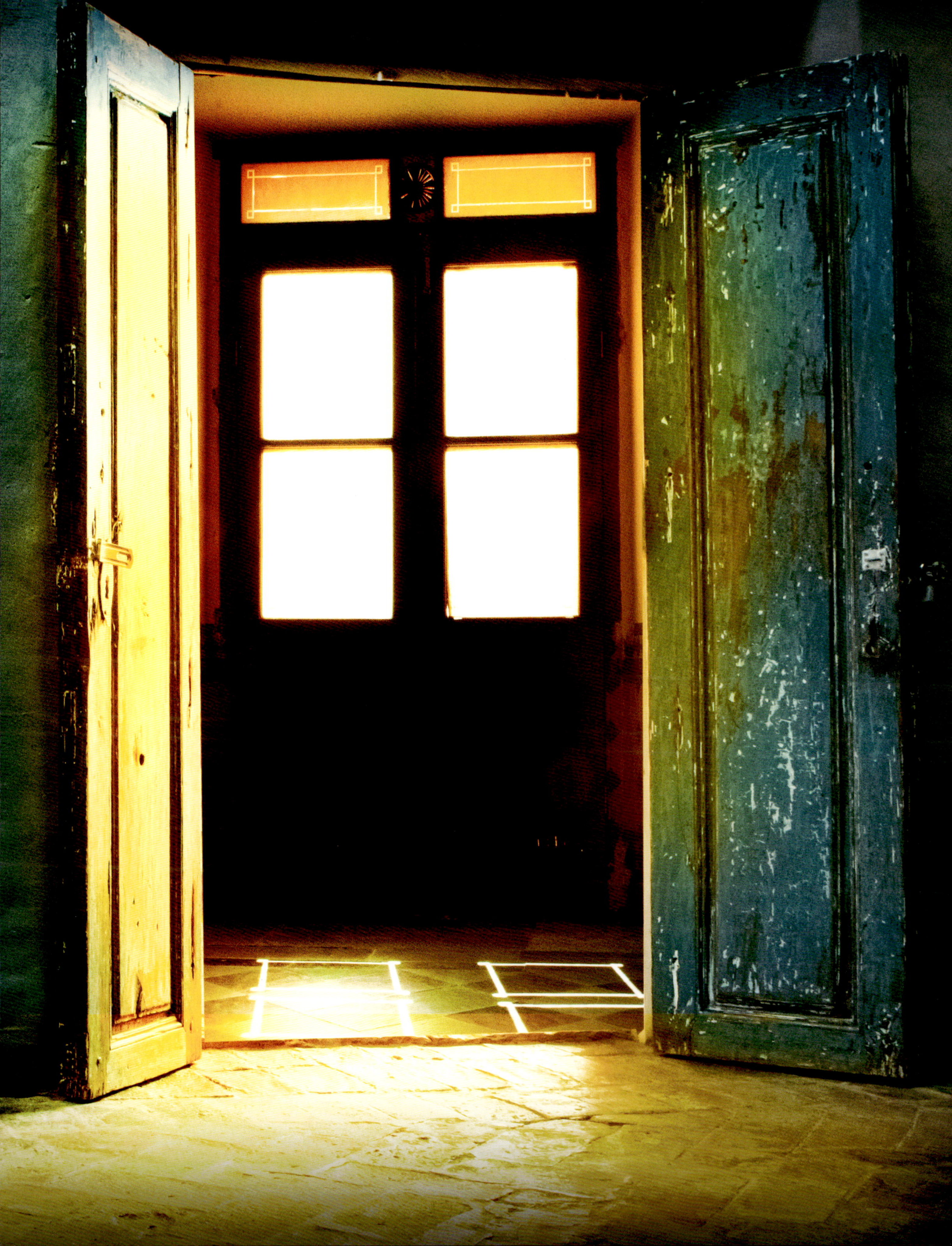

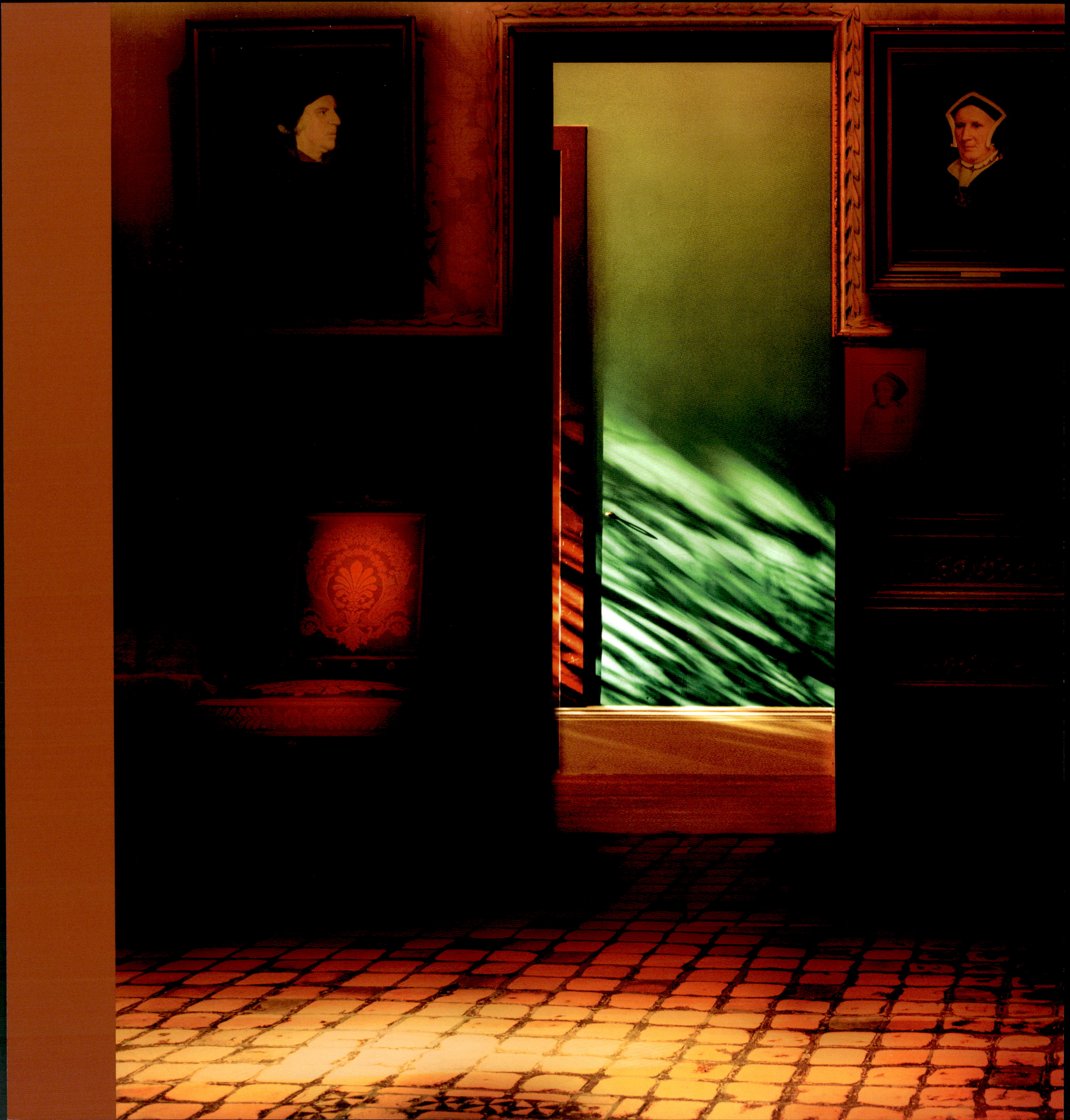

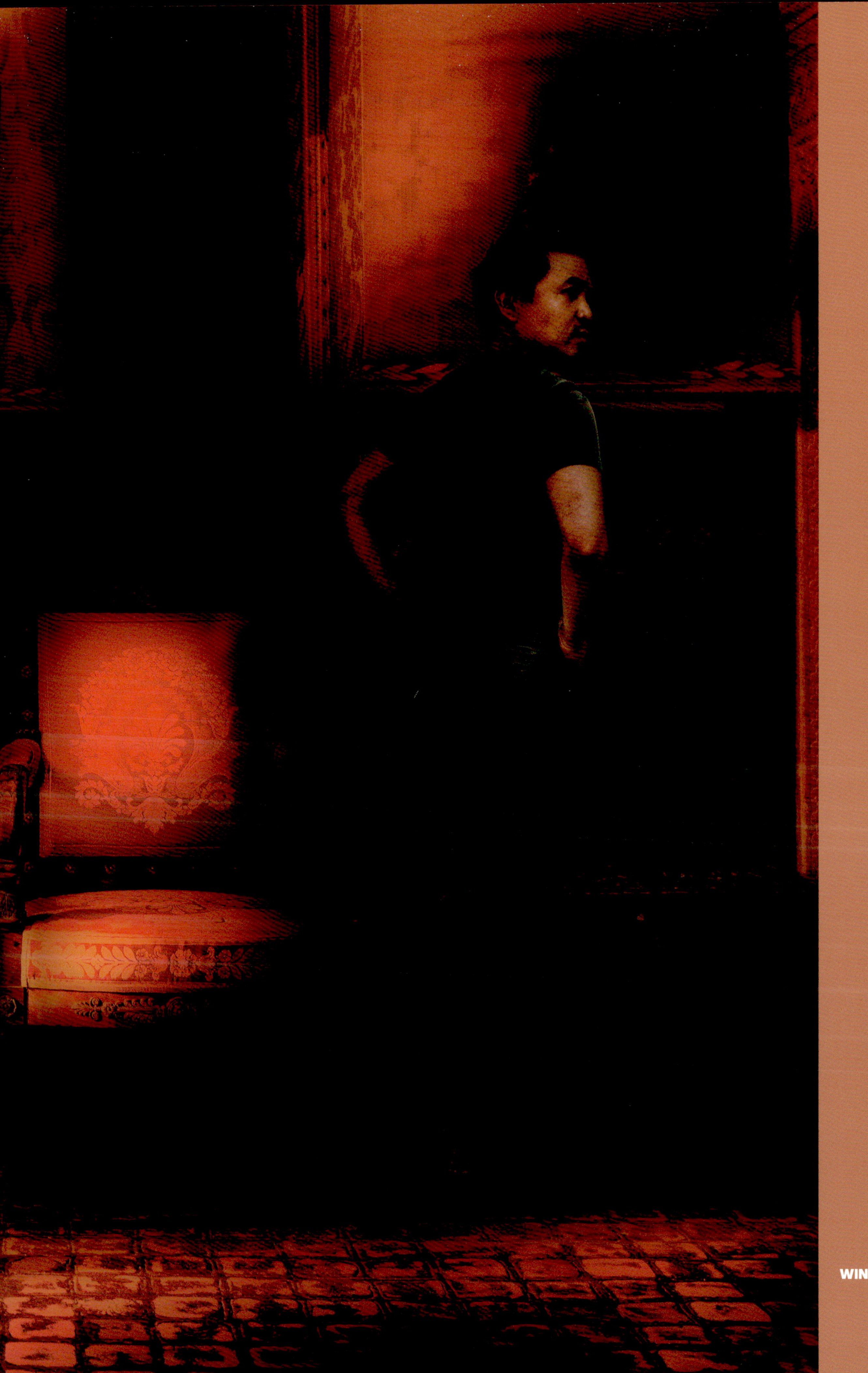

No witness here

along these corridors

of winter light

only the garbled chorus

of the mad

crying out

we are not us

Anthony James

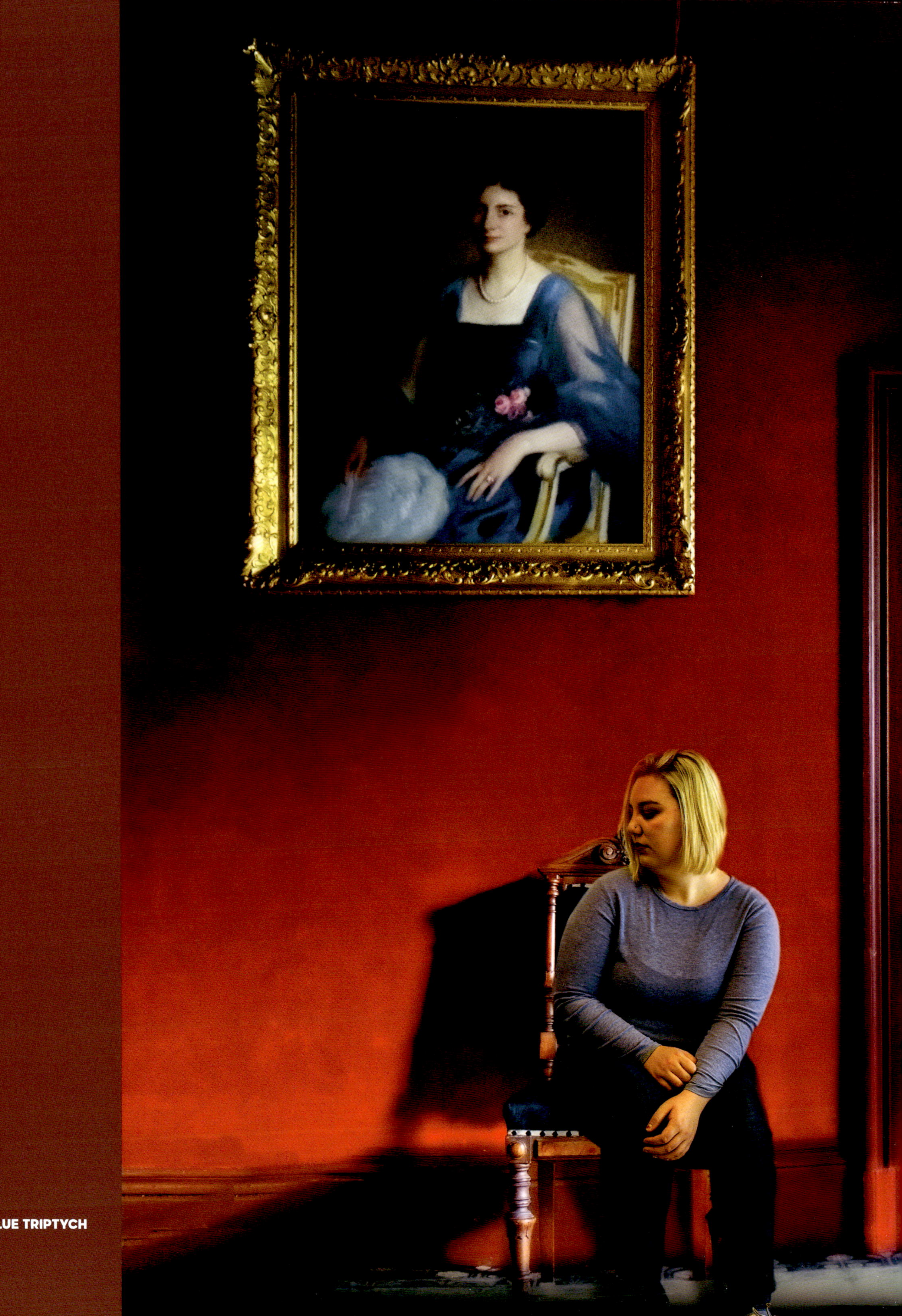

BLUE TRIPTYCH

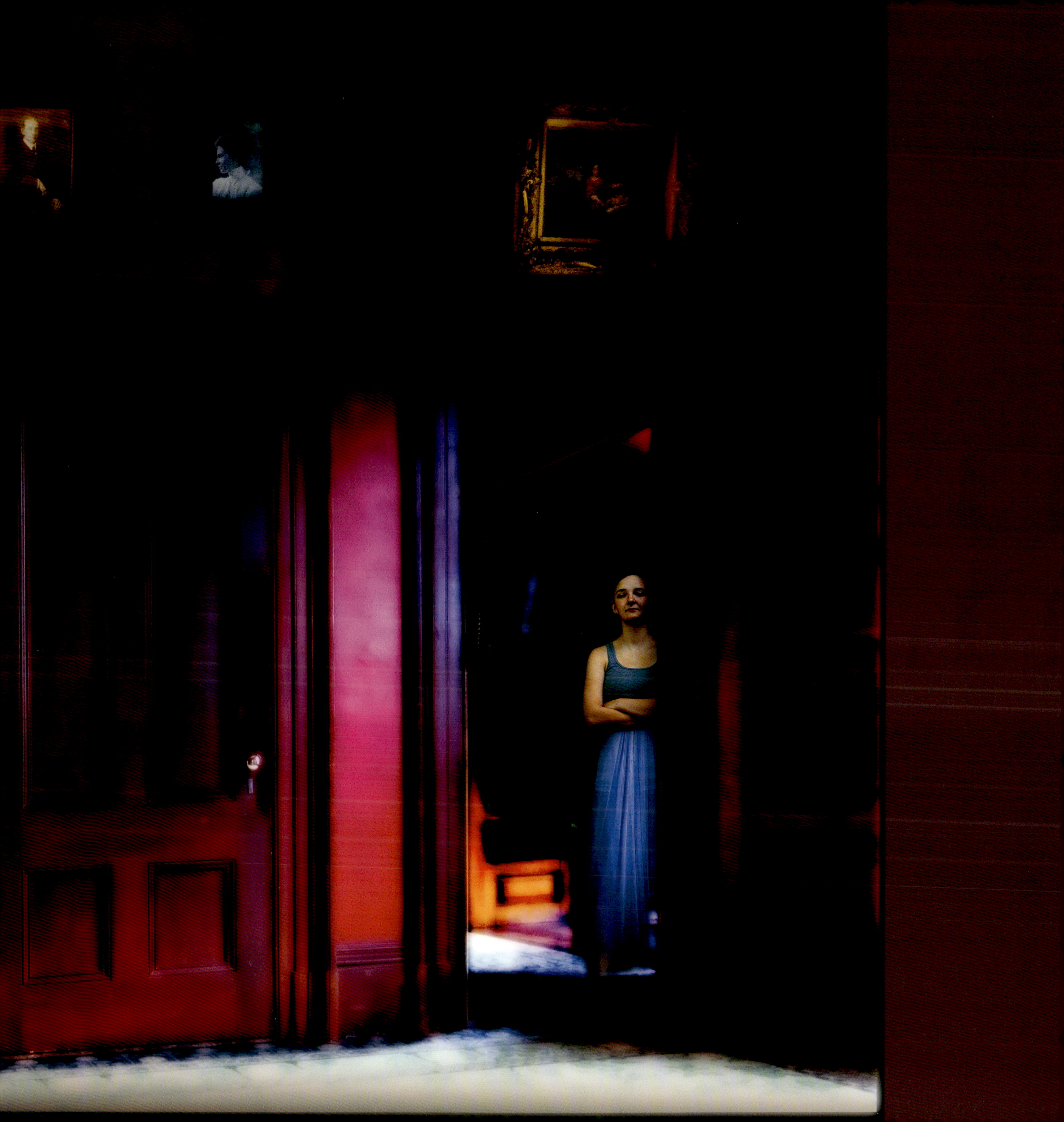

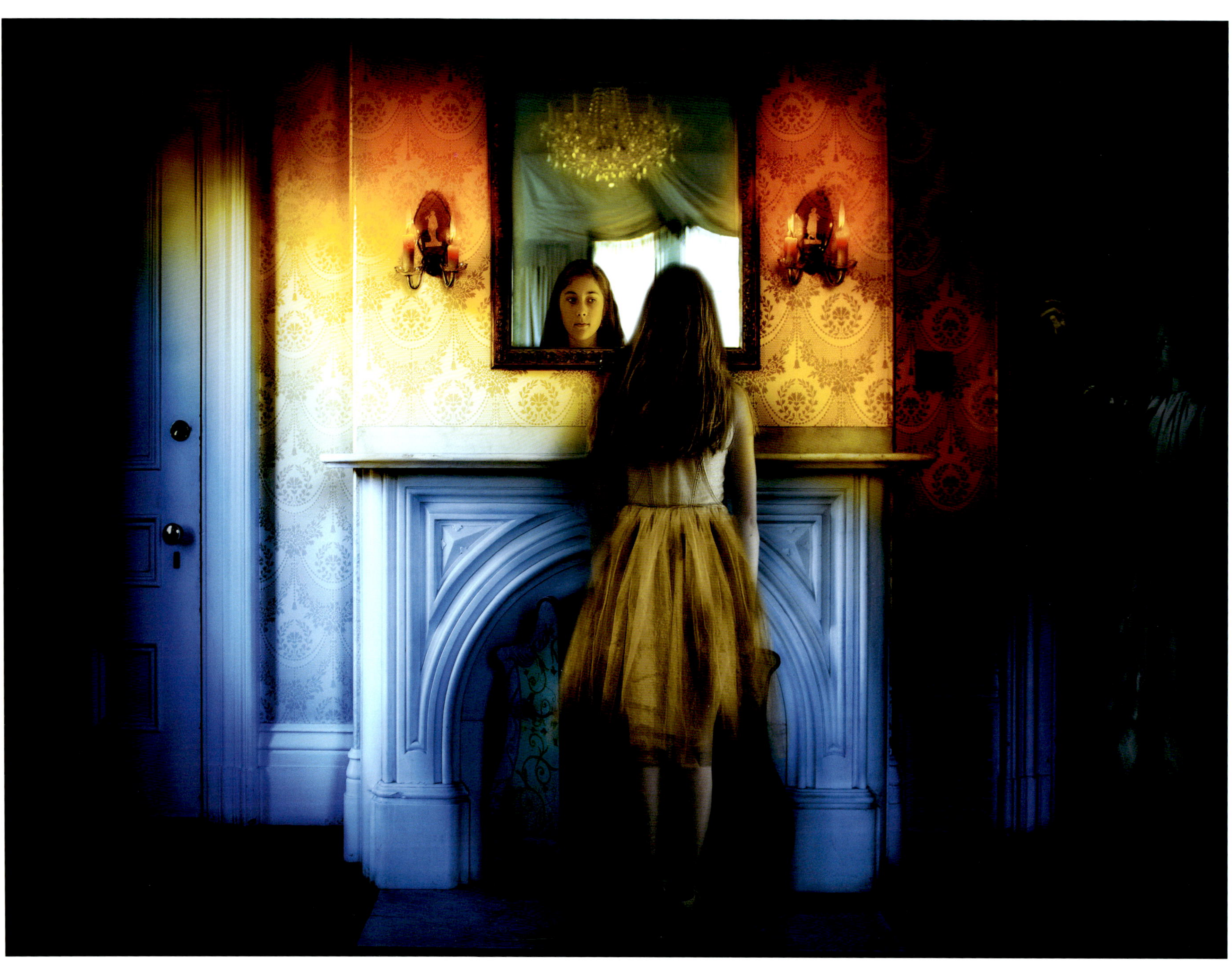

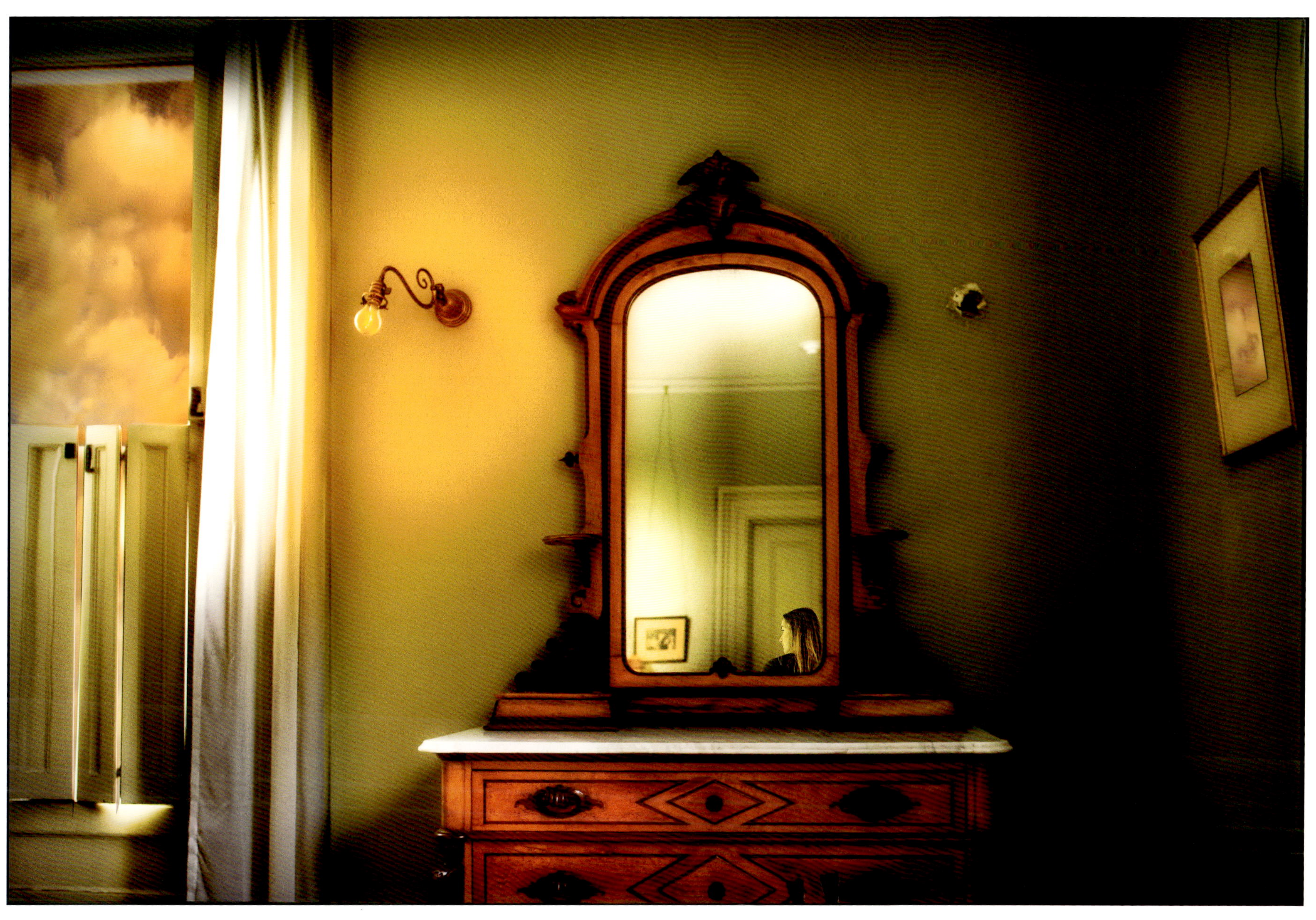

HIDDEN SPECTRAL | **GIRL IN THE MIRROR**

BLUE ROOM

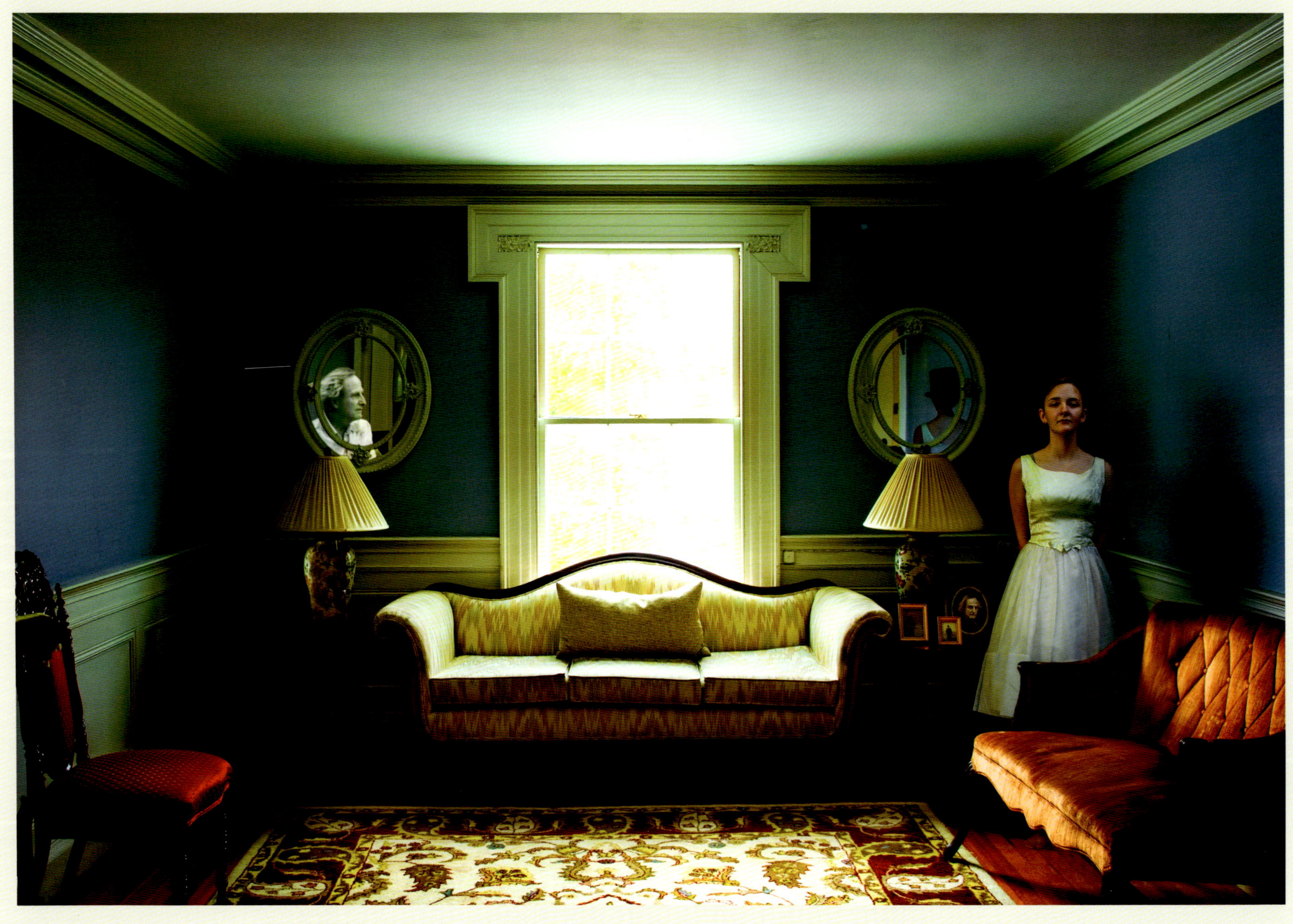

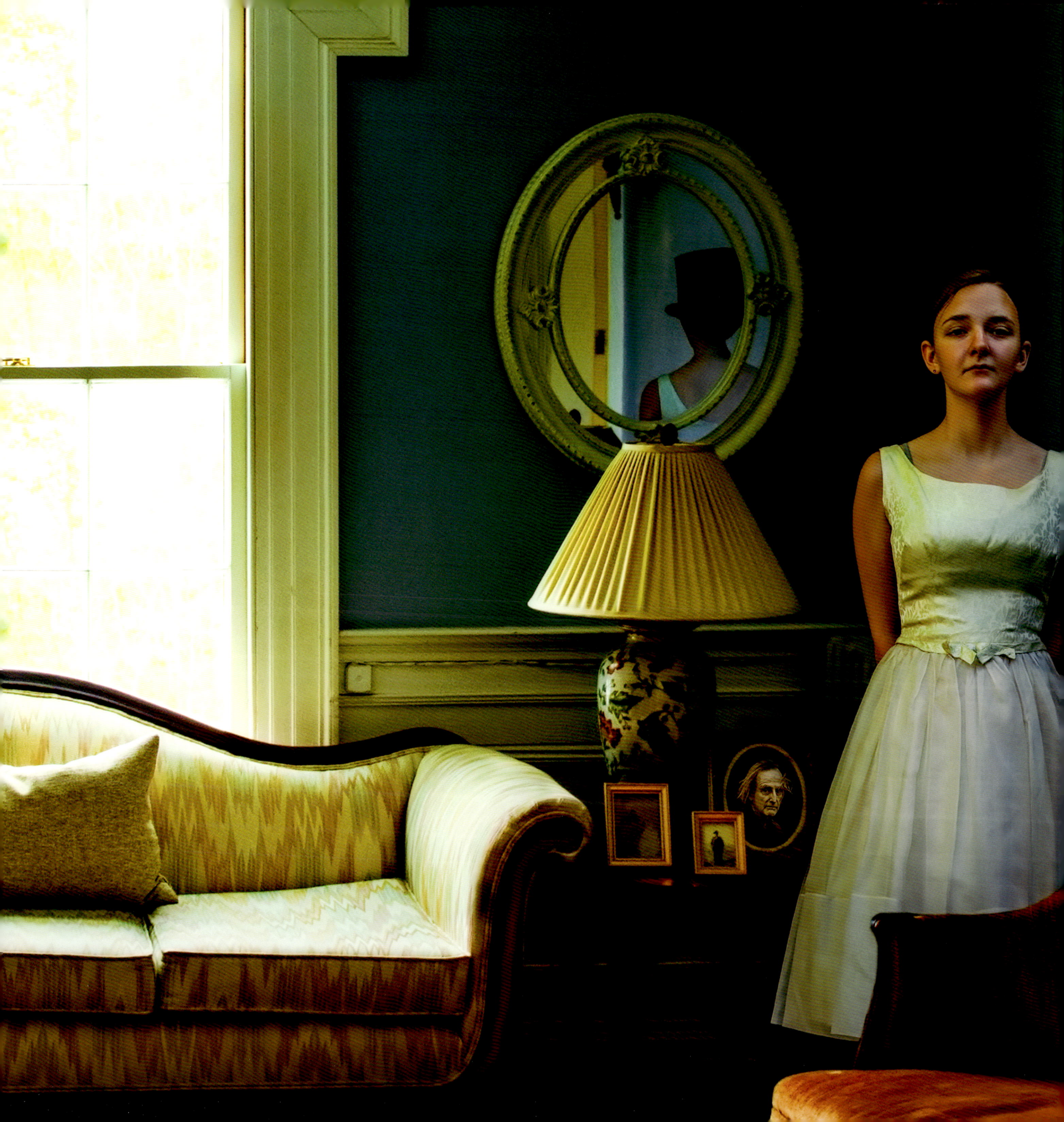

Where the sky meets sea

a girl stands by the window

washed in reverie

Nancer Ballard

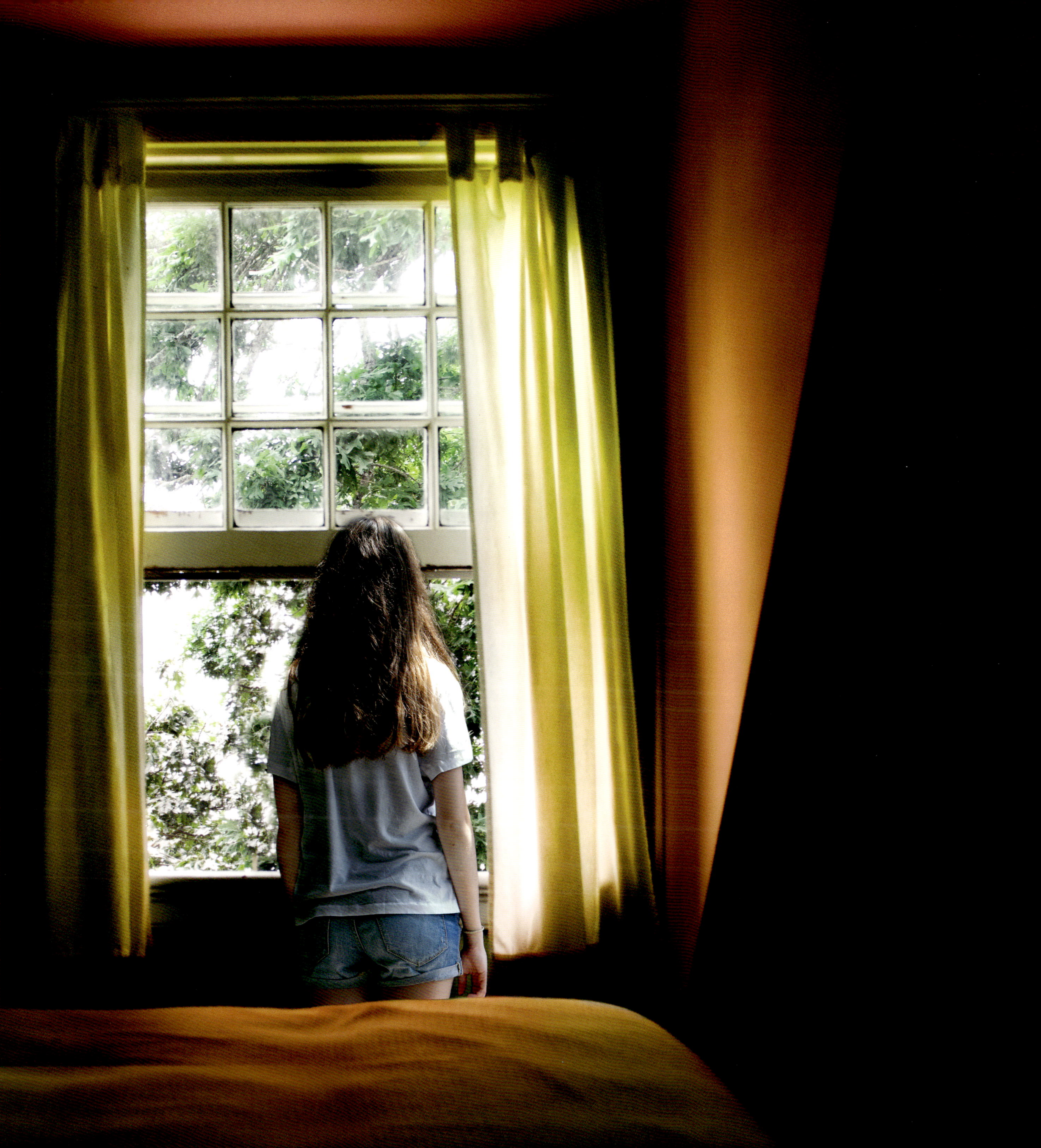

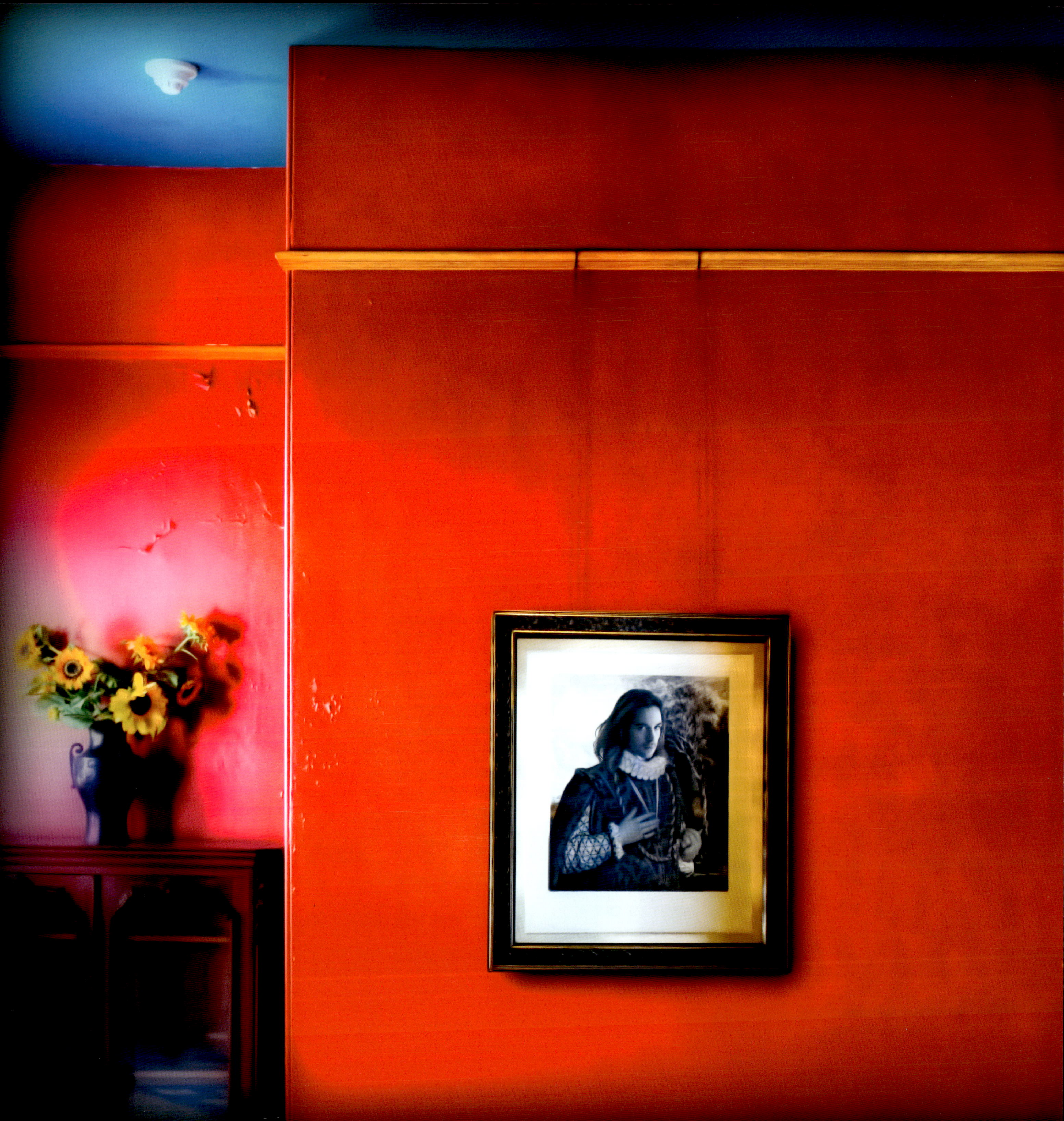

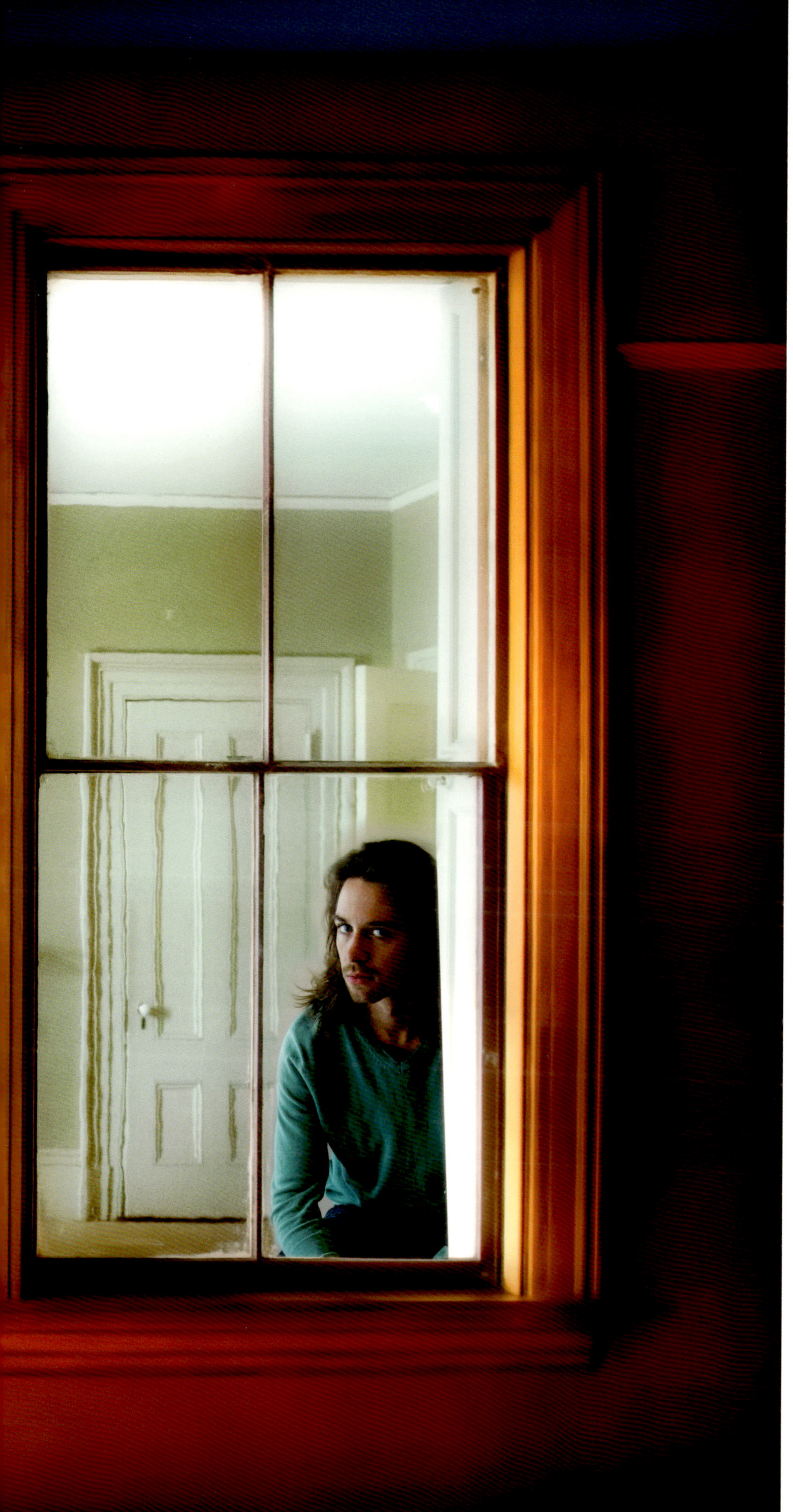

The two framed portraits hang together nicely, mounted on the red wall, two images of the same man considering himself, and us, across some **mysterious distance of time**. In one portrait he is actually behind a window outside, but actually he is inside. In another space and behind him there is a door that goes somewhere, all of it weird and enticing. The details make it rich, including yellow flowers, holding their own, horizontal yellow molding, the blue ceiling with white bulb-less fixture … and above all the loud red wall.

Peter Chermayeff

TWO PORTRAITS IN A RED ROOM

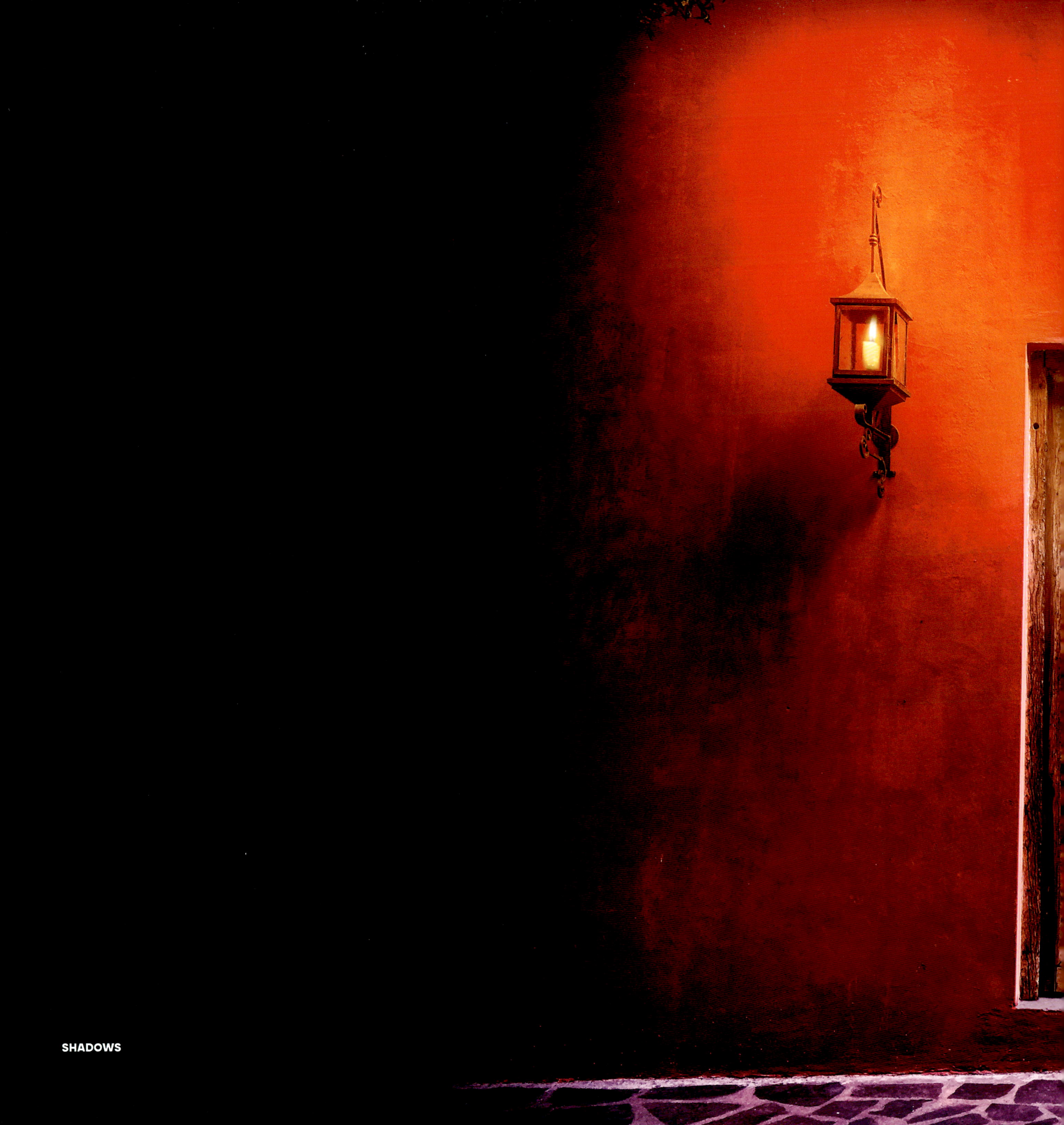

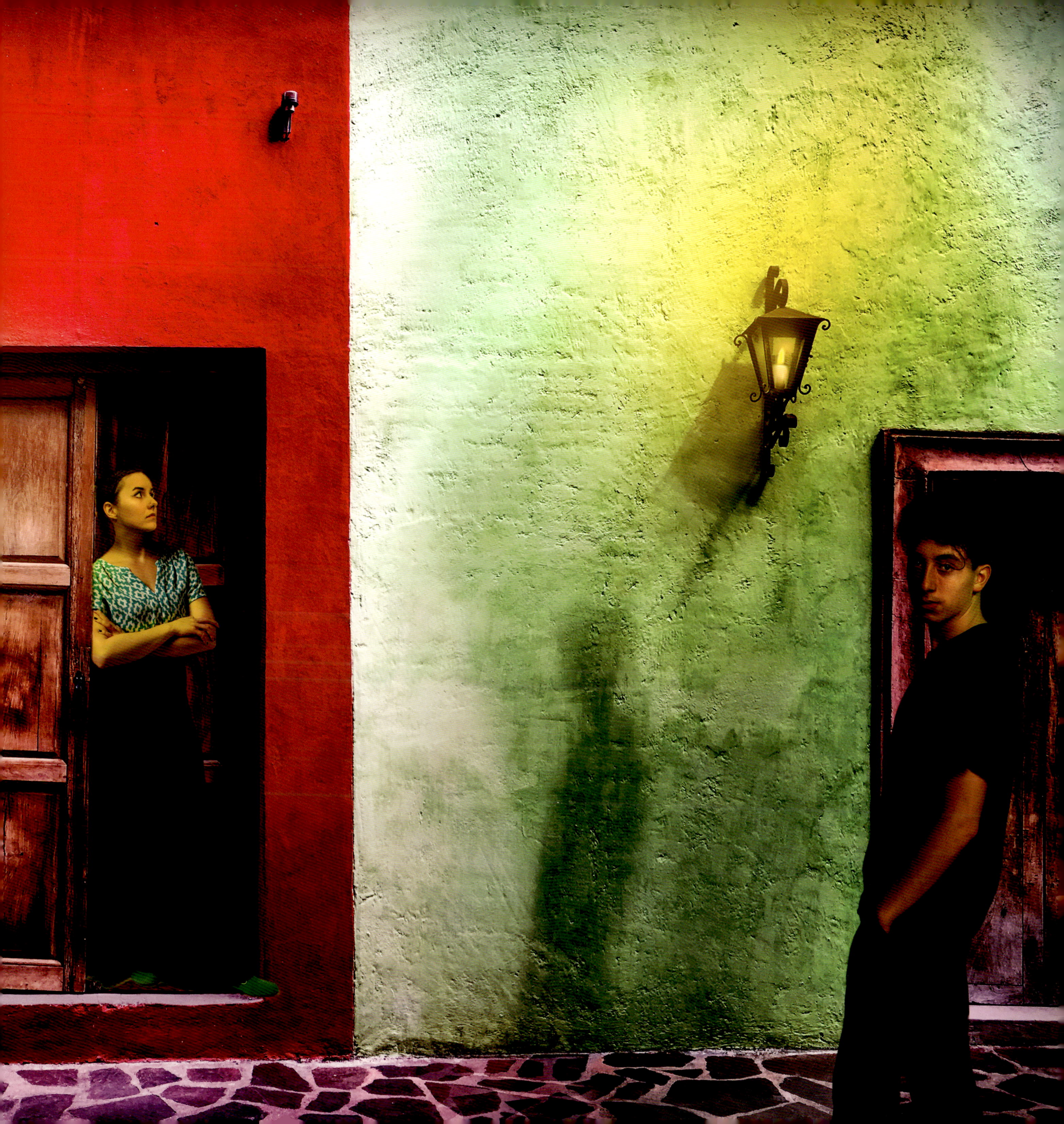

We follow the gaze of the young man sitting on the bed, which leads to a partial view of the back and arm of a person who we might assume is a man, given the well-defined arm muscles. However, all these assumptions may be wrong. Perhaps the departing person is a woman, or a transgender person. Are we so sure of the gender of the person sitting on the bed? If we leave aside all gender assumptions, we might think of all the possibilities of what action is occurring. The scene is a bedroom, so a sexual relationship is suggested. However, both figures are clothed, so a sexual act may or may not have occurred. The title of the image leads us to the theme of departure, but exactly who is departing, and what is the relationship between the two persons?

If we take the image into the realm of dreams, the scene actually begins to make more sense. In dreams, we are no longer confined to our corporal selves, and may be represented by any and all persons on the scene. The window itself is ambiguous, divided in two, displaying an area of blue atop red, orange, complementary colors, cool and warm, passionate and reserved. The person on the bed and the person leaving the frame may in fact be the same person, one staying, the other leaving. I see opposite personality types on display—passive and active, introverted and extroverted, timid and fearless. We can delve deeper into our dual natures: **anima and animus, ego and shadow, good and evil.** In our dreams, we can freely explore all the aspects of the self, and play out all the roles required of a given scene. We can be all things at once.

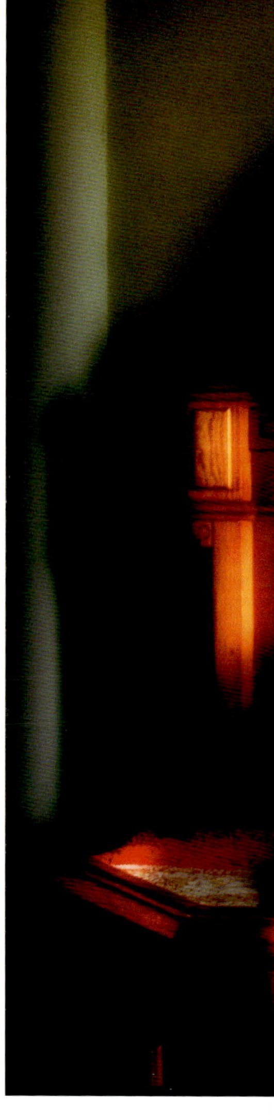

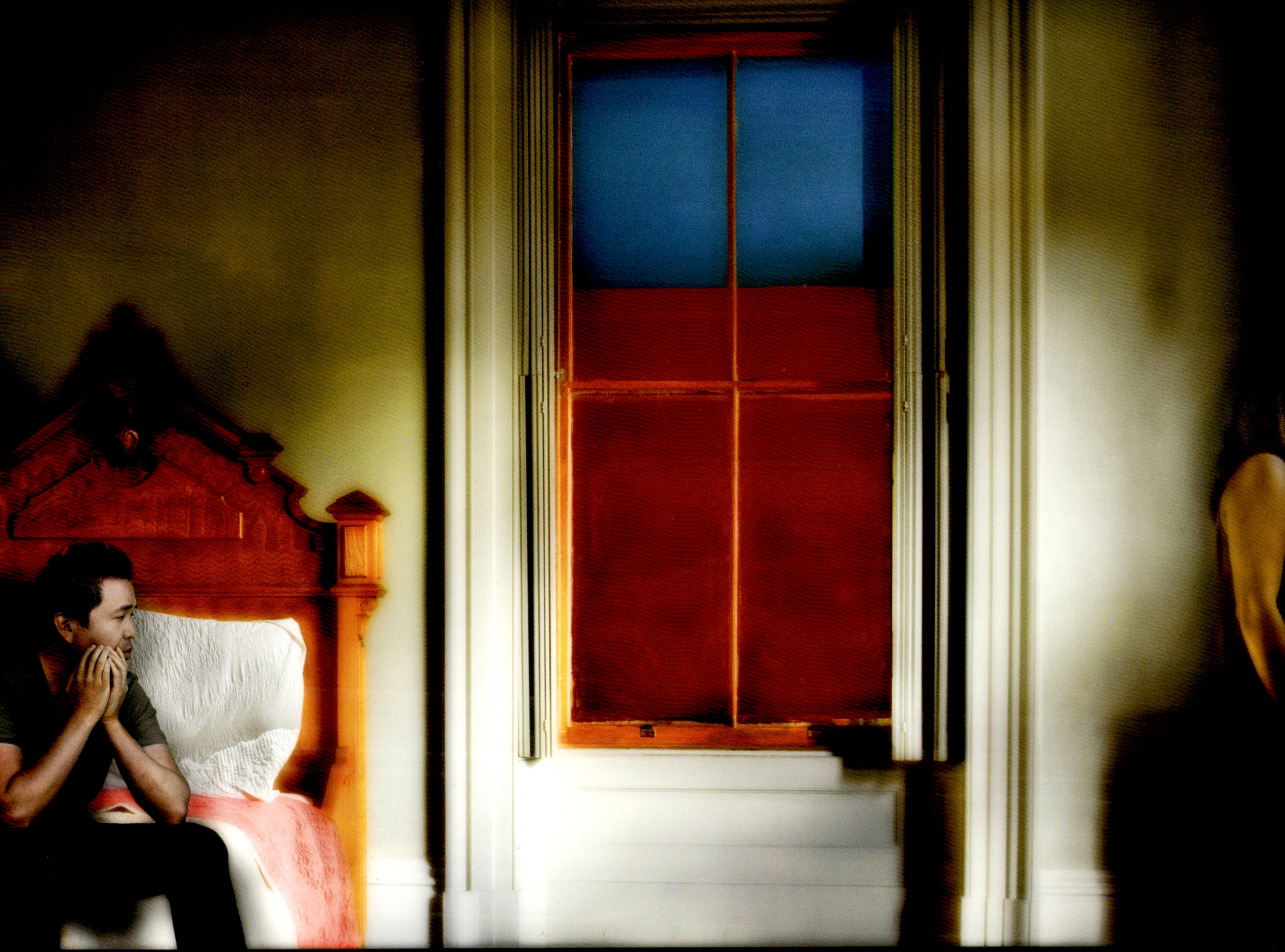

As I gaze at the image on this
page, I see a person struggling
with the process of development,
at a critical inflection point:
growth versus stagnation.

The fortunate choose growth.

David Weinberg

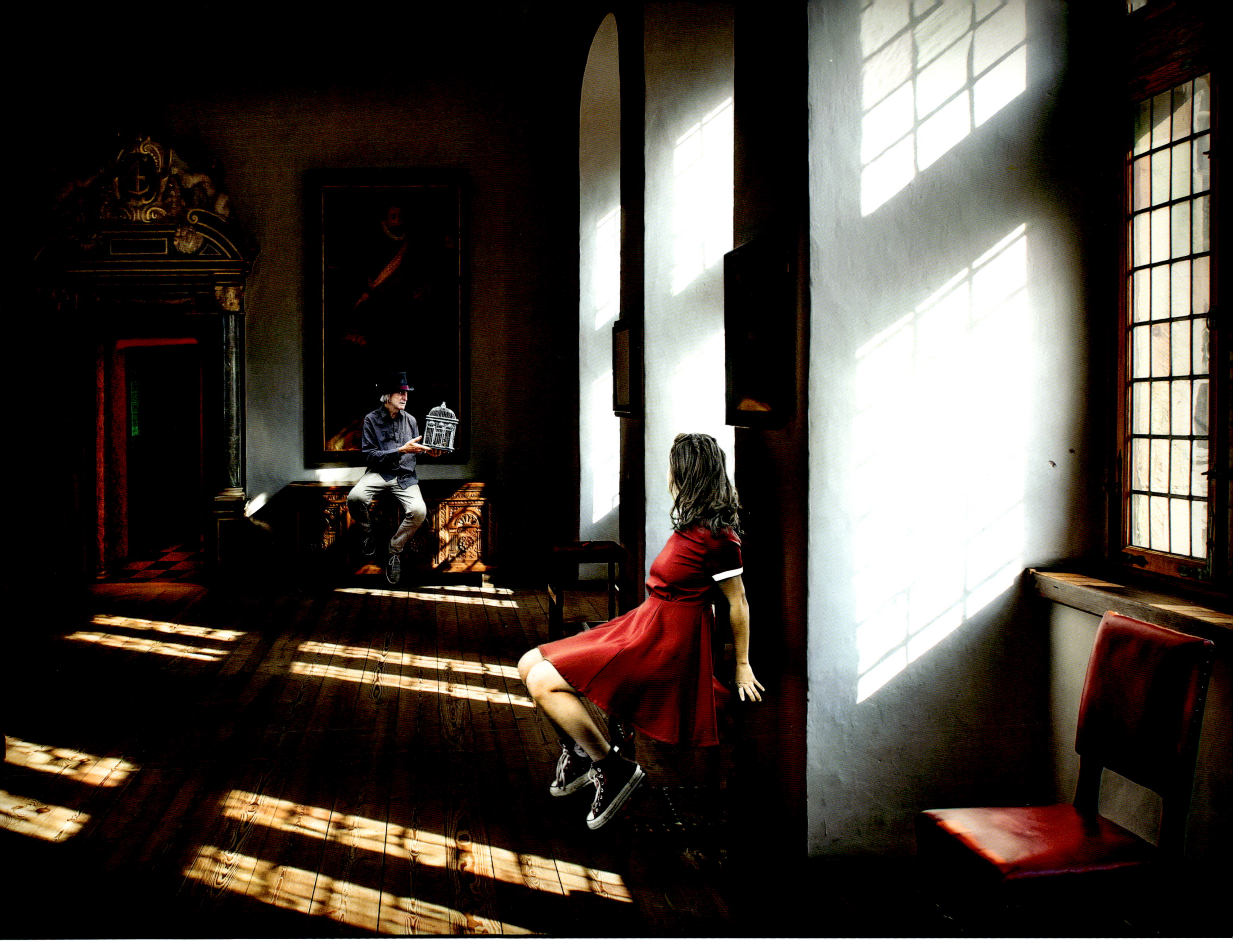

The brilliance of Fran Forman's art is always the story. As the narrative draws us in, our tendencies to critique fade. The elements of composition, technique, and technical competence, while handled masterfully in her photographic collages, hide quietly behind the stage curtain as we are captivated by the drama—or comedy—which unfolds in front.

Suspicious Visitor is a fine example of story-creation. Art often seems more comfortable if the principal elements are odd in number, three rather than two for example. I wondered why this collage with two people worked for me and decided it was the implied presence of a third person in the foreground chair. The story evolved as my eyes followed the diagonal from the chair to the girl to the man and back. And when I returned, I was seated in the chair, prepared for the two of them to stare at me, the third element.

So, who is the suspicious visitor:
the girl, the man, or the art critic?

Gordon Saperia

SUSPICIOUS VISITOR

DEEP IN MY THOUGHTS IS FREEDOM.

Victor Rosario

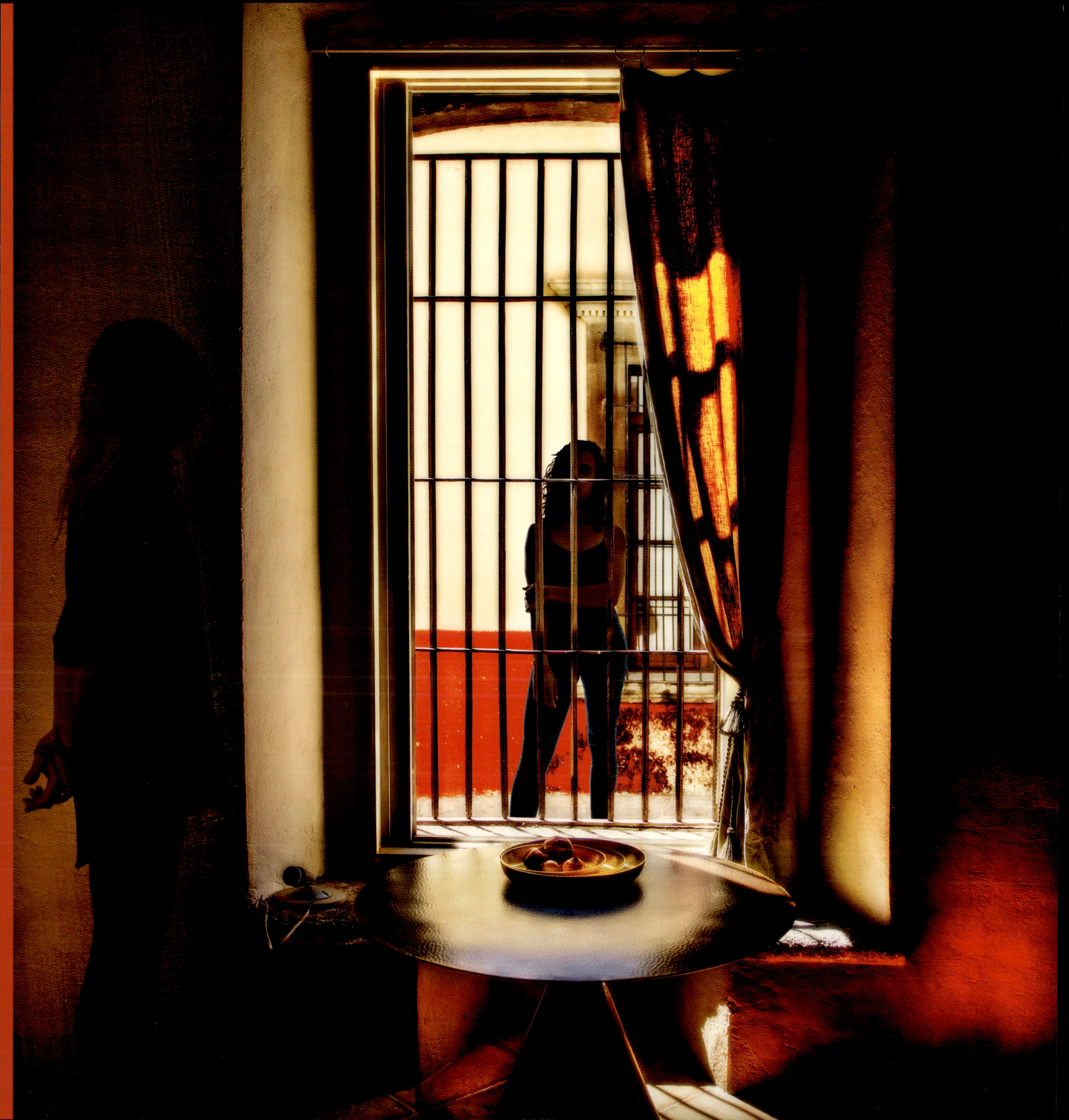

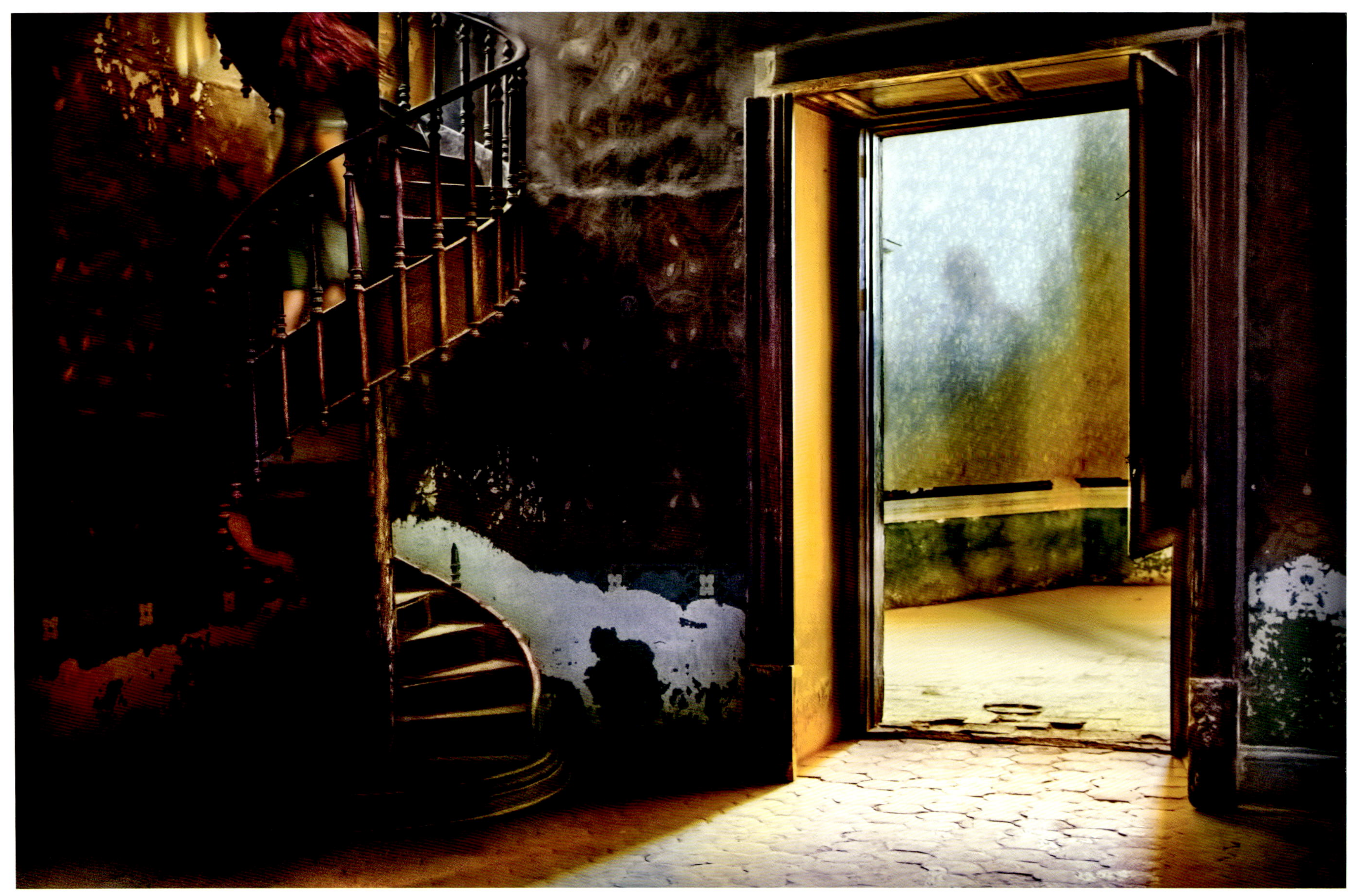

SPIRAL STAIRS

A young woman or girl ascends a spiral stairway, but does not seem to show any sense of urgency in her posture.

A shadow seems to be approaching the open doorway, or is it paused in thought or despair? Its shape is echoed in the peeling plaster near the center of the image, while other areas of decay almost look like animal totems.

This image seems to represent the elegance of decay, not only of the building, but perhaps of a relationship.

The formal composition coupled with the soft, glowing colors complete an image that is easily etched into one's memory, filled with questions but absent of any answers.

Stu Levy

A woman who lays her head on the table
because she's tired

A woman who lays her head on the table
because she's tired
of suffering

A woman lays her head on the table
because she's tired
of suffering, wondering
how much longer they can stay here

wondering whether she's going to have to
sleep with the landlord again

she lays her head on the table
she is tired of suffering
wondering if there will be a place for them, wondering
if they are going to open the border
because she's tired
of suffering, wandering, producing papers
and being told she doesn't have the right papers

and then suddenly
after a quick feel or some biting teeth
or a tongue down the gullet

suddenly the papers
are all right again

the woman lays her head on the table
she can feel a migraine coming on
and after that, she knows
she will be unsteady on her feet for days

and the daughter who watches and waits,
who believes in the new life they will have on the other side—
who dreams about studying
physical therapy, maybe, or reconstructive surgery

who believes the border will open again
any day now, soon.

Monica Raymond

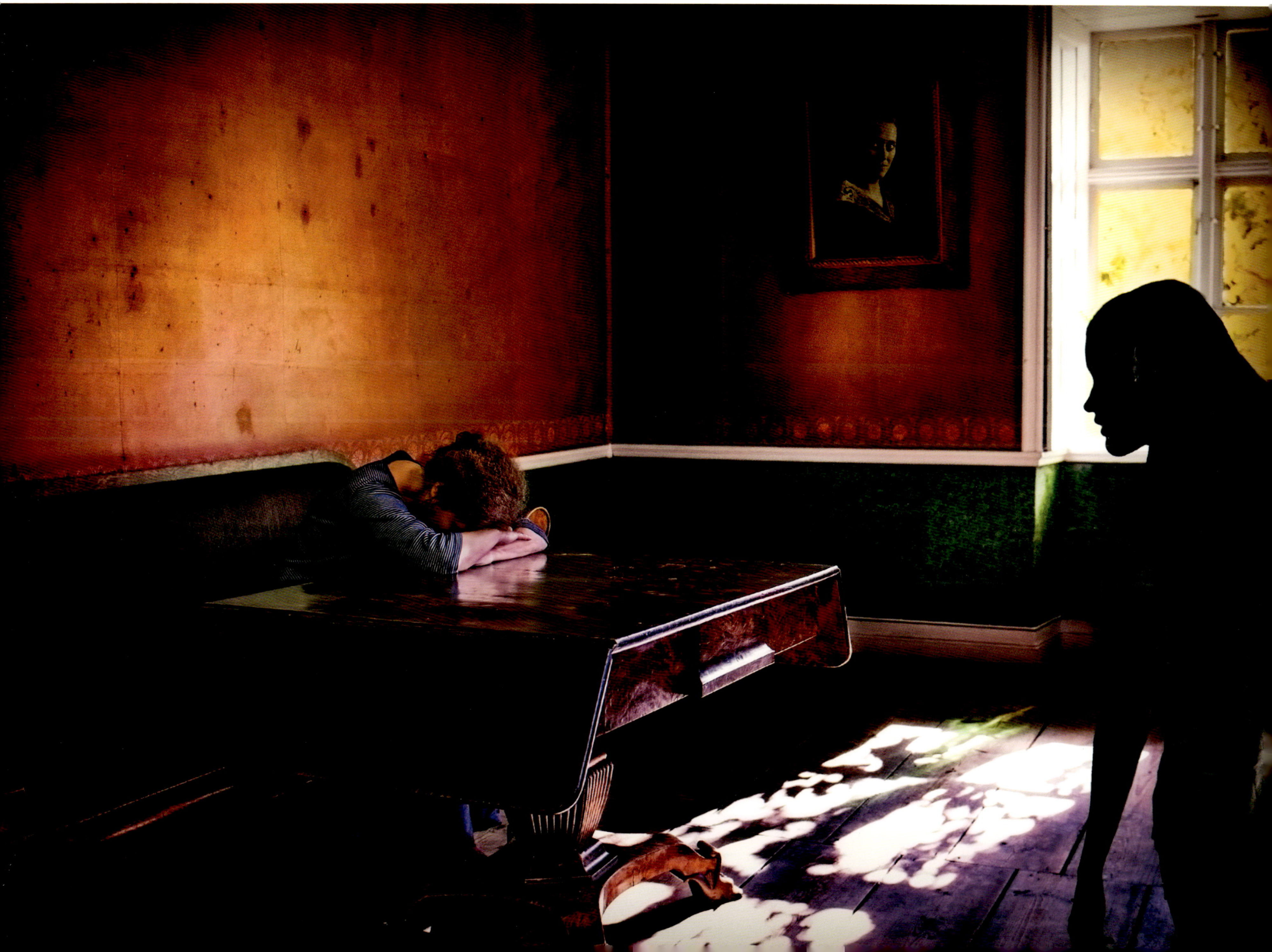

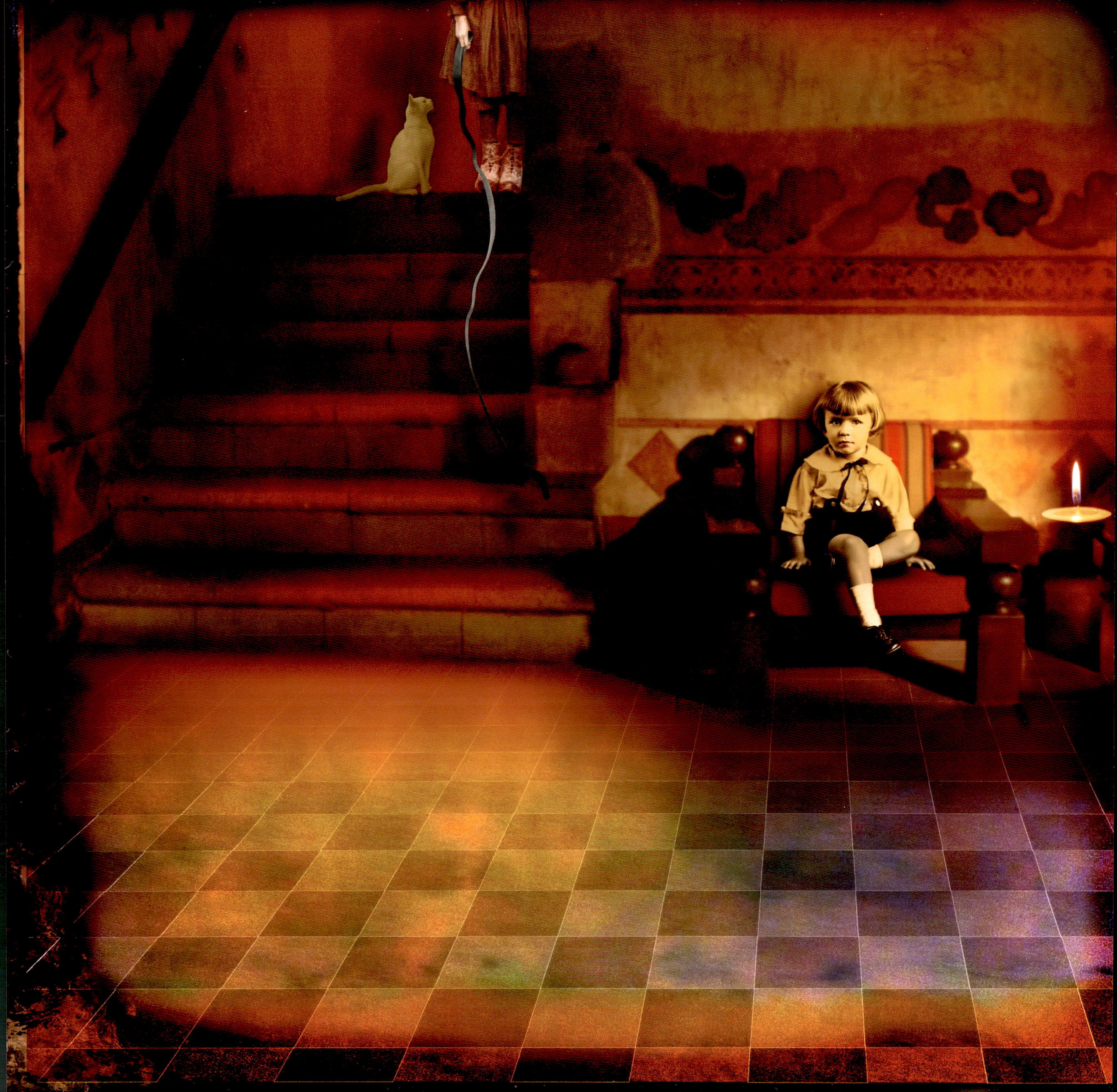

IN MY MIND I OFTEN HAVE

DIFFICULTY WITH MEMORIES—

did they come from dreams or did they really happen? Is this a real memory or the result of my mind creating an image from stories my mother told me and has the element of hope coloured and arranged the image to make it better than what actually happened? Some people can't live with doubt but for me it is like the background music of life. I don't care what happened, **LET ME LIVE IN MY MEMORIES.**

Roger Watson

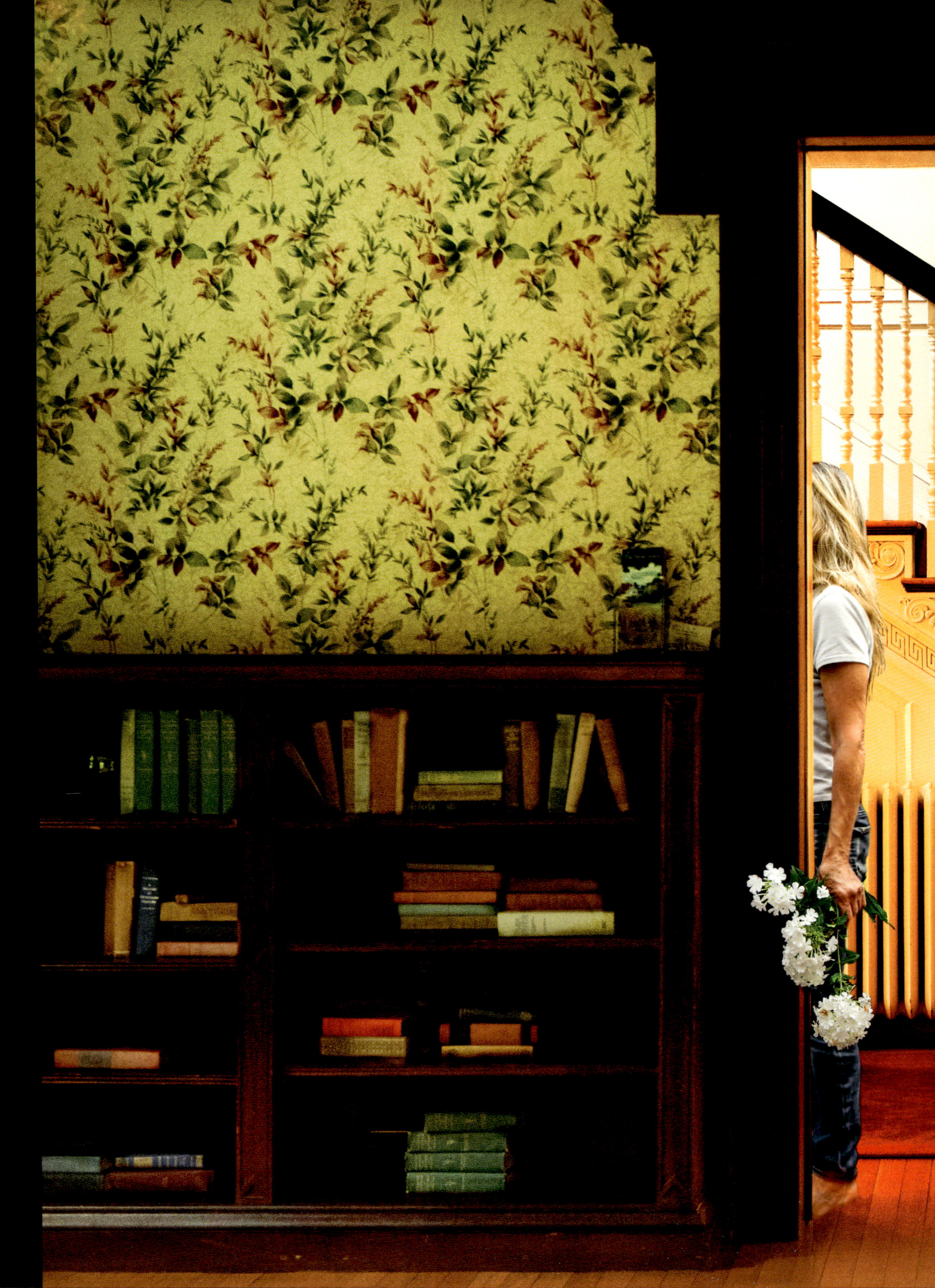

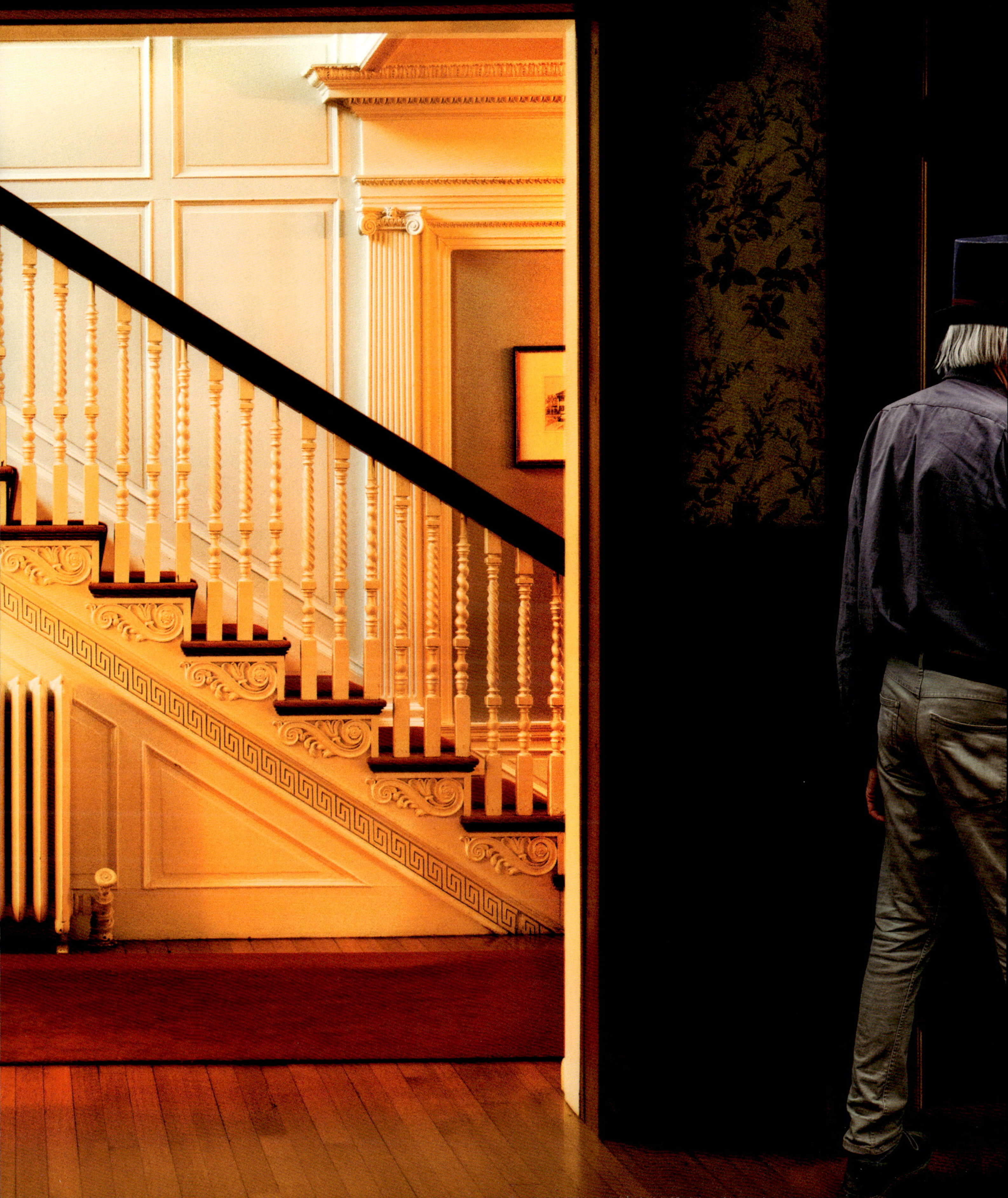

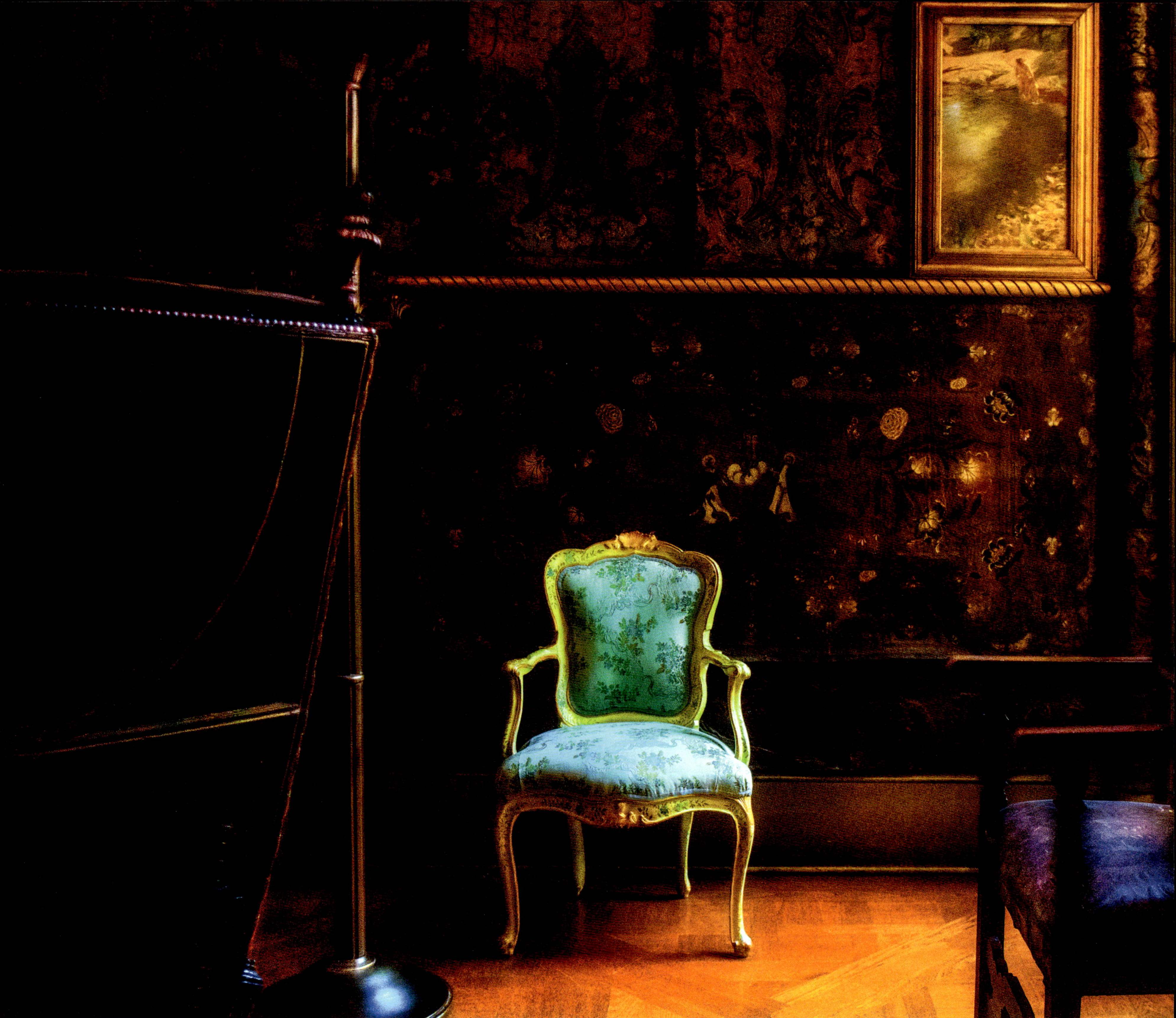

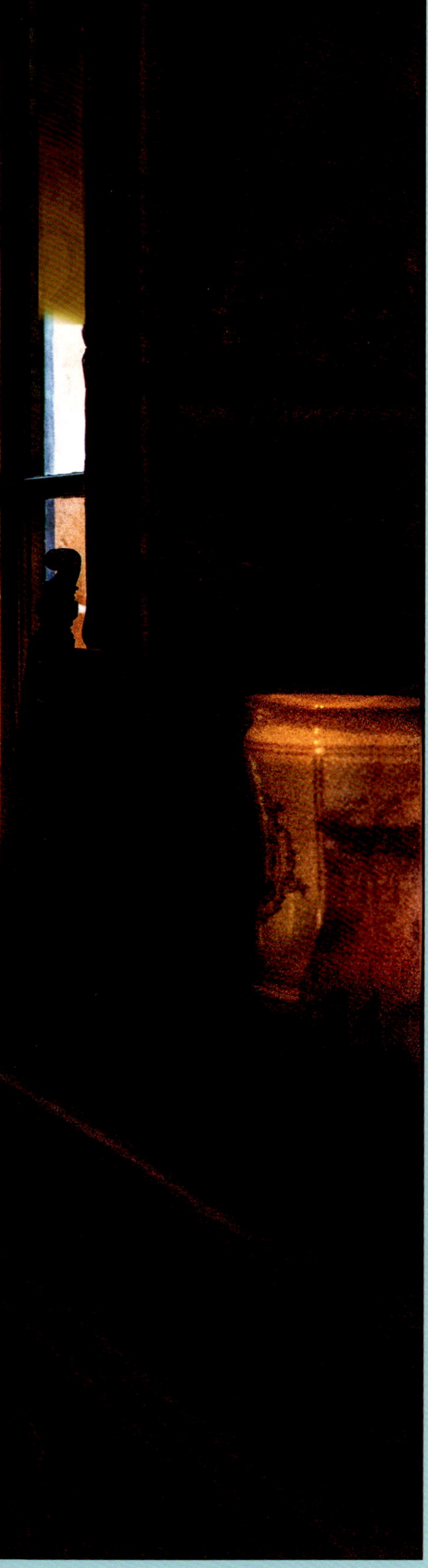

Infinite teal
color of peacock breast

with my carved arms
and silk upholstery,

I stand amid the wreckage
of Dresden, Kabul,

pristino as that Black
Madonna,

untouched
by typhoon.

There is the glamor
of ruins, and there

is the glamor
of glamor.

I stand
at the crossroads

by the abraded
wall.

No more
upper stories.

If there's one
good thing

came out
of these wars, it's that

they're blasted, no more
gods, no fates, no masters,

no Yodas, Merlins,
not even any

Cassandras. Just
décor's

left, and tales
of daring escapes.

Sit down.
Take your ease

on this
street

where all
containment

all leisure
and logic's

blasted
away.

See who comes
beside

you, to tell
the story.

Monica Raymond

BLUE CHAIR

There are many ways one could react to this image. Objectively, we see a side view of a staircase, which turns toward us at a landing, leading to a few more visible steps below. On the landing, poised atop the step, is the figure of a barefoot woman wearing a delicate dress seen from the waist down, appearing ready to continue her descent. The stairs look old, of the type one would see in a mansion or other stately building, and the walls and steps look faded and distressed, evidence of years of use and neglect, a kind of elegant decay. The beauty of this image lies not only in its color and composition, but in its ambiguity.

We naturally react to a scene containing action by creating a narrative around it. Superficially, this appears to be a young woman, light on her feet, enjoying the bounce and rhythm of her descent as she dances her way to the bottom, as a young person might do—a very romantic vision. However, the muted purple of her dress gives way to red along the hemline, the details blurred by the motion. Is this a floral pattern, or are these blood-red blotches something more disturbing? This image brings to mind times I have mistakenly interpreted a sound as laughter, only to realize later that it was the sound of crying. This light, romantic moment—could it instead be a young woman in distress, blood spattered on her dress, fleeing down the stairs, trying to outrace gravity and on the thin edge of disaster?

If this were a dream, the stairs have great symbolic significance. A dream of ascending stairs usually is interpreted as symbolizing a desire to move ahead in life, to embrace the future. Descending usually is interpreted as regressive, and in the context of an old home, symbolizes re-visiting the past. This young woman, quickly descending the stairs, may in fact be fleeing, rather than simply descending. The splashes of red on her dress signal danger.

David Weinberg

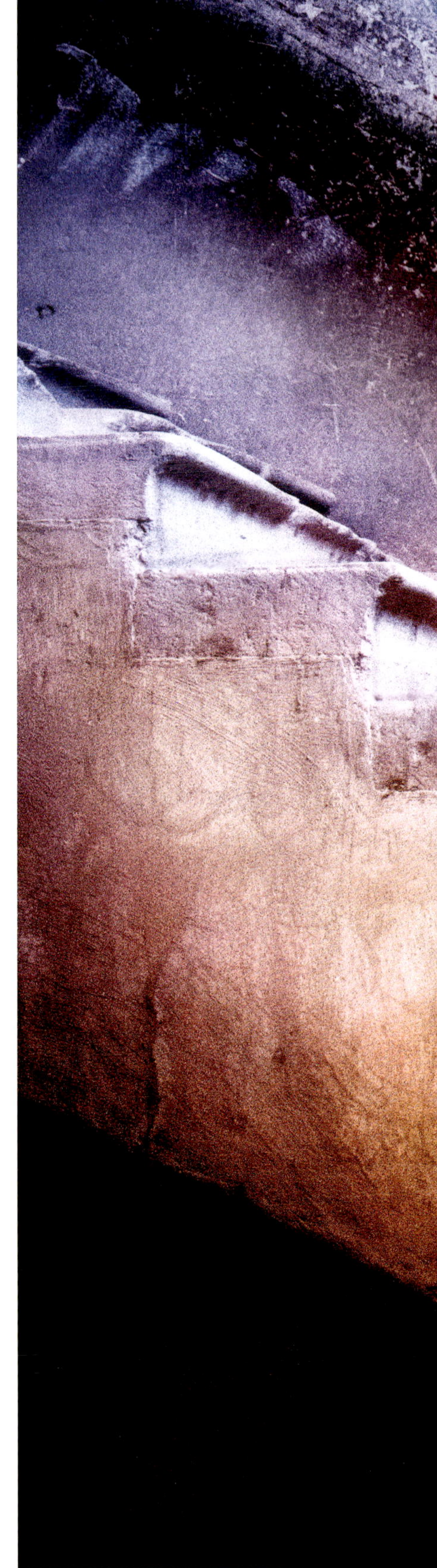

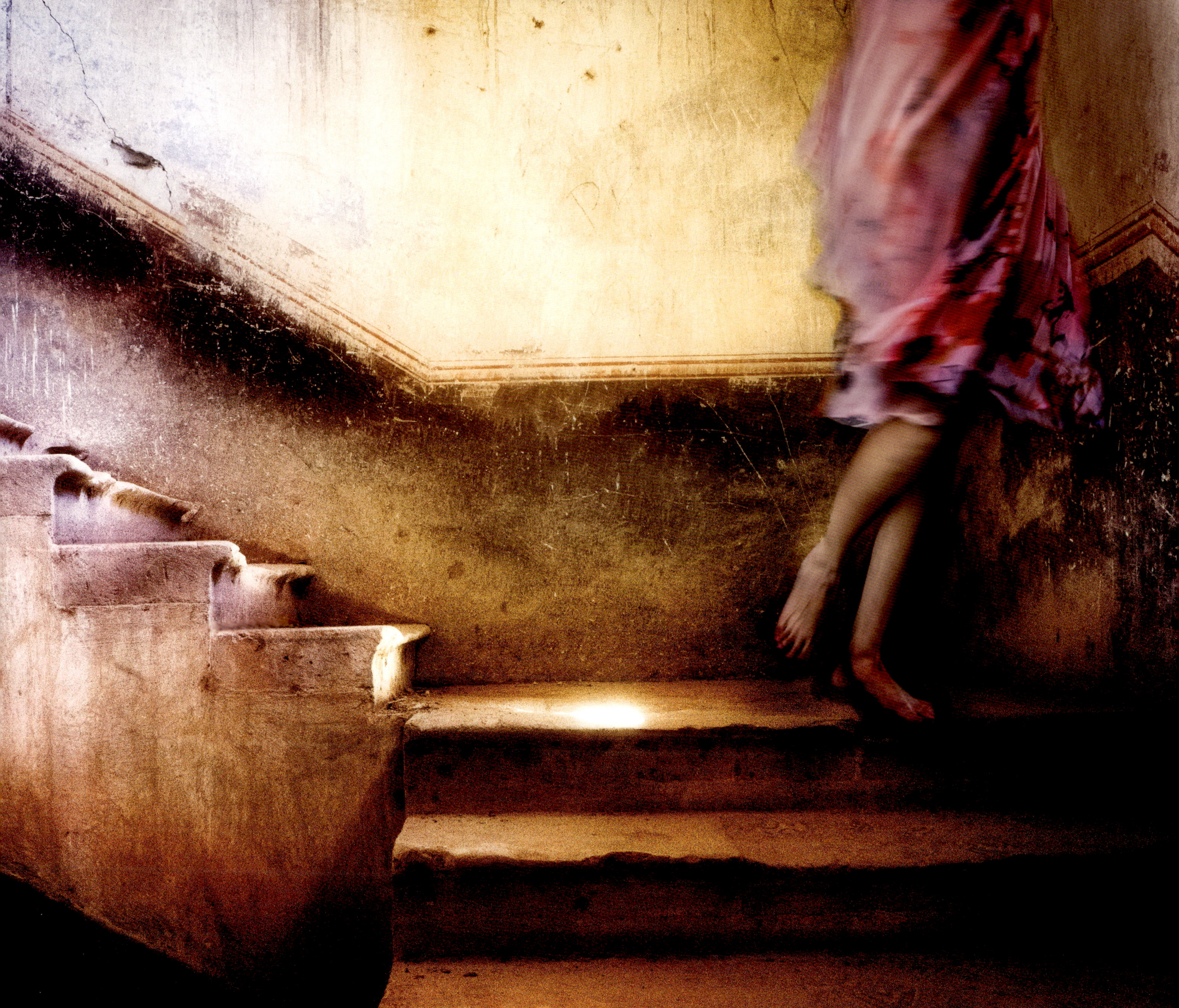

“REALISM IS A BAD WORD.

I SEE NO LINE BETWEEN THE IMAGINARY AND THE REAL.” – Frederico Fellini

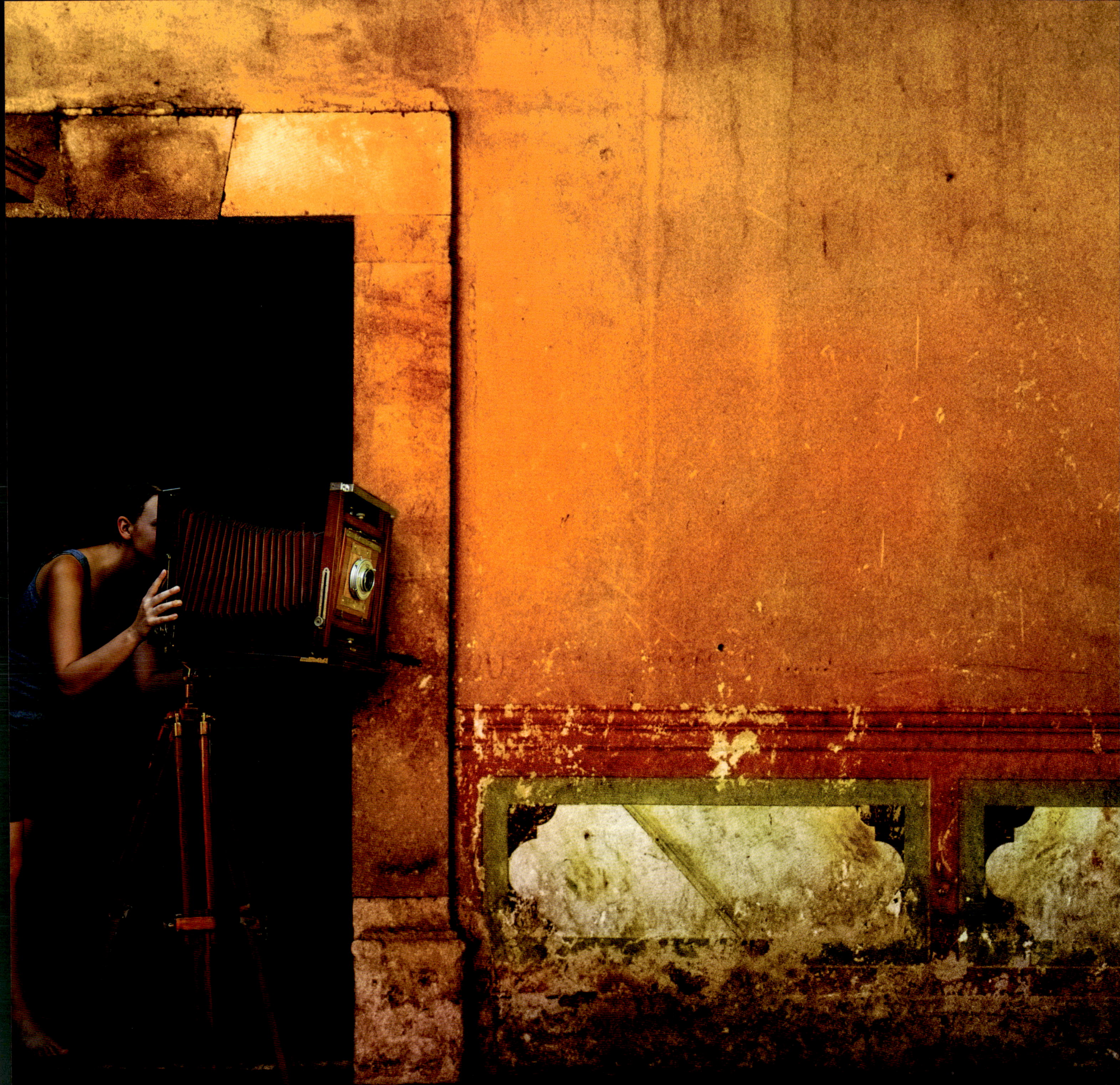

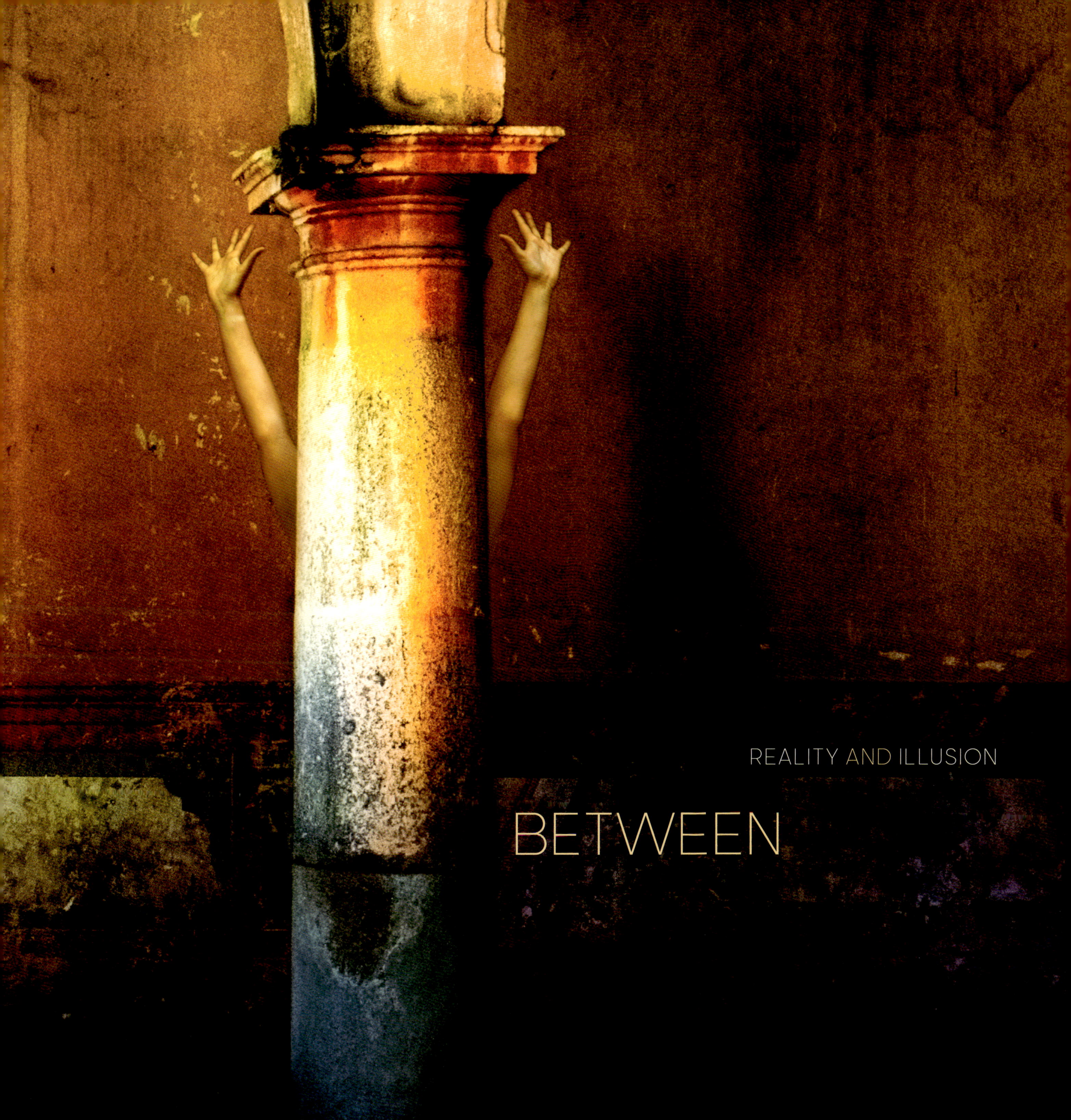
REALITY AND ILLUSION
BETWEEN

The first thing to praise about *Door to the Sea* is the intensity of the colors, the richness of them. Part of the explanation of Fran Forman's rich colors lies in her generous use of Black. Manet once opined that Black was the Queen of Colors, and Fran proves him right. Of course, colors this rich do not just happen; skillful artistic artifice lies behind their production.

Note also the skillful artifice in the sequencing of the colors, which go from cool to warm as one reads the image from left to right. Indeed, the colors are almost too perfect in their sequencing. All of the details could be examples of photo-realism, but it seems surreal that they are all so perfectly sequenced.

However, the greatest swirl of magic lies in the surreal light that suffuses the image. The oddest thing about the light is that there is no sensible answer to the question: where does the light come from? The bright areas are too bright to have been lit by the soft twilight outside the windows; furthermore, these bright areas could not have been lit by a strong light from within the house, since the shadows are falling the wrong way; the shadows run from outside in. So the light is truly impossible, if we follow standard optical laws. But the laws of physical optics are not the laws of art.

Among the laws of art, there is a fundamental principle that **the best light is light that seems interior to the image**, that is, light that comes to us from within the image and reaches out to us. To be sure, there are many excellent paintings and photographs wherein the light is cast upon the scene from some vantage point outside the frame; we often understand such art with ease. Even so, I think there is a special magic that infuses any image in which the light comes to us from within the frame. *Door to the Sea* powerfully embodies this magic.

Lash LaRue

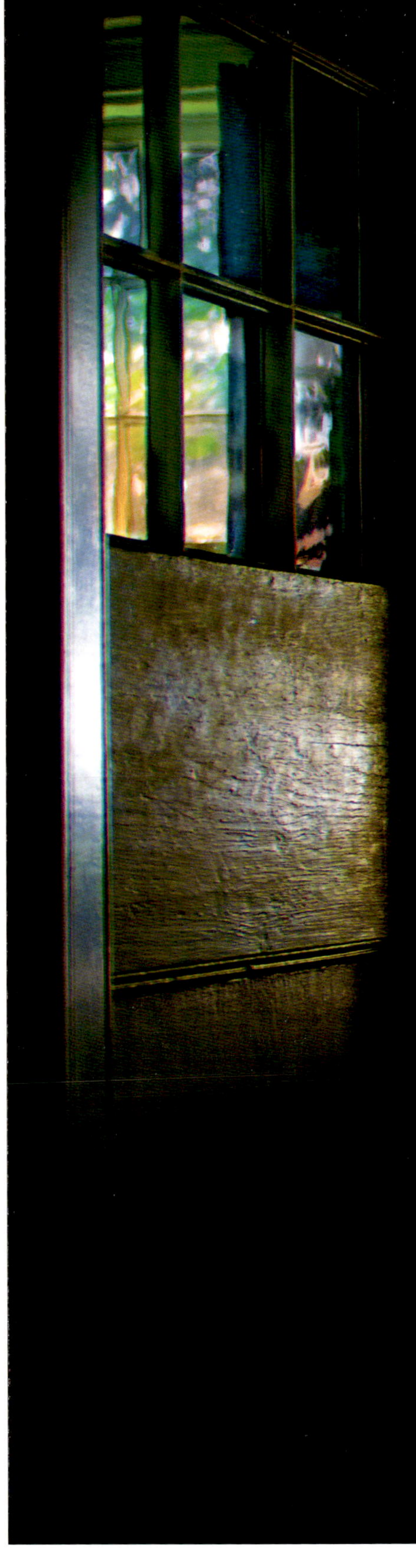

DOOR TO THE SEA

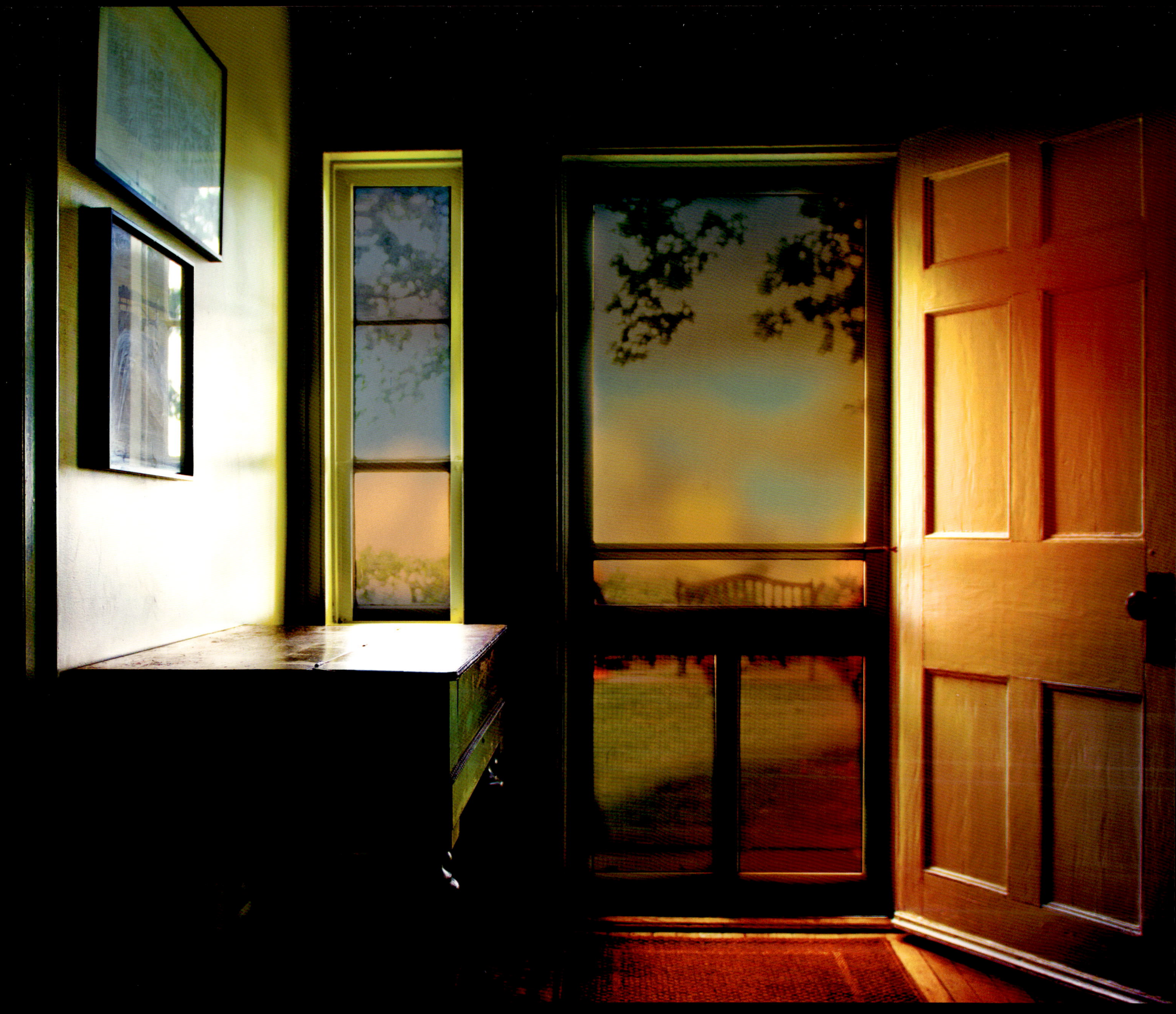

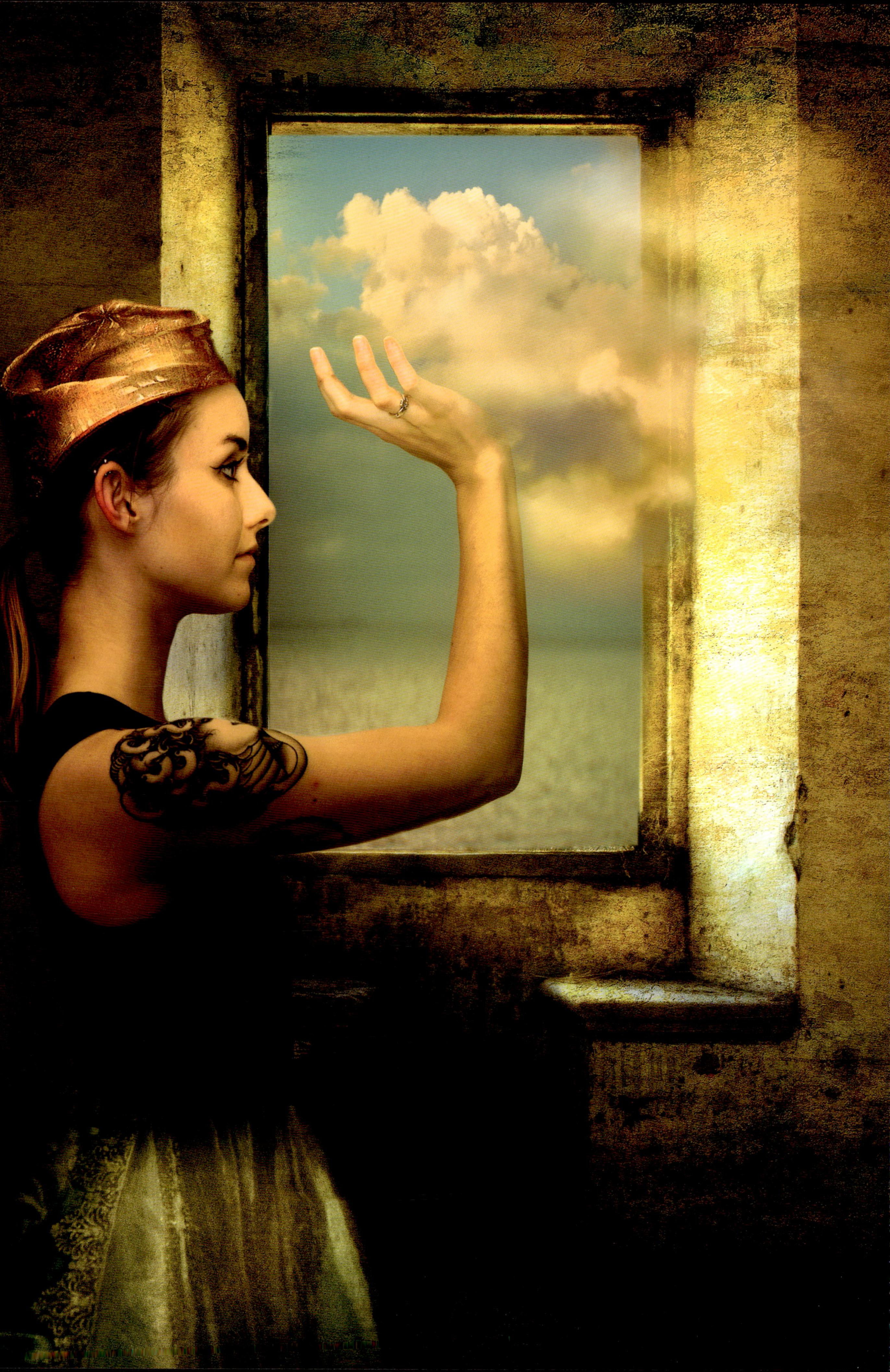

Children of the chorus

lost in the old songs
of our yesterdays

take me by the hand
singing

and dance me home

Anthony James

I go outside the lit house
and a little bit
of the light

of the lit house
comes with me.

Though storm clouds
belly purple,
and the dusk hills
sprawls of ink,

the green black bush
a dragon tracery
of iron filings,

still I am
a small taper
flaxen and lit.

But how long can this last?

Under its two chimneys,
the lit house winks at me.

From one of its two windows,
the lit house winks
sinking beneath the hill.

Monica Raymond

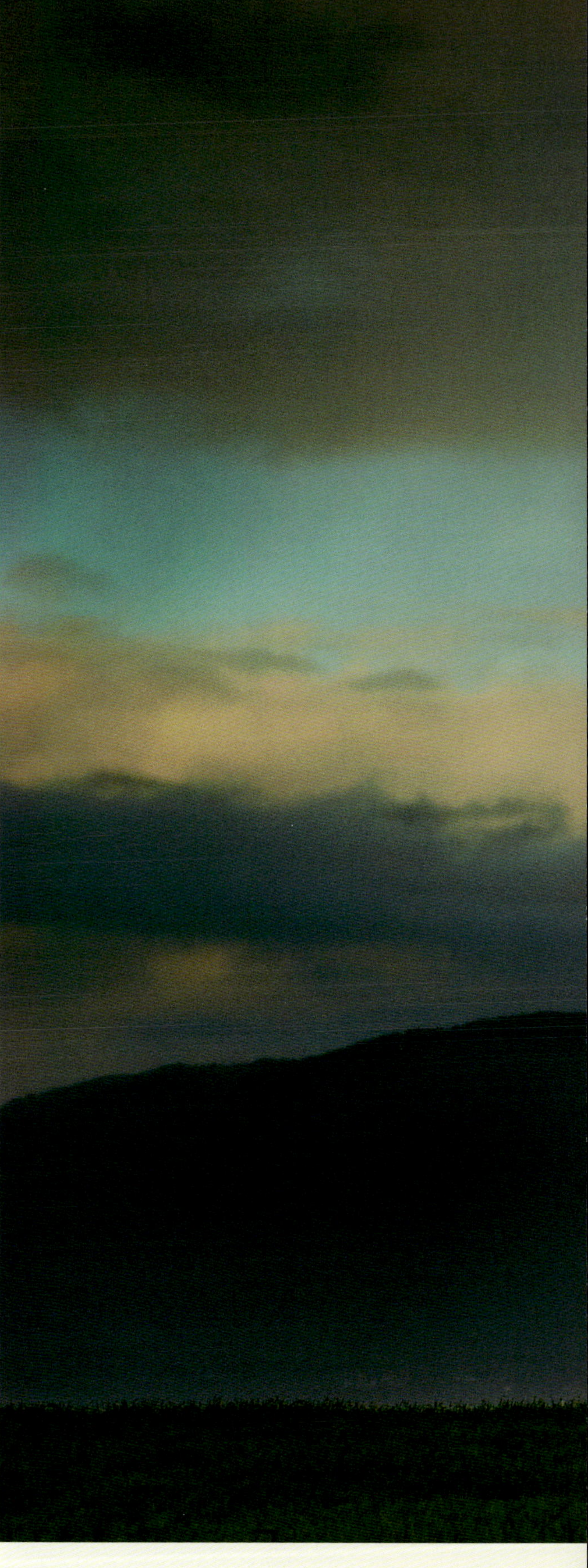

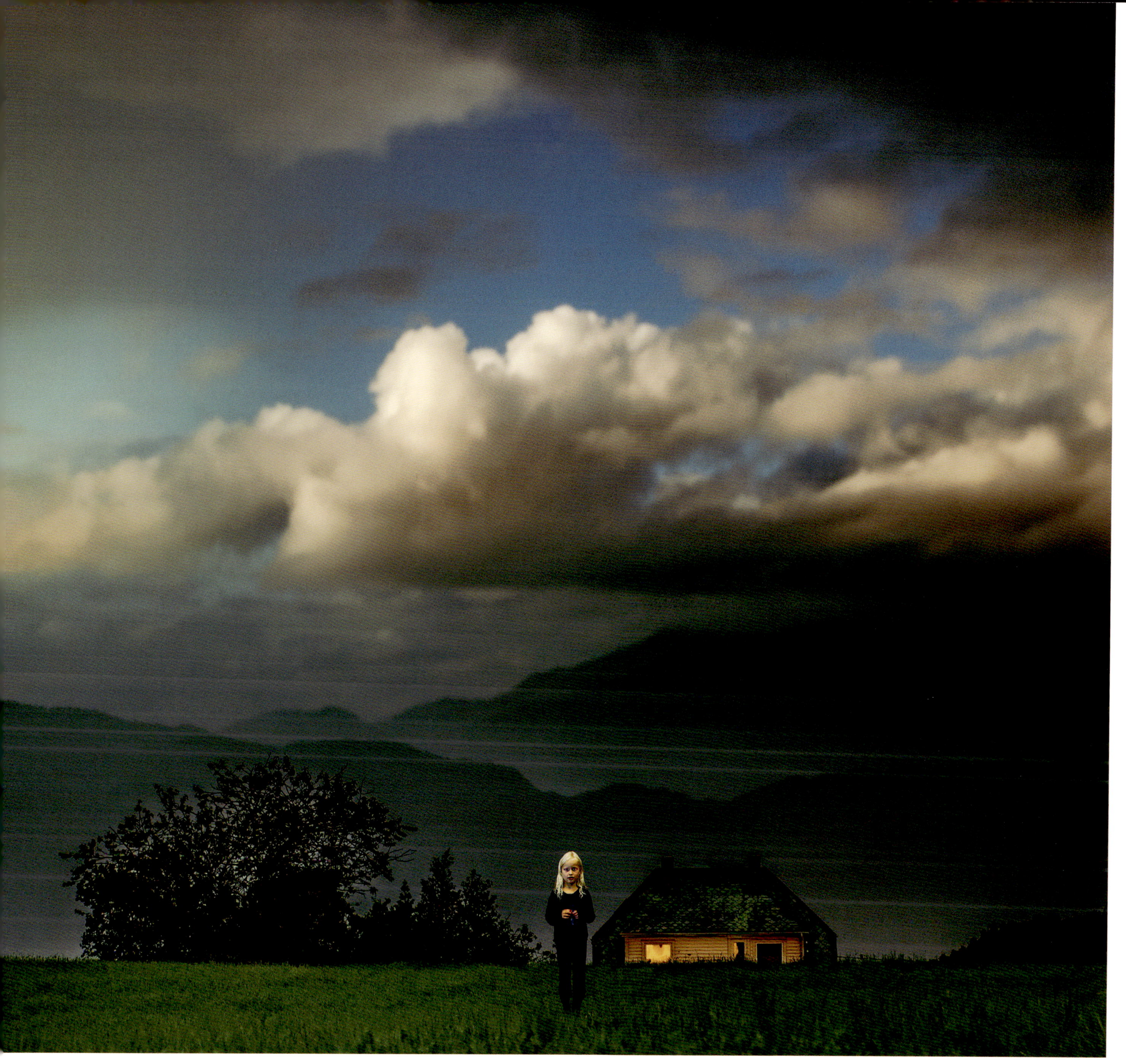

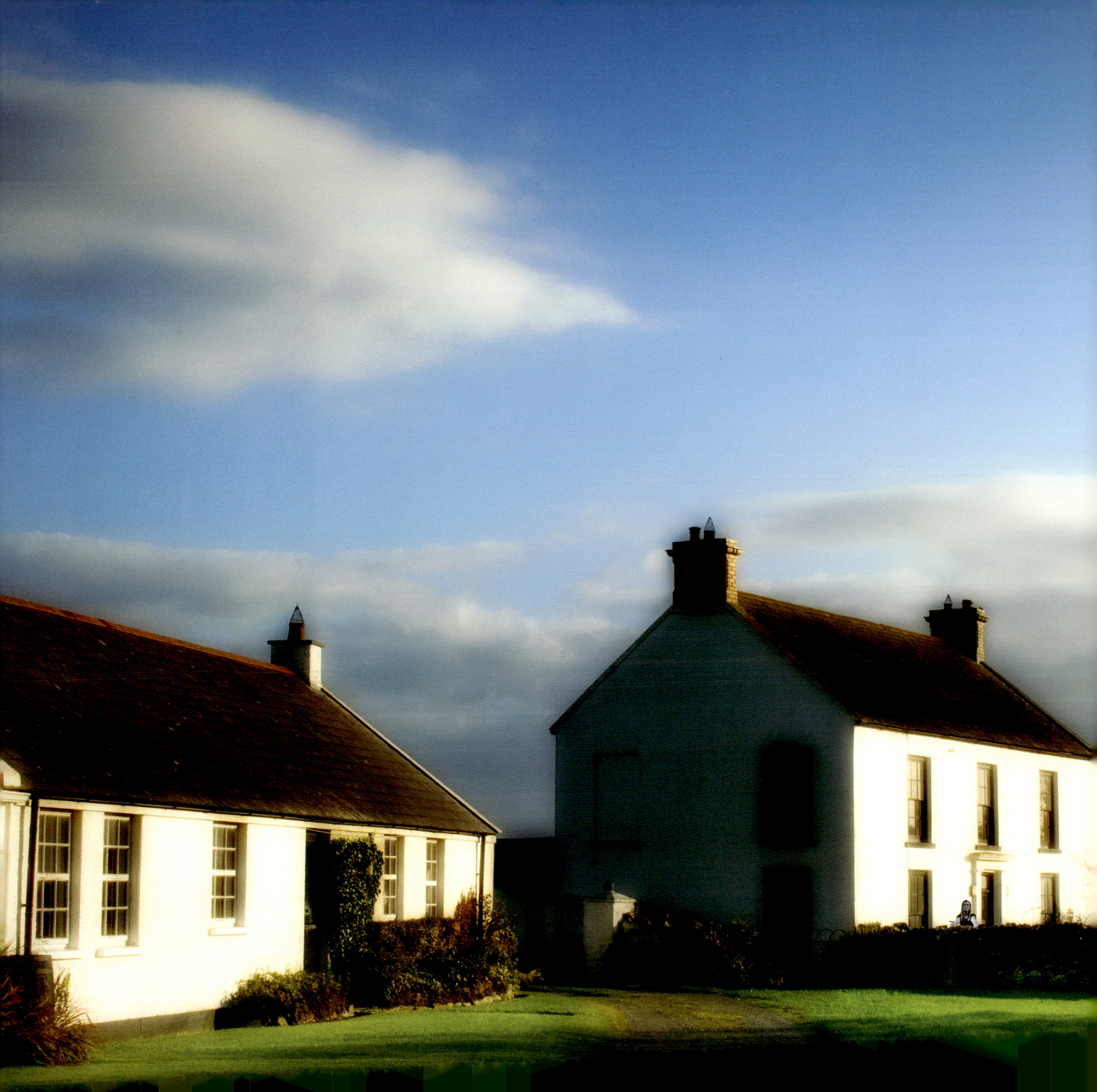

HOPPER IN KEARNEY

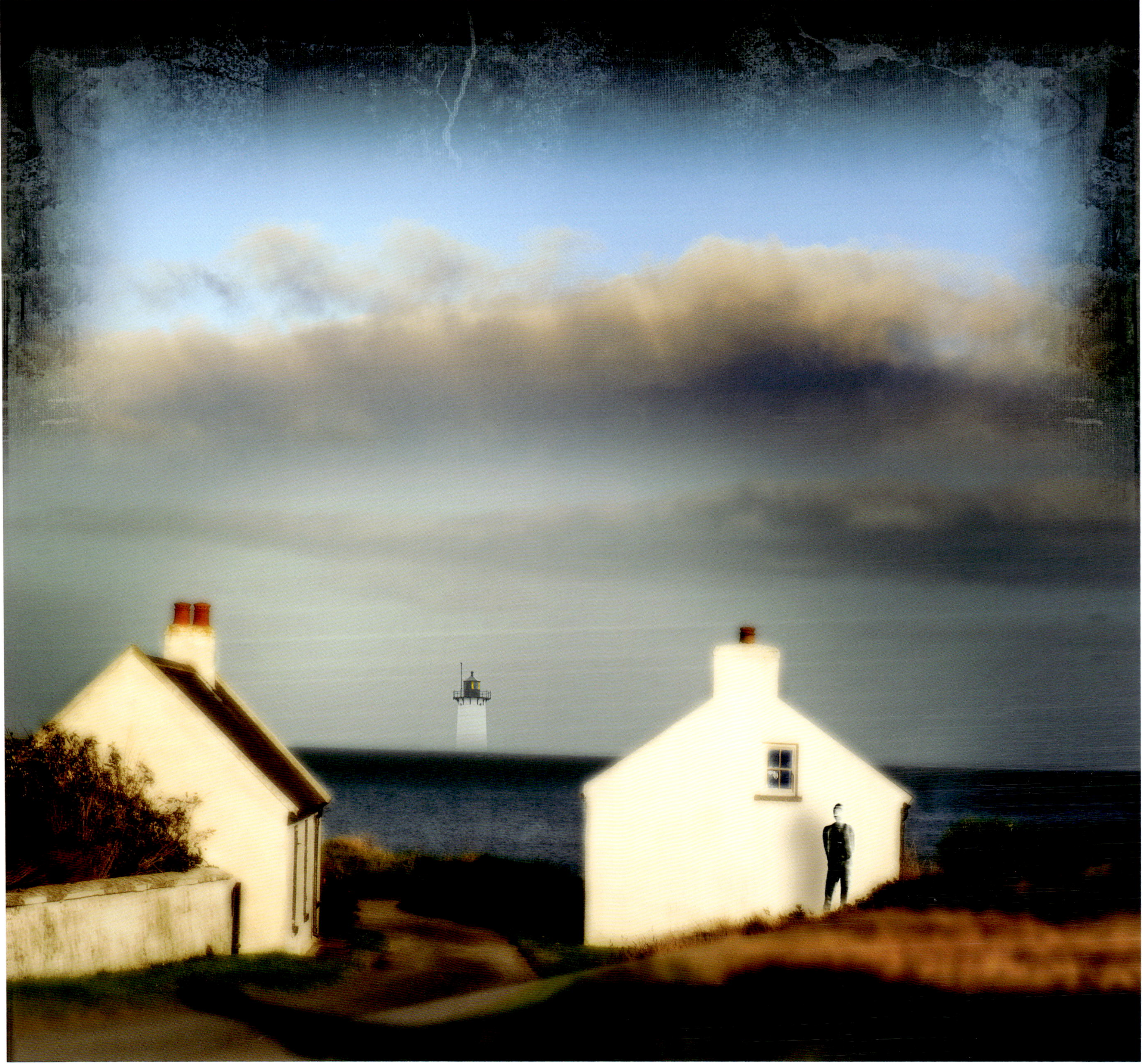

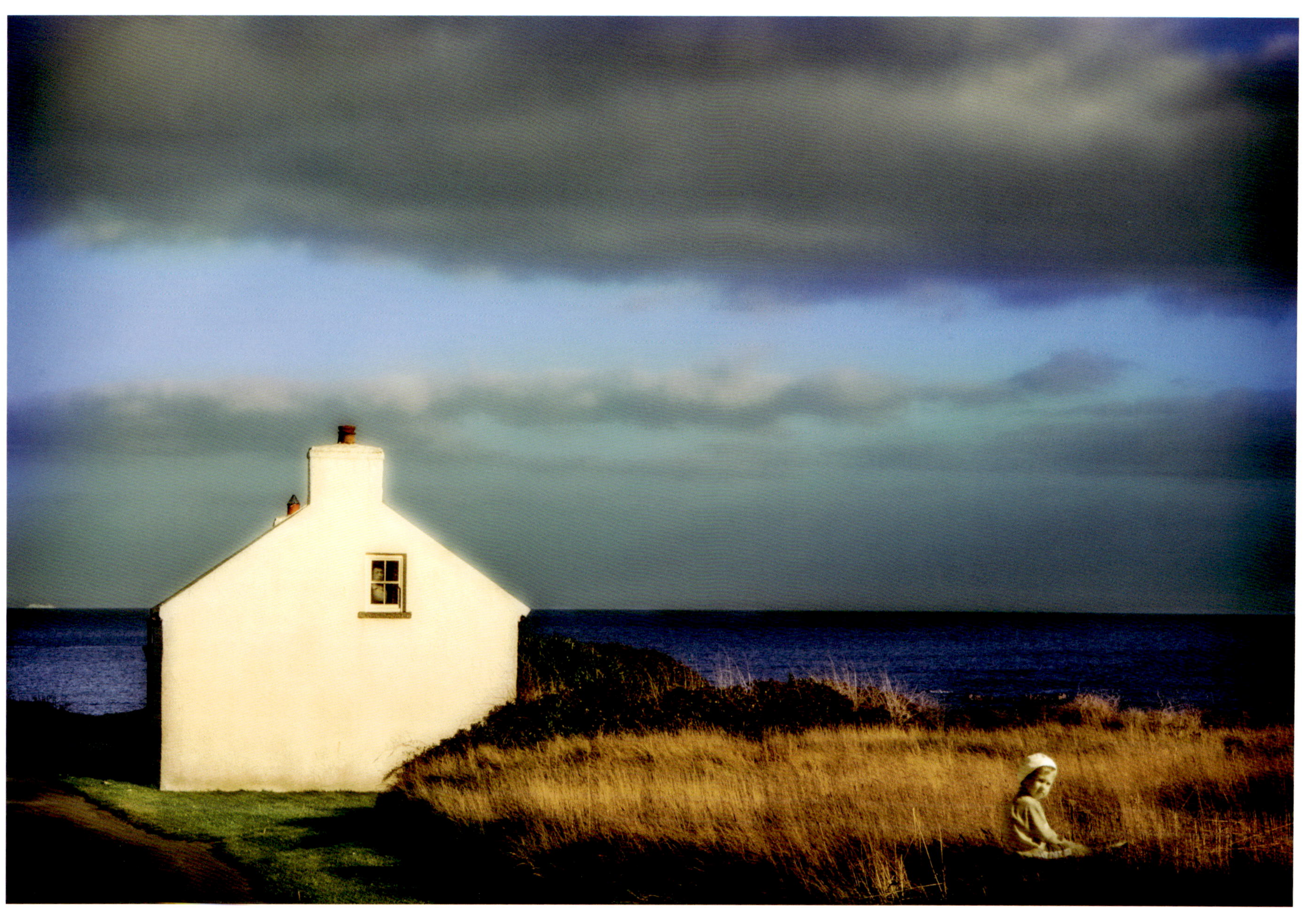

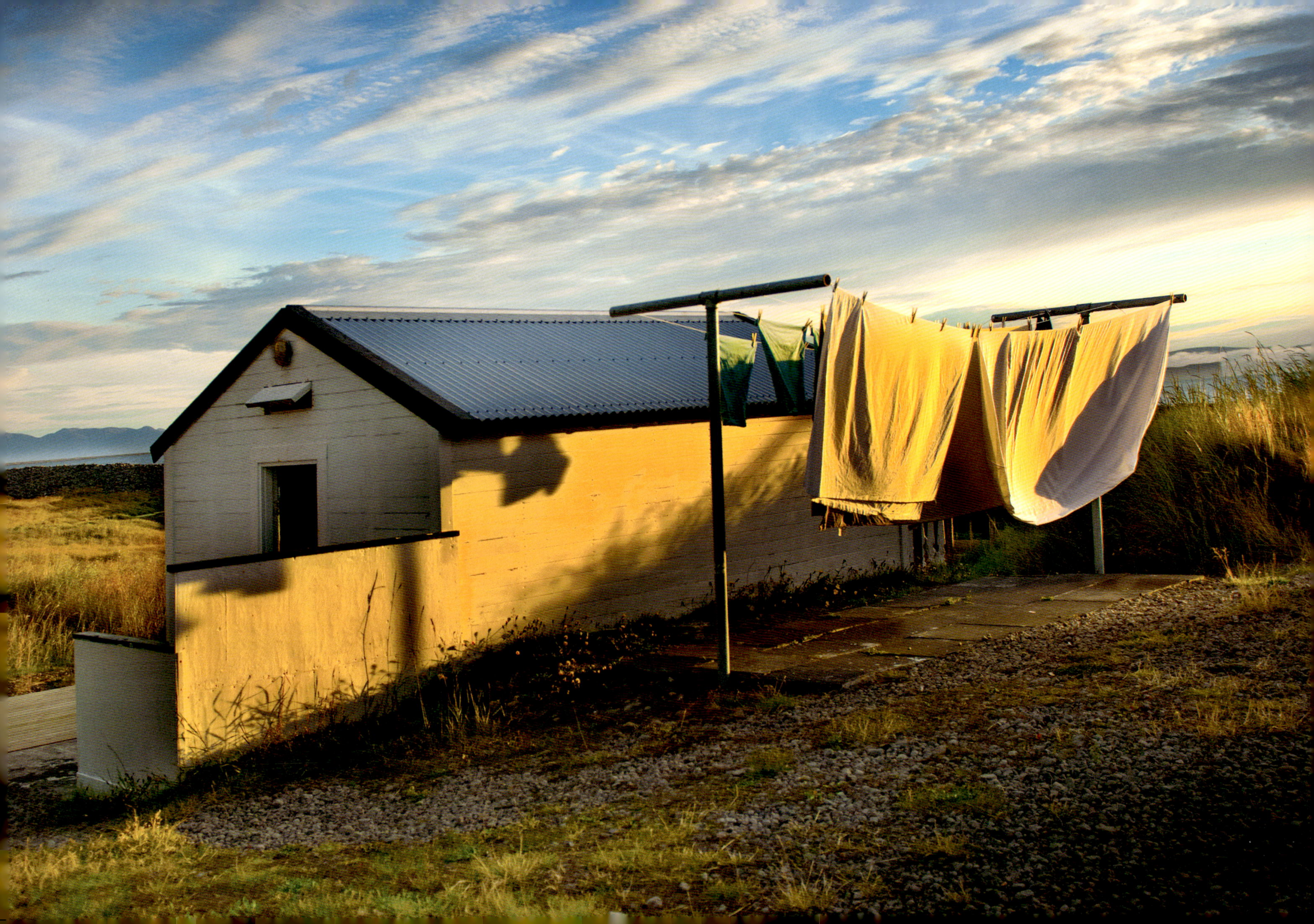

Down from the north
winds plaintive
across the pale stubble
of empty fields
your fading footprints
vagrant at dusk
your small fate on its knees
exhausted under unknown skies

beneath the starry skull
of night
you sleep
in the arms
of no one

Anthony James

GREENLAND TWILIGHT

WHAT HAS HAPPENED HERE? HAS THE YOUNG GIRL SET THE BLACK BIRD FREE OR HAS IT ESCAPED?

Either way the power of its newfound freedom is clear. The bird cannot be put back.

Two witnesses look on and can confirm the impossibility of the bird's capture.

The viewer is left to guess what the girl feels in this unbounded, unscripted escape.

Is she thrilled, terrified, exhilarated, fearful, or satisfied? Any one of these is possible.

The metaphor of release and flight is the story. What may happen next?

Gordon Chase

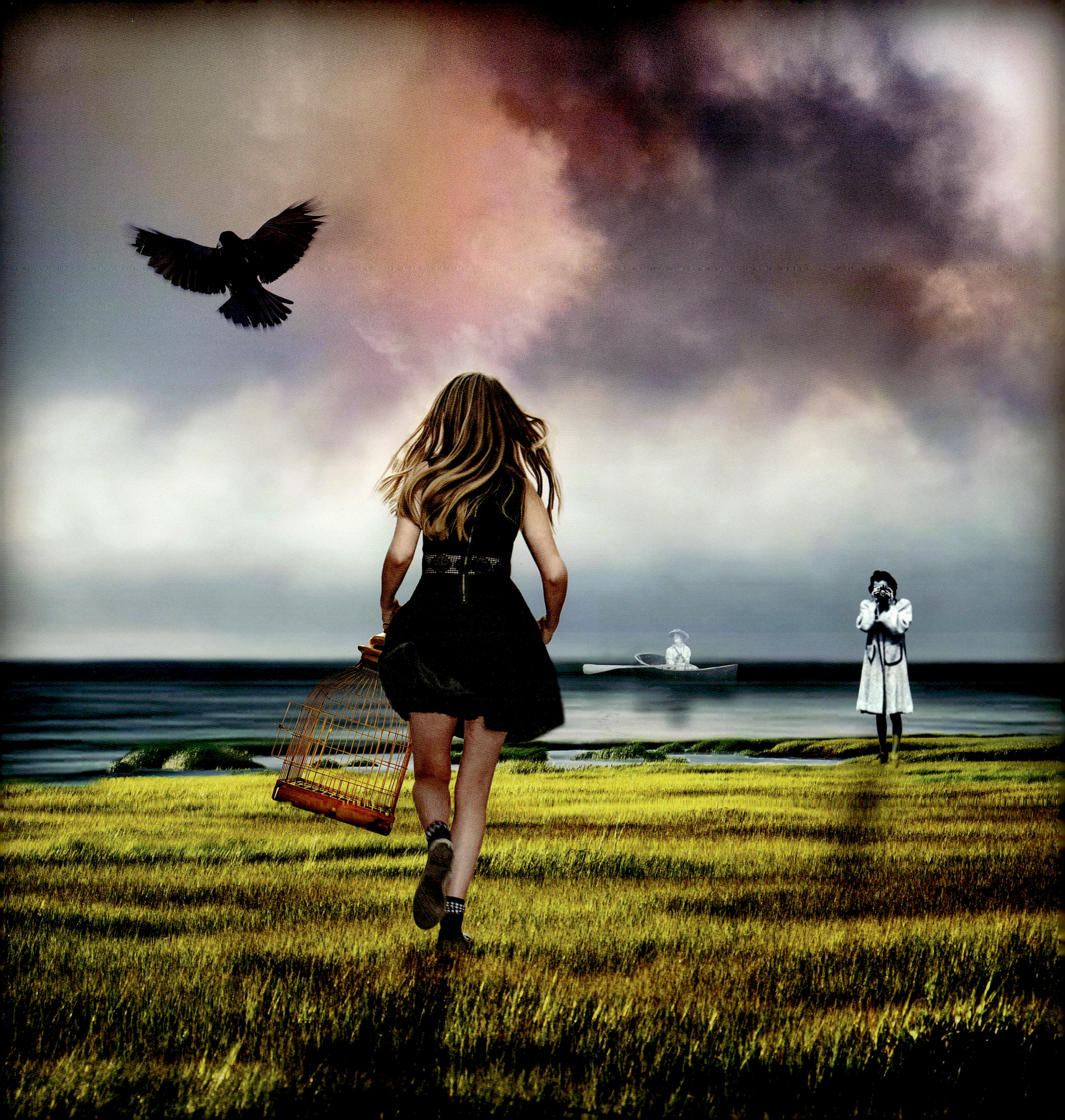

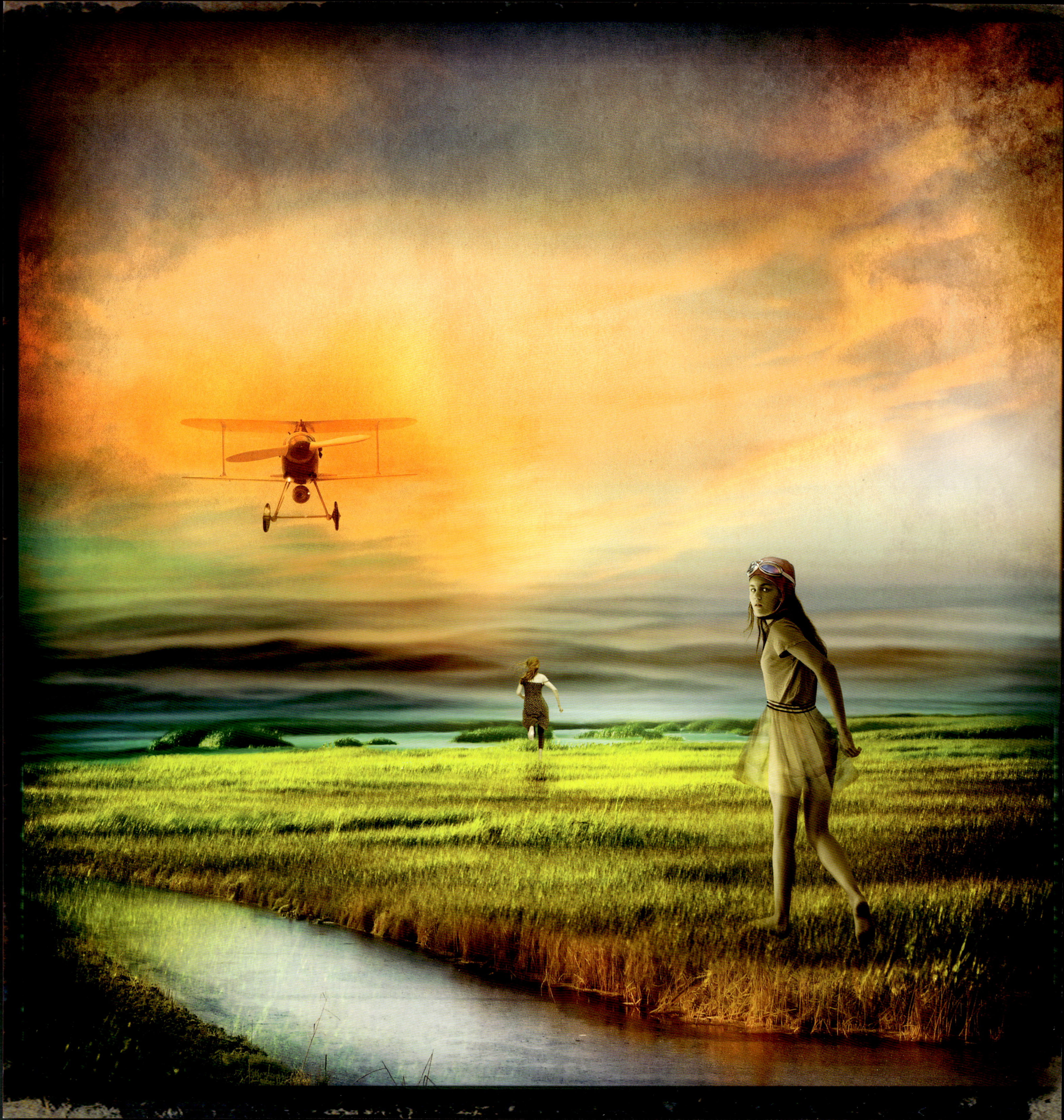

LANDING

The bumblebee light
of the future

Romantic, your sister
rushes the shore—
dolphin flanks
of the rising tide.

You've got your
goggles on,
little aviatrix,
hop on!

Wary, you look back at me.
You already see
what's coming.

Monica Raymond

It's one of those beautiful September mornings. The air is crisp. Clouds approach from the north. You're in your car, driving, somewhere. To work? To meet a friend for breakfast? You hear a ringing sound. Is it the radio? Your phone? You reach for the phone, still happy. The voice on the other end is vaguely recognizable, but distant, muffled. Then you hear the sobbing, and you know your life will be altered …

forever.

Anon.

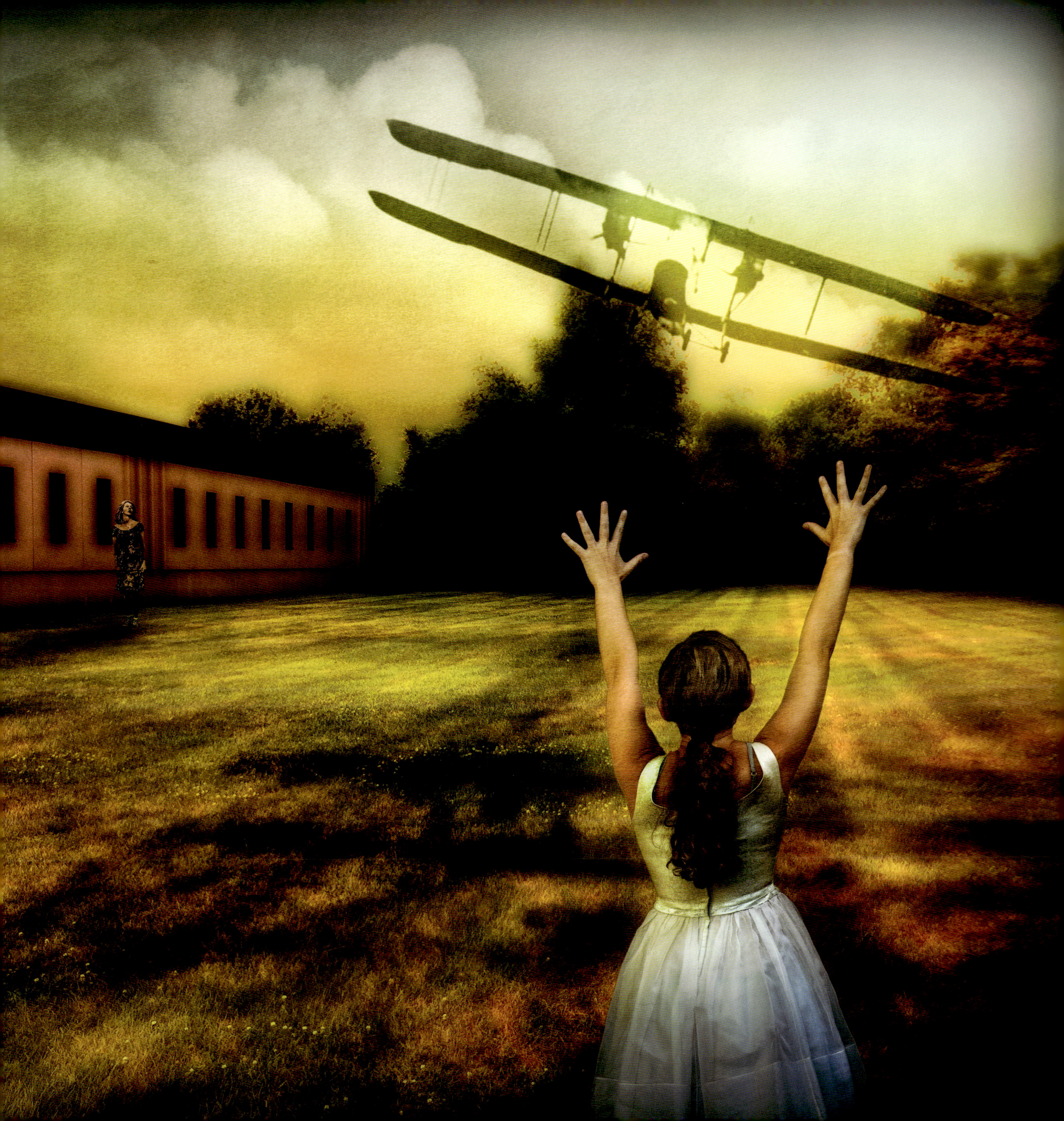

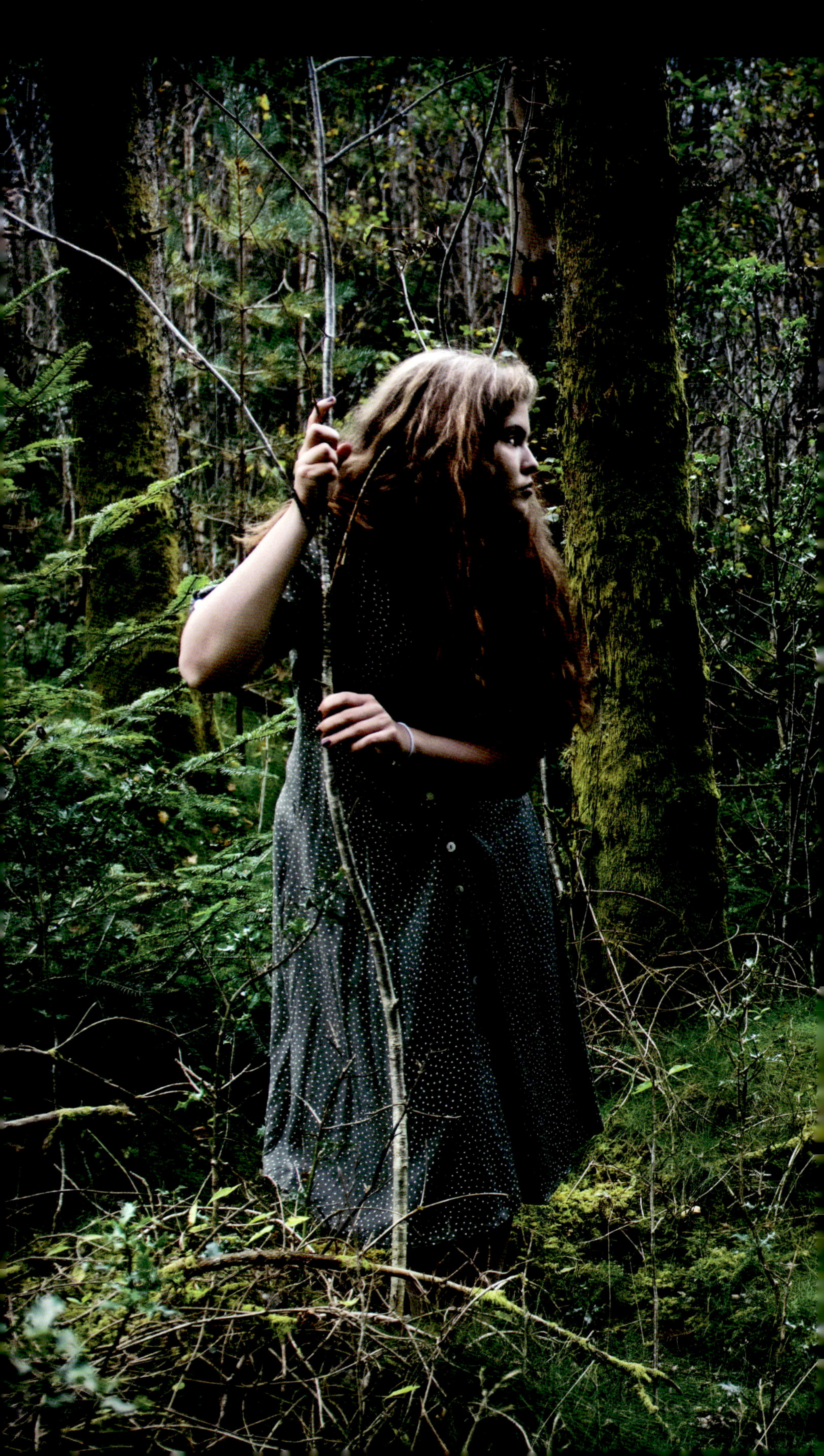

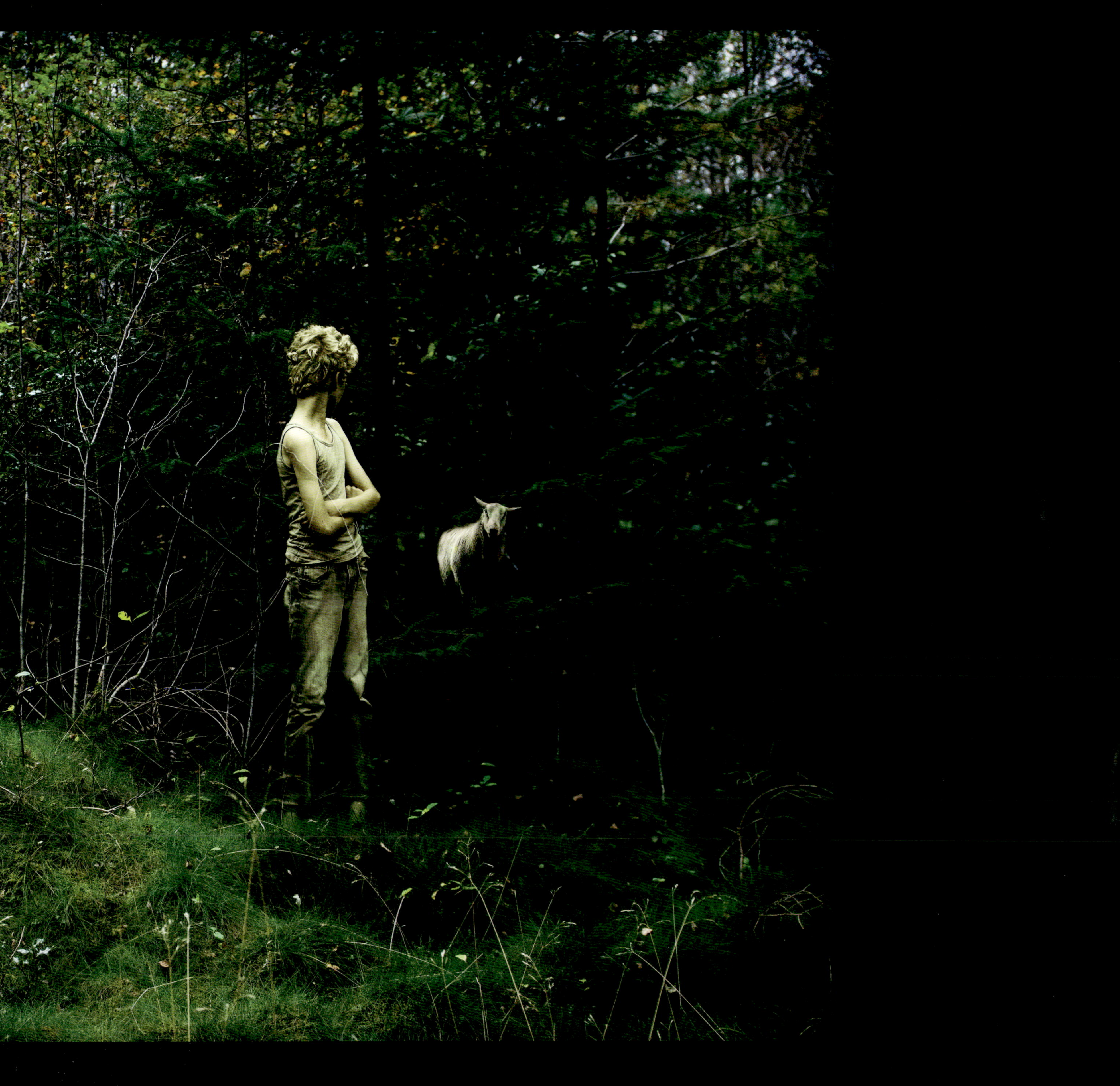

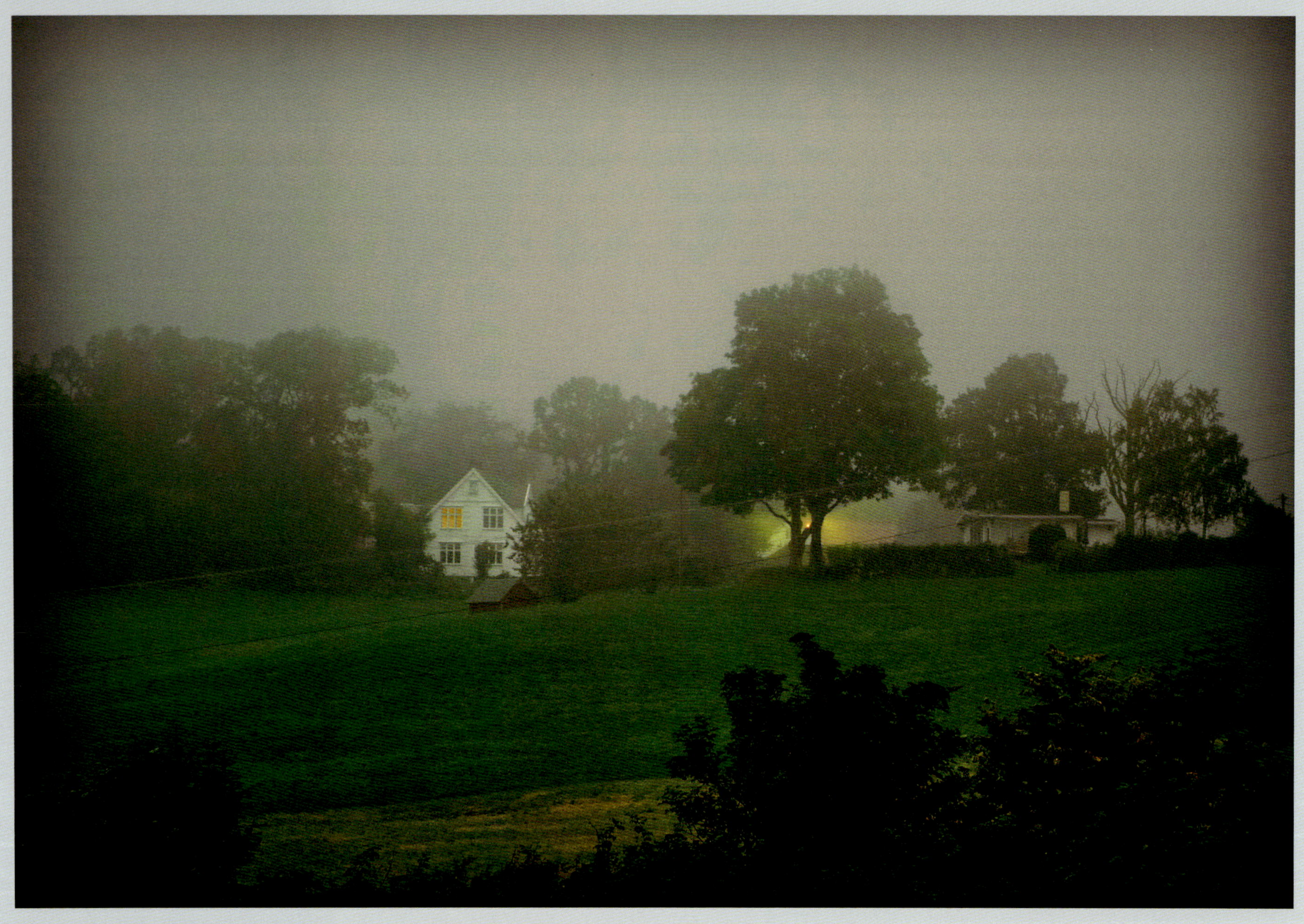

HOUSE IN THE MIST

I don't have allergies here. It takes me a while to notice that, but once I do, it's all I can think about. In the real world, when I run my hands through blades of soft grass, I am left with small red dots on my skin and a desperate need to scratch the gaps between my fingers. I sneeze almost instantly. My eyes water.

But here, I can breathe. My skin feels dewy.

I stop for a moment to place my palms on the ground for a second time, testing the limits. The blades are wet.

It's sweater-no-jacket weather.

I have been walking for at least two miles by the time I see the house. My legs are not tired, though. I am not thirsty.

These are the first homes I've seen. From behind the trees, I notice that the bigger one has a light on.

She is in there, I think, and then I steel myself, preparing for what I might find.

Sometimes, while my eyes move rapidly under my lids, I see my mother in a department store elevator. Or in our old home in Maryland. Or at a lively dinner party. We communicate with our mouths closed, a special telepathy reserved for sleep.

Often she explains that she has been given a reprieve from death for just one night, but instead of enjoying her—instead of breathing with her in the moment—I ask her how we can extend it to two. To triple our time together. To quadruple it. She grows tired and frustrated with me because that was never the point.

But as I approach this house, I can tell the experience is going to be different. I'm visiting her instead of the other way around.

I think she lives here now.

I don't know how or why she has summoned me, but I am certain that this is her doing. I know that when I arrive, she will be warming up a loaf of sourdough bread. We will eat it plain. "Like we're in Paris," she will say.

I know the song that will fill the house. I know that the window ledges will be lined with oddly shaped rocks she found on the lawn.

THE LIGHT IN THE WINDOW SHINES BRIGHTER AS I APPROACH. **I CAN'T HELP MYSELF FROM RUNNING TOWARD IT.**

Meredith Goldstein

"Gertie's back again," Zee said, looking out from the window. It was the name we'd given the Rhinoceros who wandered into our yard from time to time. We didn't know what Gertie was at first, so we had to ask our mother and she said she remembered it looked like an animal that had gone extinct when her mother was little.

We no longer had computers to help us since the Lessening, but that was way before Lisa and I were born. Mom said they were like little squares in your pocket that could help you look up anything in the world, but most people just looked at photos of cats or images of food. That seems cruel to show off food others may not have, but I guess people were a little silly back then. They also had more food.

I joined my sister at the window and took in Gertie's slow movements. I liked that she walked at an easy pace, unlike the six-foot tarantulas that scurried every which way and didn't give much though to whether they were knocking over your mailbox.

"I'm going to go talk to her," Zee said.

"What? Mom said we shouldn't! It might be dangerous," I said.

"Everything's dangerous Bee," Zee said with a shrug. She wasn't wrong. We couldn't go outside when it rained, what with all the acid. Plus we had to avoid staying in the sun too long. If you were out there without bubble blockers for more than half an hour you could start to burn. Mom still has a small hole in her hand when she was tending to the super soybean garden, so now she wears gloves all the time.

My sister walked out and I watched her approach the creature. Gertie's skin looked tough, like it could withstand the elements. Maybe that's why Zee felt like she could touch her. They were both resilient. They both had strength that the rest of us didn't.

Sara Farizan

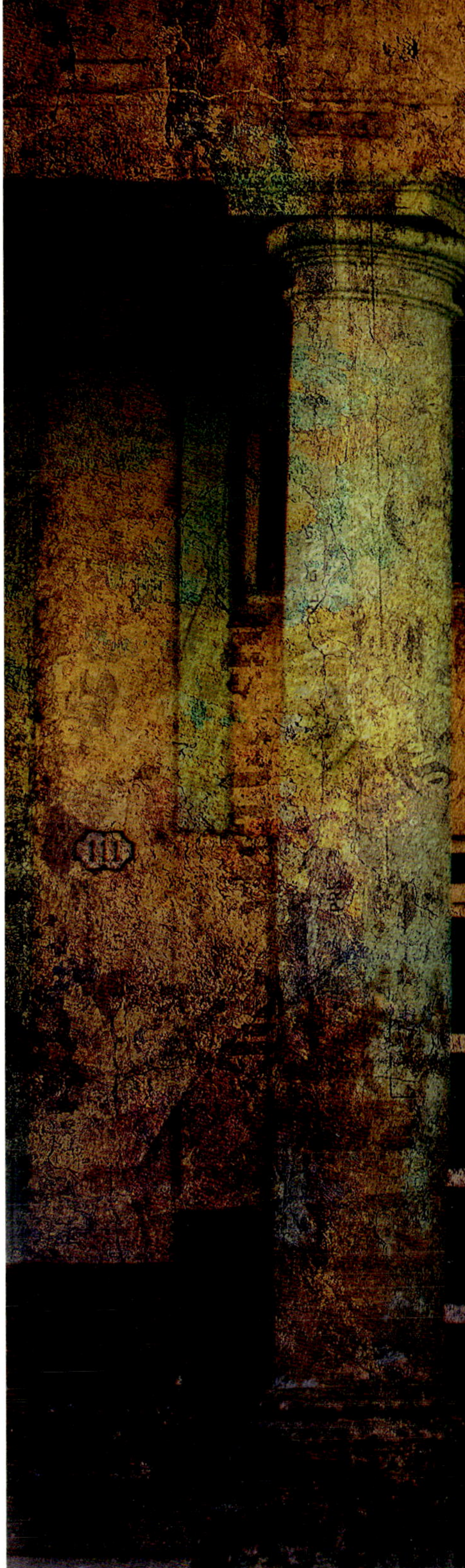

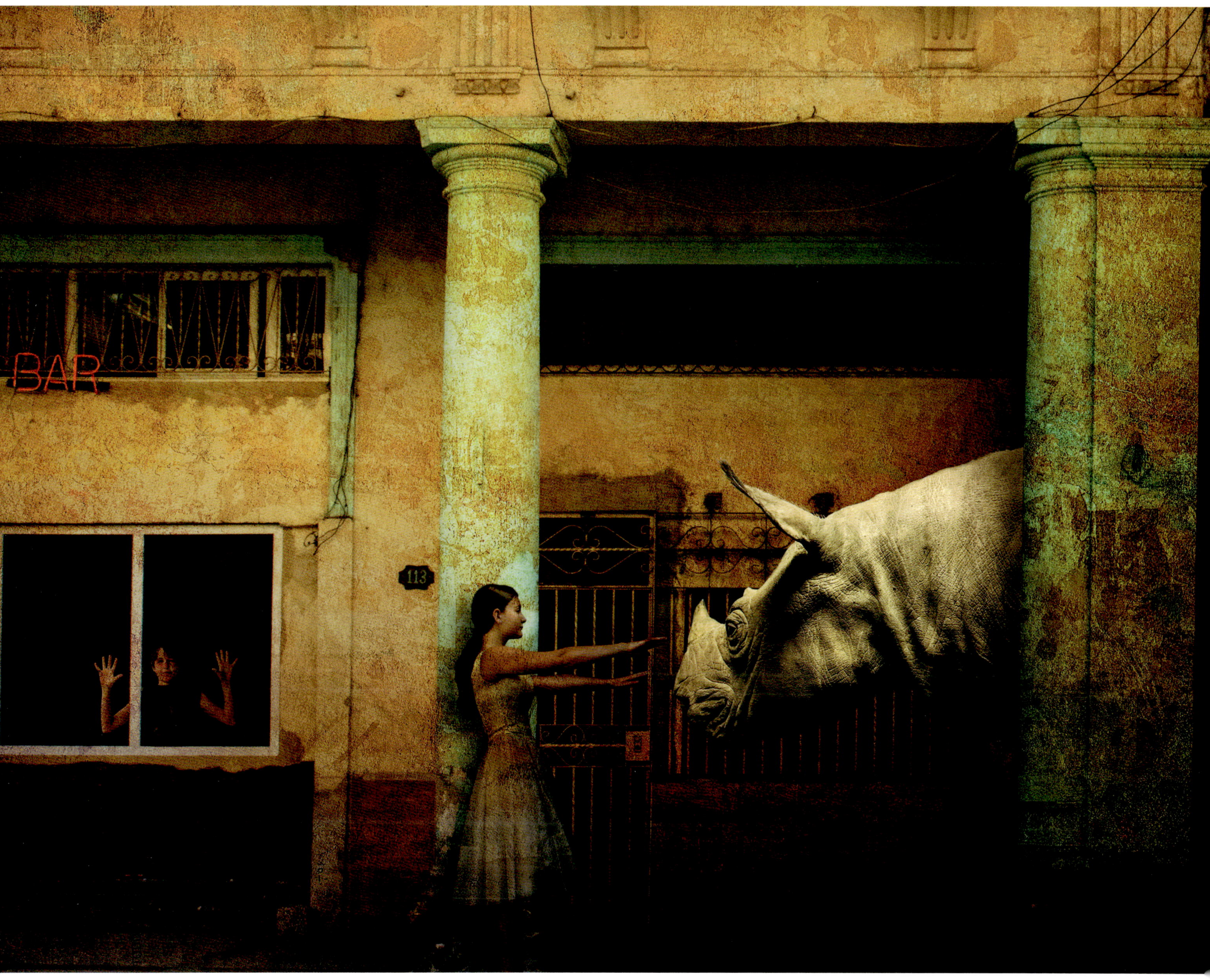
BAR
113

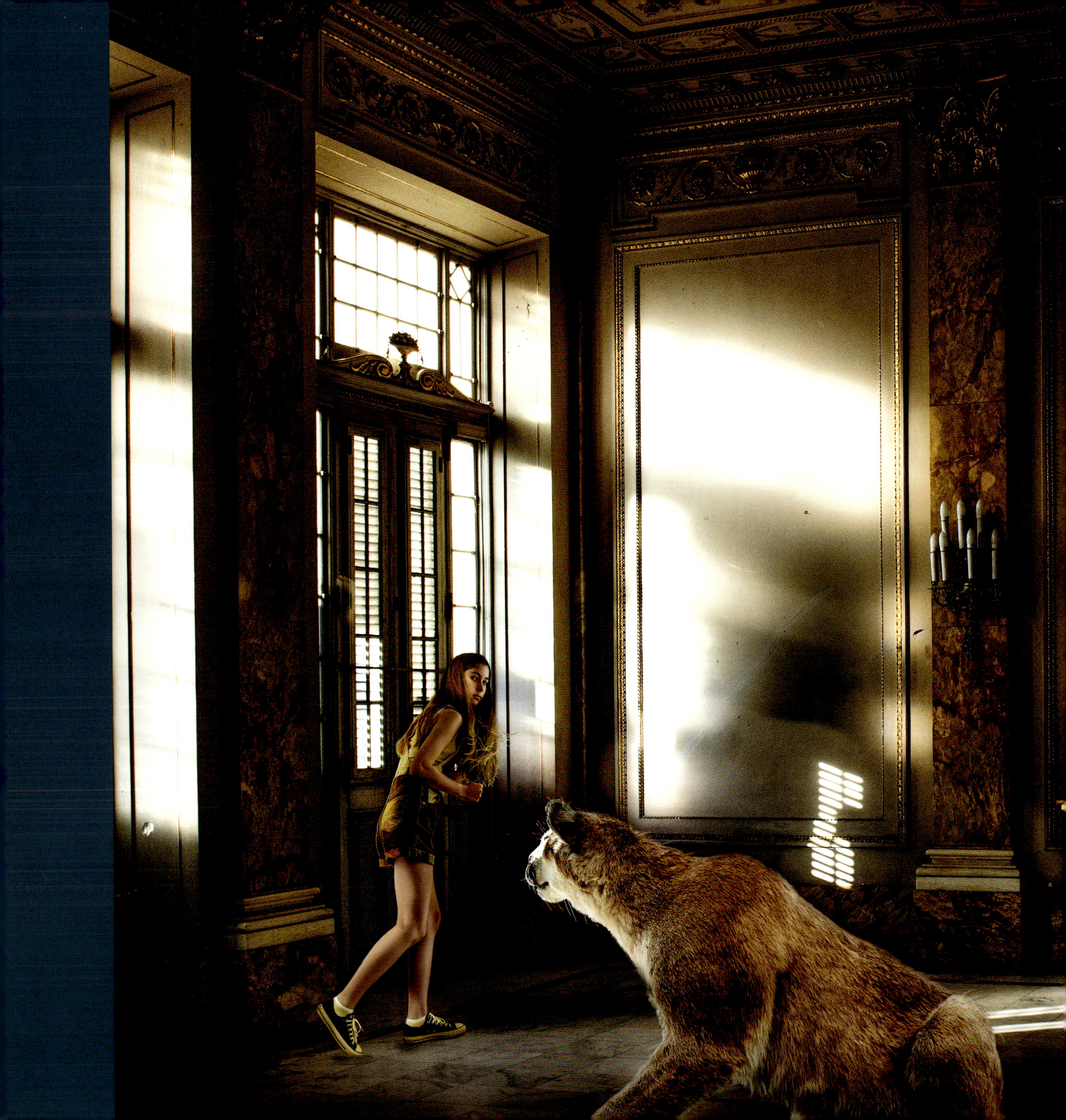

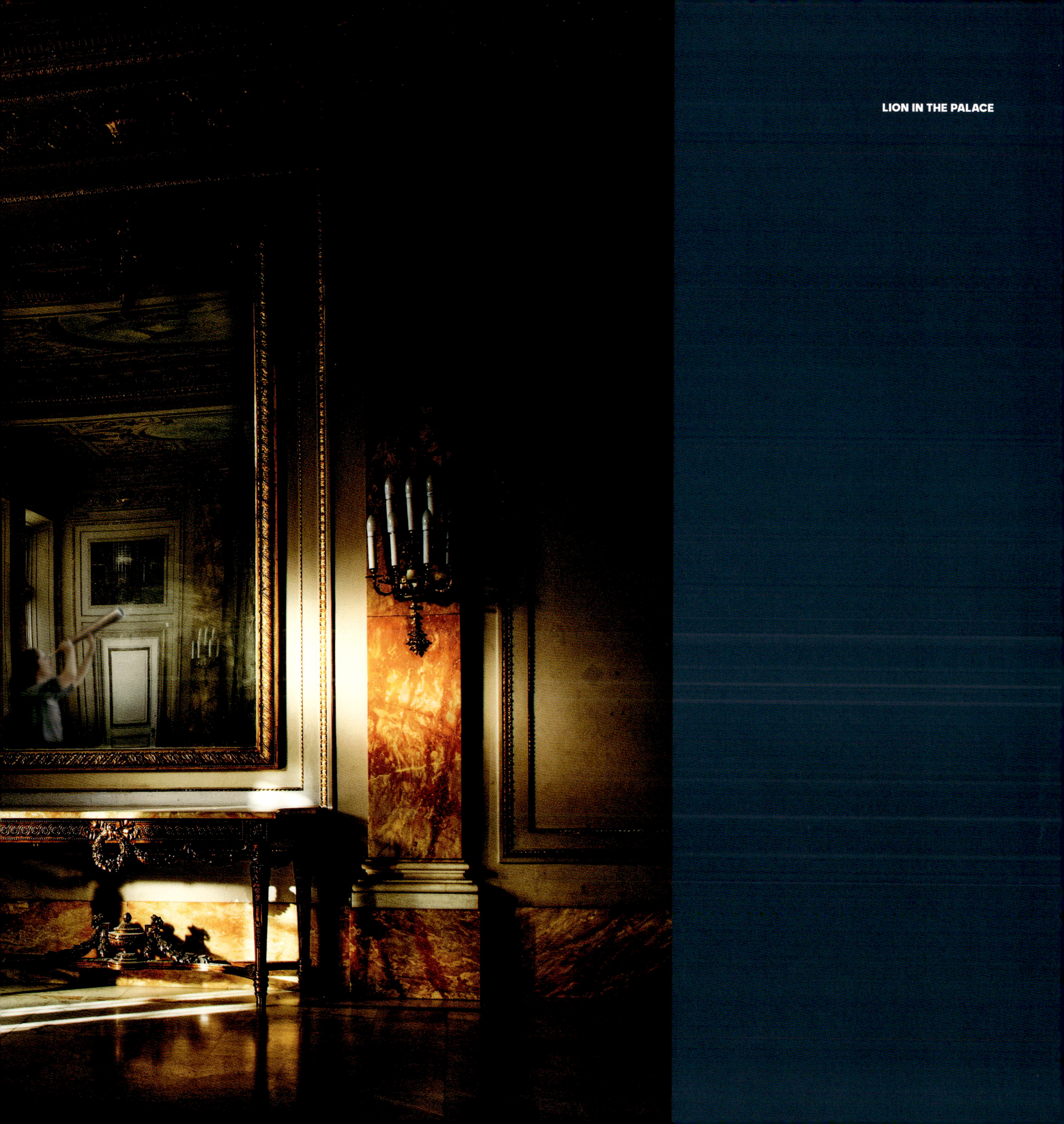
LION IN THE PALACE

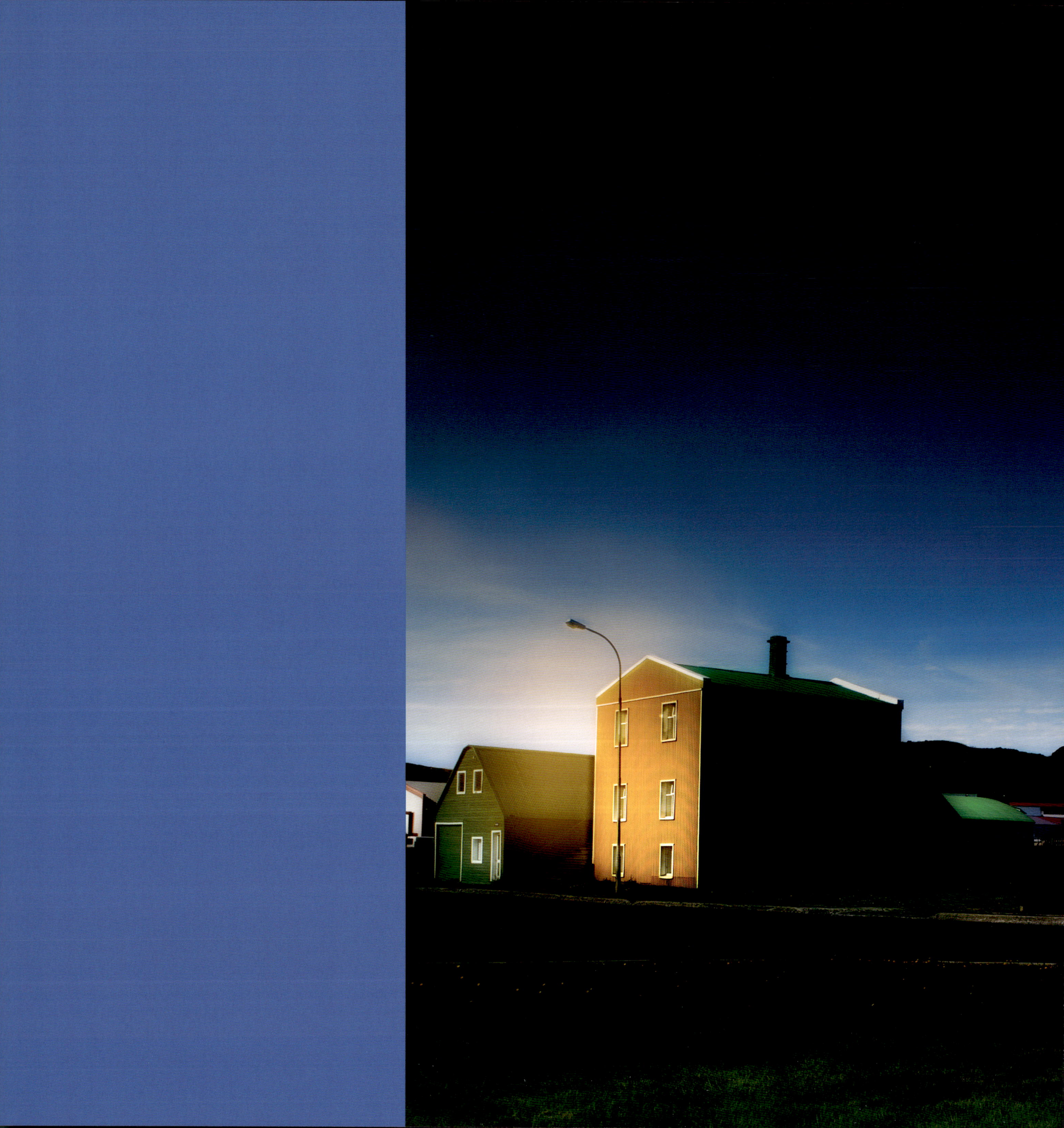

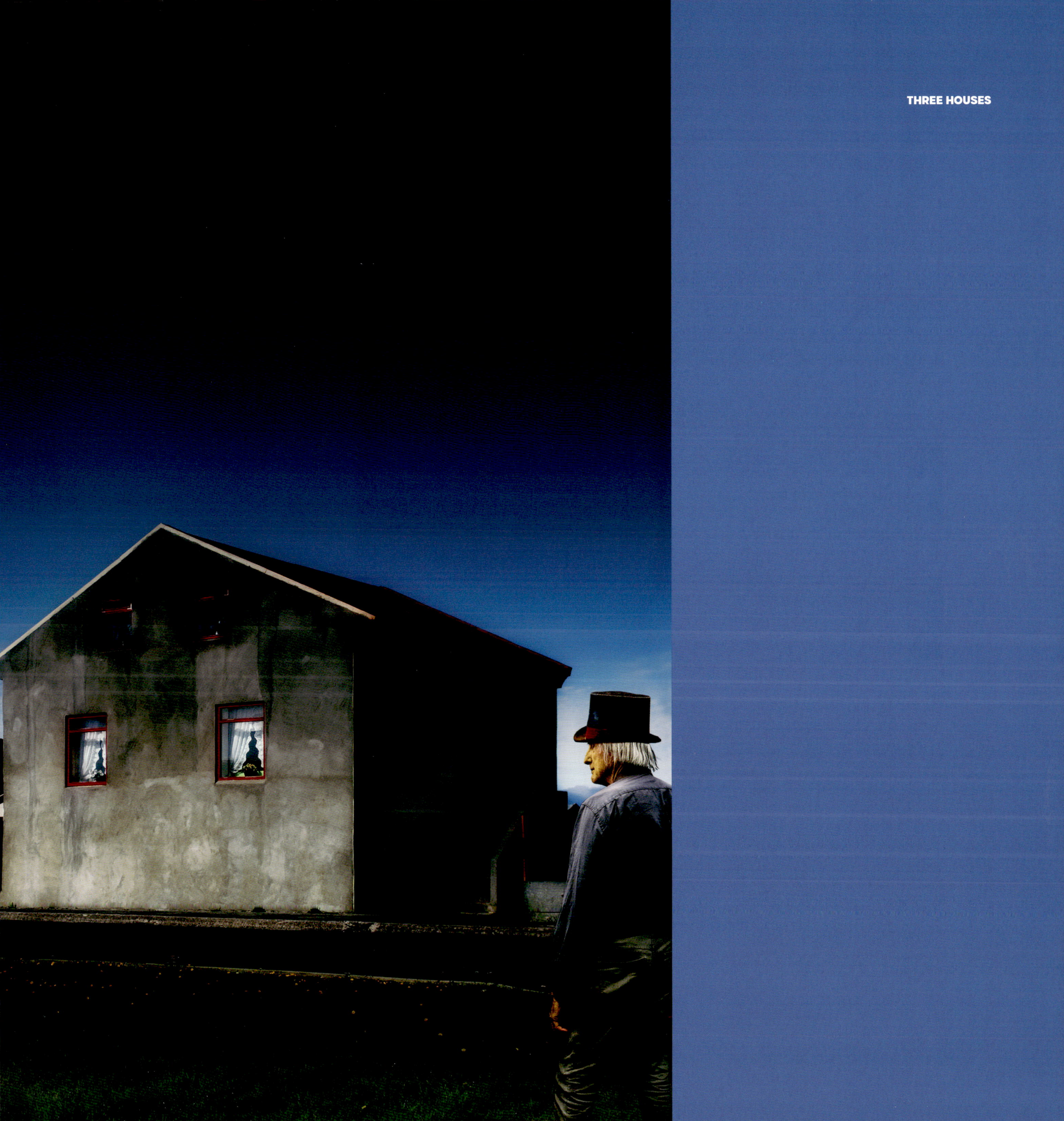

THREE HOUSES

ABANDONED

Unhinged, cast about
seeking, looking for.

Not I.
They.

Not FOR me, popped upped
bubbles,
Cellular.
Once, through my embrace,
Sinned through.

Opened and entered,
No more.
Mythical Siri-bdus!
Giving but a naught.

I am here. Built
Into this world, unborn.
Memory,
whim-ed of, printed.

No! I squeak,
Not calling. Crack,
Moan, crumble, bake,
FOR the spot. I am.

Left, split, righted by soil.
Remember me not.
Send bloodless hounds
For my fled bones.

Amnon Lourie

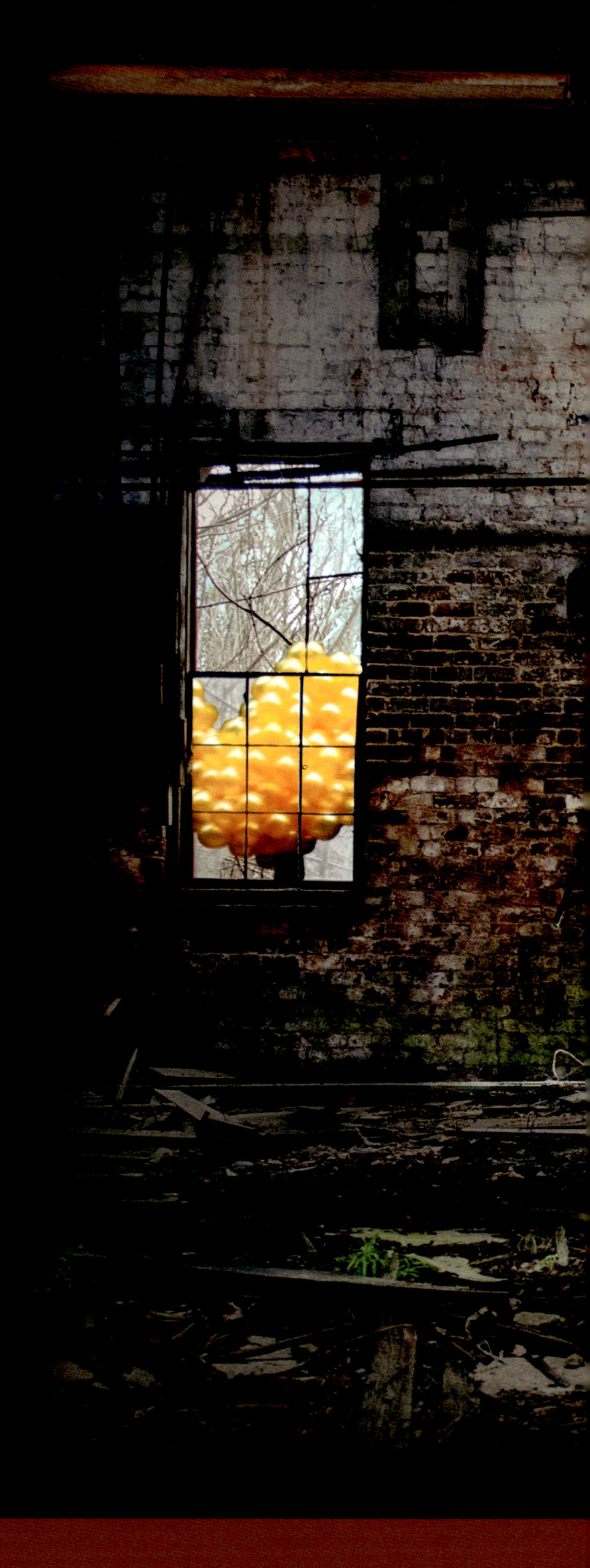

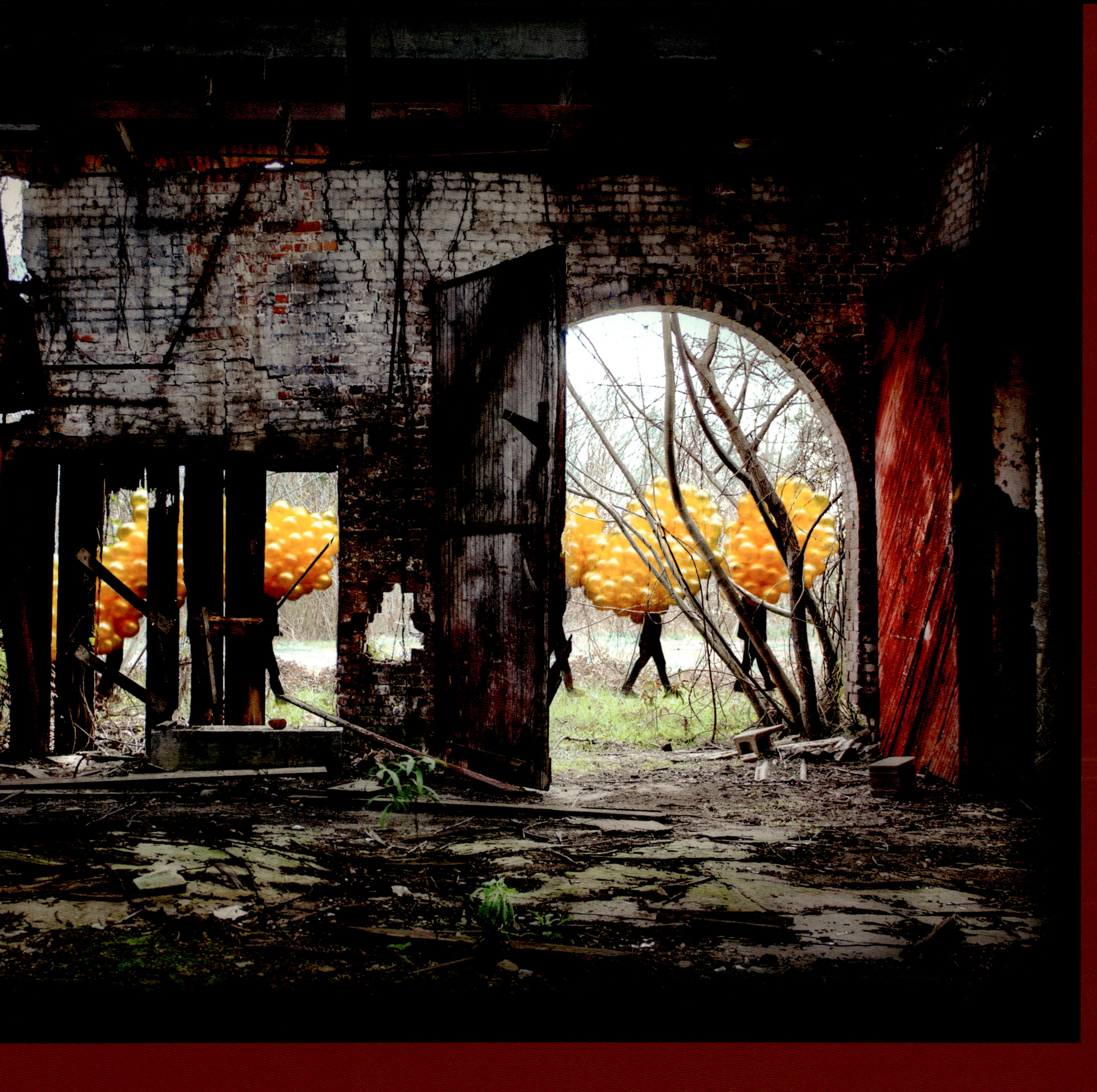

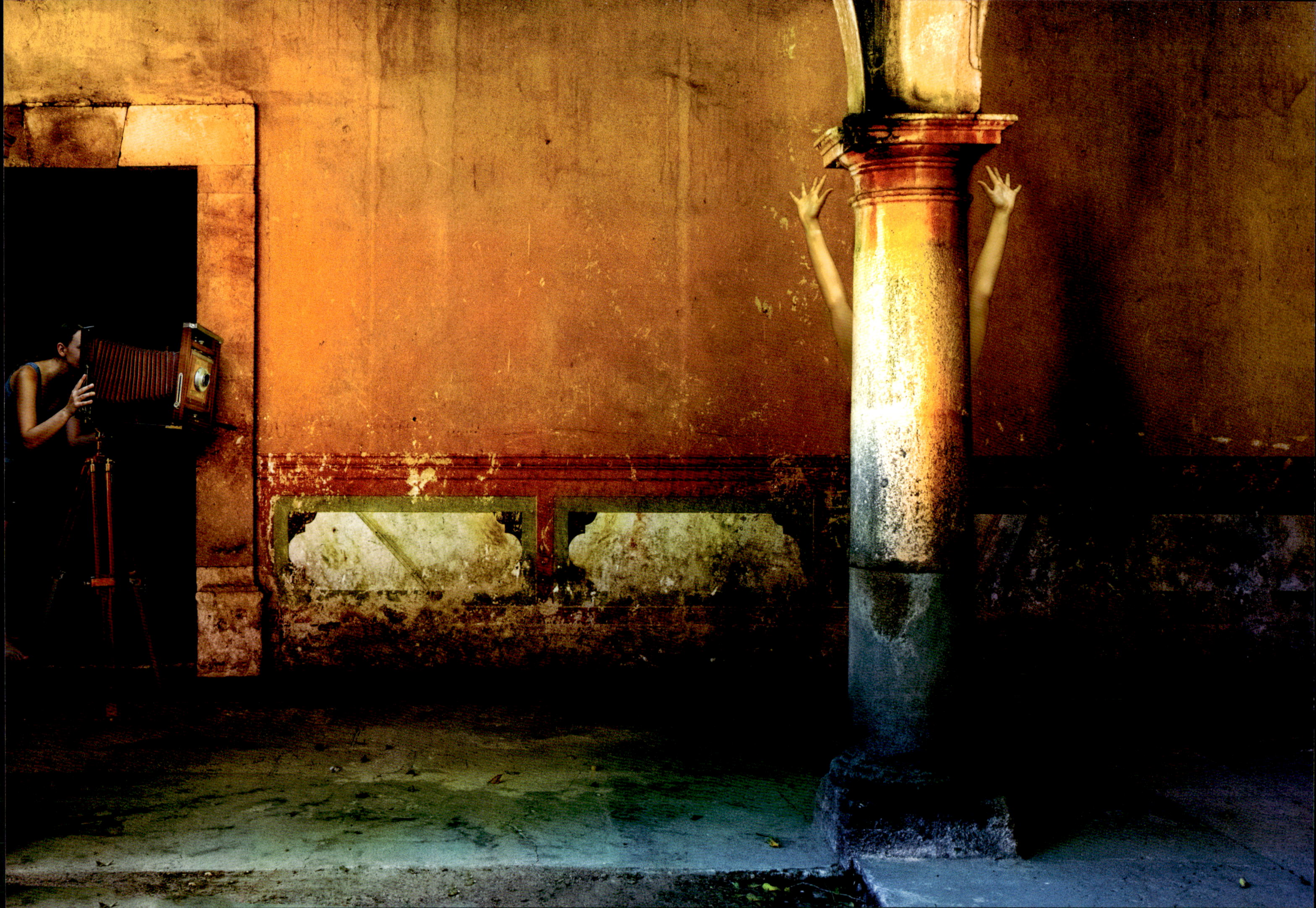

So when my older sister gets into photography, she can't just do it like a *normal* person with a Pentax or her phone—no, she has to go off the deep end, with glass plates, collodion printing in our shower/darkroom, and a box on her head as if she were Matthew Brady at Gettsyburg. But all this is actually good, because it slows her down; all this means I can hear her coming from, like, a mile away. Which is good, because she seems to have decided on me as the subject of her photo essay, which judging from the set-ups where she tries to catch me, seems to be some sort of soft-focus soft-core young woman coming of age *deshabille* snap crackle and pop. Don't get me wrong, I don't think she means to sell under-the-counter to some skeezix so old and crinkly he forgets what he even has in his underwear and therefore needs extreme measures. No, I think she thinks it's AHRT, with a capital A, H, R, T. I think she even thinks she's making a statement, the female gaze or whatever. But her motives don't particularly interest me. Point is, I haven't been consulted. Consent. With a capital C. See? I feel like I'm being stalked. But never mind, I have my own ways of getting around her *projecto*, even if she doesn't get that that I'm doing it, and just thinks I'm squirmy or hyper or a klutz or ADD-ish or whatever.

For example, she likes to sneak into my room just as I'm dozing off to sleep, after I've turned off the night light. I'm imagining she wants a shot of me dreamy and disheveled, hair loose on the pillow, dewy lips parted, blah blah blah. The way I nip this in the bud is, before I nod out, I put on my Mexican mask I have in the shape of a giant water bug. Copper foil. It's satisfyingly Gregory enough to give her a start. One time she actually reached down to pull it aside, but I shook my head, so it moved and gave a little foil, like whoosh, and she backed off. Maybe she actually thought it was a giant water bug. Or who knows? Maybe she took the photo after all. Maybe I'm inadvertently collaborating on a series much weirder than anything she thought she'd take.

Look at this picture Lucas snapped just this afternoon. We were playing scrabble when we heard her lumbering around. I realized I was in the exact pose I knew she'd love, leaning on one elbow, staring meditatively at my letters (an X, a G, a P, a T, and a couple of miscellaneous vowels), mouth partway open, bangs falling over my thick dark-framed glasses as they slid down my nose. I had to spring into action, darting behind the pillar (knocking my tiles to the floor and completely ruining the game, but oh well) and fortunately, because we live in this in this whackadoodle antique rehab monstrosity, there's usually some convenient half door or column or turret behind which to hide.

I flung my arms out from behind the pillar, but my face and body are obscured, and my limbs are so creepily white and electric they look like the feelers of some weird beetle, the spinnerets of some weird white spider. I am happy with it. If you think the insect thing is a motif, you're right. But I haven't figured out exactly where I'm going with it yet.

But I will not be her ingénue. Her nymphet.

Monica Raymond

SAILBOAT

MOST OF MY DREAMS ARE FILLED WITH ARCHITECTURAL PATHWAYS AND DOORWAYS THAT LEAD TO OTHER WORLDS.

When I look at this image I'm immediately called into my own dream-time. I feel a sense of wonder—more than mere curiosity. I am this Alice in Wonderland; pulled by the light to take the next step and dive into the water. Let the adventure begin.

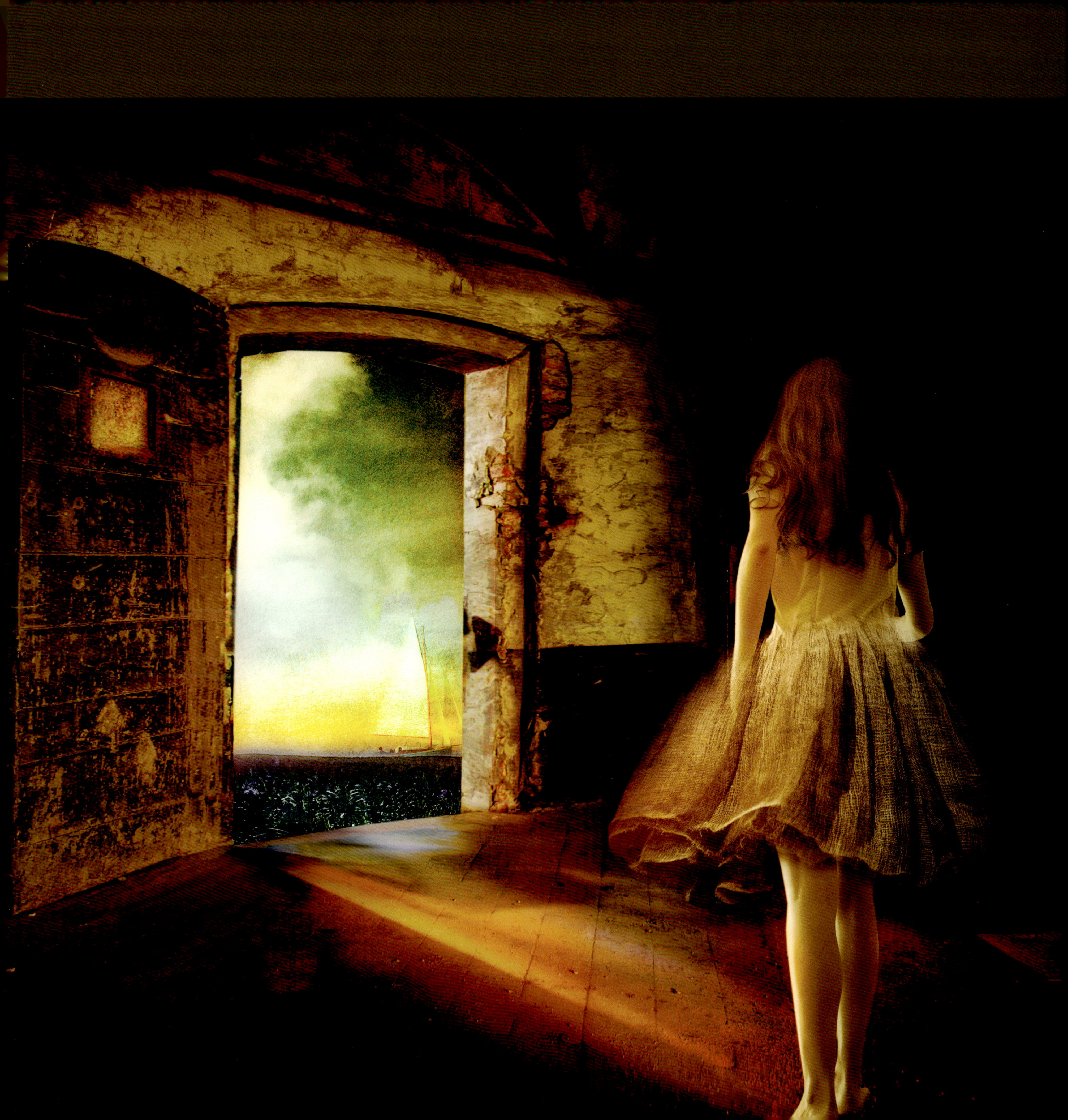

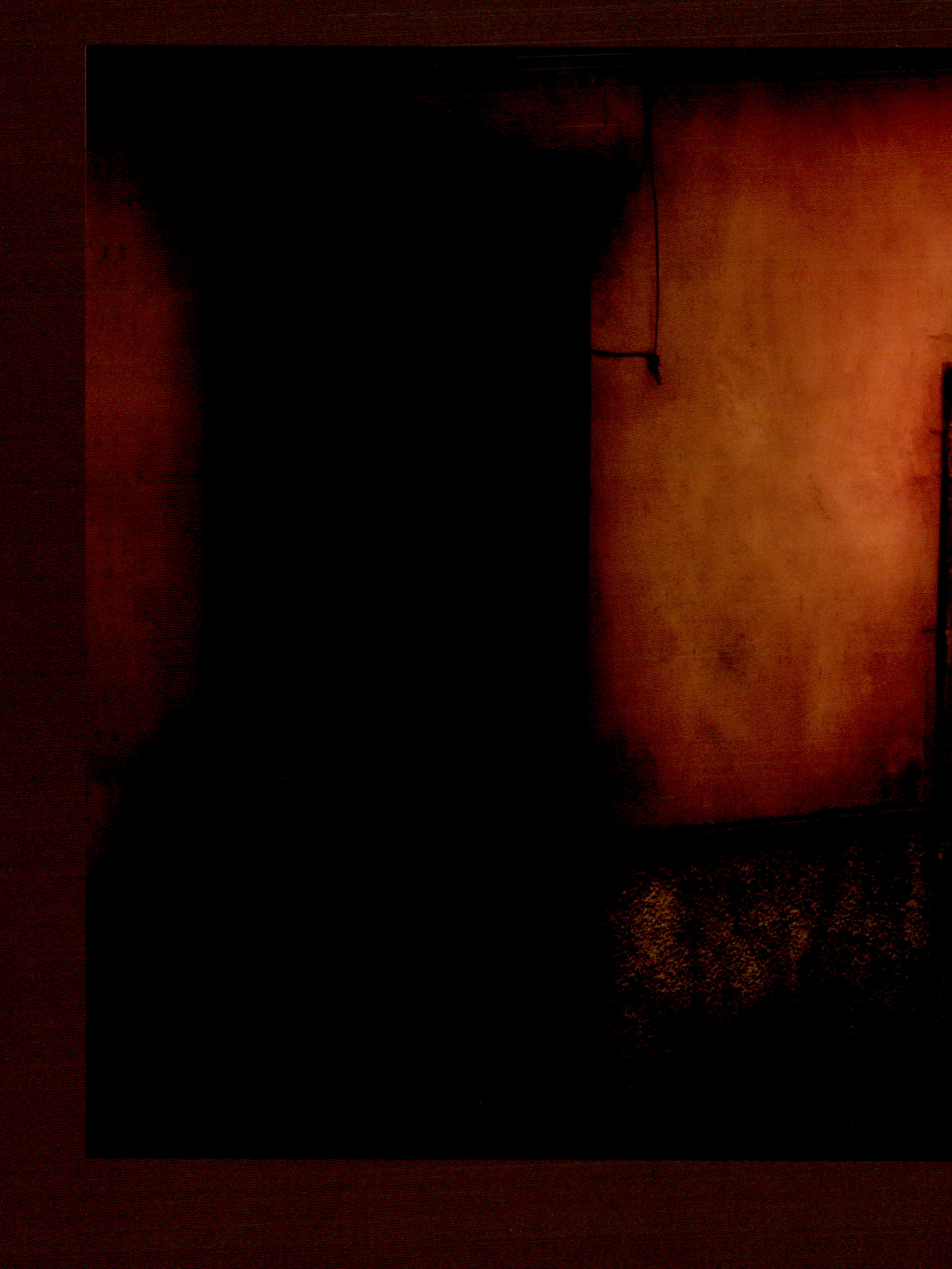

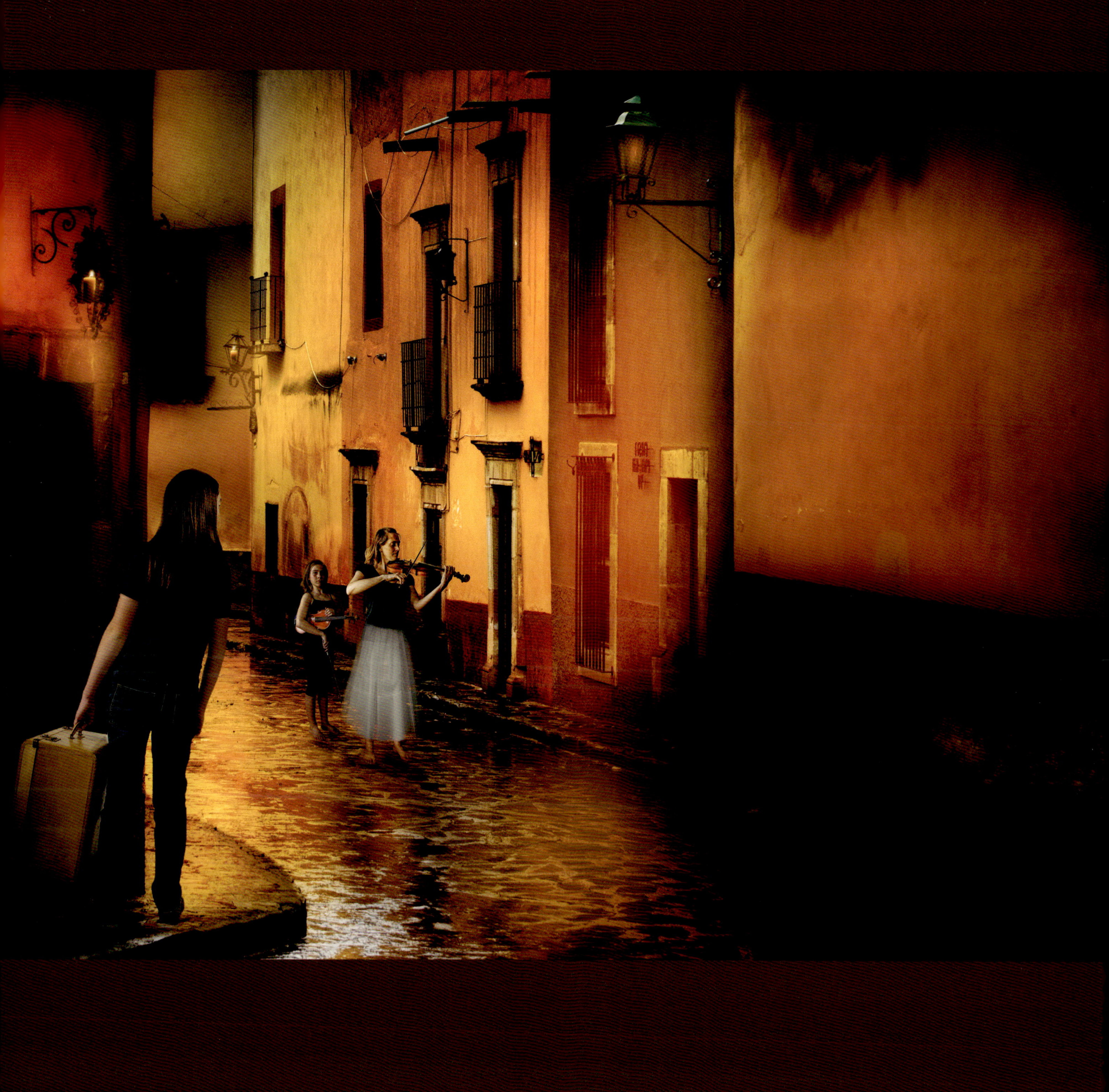

The evening starling

knows all of life's mysteries

but declines to tell

Nancer Ballard

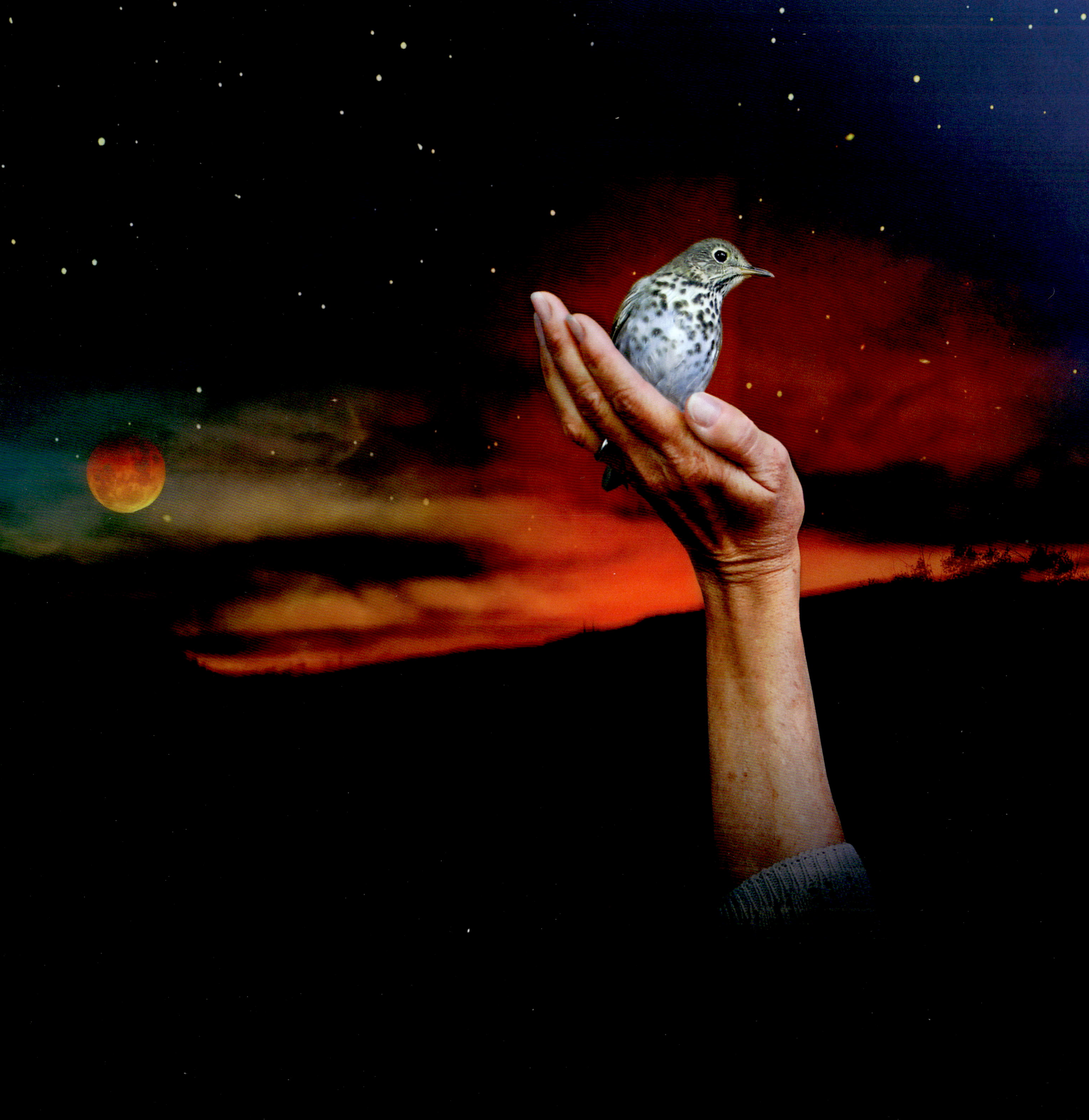

PLATES

I.

II.

III.

IV.

V.

THE LIMINAL PHOTO PAINTINGS OF FRAN FORMAN

BETWEEN TWO NOTES—THE TITLE IS A VERBAL COLLAGE

—**IS A CELEBRATION OF IMAGE COUPLING BY ARTIST FRAN FORMAN,** WHO MAKES EXQUISITE, EVOCATIVE COLLAGES.

Collage, a practice with ancient roots and countless historical precedents in most, if not all, cultures around the world, came into vogue in 1912 in the respective studios of Pablo Picasso and Georges Braque. The subsequent "revolution of papier collé," to borrow Diane Waldman's phrase, yielded a modernist explosion of genres too numerous to comprehensively catalog here. In 1990, a new strain of collage emerged, expanding the panoply of analog applications to include the parallel universe of virtual collage. In the analog sense, collages are made by physical, primarily additive processes in which myriad papers, typically not made in the artist's studio, are glued to a support to form a composite whole in actual time and space. In the virtual sense, digital collages are assembled by computer-generated imaging, in which stacked layers of imagery can be made opaque or translucent, and any object may be isolated, manipulated, enhanced, edited, cloned, or morphed; the final combined image remains virtual until or unless it is printed and made physical.

Fran Forman is a pioneer of digital collage, binding her imagery into seamless wholes, with a particular dedication to timelessness and memory. Her work is packed with scavenged images of things that seem inseparable, despite their disparate origins—things that were never intended to be together until the artist assembled them, and whose coupling establishes harmonic resonances that haunt the mind and cling sweetly to memory.

Forman's work may be simple or complex depending on the individual image, but her color, light, and mood register in the mind's eye long before recognition of the individuals, things, and spaces she incorporates.

The exquisite color and depicted light within her work imbue viewers' eyes with lush pictorial realities that call to mind certain times of day and qualities of lighting—dawn, the high afternoon, dusk, the candle-lit interior, the unified glow of backlit fog, the clouded sky just after rain. Forman's light is iconic light.

Her sense of light might well be compared to the saturated canvases of Maxfield Parrish. But unlike Parrish's fanciful imaginings, Forman's paintings feel familiar, grounded in experience, the stuff of personal recollections. Perhaps Forman's imagery is lasting and haunting because as children, young adults, or veterans of the world, none of us can forget the protracted moments when we notice something for the first time. Forman has located her imagery within such moments.

A scavenger, collector, and curator of the exquisite, she regularly visits historic buildings, always with an eye to transform and combine. Forman's compositions, with their union of antique and contemporary imagery, are unabashed amalgams of interwoven histories. While Forman uses modern tools to capture contemporary images, the High Renaissance provides her with a particular interest. Amid the innovation of Dutch landscape and the introspection of Dutch portraiture, with its candle and fireplace light, Forman finds themes of loss, longing, unexpected happenstance, sustained suspension, and mystery.

Although the artist's titles may lead the associative and imaginative mind in one direction or another, the work does not so much point to specific events as much as to the space and time *between* them. Her work in general always seems to depict twilight hours—neither day nor night, not quite the past and not yet the future, but rather the frozen moments we find ourselves lingering in and wanting not to end.

Todd Bartel with Eli Keehn

I LOVE MAKING PICTURES.

ALL MY LIFE, IT HAS BEEN **MY HOBBY, MY OBSESSION, MY MEANS OF PROCRASTINATION, MY TORMENT**, AND **MY SALVATION.**

AFTERWORD

I create images because I love to look at images. Now I take photographs, combine and manipulate, paint and alter, fuse photographs with painting, reality with fiction—whatever it takes to tell a story. It seems that, although unconscious, I'm always looking for relationships and connections—between humans, the natural and built environments, other species, past generations and periods, and especially in tone and color.

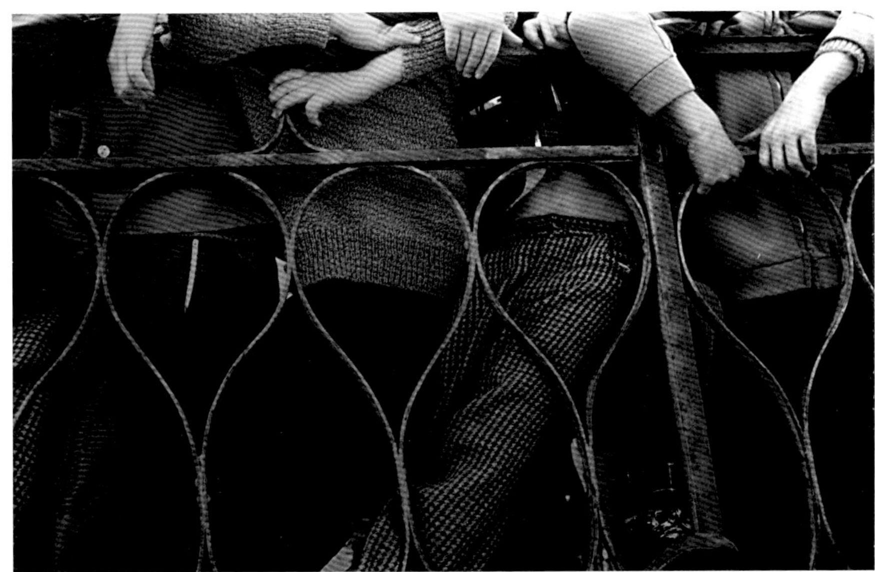

Figure 1 | 1974

A Little Background

As a child in Baltimore, I drew constantly—on papers my father brought back from his paper-supply warehouse and in the margins of my school books. Mostly I drew faces. For my 13th birthday, I asked my parents for a subscription to *Look* magazine; I thought their photographs were even better than those I saw in *Life*, and I copied these photographs, paying special attention to the faces and shading. This was my art education, and from those mid-century photographic masters, I absorbed a sense of composition through the use of light and shadow, balance and symmetry. I sensed that a photograph could make me feel ... something. To this day, I remember the emotional impact of the exhibit, *The Family of Man*, at The Baltimore Museum of Art.

It was assumed that I would "do something with my art" when I grew up. But my growing up took a long time and was subsumed by getting caught up in the remarkable cultural and social shifts of the '60s. Making art seemed too individualistic when we were trying to "change the world." I became a foot-soldier in the protest movements, studied sociology and anthropology, and then became a social worker.

Eventually, what had deteriorated into mindless doodling returned to actual picture-making. Encouraged by friends to "do something with my art," I experimented with different forms of making art. I traveled extensively and took a little camera along to record my adventures. Often, I'd take a "bad" photograph, and these mistakes helped teach me to look and see. (One in particular still hangs on my wall.—*Figure 1*)

During a planned but aborted trip around the world, I lived on a kibbutz in northern Israel, and one of my jobs was to paint the interior walls of a bomb shelter. Coming up one day for light and air, I met a visitor who was teaching graphic design in Jerusalem. What's graphic design? I asked. As he explained how graphic design is the intersection of fine art, commerce, communication, and psychology, I became hooked. Immediately, I changed course—literally and figuratively—and decided to return to the States and become a graphic designer.

While preparing a portfolio for admission to an MFA program, I spent solitary hours in a darkroom at MIT, again finding joy and salvation in the creation of an image. I understood that a photograph could tell a story better than I could draw one. Most of my photographs featured a solitary figure in movement (usually me), often leaving the frame; in fact, I felt constrained by the frame.

My time in graduate school was also spent in the darkroom, until late in the second year I realized I needed to learn the mechanics of design so I could actually get a job. Aside from occasional collage-making at night, photography was put on hold … for over a decade.

While working part-time as a designer and raising two young daughters, graphic design rapidly shifted to digital technology, and I found myself left behind in the analog world of Rubylith, exacto blades, and typesetting. In 1989, I began using a computer to draw pictures and soon after was introduced to a new and at the time revolutionary program developed for photo-retouchers–Photoshop. Immediately, I was back in the world of photography, and in this case, manipulating them on a computer. I had recently inherited a treasure trove of old photographs from my mother and I bought my first scanner—for $1000! I combined images of my ancestors with those of my children—past meets present—and found a way to keep my mother in my life, pixel by pixel. I delved into archival material, incorporating ephemera with my images. Thus began my return to an artistic life where I could integrate my love of drawing and photography. This early personal work was an attempt to forge a connection and blur the boundaries between generations, species, and the natural world, where memories, whimsy, and fragments of dreams collided.

Work for hire led me to create and design CD-roms for the Jack Kerouac estate, for a local history museum, for various businesses, and eventually, for AOL-Time Warner, and for a visually rich website devoted to the African diaspora.

Eventually, events and circumstances shifted my art-making back to a deeper place, suggesting a convergence of sometimes unwelcome random events. Existential crises in my family darkened my images. My concern for the future of our country began to seep into my image-making. And as a Jew born in the 1940s, I had the sense of foreboding that is deep in the collective DNA: a memory of displacement—that our secure foundations could collapse at any time.

As my art-making evolved, my shadows darkened and my colors exploded. My recent images suggest a paradox between the seemingly solid structures of our lives and the insecurity and fragility that lie within. They dwell in that in-between place, neither dark nor light, movement nor stasis, old nor young, superficially safe yet vulnerable.

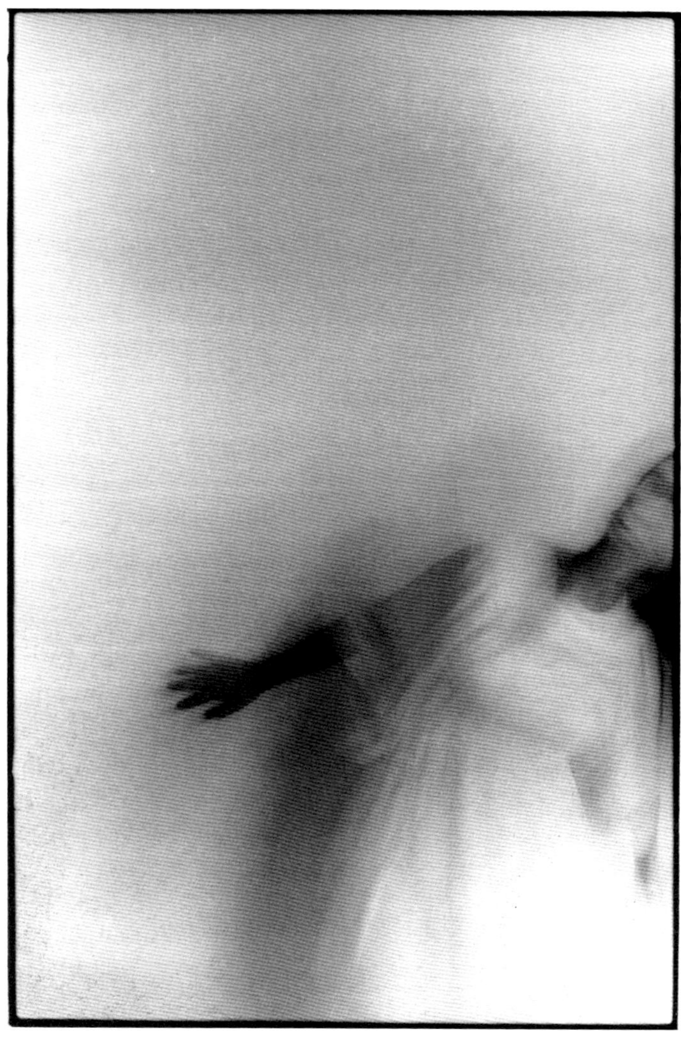

Figure 2 | 1975

None of this was conscious, of course, but I now see the same story in my art being renewed and re-invented.

I became enamored with the effects of chiaroscuro and shifting light, of mid-17th-century northern European painters who created interior scenes and light intensive portraits, of Caravaggio and of Edward Hopper who elevated the solitary figure and created a geometry with light and shadow, of the surrealism of Duane Michaels and the constructed tableaux of Gregory Crewdson, and of course, cinematographers who express in-between moments and use light and shadow to increase tension: Michael Haneke, Errol Morris, Dario Argento. Explosive use of color, of heightened shadows, of shocks of light—all become characters in the image. And my heightened use of chiaroscuro may also reflect my understanding that, for me, time is running out.

Like someone losing one's sense of taste and therefore demanding greater amounts of salt, I now demand color, symmetry, light, and contrast.

Notes on Process

My image-making is referred to as "photo-painting," and indeed, I work like a painter who has a palette of colors available, and then begins to apply one color, then another, always considering how they relate and alter. In my case, it's the interaction and relationship of image, color, and texture that intrigues me.

My method could also be compared to a choreographer; she has a finite number of dancers to work with, she has music, and she has a stage. She directs the dancers by manipulating their movements in relationship to the music and each other in space. Another analogy might be to jazz musicians "call and response," where they experiment and improvise, allowing the elements of the composition to engage with each other.

I maintain a huge library of photographs that I've shot or, if they're archival, scanned. I begin to create an image with a preconceived notion, choosing a selected group of images in the service of an idea. I wield my stylus like a paint-brush, drawing, painting and manipulating fragments and shards of photographs, trying to make an image that is beautiful, mysterious, and revealing of secrets.

The process is not random but it is intuitive, organic, sometimes rooted in my interest in art history. In creating each visual narrative, I consider not only the individual components and their relationships but also color, composition, contrast, texture, and scale. I allow the images to direct the process, with my subconscious in command. Quite often, the image moves in a different direction and the narrative shifts.

In all cases, **it's about relationships in the service of telling a story and being willing to welcome the unexpected relationships that invariably occur.**

Fran Forman

IN CONVERSATION WITH

Jane Fulton Alt | Fine Art Photographer
Nancer Ballard | Poet and writer
Todd Bartel | Gallerist, Teacher
Nadine Boughton | Artist
Gordon Chase | Teacher, Artist
Peter Chermayeff | Architect
Judy Dushku | Professor
Katrin Eismann | Artist, Author, Educator
Sara Farizan | Author
Larry Fink | Photographer
Meredith Goldstein | Author, Columnist
Jamie Gordon | Visual Artist
Cat Gwynn | Author, Photographer
David Gullette | Poet
Sarah Hadley | Photographer
Barbara Hill | Political Activist
Anthony James | Poet
Sandra Klein | Fine Art Photographer
Lash LaRue | Professor of Law, Photographer
Stu Levy | Photographer
Amnon Lourie | Filmmaker
Reinhold Mahler | Teacher of Architecture
Andrea Petersen | Attorney
David Ray | Computer Scientist
Monica Raymond | Interdisciplinary Artist
Victor Rosario | Prison Ministry, exonerated after 32 years in prison
Gordon Saperia | Photographer
Vicky Stromee | Fine Art Photographer
Roger Watson | Curator, The Fox Talbot Museum
David Weinberg | Photographer

ACKNOWLEDGMENTS

It's a cliché that 'it takes a village', but in putting together a book such as this, it's certainly true of at least a hamlet. Much gratitude to Don Linn and Unicorn for enthusiastically embracing and shepherding this project, and to Tom Chambers for the introduction. Thanks to Connie Hwang for patiently and brilliantly interpreting my desire to integrate word and image and for becoming my life-long friend. And many thanks to Tom Hummel of CrashPaper for his expertise. I am grateful to The Puffin Foundation for its encouragement and support of artists and social justice.

My many years as a Scholar at the Women's Studies Research Center at Brandeis University have provided support and collegiality, with specific thanks to filmmaker Laurie Kahn and to poets Monica Raymond, Nancer Ballard and to David Gullette , our honorary colleague at the WSRC. A special shout-out with gratitude to an old friend who has made her life's mission to embrace and support all the arts, Barbara Hill. Thank you, Todd Hido and Aperture Books for your words that perfectly articulate the artist's gratitude to the viewer. I am awed by the contribution that Paula Tognarelli, as Director of The Griffin Museum of Photography, has made to the local and national photographic community; Paula, thank you for your support and encouragement over the years, and for your suggestion that this should be a book. Thanks to the curators, gallerists, and bloggers who have featured my work over the past many years; your enthusiasm and support has allowed me to continue on this journey. Other colleagues have provided invaluable help, providing technical support, encouragement, or the patience to listen to me whine, complain, and occasionally to panic. Thanks for technical support to SueAnne Hodges at New England School of Photography. To Katrin Eismann, Tom Ashe, and Marko Kovacevic, gurus all at the MPS Digital Photography Department, School of Visual Arts, New York, I'm grateful for your friendship and for the many hours of your expertise. Thank you, Liz Burgess and Bernard Pucker of The Pucker Gallery. Thank you, Todd Bartel and Eli Keehn of The Cambridge School of Weston. Thanks to Mary Virginia Swanson, Nancy Hausman, Nadine Boughton, Sharon Basco and John Koch, Richard Perse, Ron Elson, and Meredith Goldstein whose opinions on all matters of word and image I greatly respect.

Many thanks to the writers who have contributed to this book and who have illustrated that art is, indeed, a conversation. I'm grateful for the time and effort you have all put into your writings. Thanks to Lucas, Julian, EmmaKate and my other models, for your patience while I fiddle with lights. Thanks also to Hannah and Tim Cassedy, to Sophie and Josh Charles, and especially to Bob Flack, for your patience, support, chauffeuring, and computer know-how ('just hit re-start').

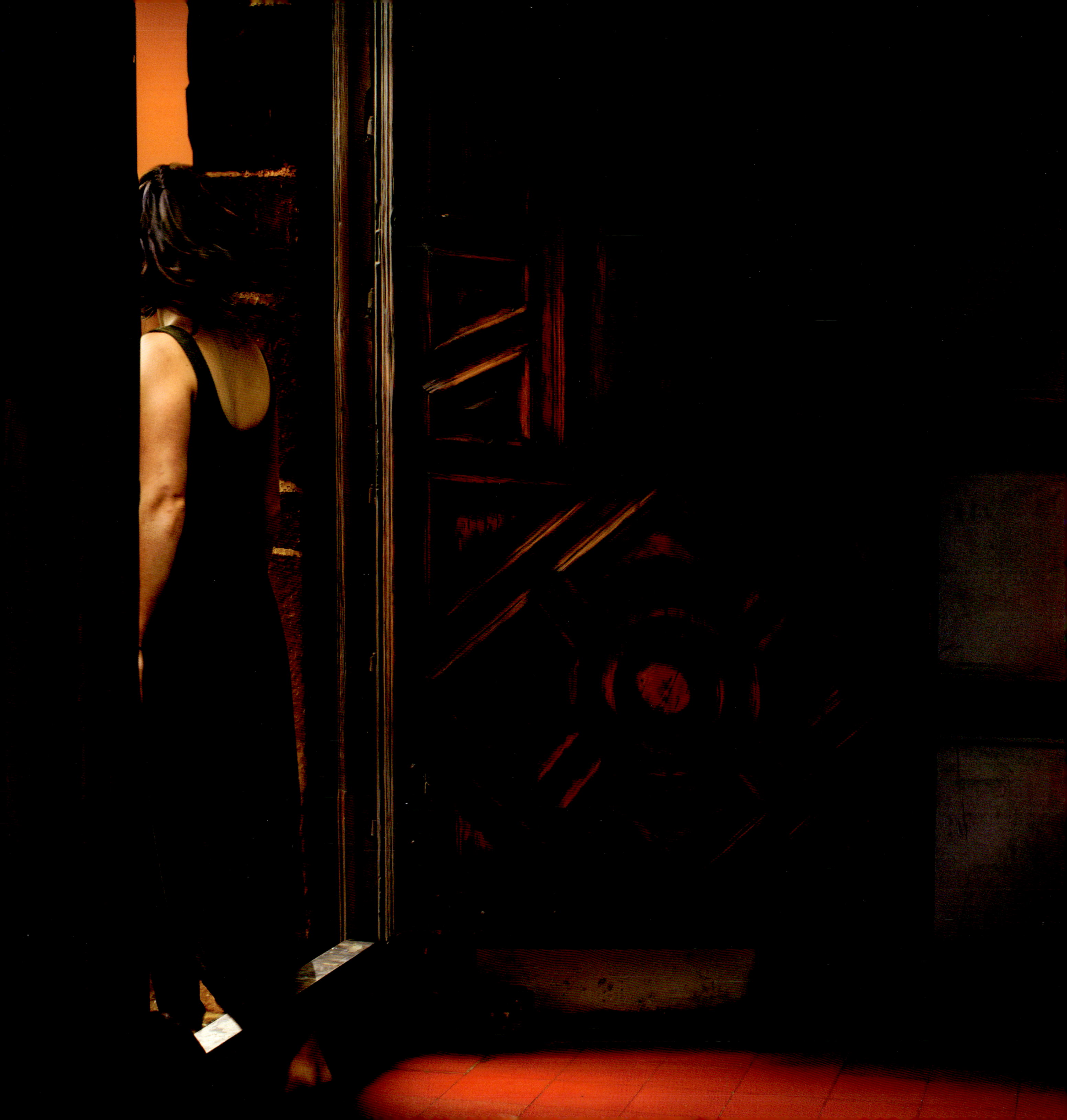